The International Library of Sociology

CRIMINAL JUSTICE AND SOCIAL RECONSTRUCTION

Founded by KARL MANNHEIM

THE SOCIOLOGY OF LAW AND CRIMINOLOGY

In 15 Volumes

I	Comparative Criminology - Part One	*Mannheim*
II	Comparative Criminology - Part Two	*Mannheim*
III	Crime: An Analytical Appraisal	*López-Rey*
IV	The Criminal Area	*Morris*
V	Criminal Justice and Social Reconstruction	*Mannheim*
VI	The Education of Borstal Boys	*Stratta*
VII	The English Prison and Borstal Systems	*Fox*
VIII	The Explanation of Criminality	*Trasler*
IX	Group Problems in Crime and Punishment	*Mannheim*
X	The Institutions of Private Law	*Renner*
XI	Juvenile Delinquency in an English Middletown	*Mannheim*
XII	Legal Aid	*Egerton*
XIII	Pentonville	*Morris et al*
XIV	Social Defence	*Ancel*
XV	Young Men in Detention Centres	*Dunlop et al*

CRIMINAL JUSTICE AND SOCIAL RECONSTRUCTION

by

HERMANN MANNHEIM

ROUTLEDGE
Taylor & Francis Group

First published in 1946
by Routledge

Reprinted in 1998, 2001 by Routledge
2 Park Square, Milton Park, Abingdon, Oxon, OX14 4RN

Transferred to Digital Printing 2007

Routledge is an imprint of the Taylor & Francis Group

British Library Cataloguing in Publication Data
A CIP catalogue record for this book
is available from the British Library

Criminal Justice and Social Reconstruction
ISBN 0-415-17736-7
The Sociology of Law and Criminology: 15 Volumes
ISBN 0-415-17832-0
The International Library of Sociology: 274 Volumes
ISBN 0-415-17838-X

Publisher's Note

The publisher has gone to great lengths to ensure the quality of this reprint but points out that some imperfections in the original may be apparent

CONTENTS

PART I. THE CRISIS IN VALUES AND THE CRIMINAL LAW

PREFACE

It is sometimes difficult for an author to remember exactly when and how his work was first conceived. The origin of the present book can, however, fairly distinctly be traced back to the following factors : First, to the incompleteness of my earlier books—*The Dilemma of Penal Reform* and *Social Aspects of Crime in England between the Wars*—an incompleteness due not only to lack of space but also to my feeling that it would have been somewhat premature at the time to draw any definite conclusions from the material collected. However, when, a few years later, in summer 1942, my colleague Dr. Karl Mannheim suggested to me that I might contribute a volume to his " International Library of Sociology and Social Reconstruction ", I welcomed his invitation as an opportunity of filling at least some of the gaps left by those earlier writings. Readers of the present volume will no doubt be aware of the links existing, for instance, between certain chapters of *Social Aspects*, especially those on " Business Administration " and similar subjects, and the economic sections of the present book ; or between the concluding Parts of the latter and of *The Dilemma.* A few lectures of a programmatic character delivered at a Summer School of the Fabian Society and at the South Place Ethical Society in London helped me further to clarify certain ideas which form the basis of the present book.

It is one of the most important functions of Criminal Justice to play some part in the great task of Education for Citizenship. The spirit of the Criminal Law and its administration should be such as to make this branch of the legal system something like a reliable guide through the chaos of modern society—certainly neither the only nor the most important educational factor of this kind but at least capable of holding its own among the many agencies at work. So far, Criminal Justice has often remained too much behind and out of touch with the progressive elements of social thought, and its approach to the problems of society has been too one-sided to make it a really living force. The present book represents a very modest and inevitably incomplete attempt to show how the work of Social Reconstruction might be reflected in the field of Criminal Justice. Of the shortcomings of this attempt and the many questions still left unanswered

I am only too painfully aware. I am equally conscious of the many criticisms which this book will inevitably provoke. It is only too likely that at least some of them will differ but little from the doubts I might have expressed myself twenty-five years ago. This will help me to understand those who will find my present views unacceptable. I am not optimistic enough to believe that these views will, in the near future, gain widespread approval. It is well known that, for reasons which would lead too far to expound here, the legal world is the slowest in making the necessary adjustments to changes in society. The great task of the future will be to separate the valuable elements in the traditional approach from the bias rooted in vested interests and sheer unreasonableness. If the book should contribute even in a small way to making this discussion as unprejudiced and as well informed as possible, it will have achieved its object.

It gives me great pleasure to dedicate this book to my colleague Professor Harold J. Laski in appreciation of his friendly interest in my work and the great kindness he has shown to me ever since I came to this country.

Without the devoted help and the persistent encouragement which I have received from my wife neither this book nor any of its predecessors could have been written.

The manuscript of the present book was completed in April, 1945; material published after that date could, therefore, as a rule, be referred to, if at all, only in footnotes.

HERMANN MANNHEIM.

THE LONDON SCHOOL OF ECONOMICS AND POLITICAL SCIENCE (UNIVERSITY OF LONDON).

January 1946.

Every generation regards as natural the institutions to which it is accustomed. Mankind, it seems, is more easily shocked by the unusual than by the shocking.

R. H. Tawney, *Equality*, p. 119.

A revolutionary moment in the world's history is a time for revolutions, not for patching.

Beveridge Report, p. 6.

Just as that bargain (with fate) is destined to be reopened in the fields of economics and politics, so, clearly, law, which is, in its ultimate substance, dependent upon these, is certain to be profoundly reconstructed in principle.

Harold J. Laski, *Parliamentary Government in England*, p. 374.

What is the good of developing child guidance, psychiatric social work and psychotherapy, if the one who is to guide is left without standards?

Moral commands which can no longer be fulfilled because they have lost touch with reality, make for an increase in law-breakers and for a diminishing loyalty to law in general. . . .

To us the question is, therefore, not so much whether we can do without conventions and repressions, but whether we can make clear distinctions between taboos, which are nothing but a burden to the mind, and reasonable principles without which a society cannot survive. . . . A successful society will economize as much as possible in the use of prohibitions and repression.

Karl Mannheim, *Diagnosis of our Time*, pp. 25, 78, 82.

It seems that the primitive elements of criminal law are slower to disappear than the primitive elements of any other branch of law.

C. K. Allen, *Legal Duties*, p. 222.

Criminal proceedings are, as compared with civil proceedings, ineffective. For their very severity detracts from their utility.

A. V. Dicey, *Law and Opinion*, p. xlvii.

Why, then, generally speaking, have administrative techniques developed? Because the rules of the criminal law have been less adequate to meet many of the complex problems of modern economic society than administrative procedures.

Nathaniel Cantor, *Crime and Society*, p. 368.

No procedures are regarded as fundamental in an age when men are battling about the purposes to which they should be devoted. Legal forms are respected when men feel that they have the great ends of life in common.

Harold J. Laski, *Reflections on the Revolution of our Time*, pp. 15–16.

The time has probably come for the problems of modern government to be approached with reference to functions rather than generalised principles.

E. C. S. Wade, Preface to 9th ed. of A. V. Dicey, *Law of the Constitution*, p. xvi.

The doctrine of the separation of powers is not sacrosanct. . . . If the particular task is not suited to the ordinary Courts of Law, it may properly be assigned to some special tribunal already existing or to be newly created for the purpose, which is better adapted in personnel or procedure.

Report of Committee on Ministers' Powers, pp. 94–5.

The ultimate safeguard of freedom against the power-loving bureaucrat depends on what kind of people we are.

Barbara Wootton in *Can Planning be Democratic?*, pp. 52–3.

The only cure for the insufficiency of science is more science.

Julian Huxley, *On Living in a Revolution*, p. 46.

CRIMINAL JUSTICE AND SOCIAL RECONSTRUCTION

INTRODUCTION

In the critical period after the war, the problem of crime can be expected to absorb many of the energies devoted to the task of social reconstruction. The rise in criminal activities which, in one form or another, is almost inevitable after such an earthquake will mean much hard work for courts and administrators of criminal justice. That the penal system in practically every country will have to be modernized nobody is likely to deny. It is, however, the main purpose of the present book to show that much more is required in the name of social reconstruction than only a reform of penal systems.

Apart from the deplorable setbacks due to the world wars, the reform of penal methods has, in many countries, made considerable headway in recent times. Of the criminal law itself, however, the same can, unfortunately, not be said. In the minds of the man in the street as well as of the expert the desire for an improvement of penal methods has almost completely overshadowed the interest in an equally thorough overhauling of the criminal law. We have made considerable efforts to discover what sort of person the offender is and why he has broken the law, and we rack our brains to find out what to do with him. This, however, is not enough. Hardly ever do we pause for a moment to examine critically the contents of that very law the existence of which alone makes it possible for the individual to offend against it. Any new ideas that have made their appearance in the field of the criminal law within the past fifty years have been largely confined to questions of treatment. The great movement from the doctrines of the classical school to those of the sociological school which has taken place during that period has first and foremost meant the replacement of the aim of retribution by that of reformation; the more scientific and humane treatment of the juvenile and the mentally abnormal offender; the working out of more efficient methods of dealing with the habitual criminal; the widening of the scope of judicial discretion ; the opening up of such new avenues as Probation, Parole, and others. In addition, there have been certain improvements in legislative technique, with a view to simplifying the definitions of individual crimes and to eliminating unnecessary distinctions and cumbersome casuistry. Nowhere, however, except in Soviet Russia, have we seen undertaken that re-thinking of the entire system of values without which all those other reforms will remain incomplete and more or less disappointing. Technically feasible though it may be to improve the existing methods of dealing with those who have broken an out-of date or unfair criminal statute, it would hardly be practical politics to neglect that part of the structure on which the whole building is based. Before we begin to consider how convicted law-breakers should be treated in prison or on probation, an analysis should therefore be made of those actions for which a prison sentence or a probation order may be the legal consequence.

As a matter of fact, even in countries such as Great Britain and the United States which stand in the forefront of the modern penal reform movement, that movement has as yet not penetrated far enough to reach the criminal law proper.[1] It is, however, unthinkable that in an era of planning extending over the whole of the social system this special task should be persistently evaded. The criminal law has, quite rightly, been called one of the most faithful mirrors of a given civilization, reflecting the fundamental values on which the latter rests. Whenever these values change, the criminal law must follow suit. The present crisis in values, one of the greatest in human history, cannot fail to have profound repercussions in this field. It is one of the principal objects of the present book to consider these repercussions one by one and to discuss the practical consequences which, sooner or later, will have to be drawn from them.

Closer examination reveals that any attempt to reconstruct the criminal law has to face at least two basic problems :

1. We have to make up our minds as to what we regard as the *most important values* in a reconstructed world ;
2. We have to decide whether these values should be *protected by the means at the disposal of the criminal law*, or whether their protection should be left to agencies of a different character.

The first point involves a reconsideration of our *system of*

[1] See also D. Seaborne Davies, *The Nineteenth Century and After*, April 1937, pp. 530 et seq.

values ; the second makes necessary a new demarcation of the *scope of the criminal law.* This is certainly not the only branch of the law where the task of the legislator is a dual one ; nowhere else, however, does this dualism of problems emerge so clearly : first, to lay down a policy, and, then, to decide whether this policy should be carried out by penal methods ; for instance, should strikes be made illegal, and, if so, should strikers be punished or, better, be dealt with in a different way?

There remains, however, a third question to be answered. Having come to the conclusion that society should protect a certain good by means of the criminal law, we still have to ask whether the solution of each and every single problem that might arise from this policy should be the duty of the criminal law and the criminal courts, or whether at least certain aspects might better be left to other agencies. Strikes, for instance, might be made criminal offences only if entered into in defiance of some administrative procedure aiming at a peaceful settlement of labour disputes. It might be left to an administrative board to judge the merits or otherwise of the dispute, whereas the criminal law and the criminal courts are expected not to lay down their own line of policy, but merely to carry out the policy of another government department. This has been done, for instance, for conscientious objectors under the Military Training Act, 1939.

The Crisis in Values

The crisis in values which confronts the criminal law of to-day is by no means of recent origin. Like the present rise in crime, it has not been produced by the war, though the war may have aggravated certain pre-existing tendencies. It concerns not merely the one or the other of the values which are safeguarded by the criminal law ; it concerns all of them with hardly any exception. To a greater or smaller extent, in every country the criminal law has in essential parts become out of date. Instead of being a living organism, supported by the confidence of all sections of the community and developing according to the practical and ideological needs of the time, it presents itself as a petrified body, unable to cope with the endless variety of problems created by an ever-changing world and kept alive mainly by tradition, habit, and inertia. Methods of treating the lawbreaker, antiquated as many of them still are, have been and are being modernized in a hundred ways—

definitions of what constitutes a crime, however, have, for the greater part remained fundamentally the same for centuries. In the criminal law, man has forged one of his most formidable weapons, but without any consistent ideas, it seems, when and for what purposes this instrument should be used ; without any philosophy or even technology to guide him ; and wholly unrelated to other similar weapons in his hands. Civil Law, Criminal Law, Administrative Law—Army, Navy, and Air Force—the tools are in existence, but there is no joint General Staff, nor even a Chief of Combined Operations, to co-ordinate the three services and to use each of them to the best possible purpose. Each system of criminal law is derived from a particular ideology ; if this ideology ceases to function, the criminal law related to it will become unworkable. Each system of criminal law is likewise attuned to a particular set of vested interests ; if this should become obsolete and has to be replaced by a different set of interests, corresponding adjustments will have to be made in the sphere of the criminal law. " Here is our biggest need ; the need of values and standards which are more than mere habits, which go down below the soil of custom into the rock of clear conviction and are founded in a philosophy of life ".[1] For such reasons it would seem imperative that each successive generation should realize its duty to work out afresh its views on the problem of crime and turn these views into the small coin of legislation, instead of retaining unchanged, as a matter of course, the law inherited from its predecessors. In doing so, it will be wise to be guided by Mr. Justice Holmes's suggestion, expressing what has been in the minds of many of us who have devoted long years of theoretical study and practical work to the subject, that " half the criminal law may do more harm than good ".[2]

In the following chapters it is proposed to pass in review some of the basic values of present-day society and to inquire whether their treatment by the criminal law is still in harmony with the functions they have to fulfil in our society or whether any pre-existent harmony may have been destroyed by the revolution which is going on before our eyes. Naturally, for reasons of space, this survey cannot be anything like exhaustive. Moreover, as it is intended for the general public rather than for a small circle of professional lawyers only it has to be, as

[1] Sir Richard Livingstone, *Education for a World Adrift* (1943), p. xiii.
[2] *Collected Legal Papers*, p. 139.

much as possible, free from legal technicalities. At the same time, it is our aim to provide the practical worker in this field with some of the elements at least of a social philosophy related to the application of the criminal law. For him it is not enough to possess a technique of social case work and some knowledge of criminology and criminal procedure, with a smattering of a few fashionable psychological theories based on traditional moral and religious conceptions which may have become out of tune with the beliefs of those among whom he has to work.

It is the great weakness of the criminal law, a weakness, by the way, which it shares with many other and more distinguished branches of human thought, that its basic conception is not clearly definable. Nobody knows for certain the meaning of " crime ", apart from the purely tautological and therefore useless interpretation that it is " something which violates the criminal law ". Having sacrificed the close relationship with moral and religious principles which characterized the pre-scientific phases of the criminal law, we have now largely to rely on the sociological interpretation. Crime is *anti-social behaviour,* and no form of human behaviour which is not anti-social should ever be treated as a crime. Any violation of this rule indicates either a mistake on the part of the legislator or his deliberate failure to break with an out-of-date tradition.

The reverse, however, is far from true. There are very many types of anti-social behaviour which are not, and many others which should not be, crimes. A number of reasons can be given for this. First, the anti-social character of many human activities, as, for instance, of certain business transactions or methods of business organization, such as attempts to monopolize a branch of trade, may for a long while remain hidden from the eyes of the legislator and the public. Secondly, different social classes within the community may hold opposite views about the merits or otherwise of this or that form of human activity, whether it may be betting and gambling, or some aspects of the stock exchange business, or strikes, sleeping out, and dozens of others. Since, in a democracy, the efficient administration of criminal justice has to depend on the widest possible backing of the community at large, any such divergence of opinion will make the lawgiver reluctant to resort to penal methods. A third point : Even where universal agreement does exist as to the anti-social character of certain forms of behaviour, they may be regarded as unsuitable objects of the criminal law, either because penalizing them would mean interfering too much with the private lives of individuals, or because it would be technically too difficult. Prostitution, drunkenness in private homes, adultery, neglect of family may belong to the former category, whereas large-scale and highly complicated anti-social business practices, evasions of taxation laws, and the like may be examples of the latter. The punishment of anti-social behaviour, it must be borne in mind, cannot be regarded as an absolute value, and the advantages which it may entail to the community have carefully to be balanced against the potential harm. We no longer believe in *fiat justitia, pereat mundus*. Wartime legislation, or failure to legislate, presents many examples to show the practical working of the first-mentioned principle. From Regulation 33B on the compulsory treatment of venereal diseases, on the one hand, to the refusal on the part of the Government to make a "No-treating Order" or to prevent waste of fuel by penal methods—rightly or wrongly, the argument centres around the idea that the penal law, unless there is no other alternative, should not intrude into the private homes and lives of individuals. Of still greater practical significance is the second category: anti-social activities too complex to be dealt with by the criminal law. For a full appreciation of the havoc which they have played with the administration of criminal justice it will become necessary to pass in review some of the traditional principles of law and procedure on which that administration is based.

PART I. THE CRISIS IN VALUES AND THE CRIMINAL LAW

SECTION ONE. THE PROTECTION OF HUMAN LIFE

Chapter 1

THE INDIVIDUALISTIC ASPECT

Crime is anti-social behaviour—anti-social behaviour is directed against certain fundamental values. A critical analysis of the present criminal law has, therefore, to examine whether it offers the necessary legal protection to the fundamental values of human society.

Among these values, *human life* may appear to be the least controversial. In fact, however, there have been considerable changes in emphasis, which may easily be overlooked or, on the other hand, exaggerated by the casual observer. To grasp their meaning and implications we have to realize that the whole issue has to be divided into two groups of problems, of which one bears an individualistic, and the other a collectivistic character. The first group is discussed in the present chapter, the second group in Chapters 2 and 3.

The individualistic aspect is concerned with the protection of human life from attacks of an individualistic character and, on the other hand, with its sacrifice on equally individualistic grounds.

A. Homicide.

There is first the question of how to protect human life against deliberate attacks arising from individualistic incentives such as hatred, jealousy, aggressiveness, acquisitiveness, and similar psychological conditions, or against attacks due to drunkenness or other pathological states of mind. This is the realm of the old traditional categories of crime against the person, —murder, manslaughter, wounding, assault. Here, the position in general seems to have changed comparatively little. In this respect at least, human nature is still very much the same as it used to be a few thousand years ago. The techniques and the frequency of these crimes have, of course, undergone very many, and sometimes violent, changes, and so have the methods of punishment applied. It would be a mistake to assume that murder has invariably been treated as the most heinous of all crimes. At least in ancient legal systems, as well as in primitive societies, we find so many exceptions to that rule that to describe them in detail would require a history of the criminal law. In modern law, the most conspicuous exception is Russia. According to her Penal Code of 1926, the " supreme measure of social defence ", i.e. the death penalty, is reserved for crimes other than murder, for which latter the maximum penalty is loss of liberty for ten years. This is by no means an innovation of the present régime ; the position was essentially the same before the Bolshevist Revolution. What may be the explanation? Sir John Maynard,[1] among other writers, has drawn attention to what he regards as a " high degree of indifference to human life " among Russians, strangely enough coupled with " a special susceptibility to the legal enforcement . . . of the capital sentence ". He quotes Kerensky's statement that " killing by terror or mass execution is another matter . . . but it is practically impossible to carry out a judicial death sentence in Russia ". The traditional distrust of the State among Russians, which Sir John Maynard regards as the explanation, has disappeared, and with it that susceptibility to the death sentence as such. The tendency to place crimes against human life only second in the order of gravity, however, has remained. The reason is that mysticism which dominates, as strongly as ever, the Russian soul, now coupled with the conviction that nothing that belongs to the individual can be put on an equal footing with the interests of the community as a whole. Highly individualistic motives such as jealousy, which in the old Russia of Dostoievsky's *House of the Dead*, just as in other countries, usually mitigated the penalty, are an aggravating circumstance in Soviet Russia.[2]

In periods of peace, social stability and economic prosperity, crimes of violence go down, and penal reformers find it easier to advocate progressive measures of treatment such as the abolition of the death penalty. The question whether great wars must necessarily lead to a wholesale weakening of the respect for human life has not been conclusively answered by the first world war. After 1918, the increase in crimes of violence was mainly confined to those countries which had lost the war, whereas in

[1] *The Russian Peasant and Other Studies*, pp. 175 and 189.
[2] Penal Code, art. 136 ; Ella Winter, *Red Virtue*, p. 192.

the victorious countries even an improvement took place.[1] The outlook for the time after the 1939–45 war with its vastly greater cruelty and destruction of material and spiritual values is, however, undeniably much darker. It would mean asking too much of human nature to assume that, as the accumulated effect of the events of the past thirty years, life should not have become cheaper in the eyes of the masses. If Alva Myrdal [2] claims for her native Sweden that " Patterns of normality and lawfulness have gradually been firmly fixed. Killing other human beings is considered simply not good form ", we cannot expect this to be equally true of nations that have gone through the experiences of two world wars. Bovet could still express the optimistic view that children remain unharmed by the picture of violence and indifference to suffering which is daily before their eyes, provided they have once firmly grasped the general principle of the sanctity of human life.[3] The exceptions to that principle, however, have become so glaring and so frequent in recent times that people whose belief in fundamental ethical values is not particularly strong may lose sight of the principle itself. It is nothing new, of course, that " *das Leben ist der Güter höchstes nicht* ", and we regard it as justifiable to require the individual to sacrifice his own life or to take the lives of others for the sake of higher values. If only we could always be sure what these higher values are. The recent discussion on the ethics of bombing great works of art and architecture in order to spare the lives of allied soldiers has revealed something of the doubts and the uneasiness existing on that score. These are matters of high policy outside the scope of the criminal law and, as a rule, but little affecting the behaviour of private individuals as such. The time has come, however, when private individuals may require, for issues vitally concerning their daily lives, some better guidance than they can get from the present law.

The question of how far human life might be sacrificed on individualistic grounds leads to a reconsideration of our attitude to *Suicide* and *Death-Pacts*, and to the movement in favour of *Euthanasia*.

[1] See the author's *Social Aspects of Crime in England between the Wars*, pp. 105, 122 and 177; *War and Crime*, pp. 71, 91 ff., 126.

[2] *Nation and Family* (International Library of Sociology and Social Reconstruction) (1941), p. 11.

[3] See the author's *War and Crime*, p. 127, where the theory is tentatively put forward that war may act as a safety-valve for crimes of violence. It may be doubtful, however, whether this theory will remain applicable to prolonged warfare under conditions of unmitigated cruelty.

B. Suicide.

Suicide is something in the nature of a test-case. In his treatment of suicide, more than in that of many other offences of much greater practical significance, the legislator can show whether he realizes that life is no longer regarded as an absolute value ; whether he has grasped the difference between law and morality and the limitations and purposes of the criminal law and of the penal system. The demand for the abolition of all penal sanctions attached to suicide or attempted suicide means no approval of self-destruction ; nor does it imply any disregard of human life or any claim that the State should never be allowed to interfere in this sphere. In no way does it represent the mere expression of an individualistic and, in a purely negative sense, liberalistic policy. True as it is, that individualists and liberals are also in favour of such abolition, it is significant that the Criminal Codes of no totalitarian State, be it Soviet, German or Italian, penalize attempted suicide. In every strong community, totalitarian or liberal, suicide will be regarded as undesirable and, as a rule, even as anti-social, since it may weaken the productive potential of State and Society and is indicative of the absence of that optimistic attitude to life which is essential for their well-being. If it becomes a mass phenomenon, as it has in certain periods of human history, it must inevitably undermine the foundations of the whole body politic. True as all this is, we are, however, forced to admit that suicide belongs to those anti-social actions which cannot be fought with the weapons at the disposal of modern criminal law. In a penal system that is not excessively cruel or stigmatizing, punishment cannot act as a deterrent on an individual who has already shown his readiness to throw away his life. Can it be of any value as a reformatory and re-educative measure ? It has recently been argued by experts of progressive and humanitarian views [1] that criminal proceedings under an enlightened penal system offer the best opportunity to ensure that persons with suicidal tendencies are properly looked after and treated at a time when they are most in need of physical and mental care. Such arguments, if actually true, are nothing but a serious indictment of the existing system of social, and particularly mental health, services. It should not be beyond the

[1] W. Norwood East, *Medical Aspects of Crime*, p. 142 ; Douglas Kerr, *Edinburgh Medical Journal*, 1942, p. 489. Against the present practice Sir Cecil T. Carr, *Concerning English Administrative Law*, p. 109.

wits of men to devise an adequate scheme dealing with human problems of this kind outside the criminal law. Those in charge of the practical administration of English criminal justice have, to a considerable extent, drawn the consequences from this state of affairs by abstaining from any prosecution in the great majority of cases. In 1938, the last year for which Criminal Statistics for England and Wales have been published, out of 3,303 persons known to the police as having attempted suicide only 616 (12 of them juveniles) were proceeded against, of whom 47 were found not guilty, whereas 25 were sentenced to imprisonment, 181 placed on probation, 4 were sent to Institutions for Defectives, and most of the other cases were either simply bound over or dismissed.[1] What a waste of time and labour must have been involved even in this moderate proportion of prosecutions ! Any kind of social, psychological, or psychiatric diagnosis and treatment which was necessary might have been much more effectively carried out without all the stigmatizing paraphernalia of criminal procedure. Realizing the boundaries of the criminal law, Soviet Russia, though strongly disapproving of a "way out which is sought only by tired and weak people,"[2] has omitted attempted suicide from her Penal Code. If English law and the Codes of a few states of the U.S.A. still take up a different attitude this can be ascribed only to the influence of the Churches, whereas the Indian Penal Code has simply followed the English model. Even among the great religions of the world, however, there has by no means been anything like uniformity in this respect.[3] Apart from Christianity, Judaism and Mohammedanism with their uncompromising condemnation of suicide, we find a considerable variety of views, not even counting such extreme institutionalized forms as the Japanese *harakiri* and the Indian *suttee*. "The self-effacement or self-abasement preached by religions has often provided an impulse under which people may and actually do commit suicide," says an Indian writer.[4] Where

[1] In the same year, Coroners returned 5,263 verdicts of suicide.

[2] Emelyan Yaroslavsky, quoted by the Webbs, *Soviet Communism*, Vol. II, 1062. See also Ella Winter, *Red Virtue* (1933), pp. 65 et seq.

[3] See art. "Suicide" in the *Encycl. of Religion and Ethics*, edited by James Hastings (1921). In the corresponding article in the *Catholic Encycl.* (1912) four types of suicide are distinguished ; positive and direct ; positive and indirect ; negative and direct ; negative and indirect.

[4] Abul Hasanat, *Crime and Criminal Justice* (1939) App. B, p. 66. P. Thomas, *Women and Marriage in India* (1939), pp. 89 et seq., suggests that *suttee* or *sati*, before becoming a religious duty, was originally a male invention to put a stop to the female practice of husband-murder which preceded it.

it did exist religious pressure has, however, much better than legal penalties succeeded in suppressing suicidal tendencies. Although it would be misleading to explain the differences in the frequency of suicides exclusively in terms of the religious factor,[1] it is not without interest to compare the extremely low rate of 14 suicides per million inhabitants in a strictly Mohammedan country as Egypt, where attempted suicide is not a legal offence, or even the rate of 101 in Scotland, where it is an offence only "if it alarms the lieges", with the rate of 126 in England and Wales. In Russia the rate was 86 in 1922–4, in Germany 266 and in Austria 372, both in 1927–31. The low Russian rate has apparently nothing to do with the present régime ; in the last decade of the nineteenth century, when it was 84 in England, it was 32 in Russia [2]. Comparative figures of this kind do not make it appear likely that the treatment of suicide as a crime possesses considerable educational value as "its prohibition speaks with all the authority that comes from the voice of the recorded law".[3] At a time when the law has to struggle hard to preserve even a fraction of its former dignity, unwarranted prohibitions of this kind may easily bring it into disrepute.

To abolish the punishment of suicide does not necessarily imply that other persons who participate in the act should go scot free as well. Nevertheless, English law, which treats anyone who incites another person to commit suicide as guilty of murder,[4] seems, as a general rule, much too severe. Cases of this kind may differ considerably in gravity according to the motives of the instigator. Some modern Criminal Codes threaten, therefore, merely imprisonment up to five or seven years, and even this only in the case of certain aggravating circumstances, as for instance, if cruel methods are used, or the instigator's motives are bad, or if the suicide is under age or

[1] The interesting fact that the suicide rate for Jews in Russia rose from 46 in 1849–55 to 416 in 1919–23, whereas the corresponding figures for Roman Catholics in Prussia were 50 and 105, is certainly not exclusively the result of a weakening of the religious influence. These and the following statistical data are taken from the art. "*Selbstmord*" in the *Handwörterbuch der Kriminologie*, Vol. II, pp. 546 et seq.

[2] *Catholic Encycl.*, art. "Suicide".

[3] E. Manson, "Suicide as a Crime", *Journal of Comparative Legislation and Intern. Law*, New Series, Vol. I (1899), p. 319.

[4] Kenny, *Outlines of Criminal Law*, 14th ed., p. 115 ; Halsbury, *Laws of England*, Vol. IX, No. 1162. However, "in R. *v.* Leddington, 1839, 9 C.B.P. 79, a man was charged with inciting a man to commit suicide, and Alderson, B., directed an acquittal, saying, 'This is a case which by law we cannot try.' The reasons for this direction are not given, and a note to the case does not make them clear." (Stephen, *Digest of the Criminal Law*, 6th ed., 1904, p. 39, fn. 2).

incapable of understanding the significance of his action.[1] Persons who merely aid and abet the suicide go usually altogether unpunished.

More complex is the position in the case of so-called *death pacts.*[2] If two persons agree to die together but one of them survives, or if one of the participants is selected to kill the other and himself and survives, the survivor is treated as a murderer in English law.[3] This, again, does not sufficiently take into account the peculiar psychological aspects of the situation—provided the survivor has throughout acted in good faith. Of course, no law recognizes the right of an individual to authorize another person to kill him.[4] This is true even of those legal systems which do not punish suicide, since there are obvious differences between taking one's own life and using the services of another person for the purpose. Should the actor, however, be treated exactly like an ordinary murderer? In certain Penal Codes, special provisions have been made in his favour, provided he acts not only with the consent but at the serious request of the other person. In this case, the penalty which would have been incurred if the action had been committed without such a request is considerably mitigated.[5] The same should apply, perhaps even to a higher degree, to death-pacts concluded and, as far as possible, carried out in good faith. The Chinese Code goes so far as to provide that the penalty may here be altogether remitted (art. 275). If English law would accord to the criminal courts in cases of murder the same wide discretion in their choice of the penalty which they enjoy in cases of manslaughter, the main difficulty would probably be solved.

C. Euthanasia.

It is comparatively easy to argue against the punishment of attempted suicide and even in favour of more lenient treatment of homicide committed at the request of the victim, but more

[1] See Russia, art. 141 ; Switzerland, art. 115. Italy, art. 580, and China, art. 275, have no such restrictions, but even here the penalty is much more lenient than that of murder.

[2] On the Japanese *Shinju* see *Encycl. of Religion and Ethics*, loco cit., p. 38.

[3] Kenny, loco cit. ; Halsbury, loco cit.

[4] Stephen, *Digest of the Criminal Law*, 6th ed. 1904, art. 228.

[5] See for instance, Italian Code, art. 579 ; Swiss Code, art. 114 ; Chinese Code, art. 275 ; Polish Code, art. 227 ; (Pre-Nazi) German Code, art. 216. The Nazi ideology is against such provisions ; see Gleispach, *Der Besondere Teil des Strafrechts*, p. 258.

difficult to defend the complete legalization of *Euthanasia*. This means the killing of another human being at his serious request for one specific reason, namely, to save him from a painful and incurable disease. The idea of euthanasia has individualistic and humanitarian roots. English law makes no provision for such cases; the general principle, already mentioned, that nobody can lawfully authorize another person to kill him being applicable regardless of any humanitarian motives. It may be true that, as Dr. Harry Roberts suggests,[1] in its practical administration English law shows "more common sense" in the matter "than is generally recognized", which apparently means that juries sometimes find such offenders "not guilty" in spite of sufficient evidence to the contrary.[2] Of the above-mentioned foreign codes which contain provisions mitigating the ordinary penalties for murder if the act is committed at the serious request of the victim not a single one refers to the special case of euthanasia, with the exception of the Polish Code which mentions "compassion" as the required motive. The adherents of the idea of euthanasia cannot be satisfied with the present legal position; they urge that a distinction should be made between this and other cases of killing at the request of the victim and that euthanasia should not merely be treated with greater leniency than ordinary homicide, but be made altogether lawful. It is generally admitted that such a sweeping change in the law can be justified only if strong safeguards are provided against possible abuses. In the "Voluntary Euthanasia (Legislation) Bill", worked out by the "Voluntary Euthanasia Legislation Society" and introduced in the House of Lords in 1936, an attempt was made to provide such safeguards.[3] The Bill was rejected, but the movement will probably be revived at some later stage. Its basic idea is that the decision as to whether, in a given case, euthanasia is justified should be transferred, together with the legal responsibility for it, from the individual upon whose shoulders it rests under the present law to a body of experts. Moreover, the decision whether euthanasia is lawful in a given case should, wherever possible, be taken before, instead of after, the event. If these experts give

[1] *Euthanasia and other Aspects of Life and Death* (1936), p. 4.

[2] See also the case in *The Times* of August 31, 1945, where a Coroner's Jury refused to use the word "murder".

[3] The Bill is reproduced by Dr. Roberts, op. cit., pp. 19–26. A brief history of the movement, extending from Seneca, via Thomas More, to Dean Inge, is given in Dr. C. Killick Millard's lecture "The Movement in Favour of Voluntary Euthanasia", delivered before the Leicester Literary and Philosophical Society, Jan. 27, 1936.

permission to carry out euthanasia their permit may, however, be cancelled by a court of summary jurisdiction at the request of the nearest relative of the patient if the court holds that the legal conditions are not fulfilled.

Euthanasia has been attacked mainly from two different quarters : by members of the Catholic Church and by adherents of traditional liberalism.

The attitude of the Catholic Church has been forcefully expressed, for instance, in a book by Father Bonnar [1] : Euthanasia, or, as he prefers to call it, " suicide-cum-murder ", is, he argues, " neither new nor clever " (as if this were of any significance—for those who propagate the idea it is a matter of conscience, not of fashionableness or cleverness). His other arguments are more to the point. Though human suffering should, wherever possible, be lessened, it is not justifiable to terminate a person's life merely because of his suffering. Granted that not all human lives are equally valuable for the community, they are, nevertheless, equally sacred in the sense that " God has reserved to Himself the right to dispose of such things as are sacred ". Of the difficulties arising from the fact that the infliction of the Death Penalty and killing in war are permitted by the Church, the author disposes by establishing the exception that " the sanctity—i.e., inviolability—of human life appears in God's Revelation as being wiped out by the commission of certain atrocious crimes. . . . No other permission to kill exists or can exist : and human life must be as sacred to the individual himself as to others." It goes without saying that no compromise will ever be reached between this view and the euthanasia movement. With Dr. Bonnar's other argument, i.e., his anxiety that the Bill of 1936 might represent merely the first step " in the grisly dance of death ", we shall deal later.

Although this anxiety is shared by Dr. Harry Roberts, his other objections are of an altogether different character. He is not opposed to euthanasia as such ; he even admits that " the issue can scarcely be that of the sacredness of life " ; what he dislikes is the proposal to surround it with an atmosphere of formality and with all the paraphernalia of officialdom. What has

[1] *The Catholic Doctor*, by Fr. A. Bonnar, O.F.M., D.D. Quotations are from the second edition, 1939, Chapter X. An exhaustive monograph on the problem, also written from the point of view of the Catholic Church, is *Die Euthanasie und die Heiligkeit des Lebens*, by Franz Walter, Prof. of Theology at Munich University (Munich, Max Hueber, 1935, 684 pp.), where the very extensive German literature on the subject is discussed.

to be done should be decided upon and carried out by the individual according to his own conscience, at his own risk and without official interference. "As a human being and a citizen, a man may act as his judgment and conscience dictate; and, if this involves breaking the law, he must be prepared to bear the penalty if he does so." With this attitude we have every sympathy, but does it go far enough and does it really solve the problem? [1] Can we always be sure to be surrounded by heroes willing to run the risk which the present law involves? And even if we were, would it be fair to expect from our fellow human beings such a sacrifice? This in particular as there is at present no way of finding out in advance how such an action might be later treated in a court of law. Dr. Roberts's view clearly reflects the romantic spirit of a bygone age and of a law which is tolerable only on the understanding that it will not be carried out. Of a law, moreover, that places those who have to administer it in the embarrassing position of having to punish after the event, instead of being able to advise and to guide at a time when it is not yet too late. Generally speaking, this is one of the great weaknesses of the criminal law, and one of the principal reasons why legal disputes should, as much as possible, be transferred from the criminal to the administrative branch of the law. Even so, plenty of opportunity will remain for the private citizen, and in particular for the doctor, to exercise their own judgment and to act according to their individual consciences. In the first instance, even if the Bill of 1936 or a similar one should become law, nobody will be forced to avail himself of the facilities provided by it. Neither patient nor doctor will be prevented from having recourse to the present procedure. One might say, therefore, that with the passing of the Bill provision will have been made for every taste, for those who like taking risks and for those whose motto is "safety first". The very fact that no application was made beforehand, may, it is true, create a certain prejudice against those who prefer to practise euthanasia on individual lines. Provided the law of murder will be made to

[1] Judge W. G. Earengay, in his admirable paper on "Voluntary Euthanasia" in the *Medico-legal Review*, April 1940, pp. 91 et seq., writes in defence of the Bill: "The claim made by Lord Dawson (in the House of Lords' Debate) that it is entirely a matter between the patient and his doctor . . . is another instance of the different point of view between law and medicine. According to the present state of the law this question does *not* belong solely to 'the wisdom and conscience of the medical profession'; the realm of law is not to be excluded by the desires of a particular profession, however eminent" (p. 100).—G. Bernard Shaw, *Everybody's Political What's What* (1944), p. 283, is also in favour of euthanasia.

conform with modern ideas, or a provision on the model of the Continental Codes referred to above will be added, this should, however, entail no undue hardship for those individualistic diehards who prefer thrill to safety.

Chapter 2

THE COLLECTIVISTIC ASPECT: THE POPULATION PROBLEM AND THE CRIMINAL LAW

The collectivistic aspect involves the sifting of the human material to be used for the construction of the new World Order. Here, the issue at stake is when and how human life has to be protected or sacrificed by the criminal law, not as in our foregoing discussion in the interest of the individual but for the benefit of the community at large. It is, in fact, the population problem itself, seen from the point of view of the criminal law, that is involved, and the questions to be discussed under this heading are: the extermination of lives useless for the community; sterilization and castration; birth control and abortion.

A. The Extermination of Socially Useless Lives.

Extermination of human beings who are of no use for the progress of the community: child exposure or infanticide, and the abandonment or killing of aged and infirm persons.

This is the collectivistic analogue to euthanasia. Whereas the motive there was the individualistic wish to shorten unnecessary agony—mercy is the keynote of the movement, says Dr. Millard—the aim is now to rid the community of a member who is not an asset but only a burden or a danger. Again, one might say, the idea of destroying such lives is " neither new nor clever ". As history shows, very few civilizations have been entirely free from temptations of this kind.[1]

For primitive communities, anthropologists have amassed material to show that infanticide and parricide have been frequently practised by them mainly from sheer economic necessity, or from superstition, as is shown in the killing of twins [2] or of children born feet first,[3] or for eugenic reasons, as in Sparta.

[1] Art. " Abandonment and Exposure " in *Encycl. of Religion and Ethics*, Vol. I (1908); E. Westermarck, *The Origin and Development of Moral Ideas*, Vol. I (1906), Chapter XVII; Prince Peter Kropotkin, *Mutual Aid* (Pelican Edition), pp. 92 et seq.; Raymond Firth, *We, The Tikopia* (1936), p. 527. E. Adamson Hoebel, " Law-ways of the Primitive Eskimos ", *Journal of Criminal Law and Criminology*, Vol. XXXI, No. 6, March–April 1941; T. R. Glover, *The Challenge of the Greek and other Essays* (1942), p. 87.

[2] Westermarck, op. cit., Vol. I, p. 385; Julian Huxley, *African View*.

[3] I. Schapera, *Married Life in an African Tribe* (1939), p. 225.

There is, however, not always a clearcut line of demarcation between these collectivistic arguments and euthanasia, and as Westermarck suggests, people who have acquired a certain wealth may continue the old practice now for humanitarian reasons instead of economic necessity.

Among modern civilized communities, there seems to be little evidence of any organized system of killing human beings without their consent for the sole reason of their being unable to contribute to the well-being of the community. Dr. Bonnar [1] quotes the late Lord Moynihan, the then President of the Voluntary Euthanasia Legalization Society, as stating in his Inaugural Address : "There are doubtless cases of mongolian idiocy, or of mental defects of one kind or another that may possibly come for discussion." No action has, however, so far been taken to deal with them on similar lines as proposed in the Euthanasia Bill. The Nazis, by practising the large-scale extermination of politically or racially "undesirables", have probably stifled any tendencies of this kind among other nations, and it has come to be recognized that the shaping of human material in the interest of a reasonable and scientific population policy is tolerable only if it begins at an earlier stage. As Dr. Leonard Darwin [2] has said, "we must never attempt to act through the agency of the death rate, but only through that of the birth rate". This leads to the problems of sterilization, birth control and abortion.

B. Sterilization and Castration.

Sterilization is an operation to deprive the patient of his faculty of procreation, whereas castration is intended to rob him of his faculty of cohabitation as well. The surgical methods used at present are : for sterilization vasectomy in the case of males, salpingectomy in the case of females, and for castration removal of the reproductive glands, i.e., of the testes of the male and of the ovaries of the female. Before vasectomy and salpingectomy became known at the end of the last century, only castration could be performed. It is therefore mainly due to recent progress in surgery and medicine that the problem has become one of practical politics even in countries where castration, as the physically and psychologically much more drastic method, would have hardly any chance.

Why are these operations of interest to the criminal lawyer

[1] Op. cit., p. 100. [2] *The Need for Eugenic Reform* (1926), p. 171.

and criminologist, what is their purpose and what is the part the criminal law has to play in the matter? Could it not possibly be argued here as in similar cases, such as abortion, that all these are questions better to be left to the biologist and the medical expert, to the social scientist and the politician? On the other hand, a distinguished biologist, Professor Haldane, has already refused to shoulder this responsibility,[1] and it is, in fact, one which can be borne only by all those professions jointly with the indispensable support of the public at large. The specific part which the criminal law has to play in the matter is, however, clear enough.

(1) There is first the *preventative* idea in its widest sense, i.e., sterilization for therapeutic or eugenic, social or economic reasons, and for the prevention of crime. As things are, it is within the framework of the criminal law that the decision has to be taken whether, and in which cases, sterilization and castration should be made lawful for the future well-being of the individual and society. An explicit ruling is needed, as without it the legal position would at least be doubtful. According to general principles of law, such operations interfere with the integrity of the human body, and, performed without the patient's consent, they would constitute offences against the person. Even his consent, however, does not completely clear the way, since it is a fairly universally recognized principle of criminal law that a consent to the infliction of bodily harm is null and void if its effects are against the public interest. This is one of the exceptions to the rule *volenti non fit injuria*;[2] it is, however, as the reference to the "public interest" shows, less uncompromising than in cases involving the destruction of human life. It all depends, therefore, on the general attitude of the law to the merits or otherwise of sterilization and castration, and, as the formula "public interest" is too vague and ambiguous, no surgeon will feel safe without explicit statutory regulation. Havelock Ellis[3] disputed that. He maintained that legal regulation was no more

[1] *Heredity and Politics*, p. 80.

[2] The formulation of this principle differs in different countries. According to English law, "nobody has a right to consent to the infliction upon himself of bodily harm amounting to a maim, for any purpose injurious to the public" (Stephen, *Digest*, art. 228.) The conception of "maim", the old mayhem, means the deprivation of the use of any member of a man's body "which he can use in fighting, or by the loss of which he is generally and permanently weakened" (Stephen, art. 227) and has its origin apparently in military needs. Castration, according to Stephen, is a maim; if sterilization not amounting to castration had been known to him, he would no doubt have included it as well.

[3] *Sex in Relation to Society* (1937), p. 486.

needed for sterilization than for any other surgical operation or for a haircut. " It is only on the legal aptitude to find quibbles, and by farcical perversions of antiquated laws, that some lawyers rely for this argument," he writes. There is a certain amount of truth in this. On general principles of law it might well be argued that no action can ever be punishable if its net result is in the best interest of society. As, however, individual views as to what is in the interest of society are likely to differ, the only safe method to exclude doubts is by way of explicit regulation ; however, even given such regulations, it will still remain the task of the criminal court to decide whether an individual operation falls within their scope. Whereas the Italian Penal Code, art. 552, expressly prohibits acts directed to render a person impotent to procreate, a number of countries possess statutes, to be discussed later, which make them lawful in certain circumstances. In English law the question has not yet been tackled by the legislator. The " Report of the Departmental Committee on Sterilisation ",[1] the so-called Brock Report, came to the conclusion that, in spite of some doubts, sterilization had to be regarded as illegal unless " necessary for the patient's health " (therapeutic sterilization).[2] Although the Report expressed no views as to the legal position of castration, it is obvious that castration, constituting a much more serious measure, cannot be permissible where even sterilization is prohibited.

For the legislator of the future, therefore, the matter boils down to the question whether " eugenic " sterilization should be permitted. In its racial aspects, it rests on the belief that individuals suffering from certain physical or mental deficiencies are likely to transmit them to subsequent generations. On the social side, preventive measures of this kind may find their justification in the fact that such persons are usually incapable of taking adequate care of their children and of giving them a proper upbringing.

Castration, in particular, has further been justified as preventing sexual offenders from repeating their crimes, either by making it physically impossible for them to offend or by effecting such a change in their personality that they do not want to offend again.

[1] 1934, Cmd. 4485, pp. 6 and 39.

[2] No further explanation of the latter term is given. Catholic teaching, however, makes a distinction, permitting sterilization only if required to cure some illness from which the patient is already suffering, not, however, in order to prevent a pregnancy which might in future endanger life or health of the woman. See A. Bonnar, *The Catholic Doctor*, p. 116.

(2) There is, secondly, the purely *punitive* aspect. Sterilization and castration may both be used as penalties for certain crimes, mainly sexual, and in past ages castration has in fact not infrequently been so applied, as an expression of the idea that the penalty should, as closely as possible, reflect the nature of the crime and that, in particular, that part of the offender's body should suffer which was used for the commission of the crime.

The criminologist, who is interested in the causation and prevention of crime, looks at sterilization and castration chiefly as measures intended to eliminate certain potential causes of misbehaviour, either by transforming the patient himself or by preventing the procreation of potentially delinquent children. Controversial as may be the extent to which mental defectives and certain categories of psychotics contribute to the annual budget of crime, it is beyond doubt that their contribution and that of their offspring considerably exceed the average rate.

Surely such considerations show that there is no other point where the criminal law reformer will have to face issues more delicate and more responsible. If the post-war world is going to be a planned world, and if a planned world means, before anything else, a well-planned population, this, it may be argued, is a part of the scheme where no progress can be achieved without the assistance of the criminal law. It is therefore indispensable to review somewhat more fully the present position, the possibilities and limitations of sterilization.

Here, as everywhere in the realm of ideas, it is the great tragedy of Nazi rule that it has besmirched whatever it has touched.[1] Sterilization, glorified and excessively applied by the Nazis and, with almost equal vigour, condemned by the Catholic Church,[2] has thereby become one of those measures of social reconstruction which can hardly be discussed without encountering the strongest prejudices. All the more would it seem necessary to present an unbiased evaluation of the existing evidence.

It is perhaps not altogether superfluous to recall the fact that legislation on the subject did not begin in Nazi Germany,

[1] Professor J. B. S. Haldane, *Heredity and Politics* (1938), p. 15, prefers "not to quote the German law on the subject because it is inevitable that to do so would give rise to a certain amount of prejudice".

[2] Father Bonnar, *The Catholic Doctor*, pp. 111 et seq., although professing to deal with the problem unprejudiced by his strong religious objections to sterilization, completely ignores the existing American, Scandinavian and Swiss evidence and indulges in vastly exaggerated estimates of the number of persons "who can immediately be marked down for the surgeon's knife".

but in the United States.[1] In 1907, more than a quarter of a century before the passing of the Nazi statutes of 1933 and 1934, the first Sterilization Act came into force in the State of Indiana. It was declared unconstitutional in 1921, but another Act was passed in 1927 and is still in force. By 1915, thirteen States of the U.S.A. had passed such Acts, and the Brock Report 1934,[2] that admirable exposition of the semi-official English view, registers even thirty States, three of which have in the meantime repealed their statutes. For reasons of space, not even a summary of the contents of these Acts can here be attempted. The brief notes given in the Brook Report show that most of them provide for voluntary and compulsory sterilization of certain categories of insanes, mental defectives, and in some cases of sexual offenders, in institutions; in a few States also outside institutions. The Oklahoma Statute of 1931, which permits sterilization after two or more convictions of "felonies involving moral turpitude" has been declared unconstitutional by the Supreme Court in 1942.[3] Several States permit also castration, which, however, has been performed only in a few hundred cases. The total number of sterilizations carried out in all States up to January 1, 1933, is given by the Brock Report as 16,066 (6,999 males and 9,067 females), all of which except about 300 were institution cases. Professor Walter Reckless, in 1940, gives a figure of 25,403 operations.[4] All sources agree that California has made by far the greatest use of sterilization (over 11,000 operations up to January 1, 1937). The comparative smallness of these figures may be due partly to the great care with which decisions are taken, and partly to the fear of the responsible authorities that the statute concerned might one day be declared to be unconstitutional. Through the decision of the Supreme Court of the United States in Buck *v.* Bell, 274 U.S. 200 (1927), upholding the constitutionality of the Virginia Statute, this danger, it is true, has been greatly reduced. It was that decision which contains Mr. Justice Holmes's famous remark: "It is better for all the world, if instead of waiting to execute degenerate offsprings for

[1] An excellent account of the history of the American sterilization movement is given in Arthur E. Fink, *Causes of Crime.* "*Biological Theories in the United States 1800–1915*" (1938), Chapter IX. See also Walter Reckless, *Criminal Behavior* (1940), pp. 411 et seq., and J. H. Landman, *Human Sterilization* (1932).

[2] Report of the Departmental Committee on Sterilization (1934, Cmd. 4485), pp. 34–5, 109–12. See also the more recent summary in *Journal of Comp. Legisl. and Intern. Law*, 3rd Series, Vol. 23 (1941), p. 191.

[3] Barnes-Teeters, *New Horizons in Criminology*, p. 180 fn. 71.

[4] *Criminal Behavior*, p. 414.

crime, or let them starve for their imbecility, society can prevent those who are manifestly unfit from continuing their kind. . . . Three generations of imbeciles are enough."

Among the *Scandinavian* countries, *Denmark* has been the pioneer. As she has had the longest experience in this field in Europe (apart from the Canton of Vaud in Switzerland) and has amended her law several times, Denmark may be treated more fully. Her first Sterilization Act of 1929 [1] permitted " operations on the sexual organs " of persons " whose abnormally developed sexual strength and tendencies predispose them to commit crimes and who thereby become a danger to themselves and to the general public " (sect. 1.), and of " psychically abnormal persons who are under the control of a State Institution, or an Institution recognized under sect. 61 of the Poor Law of April 9, 1891, and in whose case it may be considered especially important for the general public and advantageous for themselves that they be rendered unable to have offspring even if they do not present the menace to public security mentioned in sect. 1 " (sect. 2). Applications could be made only by persons who had reached the age of discretion ; they had to be accompanied by a doctor's declaration and subscribed by a guardian if the applicant had been declared incapable of managing his affairs. In cases under sect. 2 the application had to come from the director of the institution and to be accompanied by a declaration from a guardian appointed for this purpose. Competent for the decision was the Minister of Justice, who had also to state the nature and scientific description of the operation. This latter provision, together with the vagueness of the term " operation on the sexual organs ", makes it clear that castration, too, came under the scope of the Act. The operation could be performed not only on persons actually convicted of sexual offences, but also on sexually abnormal persons predisposed to commit crimes not necessarily of a sexual character. Actually, as mere sterilization produces no change in the sexual urges and predispositions of the patient, it would be incapable of achieving the object for which sect. 1 is intended, and it appears that, for this reason, only castrations have been performed under that section.

In another respect, too, the Act was very wide. The term " psychically abnormal persons " in sect. 2 would, in theory,

[1] Our account of this Act is based on the English translation in the Brock Report, p. 120, from which the literal quotations are taken, and on the German translation in *Monatsschrift für Kriminalpsychologie und Strafrechtsreform* (in future quoted as *MSchrKr*), Vol. 26, p. 34.

include not only cases of mental disorder and mental deficiency but also the whole range of borderline cases and the various types of neurosis and psychopathic personality.

An authoritative and critical account of the working of this first Danish Act during its first five years has been given by Professor Knud Sand, the chairman of the Danish Medico-Legal Board.[1] Among many other data he quotes the following figures:

Castration . . .	63 men,	no women
Sterilization . . .	20 „	88 „

The men who had been castrated are all stated to have committed sexual offences, mostly of a homosexual character, assault on children, and indecent exposure, although in a few cases of elderly homosexuals no offences had so far been actually proved. In addition, many of them had also committed non-sexual offences, as for instance arson. According to their mental status, most of them were classified mental defectives (15), subnormals (10), or psychopaths (28). Of those who had been sterilized almost all were mental defectives; only three were psychopaths and two epileptics. Although the period of observation was admittedly too short for any definite conclusions, the results were stated to be almost throughout satisfactory from the point of view of the individuals concerned as well as from that of the community. According to Sand, castration had no unfavourable physical or mental after-effects; on the contrary, patients are said to have gained a feeling of security and relief from their previous fear of relapsing into crime. In only one case was a relapse into homosexual practices observed, and of twenty-two persons who had been inmates of institutions sixteen could be discharged under supervision.

The Act of 1929 was generally regarded as of an experimental character only, and after five years' of practical experience it was replaced by statutes of a considerably more radical character: an Act of 1934 [2] provided that mental defectives might be operated on even if under age and not inmates of an institution. The decision had to be taken by a court especially constituted for the purposes of the Act and consisting of a judge as chairman, an expert in social welfare and a medico-psychologist. This Act as well as the original Act of 1929 were repealed by the present Act of 1935 [3] which, in several directions, goes beyond

[1] In *MSchrKr*, Vol. 26 (1935), pp. 49–83.
[2] German translation in *MSchrKr*, Vol. 26 (1935), p. 225.
[3] German translation in *MSchrKr*, Vol. 26, p. 544.

the scope of the previous Acts. Castration, on a voluntary basis, is permitted not only if the patient, on account of his sexual impulses, is in danger of committing crime, but also if his condition causes him considerable mental pain or may endanger his social status. Moreover, for a mentally inferior person who is incapable of understanding its meaning, the application may be made by his guardian ; in the case of other persons no such substitution is permitted, but a specially appointed guardian may have to countersign. Mentally and sexually normal adults, a category not provided for by the Act of 1929, may now be sterilized if it is in the interests of the community, especially if there is a danger that their offspring may be hereditarily affected. Such individuals have to make a personal application. Competent for the decision is, as a rule, the Minister of Justice. By far the most radical provision of the Act of 1935, however, is the one which empowers the criminal court, after hearing the opinion of its advisory medical board, to order the compulsory castration of adult persons convicted of any of the following crimes : rape or attempted rape, sexual intercourse with a mentally disordered or defective or helpless woman, or with a girl under fifteen years, homosexual or other indecent acts, provided the crime was committed in circumstances which characterize the offender as a danger to others and a person whom fear of punishment will not deter from the further commission of grave sexual crimes. In the case of a woman the court has to consider that castration is a more serious operation for her than for a man.

In *Norway*, the Draft reproduced in the Brock Report became law in 1934, in a modified form.[1] Under it, a sexual operation may be performed upon any person at his request if there are important reasons for it. If the person is under twenty-one or insane or mentally defective, the consent of his guardian or of a curator, especially appointed for the purpose, is also required. In the case of insanes and low-grade mental defectives, however, the application itself may be made by the guardian, curator, or chief of police, provided there is no hope of cure or considerable improvement and if there is reason to believe that the patient will be unable to support himself and his dependants by his labour, or that he will transmit his abnormal mentality or a serious physical defect to his offspring, or that owing to his abnormal sexuality he will commit sexual crimes. Competent to give the permission and to determine the nature of the operation,

[1] German translation, *MSchrKr*, Vol. 26, p. 36.

whether sterilization or castration, is the director of the Norwegian Medical Board who is, in cases of insanes, mental defectives and persons under age, assisted by a council of four members, of whom at least two must be medical experts, one a judge and one a woman.

The *Swedish* Sterilization Act of 1934,[1] too, is in some respects different from the Draft published in the Brock Report. Its chief characteristics are these : Castration is not admitted, and the Act deals only with sterilization without consent of persons who are unable to give legally valid consent. Sterilization of other persons with their consent may be performed on adequate grounds independent of the Act, provided the operating doctor reports afterwards to the Board of Health.[2] It is important to note that " without consent " is not identical with " compulsory ". The use of force is excluded. On this point Swedish experts are unanimous.[3] They do not make it clear, however, whether the person to be sterilized has beforehand to be given some information as to the nature of the operation so that he is in the position to exercise his right of refusal. Sterilization may be performed on insane, mentally defective or otherwise abnormal persons if there are reasons to assume that they will be unable to take care of their children or that the latter will inherit their abnormalities. Competent for the decision is, as a rule, the Department of Health.

In the five years' period from January 1, 1935 to January 1, 1940,[4] 822 persons (90 men and 732 women)—80 per cent. of them mental defectives—were sterilized under the Act, whereas 1,271 persons, of whom only 5 per cent. were men, were sterilized with their consent. As Myrdal rightly observes, this striking disproportion between men and women indicates that the Act has so far been applied not so much in accordance with eugenic principles as in deference to the wishes of poor law authorities anxious to have women sterilized for whose illegitimate children they have already to pay. In spite of this, there seems to be a movement afoot in Sweden to extend the scope of the Act to borderline groups not yet included and to cases where sterilization seems advisable for other than strictly social or eugenic reasons.[5]

[1] German translation, *MSchrKr*, Vol. 26, p. 38.
[2] Prof. Nils von Hofsten in *Eugenics Review*, Vol. 29, p. 257.
[3] Alva Myrdal, *Nation and Family* (International Library of Sociology and Social Reconstruction), p. 213 ; von Hofsten, p. 257.
[4] The following figures are taken from Alva Myrdal, *Nation and Family*, p. 213 ; see also Hofsten, loco cit.
[5] Myrdal, p. 215 ; *MSchrKr*, Vol. 30 (1939), p. 61.

In *Finland*, the Act of 1935 [1] also shows considerable modifications, as compared with the Draft published in the Brock Report. Whereas the Draft mentions only sterilization, the Act, in conjunction with the accompanying Regulation,[2] explicitly admits castration of a person over twenty-one with abnormally strong or misdirected sexual instincts if he has been convicted of a crime, or attempted crime, which shows the existence of such instincts and makes him appear dangerous to others. The definition of mental deficiency in the Regulation is extremely wide, meaning an intellectual development not exceeding that of a person of fourteen years.

An interesting feature of the *Estonian* Act of 1936 is that it regulates not only sterilization but also abortion and that it is also applicable to serious physical defects if they are of a hereditary character.[3]

Summaries of the position in the Swiss cantons given in the Brock Report and in a paper by Professor Hans Maier [4] make it clear that, although only two cantons, Vaud and Berne, seem to possess special Sterilization Acts, voluntary sterilization is in fact practised, on a moderate scale, throughout the whole of the country.

The Sterilization Acts of *Alberta* (1928) and *British Columbia* (1933),[5] having the exclusive purpose of facilitating the discharge of inmates of mental hospitals, permit sterilization only with the consent of the inmate or, if he is not capable of giving such consent, with that of his relatives, guardian, or the minister.

Nazi Germany possessed three sets of enactments which are of interest in this connection (not counting statutes prohibiting marriage or sexual intercourse between Aryans and Non-Aryans) : [6]

(*a*) The Act of 24th November, 1933, concerning the Treatment of dangerous habitual Criminals and some Measures of Prevention and Reformation.

(*b*) The Act of 14th July, 1933, for the Prevention of hereditary Disease in Posterity,[7] amended by an Act of 26th July, 1935.

[1] German translation in *MSchrKr*, 1935, p. 399. [2] *MSchrKr*, 1935, p. 401.

[3] *MSchrKr*, 1937, p. 571.

[4] Brock Report, p. 114 ; *Eugenics Review*, 1934–5, p. 19, where the French text of the Act of the canton of Vaud is given.

[5] Brock Report, pp. 118–19.

[6] Although these statutes have now lost their legal force, their historical significance as a deterrent may justify the above summary, written before the collapse of Nazi Germany.

[7] English translation in Brock Report, pp. 122 et seq.

(*c*) The Act of 18th October, 1935, for the Protection of the hereditary Health (*Erbgesundheit*) of the German People (*Ehegesundheitsgesetz*).

The last-mentioned Act prohibits any marriage between two persons, one of whom suffers from an infectious disease which may endanger the health of the other or their children, or from a mental disorder which makes the marriage undesirable for the community or comes under the scope of the Act under (*b*), or is placed under guardianship; the Act under (*a*) deals with castration, and the Act under (*b*) with sterilization.

If not in theory so at least in practice, castration is treated in Germany essentially as a penal measure. Under the Act of 24th November, 1933, it can be compulsorily applied, by order of a criminal court, to male persons over the age of twenty-one convicted of rape and similar assaults on women and of indecent assaults on children; the same applies to indecent exposure, murder, manslaughter and wounding if committed in order to produce, or indulge in, sexual lust. The court can order castration only if the person is regarded as a dangerous sexual offender, and if he has committed more than one such offence. During the first four years after the passing of the Act no fewer than 1,376 men were castrated.[1] Moreover, under an amending Act of the 26th June, 1935, castration may also be carried out with the consent of the person concerned if it is necessary in order to cure him from an abnormal sexual instinct which might otherwise lead to a repetition of sexual (including homosexual) offences or wounding. It is an important feature of the Act of 1933 that it empowers the criminal courts to order castration in cases where the offender had been convicted before the coming into force of the Act. As a consequence, several hundred of old cases (439 during the first three years 1934–6) were reopened, and subsequent castration was ordered.[2]

A great deal of discussion has been carried on in German periodicals as to the success or failure of compulsory castration. Apparently, such objections as have been raised have not been directed against the thesis that castration has no evil physical consequences—it seems to be fairly generally agreed among German experts that it has none.[3] The controversy has rather centred round the question whether castration has been effective

[1] F. Exner, *Kriminalbiologie* (1939), p. 141.
[2] *MSchrKr*, 1937, p. 484.
[3] See however, *MSchrKr*, 1937, p. 3.

as a deterrent and as a preventive. To judge from such statistical figures as are available to the author, i.e., up to the end of the year 1936, the passing of the Act of 1933 did not act as a deterrent as sexual offences continued to increase, even those for which castration could be ordered.[1] By far the greatest increase, it is true, occurred in convictions for homosexual offences, for which—unless committed with boys under fourteen—castration was originally not permitted (from 853 in 1933 to 5,321 in 1936).[2] This is the reason why the amending Act of 1935 included homosexual offences, at least on a voluntary basis. Apart from its failure to bring down the general rate of sexual offences, however, it has been admitted by one of the foremost German specialists in this field [3] that castration does not always produce the extinction or even a considerable weakening of the abnormal sexual urge, and at least two cases are described where relapse into sexual criminality had taken place after castration. Another expert, however, gives figures to show that, up to 1938, out of 52 men castrated at Hamburg in 1934 or 1935 and at large ever since not a single one had relapsed into sexual crime, and only five had during that period been convicted of other, mainly economic, offences.[4] He concludes that "*Ersatz*" offences committed by compulsorily castrated sex criminals in a spirit of vengeance and hatred of society, the frequent occurrence of which had been predicted in particular by a Swiss expert,[5] had been notably absent.

The German Sterilization Act of the 14th July, 1933, has become one of the most widely discussed pieces of Nazi legislation. Its main features are generally known and need be only briefly summarized : A person suffering from a hereditary disease may be sterilized "if it may be expected with some certainty, according to the experiences of medical science, that his posterity will suffer from serious physical or mental hereditary disease". The Act contains an exclusive list of diseases which are regarded as hereditary : Innate mental deficiency ; schizophrenia ; manic-depressive insanity ; hereditary epilepsy ; hereditary (Hunting-

[1] Exner in *MSchrKr*, 1938, p. 341.

[2] In part, this increase may have been due to the widening of the scope of the law which took place in 1935.

[3] Professor von Neureiter, Director of the Board of Criminological Research in Berlin, *MSchKr*, 1938, p. 476.

[4] Dr. W. Meywerk, Director of the Crimino-biological Board in Hamburg, *MSchrKr*, 1938, p. 503. More recent statistics to the same effect are given by Dr. C. H. Rodenberg, *Deutsche Justiz*, 1942, pp. 581 et seq.

[5] Ch. Wolf, *Die Kastration bei sexuellen Perversionen und Sittlichkeitsverbrechen des Mannes*, Basle, 1934.

ton's) chorea; hereditary blindness; hereditary deafness; severe hereditary physical abnormality. In addition, persons suffering from severe alcoholism may also be sterilized. The application may be made by the person himself or, in certain cases, by his legal representative with the consent of the Court of Guardianship. Moreover, a medical officer of health or, in the case of an inmate of an institution, the Head of the institution may also apply. Competent for the decision is a special court consisting of a judge, a medical officer of health, and another doctor who is an expert on hereditary disease. There is an appeal to a higher court. If other methods prove of no avail the application of force is permissible.

Under this Act, in the first year of its existence, i.e. 1934, in no fewer than 56,244 cases (concerning 28,286 males and 27,958 females) sterilization was ordered or granted by the Court; the number of sterilizations actually performed in that year is not known.[1] To arrive at a full appreciation of this figure, it should be compared with the American and Scandinavian figures quoted above. Although it has to be borne in mind that American Sterilization Acts were introduced piecemeal, which makes it very difficult to say how many people have been covered by them at any given time, and granted also that their full application was hampered by the uncertainty of the legal position, the contrast between one year of Nazi activities and more than thirty years of American sterilization practice remains amazing. No less striking is the contrast with Danish and Swedish figures: on the basis of the German output Denmark, in proportion to her population, ought to have ordered about 2,800 sterilizations in one year, instead of 108 in five years, and even in Sweden the machinery ought to have worked fourteen times as hard to compete with Germany. If practised on such a scale, it is impossible to regard sterilization any more as a scientific measure—experts of sufficiently high standard are simply not yet available—and it must inevitably be reduced to the level of a political and class instrument. Apart from this gross quantitative abuse of a measure which ought to have been given a reasonable probationary period and apart from its wide use of compulsion, certain other features of the Act have also been severely criticized by experts,[2] as, for instance, its exclusive

[1] *Eugenics Review*, Vol. 29 (1937–8), p. 9; *MSchrKr*, 1935, p. 551.
[2] Not unanimously! Strangely enough, an author of the rank of Havelock Ellis, *Sex in Relation to Society* (1937), p. 488, could write: "In the carefully framed law

list of diseases and its unwillingness to face the problem of the carrier.[1] Although during the war, under an Emergency Decree of 31st August, 1939, sterilizations were to be performed only when the danger of dysgenic progeny was especially grave, it seems that the Act was applied almost as widely as before.[2]

This survey of the existing legislation [3] may be followed by a brief examination of the main points on which any decision will have to be based : [4]

(*a*) There seems to be fairly general agreement that a reduction in the incidence of congenital mental deficiency and of certain forms of transmissible mental disorder and physical disability can be achieved through sterilization. Much uncertainty exists, however, with regard to the length of time required. It has to be borne in mind, for instance, that mental deficiency is not always inherited, and that even of the latter category a considerable proportion will not be discovered.

According to Carr-Saunders,[5] a fairly substantial reduction in congenital mental deficiency by means of sterilization might be expected in a century or so. Haldane, who is not particularly in favour of the whole idea, estimates that the sterilization of all mental defectives would probably cut down the supply in the next generation by something like 10 per cent., whereas, on the other hand, it might prevent the birth of perhaps ten times as many normal children.[6] For certain categories, he thinks, no noticeable effect could be expected in less than thirty or forty generations.[7] Even Haldane's sceptical attitude, valuable as it is as an antidote to unwarranted optimism, cannot, however, totally obscure the fact that a slow rate of progress is better than none. Everything possible should be done to minimize

no doctrine of racial superiority was involved." Apparently, it did not occur to him that Nazi doctrine would inevitably dominate the practical application regardless of the wording of the Act.

[1] Dr. Aubrey Lewis in *Eugenics Review*, Vol. 26 (1934–5), pp. 183 et seq. and 268 et seq., and several other writers in the same periodical.

[2] *The Lancet*, 1941, II, Vol. 241, p. 379, where a few illustrative cases are quoted.

[3] In Soviet Russia, according to Dr. Doris Odlum (*The Lancet* of Nov. 3, 1934, Vol. 227, p. 1027), sterilization is legal and can be performed at the request of any woman, but is nevertheless very rarely practised.

[4] For a comprehensive analysis of the problem as a whole there is here neither space nor need, nor is the author competent to express any independent views on the biological and medical questions involved. For all details reference may be made to the Brock Report.

[5] "Human Evolution and the Control of its Future," in *Evolution, Essays on Aspects of Evolutionary Biology*, edited by G. R. de Beer (1938), p. 121.

[6] J. B. S. Haldane, *Heredity and Politics* (1938), p. 87.

[7] P. 83. For other pessimistic views see Barnes-Teeters, *New Horizons in Criminology*, (1943), p. 179.

"the dead weight of social inefficiency which is entailed by the existence in our midst of over a quarter of a million mental defectives and of a far larger number of persons who without being certifiably defective are mentally subnormal".[1]

(*b*) As a rule, no harmful physical, mental or social effects of sterilization have so far been observed, even in the case of women, where the operation is somewhat more serious than in the case of men.[2]

(*c*) In order to be acceptable to the general public the Sterilization Act will have to define, as exactly as possible, the conditions which are to be brought under its scope. Nevertheless, a certain amount of discretion will remain indispensable. "Whatever formula may be adopted to define the disorders or abnormalities which should be accepted as justifying sterilization, doubts will arise as to whether a particular case comes within the terms of the definition."[3] This all the more if the Act should contain such elastic phrases as "if it is considered especially important for the general public and advantageous for the individual" that he should be sterilized (Denmark). Haldane[4] criticizes the German Act and the Draft Bill of the Eugenics Society for permitting sterilization of a person "if it may be expected with some certainty that his posterity will suffer from serious physical or mental hereditary disease" or if he is "deemed to be likely to transmit mental deficiency . . .", instead of using more definite quantitative delimitations. In fact, however, such quantitative elements would either tend to be ignored or they would make the Act unworkable.

This question of legislative technique will become particularly difficult if, as the Brock Report[5] and the Eugenics Society recommend, carriers are to be included, since for them only definitions of an elastic character can probably be given.

Social and economic considerations can, in themselves, not be regarded as sufficient to justify even voluntary sterilization, unless they are combined with certain serious physical or mental defects of a hereditary character. It is the duty of society to find other ways of dealing with such social and economic handicaps. Lord Riddell[6] seems to be in favour of extending sterilization

[1] Brock Report, p. 55.

[2] Brock Report, p. 29. A. F. Tredgold, *Mental Deficiency* (6th ed., 1937), p. 519. Professor Haldane, p. 80, is more pessimistic in this respect than the majority of experts.

[3] Brock Report, p. 45. [4] Op. cit., p. 78. [5] Pp. 40 et seq.

[6] *Medico-legal Problems* (1929), pp. 11 et seq.

rather than birth control to women who have borne a certain number of children or who have to struggle against heavy domestic or economic handicaps. This is, however, probably more than the public will stand, and it may also be doubtful whether it would be wise to apply permanent solutions for individual problems which may be of a temporary nature only.

(*d*) There should be no castration, neither of sexual offenders, nor of other categories, neither on a compulsory nor even on a voluntary basis, unless on strictly medical grounds. Moreover, sterilization should be on a voluntary basis only. It should have no penal character whatsoever; therefore, it should not be applied to lawbreakers as such and should, in particular, not be made a condition of their discharge from a penal institution, great as the temptation may sometimes be to do so. Nor should it be restricted to inmates of institutions. In principle, hardly any controversy exists in this country on these points. The interpretation of the term "voluntary", however, presents certain difficulties. Can it be honestly applied to mental defectives who are probably the most important group of candidates for sterilization? As shown above, most of the foreign Sterilization Acts provide that their consent can be dispensed with in one way or another. The same method has been adopted in the Draft Bill of the Eugenics Society, not, however, in the Brock Report,[1] and the uncompromising attitude of the latter seems to deserve preference at least for the beginning. It avoids the repugnant use of force for the performance of the operation. (It is surprising, and perhaps significant, that so little information has so far come from abroad about practical experiences in this respect). The fear of compulsion easily deters patients from using the facilities of the medical and social services; it undermines their confidence in the doctor, and it closes avenues badly needed for the collection of scientific case histories. Even the exclusion of force, however, does not in itself altogether dispose of the criticism of the "voluntary" system made by writers otherwise so different as Haldane and Bonnar: "A dubious piece of terminology", as mental defectives can so easily be influenced.[2] Nevertheless, their arguments are basically unsound, and the Brock Report, so sarcastically treated by Bonnar, is right, though its formulation might have been somewhat different. The crux of the matter is how far it is possible to trust the expert and to

[1] See pp. 42, 47, 58 (*e*).
[2] Haldane, p. 94; similarly Bonnar, p. 114.

combine the scientific and the democratic attitude. In a democracy, one cannot go so far as to permit the expert to lay down and to enforce his own law, and, therefore, he has to be tied down to fairly strict rules and denied the use of compulsion. With such restrictions, however, he has to be trusted to apply his special knowledge conscientiously and impartially. If those writers who, with the best intentions, try to discredit the scientist in matters such as euthanasia and sterilization would only pause for a moment to reflect on the far greater powers which they have, without much ado, already conceded to the same experts in at least equally serious questions of life and death! As an alternative to the unconditional adherence to the voluntary principle, the Swedish distinction between "without consent" and compulsion might be copied, though one would like to have some information regarding the actual behaviour of persons about to be sterilized "without their consent". They ought at least to be told what is going to happen to them.

(*e*) Similar considerations apply to the much exaggerated danger that sterilization might become a measure of class discrimination, confined exclusively to the poor.[1] Surely, there is no greater danger of class discrimination involved in sterilization than in the whole legal and penal system. On this, we shall have something to say at a later stage. The arguments for and against sterilization cannot be discussed in isolation; they have to be considered in relation to the administration of justice and the social services as a whole. We do not recommend its introduction in a fascist State. On the other hand, as the Brock Report has stressed,[2] there is class distinction under the present system where only the well-to-do can obtain sterilization.

Another inconclusive argument used by Haldane is that marriage should mean a great deal more than legalized sexual intercourse without the possibility of procreation, and to reduce it to that level would be at least as anti-social as the birth of an "occasional defective". This seems to overlook the ultimate aim of sterilization which is—though this will be achieved only in the distant future—to reduce mental deficiency to such an extent as to make sterilization itself unnecessary. It is just because marriage means so much more than legalized sexual intercourse that individuals should not be prevented from

[1] Haldane, p. 98; Bonnar, p. 115: "The whole thing is simply a scheme for wholesale mass mutilation of the poor, called the 'social problem group'." Such exaggerations can hardly be taken seriously.

[2] P. 43.

marrying merely because they are unsuitable for procreation. Haldane prefers detention in institutions to sterilization and thinks it would be not more expensive. Doubtful as this may be from the financial point of view, the argument takes into account neither the loss of human happiness on the part of inmates and staffs nor the waste of human labour which could be better used for constructive purposes than for looking after people in institutions. We are of course aware of the fact that only a small proportion—the Brock Report states 3 to 5 per cent.—of inmates of institutions for mental defectives and insanes could safely be discharged after sterilization, and that in some cases sterilization may possibly be an encouragement to sexual promiscuity. However, the Brock Committee could obtain no evidence of such danger from the U.S.A. Professor Sand's Danish material shows sexual promiscuity in some cases of women discharged after sterilization ; even here, however, it cannot be said that there had been a deterioration in their behaviour. The obvious method of dealing with this particular problem is to arrange for adequate supervision after discharge—a method already embodied in some Sterilization Acts and one to which the success of the Californian Act is usually ascribed.

When, as it is to be hoped, sterilization on the lines of the Brock Report will become part of English law in the period of reconstruction, it will probably be practised on a small scale only, and from the purely quantitative point of view but little will therefore be achieved for the next few generations. Even this small-scale measure, however, will at least open up the hitherto lacking possibilities for systematic research and for prolonged study—physiological, psychological, and social—of the after-histories of sterilized persons. The first-hand material thus collected will provide a sounder basis than at present available for the decision whether and how far the scope of the Act might finally be extended, or whether even this first step will have to be undone. Without such opportunities for research experts have to rely mainly on second-hand information received from other countries. At present, it is, therefore, this first step that matters.

Chapter 3

THE COLLECTIVISTIC ASPECT (*continued*).

Birth Control and Abortion

Sterilization, as we have seen, should be confined to rigidly selected categories of individuals and to cases where the objections to parenthood are of a permanent character. There will always remain the mass problems of those who, though not generally unfit for parenthood, should have either fewer children or have them at better spaced intervals, and in their interest the twin problems of birth control and abortion will have to be solved by the legislator.

C. Birth control.

Of these two methods, *birth control*, one of the most important inventions in the history of the human race, has, on the whole, been treated more leniently by the criminal law than abortion. Indeed, in most countries the period of open criminal persecution is now largely over. Statutes prohibiting propaganda for, and the teaching and the application of, contraceptive methods, or the sale of instruments of birth control have been largely repealed or at least fallen into disuse. Nevertheless, the history of the birth control movement [1] knows of many stormy incidents, and unless certain weak spots in its ideological armour are removed it may once more become the object of violent suppression. In view of the key position which the problem is bound to occupy in the coming work of social reconstruction the present legal position in some of the more important countries may be briefly sketched. It is illuminating to trace the various stages in the gradual conversion from one extreme to the other : from wholesale persecution via partial and half-hearted toleration to complete neutrality and, finally, to positive acceptance and incorporation in a constructive scheme of population policy. Roughly speaking, three groups of countries may be distinguished :

[1] A good account of it can be found in Dr. Max Hodann's *History of Modern Morals* (1937 edition), Chapter V, with Bibliography. Moreover, art. " Birth Control " in *Encycl. of Social Sciences*, and D. V. Glass, *Population Policies and Movements in Europe* (1940), pp. 29 et seq.

(*a*) Countries where contraception is either completely or in part prohibited by the criminal law.[1]

The position in the U.S.A. is still rather confusing.[2] Under the Federal Act of 1873, the notorious Comstock Act, the mailing or importing of articles designed, adapted, or intended for the prevention of conception or the procurement of a miscarriage was prohibited under penalties. In addition, the laws of most States of the Union prohibit either any form of sale or distribution of contraceptives, or the publication of information on and advertisements of contraceptive material. In some of the laws, however, explicit exceptions are made in favour of the medical practitioner, and in the Japanese Pessaries case of 1936 the U.S. Circuit Court of Appeals excluded from the scope of the Comstock Act contraceptives which might " intelligently be employed by conscious and competent physicians for the purpose of saving life or promoting the well-being of their patients ". It has therefore been said [3] that in 38 States the law does not seriously interfere with the use of contraceptives by physicians in their medical practice. In two States, Massachusetts and Connecticut, however, the practice of the courts has in recent years become much less conciliatory. The Massachusetts Supreme Court decided in 1938 that a physician had no right to advise on birth control under any conditions whatever, and in Connecticut, the only State where the Act makes not only advice and distribution but even the use of contraceptives an offence, the Supreme Court of Errors refused in 1940 to declare the law unconstitutional. As a consequence, all birth control clinics were therefore closed in these two States. Even in New York State, however, where the law permits contraceptive advice " to cure or prevent disease ", according to Dr. R. L. Dickinson [4]

[1] The hostile attitude of the Catholic Church is explained in the Encyclical Letter of Pope Pius XI. *Casti Connubii*, of Dec. 31, 1930 (English translation published by the Catholic Truth Society). The Church of England has become less uncompromising in recent years : see *Abortion*, by Stella Browne (1935), p. 16. A full discussion of the teachings of the Roman Catholic, Anglican and Jewish Churches may be found in Claud Mullins's book *Marriage, Children, and God* (1933). On Mahatma Gandhi's views see Jawaharlal Nehru's *Autobiography*, p. 512, and Gyan Chand, *India's Teeming Millions* (1939), Chapter XII.

[2] For detailed information see Norman E. Himes, " A Decade of Progress in Birth Control ", in *Annals of the American Acad. of Pol. and Social Science*, Vol. 212, Nov. 1940 ; 45 Harvard Law Review 723 (1932) ; David Hanscom, *Journal of Criminal Law and Criminology*, Vol. XXXI, Sept. Oct. 1940, p. 312 ; 50 *Yale Law Journal* 682 (1941) ; Alec Craig, *The Banned Books of England* (1937), esp. pp. 105 et seq.

[3] Himes, loco cit. See also Frederick Osborn, Preface to *Eugenics* (1940), p. 156, and for the most recent developments H.P. Fairchild, *Annals* (Sept. 1943), p. 79.

[4] *Control of Conception* (2nd ed., 1938), pp. 295, 301.

one-third of all women who sought advice at the Birth Control Clinical Research Bureau had to be turned away though in many cases " well-defined strains on health ", such as unemployment, overcrowding, chronic alcoholism of the husband, could be found.

Italy (art. 553) and Switzerland (art. 211) prohibit certain propagandist and advertising activities in favour of birth control. Whereas the Italian Code penalizes any public propaganda, Swiss law is restricted to propaganda which violates public decency, a term equally vague as it is popular with the makers of criminal law. Similarly, sect. 235 of the Danish Penal Code punishes the offensive advertising or offering of contraceptives.[1] A French law of 1920 and a Belgian law of 1923 punish, in addition to such activities, anybody who facilitates the use of contraceptive methods.[2] In both countries, however, the laws have remained largely ineffective because of the narrow interpretation which has been applied to them. Between 1927 and 1934, only 82 persons were convicted under the French law of 1920, and 21 persons under the Belgian law of 1923.[3]

(*b*) In the second group of countries no penal provisions concerning birth control do exist. Birth control is more or less tolerated as inevitable, but its application is limited as much as possible by non-penal methods.

In Nazi Germany, for instance, no penal prohibitions have been introduced ; nevertheless, ever since the beginning of the Nazi régime a violent campaign has been carried on against any form of activity in favour of birth control, such as propaganda, advice, distribution ; and birth control clinics have been closed throughout the Reich.[4] Contraceptives are, however, available, though less easily than before 1933. Similarly, in Japan, in spite of the lack of legal prohibitions, propaganda of birth control was suppressed by the police.[5]

Although English criminal law has given up the fight against regulated birth control,[6] the idea itself has had a somewhat half-hearted reception in this country. This is apparent in

[1] *MSchrKr*, 1937, p. 575 ; Glass, *Population Policies and Movements*, p. 223.

[2] Full details on the position in France, Belgium, Germany, and the Scandinavian countries are given in an article by Dr. D. V. Glass, *The Modern Law Review*, Vol. II, 1938, pp. 97 et seq. and in his book *Population Policies and Movements in Europe* (1940).

[3] Glass, *Modern Law, Review*, pp. 111 and 112.

[4] M. Hodann, p. 206 ; Glass, *Population Policies and Movements*, p. 283, and *Modern Law Review*, p. 116 ; Clifford Kirkpatrick, *Women in Nazi Germany* (1939), p. 148 ; Osborn, op. cit., p. 170.

[5] Ryoichi Ishii, *Population Pressure and Economic Life in Japan*, (1937), p. 238.

[6] Alec Craig, *The Banned Books of England* (1937), pp. 110 et seq.

particular in the attitude of local authorities towards contraceptive advice. According to the Inter-Departmental Report on Abortion, which will be discussed later, " roughly one-third of the 408 Welfare Authorities . . . have not taken any steps to exercise their powers ", conferred upon them by the Minister of Health.[1] Moreover, these powers to give advice at Welfare Centres, Clinics, etc., appear to be fairly narrow in themselves, restricted as they are to married women, and, even for them, to cases where birth control is regarded as necessary on medical grounds. The Report itself stresses that, although local authorities should be induced to make fuller use of their existing powers, it would be undesirable " that the public health services should be utilized for the unrestricted dissemination of birth control advice ". As a consequence, in the words of Mrs. Thurtle,[2] " by being denied equality of knowledge . . . the poorer women are to have visited on them the shortcomings of their upper- and middle-class sisters ". It is thus not the criminal law but the administration that is mainly responsible for the existing local and social inequality in matters of birth control in England. In recent debates in the House of Commons the suggestion has been made, however, to reintroduce certain legal restrictions on contraceptives,[3] and the possibility can never be entirely excluded that, either as part of a programme to stem the decline in population or on moral grounds, the help of the criminal law might once more be invoked by the legislator.

(*c*) In the third group might be included all those countries where not only no difficulties whatsoever are placed in the way of birth control but where birth control is even made to play a positive part in a constructive scheme of social reform. Russia, to judge from such scanty information as is available, does not seem to belong to this category. It is true, no taboos on birth control have been erected by Russian law, even when abortion was made illegal. Nevertheless, its practical application was said, before the war, to be less widespread than in Western countries, and after 1936 " the literature on the subject suddenly disappeared from news stands and bookshops." [4]

[1] Report of 1939, Chapter VIII. In her book, *Abortion, Right or Wrong?* (1940), p. 30, Mrs. Dorothy Thurtle, who was herself a member of the Inter-Departmental Committee, states that the position is even slightly worse. See also Claud Mullins *Marriage, Children, and God,* Chapter X.

[2] Op. cit., p. 33.

[3] See Debates of July 16, 1943 : Hansard, Vol. 391, pp. 581 et seq.

[4] Maurice Hindus, *Mother Russia* (1943), p. 356 ; see also the Webbs, *Soviet Communism,* II, p. 826 ; Ella Winter, *Red Virtue,* p. 142.

The country which, at least in the theoretical sphere, has recently advanced most in this field is Sweden.[1] Not only have the repressive Acts of 1910–11, which prohibited the exhibition and advertising of contraceptives mainly with the effect of making the public aware of the existence of the latter, been repealed in 1938, the idea has even been forcefully stressed that " birth control shall be frankly declared to be good in itself. We do not want to keep up the birth rate by causing the birth of unwanted children who have to thank ignorance or bad luck for their existence ".[2] This attitude of mind can be understood only as part and parcel of Swedish foreign and domestic policy in general. While renouncing the imperialistic dreams of former centuries, this policy sees its ultimate goal in the improvement of the standard of living for a numerically fixed population within a fixed territory. Quantity is not regarded as more important than quality ; smallness breeds no inferiority complex, and there is no confusion between " greatness " and " bigness ". Consequently, the family with three or four children was regarded as the ideal by the Swedish Population Commission of 1935, and a well-planned scheme of birth control had to be worked out to achieve it.[3] Its basis is the treatment of birth control instruction not as a makeshift solution to be restricted to married women in cases of emergency at a stage when it is frequently too late, but as an indispensable element of the child's general education. It was the considered opinion of the Population Commission that any obstacles, legal, administrative, or others, put in the way of birth control knowledge, far from producing a higher birth rate, can have only harmful results. One of the most important of these results is the increase in abortion.

To the criminologist who has good reasons to regard the unwanted child as one of the most likely candidates for future delinquency [4] the Swedish policy, apart from its other merits, cannot fail to have a particularly strong appeal. While for the over-populated countries of the Far East birth control has become a matter of life or death, for Western Civilization the complete

[1] See in particular the interesting account in Alva Myrdal, *Family and Nation*, pp. 196 et seq. ; also D. V. Glass, *Population Policies and Movements*, Chapter VII.

[2] Professor Gunnar Myrdal, Stockholm, in the *Annals of the American Academy of Political and Social Science*, Vol. 197 (May 1938), p. 210.

[3] Alva Myrdal, op. cit., pp. 11, 104, 169, 196.

[4] Only recently, this point has again been stressed by Mr. Claud Mullins, *Crime and Psychology* (1943), p. 125, and more fully now in " *Why Crime ?* " (1945). Moreover, a few of his case histories seem to indicate a causal connection between ignorance about birth control and such offences as indecent exposure ; see pp. 90 and 92.

replacement of penal by scientific and educative methods is at least a *conditio sine qua non* of constructive planning. On the other hand, even the Swedish system of combining birth control with social reform may easily fail to prevent a further decline in population unless it is accompanied by such changes in moral values as are necessary in order to make procreation not only tolerable from the economic point of view, but also in other respects positively desirable.[1] In the matter of birth control, mankind has to travel from the stage of indiscriminate legal prohibition and religious taboo through a network of minor legal and administrative obstacles to the other extreme of complete freedom; from considerations of a purely quantitative character to a system which keeps the right balance between quantity and quality. For the criminal law there is no place in such a system, unless its assistance is required in the fight against commercial exploitation of this basic need of mankind. This, however, belongs to another chapter.[2]

D. Abortion.

Neither a Sterilization Act nor even a well-planned system of birth control can in themselves lead to a complete disappearance of abortion as a social problem, though they may considerably reduce its scope. Sterilization, particularly if permitted on a voluntary basis only, will be limited to a small group of individuals. Birth control is, for a variety of reasons, bound to fail in a fairly high proportion of cases. Moreover, owing to changed circumstances, a pregnancy which may have been desired at the time of conception may become an intolerable burden soon afterwards. And, finally, for certain pregnancies, as for example, in cases of rape, the question of birth control does not even arise.

At present, abortion is by far the most frequent among the more serious offences committed by women. According to *Criminal Statistics* for 1938, 10,872 females were proceeded against in that year for indictable, and 67,366 for non-indictable offences. Only 66 were charged with abortion. The Inter-Departmental Committee on Abortion, on the other hand, estimated the annual number of criminal abortions in England and Wales at approximately 40 per cent. of the total number of

[1] This is rightly stressed by R. and K. Titmuss, *Parents' Revolt* (1942), p. 115.

[2] Chapter 8 Bc (Monopoly). On certain tendencies to monopolize the production and distribution of contraceptives in the U.S.A., valued at about 250 million dollars a year, see Himes, *Annals*, Vol. 212, pp. 95–6.

abortions, which they put at between 110,000 and 150,000, i.e., at about 44,000 to 60,000.[1] It is obvious that if all these abortions would have led to convictions in the criminal courts, the pre-war sex ratio of crime, which was about 1 : 7 in favour of women, would have been completely altered. This grotesque disproportion between the frequency of abortions and the infinitesimal number of convictions [2] is in itself a serious matter. A symptom of the disregard into which the law has fallen, it was one of the main reasons for the setting up of the Inter-Departmental Committee in 1937. There is, in this country as well as abroad, hardly any other section of the criminal law that is so completely out of touch with the feelings of the masses as the law of abortion.

Even the most superficial historical or comparative analysis of the subject reveals the weakness of the foundations on which this law has been built and the extreme variety of attitudes adopted towards abortion at various times among different peoples.[3] In spite of its strong condemnation by the Church, it was not before 1803 that abortion was made a statutory offence in English law, to be tried by criminal courts, instead of by ecclesiastical courts.[4] This is remarkably late for a country which, at that time, possessed already a very elaborate system of statutory offences. " Abortion is evidently a crime without much recorded or reported history ".[5]

To say that the present law is out of touch with the realities of modern life and the feelings of the masses does not imply any wholesale and unconditional approval of the practice of abortion. We are by no means in favour of the battle-cry that " the woman's right to abortion is an absolute right up to the viability of her child, as much as the removal of a dangerously

[1] See the Report on Abortion (1939), pp. 9 and 11. These figures are probably under-estimates. Dr. Glass, *Population Policies and Movements*, p. 429, thinks it " not at all improbable that there are each year about 100,000 illegal abortions in England and Wales ". For certain other countries the numbers of induced abortions have been estimated at slightly below or even slightly above the numbers of births (see, e.g., Hodann, *History of Modern Morals*, p. 218 ; Glass, *Population Policies and Movements*, pp. 163–4). Magnus Hirschfeld, *Geschlechtskunde*, Vol. II (1928), estimated the annual number of miscarriages in Germany at 700,000, of which he classified 95 per cent. as " criminal ".

[2] Further details in the Report on Abortion, p. 45.

[3] See, for example, E. Westermarck, *Origin and Development of Moral Ideas*, Vol. I, pp. 413, et seq. ; Lecky, *History of European Morals from Augustus to Charlemagne*, Vol. II, pp. 9 et seq. ; D. Seaborne Davies, 2 *Modern Law Review* (1938), pp. 130 et seq.

[4] " Before 1803, the references to the procuring of abortion as a crime at common law . . . are not numerous and are late in date " (Report on Abortion, p. 27).

[5] Davies, p. 130.

diseased appendix ".[1] Extravagantly individualistic claims of this kind are likely to make the solution of an already over-complicated problem almost impossible. It goes without saying that in Soviet Russia such theories have never been adopted. A right understanding of the Russian law and practice between 1920 and 1936 is indispensable in order to come to a correct interpretation of the change made in 1936.[2] An outstanding characteristic of modern Russian criminal law in general is the readiness with which it is changed and adapted to new conditions. The abortion law before 1936, too, was not intended for all eternity; it was an experiment, a product of extraordinary circumstances and destined to disappear with them. Housing, food, medical service, the birth rate, foreign politics—these and many other factors were constantly in the minds of the Soviet Government when formulating the abortion policy of the day. Another important point which is easily overlooked is that even under the original Soviet law [3] abortion was by no means permitted without any restrictions. It was legal only for doctors in hospitals; not after three months of pregnancy (according to Taussig even two and a half months); for a first pregnancy only if necessary to avert serious danger to the woman's life; and not to be repeated earlier than six months after a preceding abortion (according to Dr. Odlum not more than once a year and, as a rule, altogether not more than three or four times). More important even than these legal restrictions, however, was the growing pressure on the part of State and party on women, especially if members of the Communist party, not to resort to abortion except for very good reasons. Looked at in this way, the law of 1936 was nothing but the logical consequence of the deterioration in the political and military situation on the Continent, in conjunction with the simultaneous economic and social progress in Soviet Russia.

Abortion will always remain an evil, a makeshift, and a waste, which should be reduced to the utmost minimum. The

[1] So not very long ago Miss F. W. Stella Browne in *Abortion* (1935), p. 29.

[2] A summary of the law of 1936 is given in the Report on Abortion, p. 165. The literature on abortion in Soviet Russia is very extensive. Reference may be made in particular to the following: F. J. Taussig, *Abortion, spontaneous and induced* (1936), excellent but covering only the period before 1936; S. and B. Webb, *Soviet Communism*, Vol. II, pp. 826 et seq. and 1202, with further literature; Pat Sloan, *Soviet Democracy* (1937), p. 125; M. Hindus, *Mother Russia* (1943), p. 317; M. Hodann, *History of Modern Morals* (1937), pp. 220 and 293; *Report on Abortion*, pp. 22 et seq., 84, 140, 165; Dr. Doris Odlum in the *Lancet* of Nov. 3, 1934, Vol. 227, p. 1027.

[3] See the full text of the Decree of Nov. 18, 1920 in Taussig, p. 405.

problem before us is to determine the part which the criminal law should have to play in dealing with it. This, as we tried to make clear in our introductory remarks,[1] involves in fact two different questions: first, where shall the general line of demarcation be drawn between lawful and criminal abortion? and, second, what kind of agency shall be competent to apply the general policy to individual cases?

(1) The first point makes necessary a sorting out and an evaluation of the various arguments which have been used in defence of abortion: the *therapeutic—eugenic—ethical* or *humanitarian—social, economic*, or *personal* indications (labels some of which are rather misleading).

A brief summary of the legal position in a number of countries may not be out of place:[2]

(*a*) *Therapeutic abortion*, i.e., an abortion procured by a medical practitioner to interrupt a pregnancy which is likely to endanger the woman's life or seriously to impair her health. Provided certain safeguarding provisions are observed, therapeutic abortions are explicitly declared to be lawful in the following countries: Argentine, China, Denmark, Germany, Iceland, Latvia, Poland, Rumania, Soviet Russia, Sweden, Switzerland, the majority of States in the U.S.A.,[3] and Yugo-Slavia.

In addition, in several countries, notably England, France, Belgium, and Norway, where the penal law contains no specific provisions in favour of therapeutic abortion, it is nevertheless, within limits, regarded as legally permissible.[4] In England, the famous Bourne case, 1938,[5] though greatly contributing towards the clarification of the problem, has by no means brought a complete solution. While reaffirming the legality of abortions performed for the preservation of life, it has left in doubt whether the mere protection of the woman's health can really be regarded as enjoying the same privileged treatment in English law. The Inter-Departmental Committee, in any case, described the position in this respect as still ill-defined and unsatisfactory and

[1] Above, p. 2.

[2] This summary, which makes no claim to present a complete picture, is mainly based on the *Report on Abortion*, App. 2; Glass, *Population Policies and Movements*; F. J. Taussig, *Abortion*; on material published in the *MSchrKr* and the *Eugenics Review*, and on a number of Penal Codes.

[3] See the analysis of the U.S.A. statutes by Taussig, op. cit., p. 426, and App. A.

[4] Report on Abortion, pp. 158 et seq.; Glass, *Population Policies and Movements*, pp. 157 et seq.

[5] See Report on Abortion, pp. 30 and 70; D. Seaborne Davies, loco cit.

recommended an amendment of the law to legalize abortion for serious reasons of health. There can be no doubt as to the desirability of such an amendment.

(*b*) *Eugenic abortion*, i.e., an abortion performed to prevent the birth of a child likely to inherit serious physical or mental disabilities. This, too, has been made lawful in a number of countries, though the list is considerably shorter than for therapeutic abortion : Denmark, Germany, Iceland, Latvia, Rumania, Soviet Russia, Sweden.[1] As in the case of sterilization, with which these abortion laws are sometimes organically linked up, no complete uniformity exists in defining the term " eugenic ". The principle itself, however, is sound, and it is to be regretted that the Report of 1939, not courageous enough to follow the example of the Brock Report, for reasons which cannot be regarded as adequate refused to make corresponding recommendations for abortion.[2] Although the position is not exactly the same here as for sterilization, the case for eugenic abortion when all is said, seems hardly less strong. In countries with compulsory sterilization it is easy to make abortion in such cases dependent on subsequent sterilization, but even where sterilization is on a voluntary basis it might be possible in suitable cases to permit abortion only when sterilization has been agreed to by the woman.[3]

(*c*) Abortion for *ethical* or *humanitarian* reasons : This refers to pregnancies resulting from sexual crimes, as rape, incest, unlawful carnal knowledge. Such abortions have been made lawful in Argentine, Denmark, Iceland, Latvia, Poland, and Sweden. Here again, no complete uniformity exists with regard to the scope of the exemption and the essential requirements. The attitude of the *Report on Abortion*, although sympathetic in principle, is largely negative in its practical recommendations.[4] With its view that incest should, as such, provide no justification one might possibly agree, provided eugenic abortions should become legal. Even here, if the interests of the children resulting from incestuous intercourse are duly considered, one might feel inclined to take the opposite view.[5] With regard to rape, however, the only reason why the Report felt unable to recommend any change in the law was the difficulty of securing the necessary

[1] The Report on Abortion, p. 164, and M. Hodann, *History of Modern Morals*, p. 230, further refer to the Swiss Canton of Vaud.
[2] Report on Abortion, p. 90.
[3] See also Taussig, pp. 317 et seq.
[4] Pp. 86 and 123.
[5] See the Minority Report by Mrs. Dorothy Thurtle, p. 148.

evidence at an early stage of the pregnancy. Although this is no doubt a serious obstacle, it should not be impossible to devise a special form of thorough, but at the same time speedy procedure which would do justice to the various interests concerned. Some of the existing statutes seem to require only that the crime should be reported to the Police (Sweden, Latvia), or that the Police, after investigation, should not have rejected the charge as unfounded (Denmark, Poland) while another (Iceland) requires full proof in a court of law. The best solution may be found somewhere between these extremes, in particular, if strengthened by penalties for wilfully wrong charges. In any case, therapeutic abortion should not—as the Report suggests—remain the only remedy for pregnancies resulting from rape and unlawful carnal knowledge of young girls.

(*d*) The *social, economic* and "*personal*" argument constitutes the real crux of the matter: should abortion be made lawful for reasons connected solely with the woman's social, economic, or other personal circumstances even if none of the factors under (*a*) to (*c*) are present? The *Report on Abortion*, which repudiates any such suggestion,[1] states that in none of the countries whose laws are summarized circumstances of this kind are in themselves at present recognized. This seems to be correct if explicit recognition is meant. It is true with regard not only to Russia but also to Latvia, where a provision in the Act of 1932, legalizing abortion if the child would have been a serious economic burden to the woman or her family, was dropped in 1935.[2] There is, however, as the Report admits, the Icelandic Act of 1935 which provides that decisions on the lawfulness of an abortion for therapeutic reasons should take into account the following factors: "the birth of many children at short intervals, the lapse of a short time since the last confinement, and domestic difficulties due to a large number of children, poverty or serious ill-health of other members of the family".[3] This means a combination of the therapeutic with the social-economic-personal indication. Similarly, the Danish Act of 1937 [4] provides that in the case of therapeutic abortion the woman must be given a warning about the dangers of abortion and information about the available social and medical assistance for childbirth if the danger to life or health is "not due to disease". As this can only refer to bad

[1] Report, pp. 33 et seq.; 82 et seq.; 123.
[2] Report, p. 162; *MSchrKr*, 1933, p. 205; 1935, p. 270.
[3] Report, p. 160; *MSchrKr*, 1935, p. 273.
[4] Report, p. 159; *MSchrKr*, 1937, p. 572.

economic and home conditions, which would make the birth of the child a danger to an otherwise healthy woman, it appears that this Danish Act, too, has by implication stretched the therapeutic indication so much as to include large parts of the socio-economic-personal factor.[1] It has done for the latter what the Bourne case did for rape, i.e., to bring certain categories of borderline cases under the umbrella of the therapeutic indication. Taussig,[2] too, although not in favour of admitting the socio-economic indication as such, makes so many concessions that the practical difference between his and our views is probably very slight. The Report of 1939 may perhaps have had similar intentions ; [3] in its positive recommendations it is, however, too timid and fails to face the fact that in perhaps the majority of cases " economic indications *are* medical indications ".[4] Sentences such as " In so far as those circumstances may have been directly (!) detrimental to her health, the question whether her condition in pregnancy is serious enough to justify the induction of abortion is one for medical decision ", which, instead of tackling the real issue, try to place the whole burden of responsibility on the medical profession, are far from helpful. The word " directly ", in particular, is characteristic of this attitude.

Another attempt to compromise may be found in the Swiss Federal Penal Code of 1937, art. 120, which, having first dealt with the therapeutic indication, provides that, in addition, the Court has power to reduce the penalty at its discretion if the abortion was performed " on account of another serious calamity (*schwere Notlage*) in which the pregnant woman found herself ".[5] While this formula is comprehensive enough to cover at least the most tragic cases, even for them it does not make the abortion altogether lawful.

To say, as the Report of 1939 does, that " the proper and only sound approach to the problem . . . is not to accept the desire for termination of pregnancy as ineradicable, but to attempt by social, economic and educational measures to remove the causes responsible for that desire " is one of those dangerous truisms which are too often used as an excuse for doing nothing.

[1] According to information from Danish sources reproduced by Glass, *Population Policies and Movements*, p. 323, it will be possible under the Act " to plead that a further pregnancy would have a serious effect upon the health of a woman who already has a large family and whose income is very small ".

[2] Op. cit., p. 320.

[3] See p. 86, para. 239.

[4] R. L. Dickinson, *Control of Conception* (2nd ed., 1938), p. 302.

[5] This provision is omitted in the summary given on p. 164 of the Report.

Even Alva Myrdal [1] rejects the economic indication as a confession of failure on the part of the State and society which no democratic country can afford to make. Is such an attitude really practical politics? Social evils do not cease to exist because we are ashamed of them and resolve to do our best to eliminate them. For many years to come they may remain stronger than we, and, in the meantime, the only sound approach is to tackle the problem from the other end as well. This has been the conviction of the present writer ever since, some twenty years ago, as an examining magistrate he had to investigate scores of abortion cases from the poorest quarters of Berlin. Moreover, even a substantial improvement in social and economic conditions will not be sufficient completely to remove all those factors which, in individual cases, may justify the desire for abortion.

The very close correlationship in which the socio-economic indication inevitably stands to the general social and economic standards of the country makes it necessary to define the scope of this indication in broad and elastic terms so as to enable the law to keep pace with any changes in those standards. We have already stressed the great adaptability which Soviet Russia has shown in this respect. There, the necessary adjustments in the practice of abortion could, to some extent, be carried through without corresponding changes in the law, because other instruments of social control, party pressure and political propaganda, were available. In a democracy, where these methods are less strongly developed, one may have either to resort to more frequent changes in the formulation of the law or to couch it in terms wide enough to keep pace with any social or economic, or even political, changes that may occur.

While there have been many unofficial attempts to define the socio-economic indication, very few of them have gone so far as to divorce it entirely from the therapeutic aspect. Professor Taussig, for instance, suggests the term "physical depletion of the mother", meaning "any condition that produces bodily exhaustion predisposing to disease, such as too frequent child-bearing, under-nourishment, or excessive family responsibilities".[2]

I can see no reason why the socio-economic indication should not receive the same treatment by the law as is now generally conceded to its therapeutic counterpart, provided the danger is equally serious for mother and child and cannot be overcome by adequate assistance in the socio-economic sphere. There should,

[1] *Nation and Family*, pp. 208 and 324. [2] Taussig, op. cit., p. 443.

of course, be all possible safeguards to make sure not only that the woman is given the necessary information about the economic and medical support to which she is entitled for herself and her child (Denmark), but also that such support is actually forthcoming at the time when it is needed. Moreover, the risk to the woman's health inherent in abortion even when carried out in favourable conditions [1] should be fully taken into consideration before the decision. With all these provisos, there is, however, an indisputable need for the admission of abortion on purely socio-economic reasons, at least for a transitional period. The position differs from sterilization, which, meaning finality, is unsuitable for temporary emergencies. However, the opposition to abortion on socio-economic grounds is bound to be formidable, as society can but rarely be persuaded openly to confess its failures.

Finally, there is a good case for the view, forcefully expressed in Mrs. Thurtle's Minority Report,[2] that, even in the absence of other indications, a woman should have the right to an abortion after four pregnancies (I should, however, prefer to say " after the birth of four children "). Sterilization, which has occasionally been suggested for such cases, is unsuitable because of its finality ; if the woman should have the misfortune of losing her children she may well change her mind.

(2) We can now pass to a question almost equal in importance to that of the legal definition of the various factors justifying abortion, i.e., the selection of the agency which should be competent to apply the law. Under the system at present used in most countries this agency is the criminal court, and nothing besides it. Such a system was acceptable as long as the law recognized no exceptions from the principle that abortion is a crime. The task of the court was then confined to the traditional questions of proof, of guilt, and of sentencing. As soon as the law, explicitly or by changes in the court practice, admits the possibility that, given certain conditions, abortion may be lawful, the position becomes fundamentally different.

However the various above-mentioned " indications " may be formulated, the law will always have to employ a number of broad and elastic terms, such as " serious danger to life or

[1] The literature on the subject is enormous, and it is not for the medical layman to take sides in this controversy. The medical arguments against abortion are presented, for instance, by Ludovici in *Abortion*, ed. by Stella Browne (1935), pp. 53 et seq.

[2] Report, pp. 148–9 ; also D. Thurtle, *Abortion, Right or Wrong?* (1940), p. 63.

health ",[1] or " to prevent the birth of a child with serious mental or physical defects ", or " domestic difficulties due to a large number of children, poverty, or serious ill-health of other members of the family " (to quote a few examples from foreign Acts). This means a considerable degree of latitude for those who have to interpret the law, and a corresponding degree of uncertainty for those in whose interest the legal change is made. As a further consequence, criminal courts will be burdened with a task for which they are unsuitable. There will hardly ever be an abortion case in which none of the indications admitted by the law would be set up in defence, and the court will become more and more dependent on medical, eugenic, and other experts. At the same time, judges and juries will have to assume the responsibility for the direction of considerable parts of the country's population policy, a duty for which they are constitutionally unfit. On the other hand, those to whom pregnant women turn for advice will, except for extreme cases, be in no position to foretell the probable outcome of the trial. As already stressed in another connection, it is one of the essential weaknesses of criminal procedure that it can be set in motion only after the event, and that the individual concerned has to fight for his right " with a rope around his neck ". There is no way of finding out in advance the course which the court may take when passing judgment on a certain action. To remedy this weakness, at least to some extent, certain safeguards have been incorporated in those Acts which admit the therapeutic indication. They all have in common the tendency to secure in advance so much high-class evidence for the existence of the legal requirements that in the case of a prosecution the task of the court should be made as easy as possible and its likely decision ascertainable in advance. Under these Acts, abortions are privileged only if carried out at a public hospital by an authorized doctor, after consultation with another authorized doctor (Denmark, Iceland, Sweden, some States of the U.S.A.) ; or at least by an authorized doctor in a hospital (Russia before 1936) ; or it is provided that in cases of emergency when these formalities cannot be observed the doctor should at least notify the authorities within twenty-four hours (Switzerland). The

[1] The Report of 1939, p. 72, rightly refuses to give a precise definition of the medical conditions which should justify an abortion, because " the real test . . . is not that the woman is suffering from a particular form of illness, but that the illness is likely to make the continuance of her pregnancy seriously dangerous to her life or health ".

Report of 1939, which deals very fully with this aspect of the problem,[1] recommends that, except for particularly urgent cases, the present practice of consulting a second doctor should be made a statutory duty and that the Medical Officer of Health should be notified within forty-eight hours. Failure to notify would not in itself make the operation unlawful, but would constitute a separate offence.

All these safeguards, valuable as no doubt they are, seem to be open to two criticisms : First, they are concerned solely with the therapeutic indication, and, it is true, the Report of 1939, recognizing no other indications, had no reason to make any special recommendations for them. The peculiar difficulties of the so-called ethical indication (rape, etc.) have already been referred to. If, however, the eugenic and the socio-economic indications should also be admitted, an analogous machinery would surely be required for them, where specialists on eugenics and perhaps also on social questions might have to be employed.

Our second criticism is this : Safeguards such as provided in some of the Continental Acts and as suggested in the Report, while making the position of the pregnant woman reasonably secure from the danger of criminal prosecution, place the whole responsibility on the shoulders of the private doctor. It will obviously be extremely difficult to prosecute a woman who has obtained the consent of two medical practitioners. The position of the latter, however, may well be different. Even two doctors may be accused of having acted in bad faith, and there is in fact always the danger that " a class of legalized abortionists might arise ".[2] The Report of 1939 considered, though it rejected, a suggestion that the concurrence of more than two medical practitioners should be required, and that in the case of prosecution the burden of proof should be shifted from the Crown to the defendant.[3] All this shows that complete security cannot be expected unless some more effective safeguards are devised. A similar idea may have been in the minds of those who drafted the Rumanian, Yugo-Slav and German Acts. In Rumania, a pregnancy may be terminated only with the consent of the Public Prosecutor, which is given on the production of a hospital certificate or after a consultation between the operating doctor and a specialist. In Yugo-Slavia, the decision is in the hands of

[1] Report, pp. 72 et seq., 122.
[2] *Eugenics Review*, July 1939, p. 84.
[3] Report, pp. 75 and 78.

a Committee whose chairman is the Medical Officer of Health, and in Germany, in cases of eugenic indication, a Court of Referees has to decide.[1] In Russia, too, a special Commission was appointed for the purpose in 1924.[2] In this connection, Dr. Blacker's suggestion may be mentioned to set up a Family Welfare Service which could take part in decisions on abortion.[3] Professor Taussig also seems to be in favour of such an idea, but adds, regretfully, that in the United States a Commission of this kind would probably be unable to function without interference by politicians and public grafters.[4] Since this danger is absent in England no serious obstacle to the establishment of administrative agencies seems to exist. The chairman of such a Local Board or Commission might well be the Medical Officer of Health, although the Report of 1939 does not, as a rule, consider him competent to advise on a clinical question of this kind;[5] and he may be assisted by two experts, either permanent or *ad hoc* appointed, one of them familiar with the medical questions most likely to arise, the other a specialist on eugenics or social questions, as the case may be.[6] The permission of this body would be necessary for every abortion, and its official character would be the best safeguard against collusion. Abortions performed without permission would be punishable regardless of the existence of any of the recognized indications. The Commission would have to be guided by detailed regulations which might, however, be somewhat more elastic than in the case of abortion laws to be applied by criminal courts, for the simple reason that these regulations would have to operate before, not as at present after, the abortion is actually performed. There might be an appeal against decisions refusing permission, provided that it is technically possible without too much delay. In addition to these local Commissions, there should be a Central Board whose duty it would be to lay down the general policy in accordance with the needs of the day and the contemporary state of medical, eugenic, and demographic knowledge. Any scheme of this kind will be subjected to all the traditional criticisms: too bureaucratic, too expensive, too slow, lack of sufficiently trained personnel, no

[1] Report, pp. 160, 161, 163; Taussig, op. cit., pp. 395 and 424.
[2] Taussig, pp. 405 et seq. Magnus Hirschfeld, *Geschlechtskunde*, Vol. II, p. 473.
[3] *Eugenics Review*, 1939, p. 93.
[4] Op. cit., p. 445.
[5] Report, p. 75.
[6] If the plan recently put forward by the Royal College of Obstetricians and Gynæcologists (*The Times*, June 13, 1944) should materialize to establish a comprehensive national maternity service, the Abortion Commission may have to form part of it.

privacy, too much class discrimination.[1] In fact, it will be greatly superior to the present anarchic system, which involves much more human waste without achieving anything. The question of delay is purely technical ; there is no reason why it should be insoluble. Skilled personnel is required under any conceivable system which would be equal to its task ; the need for privacy should not be unduly exaggerated, and differentiations according to wealth and social class would probably be much less pronounced than they are at present. Even the vexed question of how many repetitions of legalized abortion a woman should be allowed could be tackled by a Commission able to pursue a definite line of policy, to advise, to warn, and to forecast the likely course of events, much more easily than by a criminal court inevitably confined to the individual case in hand. In fact, the advisory functions of the Commission would probably become more important than the quasi-judicial ones, and in its official capacity it could effectively assist the efforts of private doctors to dissuade women from unjustified abortions.

Under such a system, the work of the criminal court would be limited to abortions carried out without official permission, which would have to be severely punished regardless of the presence of any indications. Even this would frequently present difficulties of the highest order : whether an abortion had actually been performed ; the question of guilt and of the participation of other persons, all of them points which a criminal court is best qualified to deal with. No longer would it be expected, however, to take a prominent part in the shaping of the country's population policy. The Central Board, on the other hand, would have the duty carefully to study the material coming to light in such proceedings in order to discover and to remedy any shortcomings in the administration of the scheme.[2]

Criminal abortions will probably remain fairly frequent for a number of years ; but they will slowly decline as a result of the educational work of the Commissions and Board and of an improvement in economic conditions and social services.

[1] See already Stella Browne, *Abortion*, p. 36.

[2] It is significant that the Committee on Abortion had to do its work apparently without any real information about the conditions brought to light by criminal proceedings. Although the annual numbers of such proceedings are very small, a systematic analysis of the circumstances of each case would no doubt yield valuable material.

APPENDIX TO SECTION ONE: CRIMINAL NEGLIGENCE

Of the questions so far discussed, sterilization and birth control bear only indirectly on the general issue of the protection of human life, as the child whose birth is made impossible by such measures has not yet become individualized. It is not his life but the interests of the potential parent and, in particular, those of the community that are protected by the present law. Outside the field of sterilization and birth control legislation, however, the criminal law has shown considerable reluctance to protect human life from attacks which are directed not against this or that individual but against undefined multitudes of persons. In English law this reluctance is particularly striking. A few examples may illustrate the state of affairs we have in mind:

In his stimulating little book *The Scientific Attitude*,[1] Dr. C. H. Waddington writes:

> The adoption of methods of thought which are commonplaces in science would bring before the bar of ethical judgment whole groups of phenomena which do not appear there now. For instance, our ethical notions are fundamentally based on a system of individual responsibility for individual acts. The principle of statistical correlation between two sets of events, although accepted in scientific practice, is not usually felt to be ethically completely valid. If a man hits a baby on the head with a hammer, we prosecute him for cruelty or murder; but if he sells dirty milk and the infant sickness or death rate goes up, we merely fine him for contravening the health laws.

And:

> The whole community of England and Wales kills 8,000 babies a year by failing to bring its infant mortality rate down to the level reached by Oslo as early as 1931, which would be perfectly feasible; but few people seem to think this a crime.

Or: Not so long ago, according to Press reports a London builder and a clerk of works were charged at the Central Criminal Court with conspiring together and with other unknown persons to defraud the Hammersmith Borough Council in connection with the erection of air-raid shelters; with conspiring to effect public mischief by building 120 shelters knowing they were deficient in structure and short of the standard of protection contained in the specifications provided; and with the manslaughter of a girl whose body (as well as the body of a soldier) was found in the ruins of one of the shelters after a bomb had fallen near it.[2]

The defendants were found "not guilty" on the first charge, but found "guilty" and each sentenced to nine months' imprisonment in the second division on the charge of conspiring to effect public mischief by building 120 air-raid shelters in such a manner that they had to be rebuilt by the council. The manslaughter charge was not

[1] Pelican Books, 1941, p. 26.
[2] See *The Times* of Jan. 15, 18, 22, 23 and Feb. 24, 1944.

further pressed by the prosecution, and the defendants were acquitted of it. The outsider who has to rely for his information only on scanty press reports might find it somewhat difficult to explain to the layman why persons guilty of conspiring to build defective air-raid shelters should not have been equally guilty of the manslaughter of persons killed in those shelters, particularly as two experts are reported to have stated that the victims would not have lost their lives had the shelters been built in accordance with the prescriptions.

During the 1943 famine in India the allegation was frequently made that the shortage of foodstuffs was partly due to profiteering and hoarding. Nothing has been heard, however, of any prosecutions of profiteers or hoarders for culpable homicide under the Indian Penal Code.

A final illustration, relating to what is probably the most notorious group of cases: manslaughter committed by negligent driving of a motor-car.

It is always the same picture: wherever the lives of an undefinable number of persons are endangered and thereby some of them actually killed through reckless and unscrupulous behaviour, the guilty are usually punished, not, as they should be, for murder or at least manslaughter, but, at best, for some comparatively minor offence of a technical nature, such as contravening the public health laws, or public mischief, profiteering, or careless driving.[1] No wonder, then, that a legal layman, like Dr. Waddington, and others with him, may get a little puzzled or even annoyed at this failure of the criminal law to afford adequate protection to life, otherwise proclaimed to be the highest of all earthly goods.

The explanation is, briefly, this: The criminal law, particularly in England, is still too much labouring under the delusion that danger to human life usually comes from overt and tangible individualistic acts directed against a specific individual, such as bodily assault, shooting, or perhaps rape, arson, or abortion. An offender who, in the course of committing any such act, causes the death of the victim will be guilty of murder or at least manslaughter. English law is, indeed, much harsher in this respect than other legal systems, adhering as it does, up to the present day, to the mediæval doctrine of "constructive murder", or, in the words of the great Italian jurists of the fourteenth century, "*versanti in re illicita imputantur omnia quae sequuntur ex delicto*".[2] There is, consequently, a serious risk of a death sentence for anybody who kills another person through one of those traditional offences, even if he had no intention whatsoever to cause death. Again, anyone who intentionally kills an unspecified number of persons, for instance, by placing a time bomb in a ship,

[1] We do not wish to imply that these offences are actually of a minor character only; they are, however, at present often treated as such.

[2] On this subject, see the author's series of articles "*Mens rea* in German and English Criminal Law", *Journal of Comparative Legislation and International Law*, Third Series, Vol. XVII (1935) and XVIII (1936); Kenny, *Outlines of Criminal Law* (11th ed. 1933), pp. 135–41. In fact, the theory of "*versanti in re illicita*" goes back even to Bernardus Papiensis' *Summa decretalium*; see Alexander Loeffler's standard work "*Die Schuldformen des Strafrechts*" (1895), p. 139.

is, quite rightly, held guilty of murder.[1] In strange contrast to this attitude stands the lenient treatment meted out to offenders who kill, or cause at least serious danger to, masses of human beings by equally modern but less tangible methods such as selling unhygienic food or milk, or hoarding, profiteering, or erecting defective air-raid shelters. Criminal law has not yet become sufficiently aware of the fact that we are living not in an individualistic but in a mass age, where everything has to be adapted to the use of mass methods. Likewise, it has not yet grasped the profundity of the revolution which Freudian psychology has brought about in our interpretation of the idea of " negligence ". Formerly a Cinderella of the criminal law, negligence has become one of its pivotal conceptions, which modern legislative technique can no longer afford to neglect. English criminal law is particularly inadequate in this respect, making no provision even for the punishment of wounding or arson committed through gross negligence. Class distinctions and prejudices may account for a great deal of this negative attitude. The conception of criminal negligence is of practical importance mainly for professional men and skilled craftsmen, and they, not the common labourer, would be the chief sufferers if the scope of that conception would be extended. On the other hand, in a legal system which deliberately uses the criminal law for specific political and administrative purposes the difference between intention and negligence will be much less pronounced.[2]

The reckless motorist is only the most frequent and most familiar representative of that new type of offender. The question when the slaughter he causes on the roads amounts to murder or manslaughter and when it should be called by less unkind names has provoked a whole stream of statutes, court decisions, and learned articles. Only in part are the difficulties which have arisen for the administration of criminal justice in this field inherent in the technical side of the matter; for the rest they are due to class prejudices.

> Even before the creation of the modern road traffic offences [writes Mr. D. Seaborne Davies],[3] English law was involved in the difficulties that many cases dealt with as manslaughters were technically murders in strict theory of law and that the law of manslaughter which was invoked to avoid the dislike of capital verdicts was itself in this undefined state. When the modern carnage on the roads became serious, the further complication arose that juries were loath to convict " nice people " of manslaughter. To meet the multiplicity of non-fatal offences and, perhaps, to provide a minor offence of which motorists could be convicted without unduly straining the susceptibilities of juries, the Road Traffic Act, 1930, created two new offences, " reckless driving " (sect. 11) and " driving without due care and attention " (sect. 12).

One might perhaps also refer to the peculiar complication created in English law by the Janus-like duplicity of the term " manslaughter ",

[1] Kenny, *Outlines*, p. 137.

[2] See below, Chapter 8.

[3] 1 *Modern Law Review* (1937), p. 243. See, moreover, Patrick Dean, " Manslaughter and Dangerous Driving ", *Law Quarterly Review*, Vol. LIII (1937), pp. 380 et seq.; J. W. C. Turner, *Cambridge Law Journal*, Vol. V (1933), pp. 61 et seq.

which, apart from being undefined, contrary to Continental conceptions covers two, from the psychological point of view entirely different, sets of offences, intentional homicide not amounting to murder, on the one hand, and killing through negligence on the other. This unfortunate duplicity has no doubt added to the already strong disinclination of juries to find " nice people " guilty of manslaughter.[1] What is urgently needed in English law is a reasonable definition of murder and manslaughter together with two new statutory offences of causing death or injuries and of seriously endangering the lives or health of human beings through negligence.[2] Without going into details, reference may be made to certain Continental and other Penal Codes which have tackled these problems.[3]

It should not be assumed, however, that such reforms will render unnecessary that host of penal provisions of a technical nature which have become a characteristic feature of modern criminal law everywhere. To return to the case referred to by Dr. Waddington, all those penal provisions in the Public Health Acts will remain indispensable for the masses of minor cases. There has to be some machinery to enable the courts to impose small penalties on sellers of unsound meat or dirty milk, or on persons suffering from infectious diseases who carry on an occupation connected with the handling of food, without having to prove any actual injuries to life or health of individuals, still less any negligence with regard to these ultimate results on the part of the offender. The careless builder who erects faulty air-raid shelters has to be punished even if, for one reason or another, it cannot be proved that he was able to foresee the fatal results of his negligence. For cases of a more serious nature, where the negligence is so considerable as to border on malice this is unsatisfactory because of the smallness of the penalties usually imposed. For the sake of a speedy administration of criminal justice, however, which would be seriously blocked if the question of guilt had to be completely cleared up in each individual case, such compromises can hardly be avoided in a mass age. All the criminal law can do is to provide a suitable choice of enactments for the protection of human life and health, ranging from deliberate attacks such as murder, manslaughter, malicious wounding, via negligent actions where the offender was able to foresee and to avoid death or injury, to contraventions of a technical character which are punishable as such, regardless of the more serious ultimate results which they may

[1] Turner, loco cit., p. 61 : " The word ' manslaughter ' suggests to many lay minds some kind of brutal criminality ; they find an incongruity in associating it with a prisoner of respectable appearance." The corresponding difficulties which have arisen in connection with the American monopoly legislation are discussed below, Chapter 8 Bc.

[2] The question whether a statutory definition of the meaning of criminal negligence itself would serve any useful purpose may remain open. See, for example, art. 18 (3) of the Swiss and art. 10(*b*) of the Russian Penal Code.

[3] See, for example, the very wide formulations in the Polish Code, art. 217, or the Indian Code, arts. 304A, 336, 337, 287, providing penalties for any kind of negligent action which endangers life or health. Most other codes enumerate specific activities which produce certain types of common danger, such as inundations, fires, railway disasters.

entail. The fact has to be faced that the criminal law, in former days mainly regarded as an annex to the law of property, has now at least as much become an annex to the administrative law, which could hardly function without this protective screen. Most of the seven or eight hundred thousand non-indictable offences which used to be dealt with by English Courts of Summary Jurisdiction before the war belonged to that category. It is not without its significance that the great opponent of the growth of administrative law in England, Dicey, was equally critical of the protective value of penal provisions attached to it.

If a law [he writes] [1] imposes a penalty on a shipowner who sends a vessel to sea before he has obtained a Board of Trade certificate of its seaworthiness, it is probable that few ships will set out on their voyage without a certificate, and it is possible that, for the moment, the number of ships which go to sea unfit to meet a storm may be diminished. These good results of State intervention are easily noticeable. That the same law may make a shipowner, who has obtained a certificate, negligent in seeing that his ship is really seaworthy, and that the certificate will in practice bar any action for real negligence, are evil results of legislation which are indirect and escape notice. Nor do most people keep in mind that State inspectors may be incompetent, careless, and even occasionally corrupt. . . .

Even where no special certificate is in question, such arguments might be used, though still less convincingly, to bring into disrepute almost the whole body of administrative law and its penal provisions. State interference, it can always be said, tends to weaken the individual's sense of responsibility by employing officials to do some part of his job. When the State sets up speed limits for motor-cars and employs policemen to enforce them, a modern Dicey might argue that this will only make the motorist more careless since he will rely on the policeman to tell him when he exceeds that limit, and policemen may be incompetent or, occasionally, even corrupt. And, if anything should happen, juries will take his part and refuse to find him guilty of manslaughter. The main fallacy of this line of approach lies in the erroneous belief that, without all this preventive apparatus set up by modern administrative and penal law, the individual citizen would conscientiously shoulder his responsibilities and everything would run smoothly. Historically and psychologically, this complacent view is unfortunately wrong. The individual left to himself has only too often made a complete mess of things, which explains the need for that preventive machinery.

[1] A. V. Dicey, *Law and Public Opinion in England during the Nineteenth Century* (1930 ed.), p. xxiv (Introduction to the second edition, 1914).

SECTION TWO. THE PROTECTION OF SEXUAL AND FAMILY LIFE

Chapter 4

SEXUAL OFFENCES, ESPECIALLY HOMOSEXUALITY

To the superficial observer, it might appear questionable whether in an analysis of crime specifically related to the task of social reconstruction *sexual crime* should be included. Is not, it might be argued, one of the chief characteristics of the sexual offender a narrowly individualistic attitude which can but little be affected by changes in the social and economic structure of society? In fact, nothing would be more erroneous, however, than such an attempt to remove the problem of sexual crime from the sociological sphere and to regard it as the exclusive domain of the psychologist and psychiatrist. It is a commonplace, strongly confirmed by the study of primitive communities, that the very conception of sexual crime depends on the views about sexual behaviour generally held in a given society. The better understanding and the more lenient treatment of sexual offenders are due not only to the progress made by the modern psychology of sex, but at least as much to the profound changes which, to some extent independent of it, the daily conduct of so-called normal men and women has undergone in the course of the present century. Soviet Russia is not the only country to demonstrate the intimate connection between sexual habits and social outlook, although probably nowhere else such a violent zig-zag course might have been possible within the brief period of twenty years.[1]

Already from the purely quantitative point of view, it would be distinctly unwise to underrate the social significance of sexual abnormality and sexual crime. Even the bare figures of *Criminal Statistics*, grotesquely unrepresentative as they are of the actual frequency of sexual offences, tell a pathetic story. In

[1] See Ella Winter, *Red Virtue* (1933), esp. Chapter VIII; S. and B. Webb, *Soviet Communism*, II, p. 1054; M. Hindus, *Mother Russia*, Chapter 25.

1938, in England and Wales 2,321 persons were found guilty of indictable sexual offences, to whom have to be added 1,931 persons dealt with for indecent exposure, 3,459 for prostitution, 228 for living on the earnings of prostitution and 217 for brothel keeping, making a total of more than 8,000 persons.[1] The proportion, per million of population, of persons tried for "unnatural offences" alone increased from 5 at the beginning of the century to 16 in 1938. In Germany, the proportion of sexual offences rose from 260 in 1931–2 to 390 in 1936, again per million of population, and that of homosexual offences alone from 14 to 102.[2] Passing from the figures of *Criminal Statistics* to the actual frequency of sexual offences, it has to be admitted that no reliable estimate will ever become possible. Granted that the ratio of "crimes cleared up" to "crimes known to the Police", as shown in *Criminal Statistics*,[3] is surprisingly favourable, the peculiar features of these offences make it highly probable that only a tiny percentage of them ever comes to the knowledge of the Police.[4] The same applies, to an even higher degree, to the incidence of sexual abnormalities, whether or not they may lead to violations of the criminal law. According to Dr. Clifford Allen,[5] estimates by various observers have ranged from 2 to 10 per cent. of the general population. Magnus Hirschfeld, on the basis of sample enquiries and questionnaires, arrived at a figure of one and a half million individuals with entirely or at least predominantly homosexual instincts in Germany,[6] and of over ten millions in the whole of Europe, and Kenneth Ingram has only recently warned us that "to-day, certainly in England and Germany, the number of homosexuals is infinitely greater than most sociologists appear to appreciate."[7] Although Hirschfeld's estimate may have been founded on somewhat rash generalizations, there is, on the other hand, a great deal of truth

[1] *Criminal Statistics* for England and Wales for the year 1938, p. xxxii and Tables AB and C. It has to be noted that this figure does not necessarily mean as many different individuals, since some of these offenders may have been found guilty more than once in the course of the year.

[2] *MSchrKr*, 1938, p. 341. See also above p. 30.

[3] *Criminal Statistics* (1938), Table XXIV.

[4] Dr. M. Marcuse, who was one of the best-known specialists on sexual perversions in pre-Nazi Germany, expressed the view that one case out of many thousands of homosexual offences is brought before the criminal courts, *Handwörterbuch der Kriminologie* (HdKr) (1933), Vol. I, p. 679.

[5] *The Sexual Perversions and Abnormalities* (1940), p. 80.

[6] *Geschlechtskunde*, Vol. I (1926), p. 575. See also Stefan Zweig's *Autobiography*, p. 228.

[7] *Sex-Morality To-Morrow* (1940), p. 102. Similarly R. v. Krafft-Ebing, *Psychopathia sexualis* (English translation, 1939), p. 351.

in his view that a sensible reform of the German criminal law relating to sexual offences might have reduced their annual figure of 16,000 (taking only the ten most frequent categories of offences) by no less than two-thirds.[1] Similar reductions could no doubt be achieved in English law, with very considerable savings in time and money, not counting the enormous amount of human misery which could thereby be avoided. This, then, is the practical significance of our scanty references to the quantitative aspects of the matter. Above all, they should remind us of the need for a re-examination of the credentials of the present law. Statutes penalizing the sexual life of men and women are justified not because we have got used to their existence, but only when and so far as they are really needed in the interests of society. Some measure of restraint will clearly remain indispensable for a long time, and there may even be a grain of truth in J. D. Unwin's contention [2] that " the limitation of sexual opportunity must be regarded as the cause of the cultural advance of mankind ". However, as limitations imposed on sexual conduct are not necessarily of a legal and penal character, even an acceptance of this theory would assist us but little in our task to draw the right line between sexual deviations which can and others which cannot be tolerated by the criminal law. In fact, Unwin's theory has to be considerably modified in the light of Freudian psychology, which should make us still more reluctant to use in this sphere the double-edged weapon of legal punishment. The New Order cannot afford to squander its energy and resources on the persecution of otherwise decent and useful members of the community, merely because their sexual behaviour differs from that of the majority. The weeding out of obsolete penal laws is not the least useful method of social reconstruction.

There are various ways of classifying sexual offences. The medico-psychologist, who is particularly interested in abnormal sexual behaviour, may distinguish according to abnormality of stimulus, of strength of urge, of mode of expression, and of its object.[3] The lawyer, who confines himself to sexual behaviour that constitutes an offence, has to use another scheme : Sexual activities may have to be suppressed by punishment if they involve

[1] *Geschlechtskunde*, Vol. III, p. 653.

[2] *Sexual Regulations and Human Behaviour* (1933), p. 59. Consequently, in his utopian *Hopousia* he stated that, " in order that the Hopousians may display the greatest possible energy, there will be more compulsory continence there than in any white man's society " (*Hopousia*, 1940).

[3] See Clifford Allen, op. cit., pp. 14–15.

(1) the use of force, intimidation, deception, or similar methods,
(2) the corruption of youth,
(3) perversion and biological waste,
(4) " indecent " acts which threaten the public order,
(5) commercialization of sex.

With few exceptions, such as the Soviet Penal Code which includes sexual offences among " Crimes against Life, Health, Liberty, and Personal Reputation ",[1] all existing Penal Codes possess special chapters dealing with this subject. A comparative survey of the present laws shows the absence of any fundamental differences with regard to the first and second of our five categories. That rape or the use of any other improper methods of achieving sexual intercourse against the will of the partner, and that sexual corruption of immature persons are serious crimes is beyond dispute. A discussion of the comparatively few points of legislative technique that are bound to arise is outside the scope of this book, with perhaps one exception: Should the exploitation for sexual purposes of a woman's economic dependence be a crime and treated like rape? This is the attitude taken in several modern Penal Codes,[2] not, however, in English law. The idea itself seems sound enough, though it may be difficult to find a suitable legislative formula. The Russian Code punishes " coercion " of a woman " by any person on whom she is dependent materially or by reason of her employment ". Even if, owing to the absence of unemployment and private employers, the average worker should be less dependent on his superiors in Russia than in some capitalist countries, it cannot always be easy for the Russian courts to decide when pressure reaches the stage of " coercion ".[3] In the draft of the German " Cartel for the Reform of the Criminal Law of Sexual Offences " it was proposed to punish coercion only when consisting in the threat to worsen the conditions of employment or to dismiss the woman altogether.[4] This, however, seems to be too narrow to be of much practical use.

Apart from this special point the real difficulties in the matter

[1] Similarly the Indian Code, Chapter XV. Most of our traditional sex offences, so far as they are punishable in India, are dealt with not in Chapter XV, but elsewhere (rape, for example, in Chapter XVI, " Offences affecting the human body ").

[2] Russia, art. 154; Switzerland, art. 197; China, art. 228; German Draft Code of 1927. Some older material in E. Wulffen, *Der Sexualverbrecher* (1922), p. 428.

[3] The formulation of the Swiss Code is, if anything, even more indefinite.

[4] See Magnus Hirschfeld, *Geschlechtskunde*, Vol. III, p. 626.

of rape and corruption of youth centre round the question of how to secure reliable evidence for such offences, and how to punish them. That, even for such a universally detested crime as rape, there are limits to the severity of punishment beyond which a civilized community may refuse to go has recently become apparent in the case of death sentences imposed by American courts-martial in Great Britain.[1] As the Secretary of the National Council for the Abolition of the Death Penalty writes, " it is significant that in the districts where the cases have been tried and the local press have fully reported on them, and where the population might reasonably be presumed to be incensed against the offender, there have been widespread spontaneous protests, by bodies of shop-stewards, groups of factory workers and many individuals ". Two points would seem to make the sociological and psychological assessment of these and other protests peculiarly complicated : the fact that some of the convicted soldiers were negroes, and, secondly, the absence of the death penalty for rape in English law. Whereas the first factor gave rise to the suspicion that the accused had been found guilty and sentenced to death mainly because of their race, the second made the imposition of such sentences particularly repugnant to the English public. It is interesting to speculate whether the reaction would have been the same without these two factors. Even so, however, the lesson for us seems to be that considerable sections of the public have by now become aware of the dangers involved and of the great need for a careful and scientific weighing of the evidence in charges of rape.[2] The next step will be to apply a similarly critical attitude to other categories of sexual offences, in particular to charges of indecent assault on young children.

Lack of space unfortunately forbids to deal in the present book with another subject closely connected with its main themes : Prostitution.

From the point of view of legal reform, next to Prostitution it is *Homosexuality* that constitutes the real crux. Probably no other penal statutes have been so bitterly attacked within the past thirty years as those dealing with " unnatural offences ". In pre-Nazi Germany, the struggle against " § 175 " had gained

[1] See *The New Statesman and Nation*, June 17, 1944, p. 399 ; June 24, 1944, pp. 417 and 421 ; *The Times*, June 19 and 23, 1944.

[2] See *Handwörterbuch der Kriminologie*, art. " Notzucht ", Vol. II, p. 227. According to certain mediæval Germanic laws, a woman who brought a charge for rape was to be believed only if, immediately after the alleged crime, she had complained to the first person she had met, with dishevelled hair and torn dress. See also E. Wulffen, *Der Sexualverbrecher* (9th ed. 1922), p. 437.

a popularity but rarely achieved for legal issues. In spite of such intensive efforts, very little has so far been done in the way of law reform, and it may be worth while, therefore, to review the various factors responsible for this failure. The most outstanding and, at the same time, most primitive among them is the disgust which is undoubtedly felt by the man in the street for anything related to homosexuality. In this connection, the term " man in the street " has to include almost anybody who has made no special study of the subject, from distinguished judges [1] to convict burglars who tend to despise their fellow prisoners of the homosexual type.[2] It is open to doubt, however, whether such an attitude may not in itself be largely due to the present wholesale stigmatization of homosexuality by the law, and therefore likely to change with it. If it should be true that the social ban is far less strong against female than against male homosexuals,[3] this would be an indication that much of the social stigma is in fact due mainly to the legal prohibition. On the other hand, occasional tactical blunders, flagrant exaggerations and undue glorifications on the part of enthusiastic reformers may have further intensified that normal feeling of disgust.

Second, the customary lack of distinction between genuine homosexual tendencies and homosexual activities not caused by such tendencies makes it easy for opponents of the reform movement to apply their whole arsenal of weapons in the wrong direction—i.e., to use in cases of genuine perversion arguments applicable only to individuals who indulge in homosexual practices without being perverts.

A third factor which deprives them of many sympathies is

[1] See, for instance, Lord Atkin in the House of Lords on July 7, 1937 (Hansard, col. 145) referring to his judicial experiences : " It is not correct to say that these cases . . . are the result of something in the nature of disease . . . they are the result of wicked impulses, which, like other wicked impulses, are capable of being controlled. . . . They can be checked by advice and by resolution." This in reply to a very moderate statement by Lord Dawson of Penn : "We now look upon homosexuality as a pathological condition. I am not at all sure that in the future it may not be regarded as an insufficiency disease, and although it is true that the law must take cognizance of it and punish it in order to act as a preventive to potential offenders, the more reasonable view is gradually being adopted that it, at any rate, has one foot in the realm of disease and is not wholly in the realm of crime." Our only comment is that we do not know the proportion of cases in which punishment acts here as a preventive. We do know, however, that judicial experience, unless it is backed by an adequate knowledge of psychology and psychiatry, cannot enable a lawyer to speak on the subject with authority.

[2] " The average thief, burglar, or pickpocket did not mix with the homos," writes Jim Phelan, *Jail Journey*, p. 292. By " average ", he means, I suppose, " professional ".

[3] East-de Hubert, *The Psychological Treatment of Crime* (1939), p. 89. See also de Hubert, *British Journal of Medical Psychology*, Vol. XVII (1938), pp. 65 et seq.

the not infrequent phenomenon of homosexuals committing sexual offences of another kind as well, particularly of a sadistic character. This should, however, not be indiscriminately exploited to the disadvantage of homosexuals as such.[1]

Passing to what is no doubt the most progressive-minded category among the opponents of law reform, we encounter the idea that under a modern penal system, with its ever-increasing opportunities for psychological treatment, it is in the best interest of the homosexual to let him participate in the blessings of that system. The fallacies of this argument are fairly obvious. In the first instance, as in the case of suicide,[2] as long as the penal system has to deal with crime in the traditional sense, it is a perversion of its true functions to use it for certain categories of human beings solely because they require medical or psychological treatment. It is moreover difficult to see why such methods of treatment should be made available only within the penal system to those who are in need of them. If the reason should be that many homosexuals are unwilling to undergo treatment unless forced to, the obvious answer is that, as a rule, psychological methods are bound to fail where a real desire to be cured is absent. The problem of the " unwilling patient " was admirably discussed some years ago in a symposium by four leading specialists.[3] For our present question, one of the principal results of that discussion seems to be that the percentage of unwilling patients among homosexuals is particularly high, the unwillingness being most pronounced among those with strong constitutional tendencies towards homosexuality. The reasons for this are obvious enough : the vacillating attitude of the criminal law and of society as revealed by history ;[4] the high cultural achievements and the moral integrity of many homosexuals ; the manifold pleasures and advantages frequently derived from their abnormal instincts—all this may be regarded by some of them as a justification of their behaviour and compensate them for any pain caused by punishment. It may be true that, as Dr. Carroll has pointed out, in certain cases coercion

[1] As East-de Hubert, op. cit. pp. 86, 88, seem to admit, the large proportion of homosexuals with other perverse activities among their cases was apparently due to the special method by which their material was selected (exclusively persons sentenced to imprisonment or penal servitude).

[2] Above, p. 10.

[3] Denis Carroll, W. H. de Hubert, J. R. Rees, and O. H. Woodcock in the *British Journal of Medical Psychology*, Vol. XVII (1938). " The majority of homosexuals do not desire to change their temperament," writes Kenneth Ingram, *Sex Morality To-morrow* (1939), p. 129.

[4] See, for example, Ruth Benedict, *Patterns of Culture*, pp. 262 et seq.

is no obstacle to treatment, and that for some patients it is even indispensable. This will, however, probably be an exceptional situation, whereas for the majority the coercive atmosphere created by the criminal law will be not only unnecessary but positively harmful.[1] The fact that his sexual activities, which he is often unable to regard as abnormal, are treated as serious crimes by the law is likely to make him profoundly anti-social and produce the mentality of an outlaw. "The moral means of correction are therefore wanting."[2] Moreover, the co-operation between the criminal court and the medico-psychologist is, without any fault of the responsible individuals, in certain respects bound to remain defective. The criminal law being as it is, no complete identity of outlook can be achieved. One and the same factor may easily assume a totally different significance in the eyes of a judge and of the medico-psychologist, and even the very object of their efforts may be different. Let us for a moment consider the indications which are regarded by the medico-psychologist as having a favourable prognostic significance, such as prevalence of environmental causes (early seduction, prolonged segregation from the opposite sex, etc.) ; or "presence of modifiable neurotic factors which have discouraged hetero-sexual interests" :[3] From the point of view of the criminal court, such factors are likely to imply the need for leniency, meaning in rare cases probation, more often short sentences of imprisonment.[4] From the point of view of the medico-psychologist, however, sentences of less than six months are regarded as "generally insufficient for psychotherapeutic treatment".[5] On the other hand, factors believed to be adverse to treatment are, among others : homosexual activities of long standing and the presence of other sexual perversions and anti-social trends—all features which make for the imposition of long terms of imprisonment, not indicated on medical grounds, in order to satisfy the traditional ideas of deterrence and retribution. East and de Hubert regard sentences of six to twelve months as most suitable, but they recognize that the actual length usually depends on "the severity of the crime, number of convictions

[1] See also Dr. Rees, loco cit., p. 69.
[2] R. v. Krafft-Ebing, *Psychopathia sexualis*, p. 578.
[3] East-de Hubert, p. 91.
[4] According to *Criminal Statistics* for 1938, probation and binding over without probation were used to any considerable extent only for the comparatively minor offence of indecency with males, not, however, for the crimes of buggery and attempted buggery.
[5] East-de Hubert, p. 158.

and other factors which have no bearing on the requirements of the offender when in prison, and thus it may prove too long or too short for useful psychiatric treatment ".[1] The very first of their illustrative cases, that of a youth aged 19 who had received three and three years' penal servitude, concurrent, for sodomy, with no aggravating features emerging from the summary given, shows the crassest possible incongruity between the psychotherapeutic situation and the length of the sentence, though it is an incongruity of a kind different from that indicated above.

Criminal courts may easily be tempted to interpret a verdict of " unsuitable for psychotherapy " as indicating a particularly heavy dose of moral wickedness in the offender. In fact, such a verdict is most likely to occur in cases of abnormal constitutional disposition where environmental factors play only a secondary rôle. There are, in other words, many homosexual offenders to whom neither treatment nor punishment should reasonably be applied,[2] and any attempt to justify prison sentences for them by reference to the possibility of treatment which such sentences entail must remain futile. " One can confidently state that one has never seen a case influenced, except for the worse, by imprisonment ", writes Dr. Clifford Allen.[3] If society has to be protected against really dangerous homosexuals it can only be through long periods of detention of a non-penal character. Even the " penal institution of a special kind " for certain abnormal types of criminals as advocated in the Report on the Psychological Treatment of Crime,[4] useful as it will no doubt be for other categories of sexual and non-sexual offenders, does not seem to be suitable for those with homosexual tendencies. While its " penal " character would give offence to those who can discover no criminal element in homosexuality as such, the fact that it would be an institution for different types of abnormal lawbreakers makes it unsuitable to receive homosexuals. An aspect which is, surprisingly enough, not even touched in the East-de Hubert Report is the psychological effect of the presence of homosexuals in an institution. The subject " Homosexuality

[1] East-de Hubert, p. 156 ; also p. 160.

[2] Krafft-Ebing, op. cit., p. 460, expressed the view that the number of cases which can be really cured would always remain limited. Although it may increase with advancing medico-psychological knowledge, for all practical purposes one has still to expect a considerable proportion of failures.

[3] *The New Statesman and Nation*, Sept. 18, 1943. Special reference may be made to the interesting correspondence which appeared in that periodical on Sept. 4, 11, 18 and 25, 1943.

[4] East-de Hubert, pp. 155, 159, 164.

and Prison " has, rightly, played a very large part in modern penological literature.[1] There are two aspects of it: the perverting effect of institutional life on the sexually normal inmate, and the special danger which the presence of homosexual prisoners constitutes in this process—" homosexuals who are formed in prison " and " homosexuals who come to prison ", to use Joseph Fishman's labels. Nobody who has read the descriptions of prison life, seen from this special angle, as given by Donald Clemmer, the sociologist who worked for nearly a decade in one of the big American prisons, or by Jim Phelan, who spent nearly thirteen years in English convict prisons as a " lifer ", can possibly approve of the present practice. As Compton Mackenzie, Kenneth Ingram, and others have pointed out, it is absurd to send homosexuals to exclusively male institutions where every inducement to continue their activities is provided for them.[2] If the homosexual has to be kept in an institution it can only be one in which the other inmates are either also homosexuals, or women, which latter alternative is probably beyond the reach of practical politics.

If, then, as has been argued here at length, prison, even with the addition of psychological treatment, is the worst possible method of dealing with homosexuals, why not, it will be asked, try probation? Probation, it is true, avoids most of the disadvantages of institutions; some part of the stigma inseparably connected with the criminal law, however, remains, and in the case of the incurable constitutional homosexual there will always be the danger that the courts, having applied probation once or perhaps twice, will eventually resort to the traditional prison sentence. Moreover, probation can only be applied with the consent of the offender, which may sometimes not be given.

The solution can be found only by going back to the fundamental question: is homosexual behaviour anti-social, and if so, is it one of those anti-social actions which should be treated as crimes? To use the fact that many homosexuals are unco-operative and do not wish to be cured to justify an affirmative

[1] See, for example, the admirable discussion in H. E. Barnes and Negley K. Teeters, *New Horizons in Criminology* (New York, 1943), pp. 618 and 888; Joseph F. Fishman, *Sex in Prison* (1934); Donald Clemmer, *The Prison Community* (1940), Chapter X; Jim Phelan's interesting *Jail Journey* (1940), may also be mentioned although the author would probably protest against any connection with " penology ", which he detests.

[2] Kenneth Ingram, *Sex-Morality To-morrow*, p. 107. See also S. H. Foulkes, *Psycho-Analysis and Crime* (1944), p. 34, and, on the other hand, W. Norwood East, *Medical Aspects of Crime*, p. 323.

answer would be illogical: if there are no other grounds on which to treat him as a criminal, why should the homosexual co-operate with the machinery of the criminal law? No; unless one identifies "anti-social" with "abnormal", which would open up extremely dangerous prospects, there is only one reason why homosexuality as such should be regarded as anti-social: its harmful consequences for the birth rate. To deny them is impossible, nor is it convincing to argue that "homosexuality can no more be condemned on that score than contraception".[1] We do condemn birth control where it is practised excessively and for no adequate reason. In fact, a number of homosexuals marry and have children,[2] but this can hardly be used as an argument in their favour—"the true crime of the homosexual is his marriage", as Magnus Hirschfeld says.[3] To be homosexual, we might say, is no more anti-social than to be tuberculous, but it is anti-social for such individuals to marry and have children, and it is also anti-social to spread the disease, or to make no serious attempt to be cured where cure may be possible.[4] One has to bear in mind, however, that there are many categories of anti-social behaviour which are, for good reasons, not punishable. The position is obviously not the same, for instance, for the patient suffering from tuberculosis or syphilis, and for the homosexual, because physical and mental treatment are of a different nature, and unwillingness may be made an offence in the case of the former but not in the case of the latter. We may now try to answer the question: when should homosexual acts be treated as a crime? It may be useful, at this stage, briefly to review the principal methods employed in different countries.[5] There are three categories of them:

(*a*) Countries where all, or at least some, homosexual activities, are punishable, even in the absence of any of the aggravating circumstances mentioned under (*c*), To this group belong, for instance, the United Kingdom, India, and the British Colonies whose Penal Codes are modelled on English law; Germany, Austria (here even between females) and, since 1934, Russia. In most of these Statutes the definitions of the prohibited activities

[1] Kenneth Ingram, op. cit., p. 122.

[2] Among the fourteen cases described by East-de Hubert, only one is stated to have had any children, though three of them were married.

[3] *Geschlechtskunde*, Vol. I, p. 573.

[4] See also R. D. Gillespie in *Mental Abnormality and Crime* (1944), p. 84; W. Norwood East in the same symposium, pp. 191 et seq.

[5] Much historical material is given in George Ives, *The Continued Extension of the Criminal Law* (privately printed, no date, 1922?), pp. 14 et seq.

are utterly inadequate, and sometimes they are even entirely absent. If English law, in the Offences against the Person Act of 1861, 24 & 25 Vict., c. 100, sect. 61, threatens with punishment "whosoever shall be convicted of the abominable crime of Buggery, committed either with mankind or with any animal", or sect. 62 "any indecent Assault upon any male person", or if the Criminal Law Amendment Act, 1885, sect. 11, punishes "any act of gross indecency" between males, or if the notorious § 175 of the German Penal Code up to 1935 used the term "*widernatürliche Unzucht*" (now only "*Unzucht*")—which may be translated as "indecency against nature"—it is obvious that such phrases are incapable of fulfilling one of the traditional functions of a criminal statute: to inform the individual citizen how far he may safely go without offending against the law.[1] No wonder, then, that the decisions of the German Supreme Court used to vacillate between a narrow interpretation, restricting the scope of § 175 to actual penetration, and a wider interpretation which included anything only remotely comparable to sexual intercourse.

In Soviet Russia whose Penal Code of 1926 had made no reference to the matter, a decree of March 1934 "without any public discussion" required the republics of the U.S.S.R. to add to their codes an article making homosexual behaviour between men, adults as well as juveniles, an offence. The Webbs suggest that this change of policy was the sequel to the discovery of centres of demoralization.[2]

(*b*) To the other extreme belong France and most of the Penal Codes based on the Code Napoléon (e.g., Egypt and, though less directly, China). In this group, no special mention is made of homosexual acts, which means that they are punishable not because of their perverse nature but only if they fall under any of the other four categories of sexual offences enumerated above (p. 63), particularly if they constitute "*un outrage public à la pudeur*" (art. 330, Code Pénal), or if the offender has "*attenté aux mœurs, en excitant, favorisant ou facilitant habituellement la débauche*

[1] See below, Part II. In this field, the art of legislative technique has made no progress since the times of the mediæval law-books. Slightly more definite are the Indian Penal Code, art. 377, "Whoever voluntarily has carnal intercourse against the order of nature with any man, woman or animal . . . (Explanation: Penetration is sufficient to constitute the carnal intercourse necessary to the offence)", and the Colonial Codes.

[2] S. and B. Webb, *Soviet Communism*, Vol. II, p. 1060 fn. 2. The full text of the decree is reproduced in the official English translation of the Soviet Penal Code, App. II.

ou la corruption de la jeunesse de l'un ou de l'autre sexe au-dessous de l'âge de vingt-un ans " (art. 334). This is the state of affairs envisaged by men like Magnus Hirschfeld and Krafft-Ebing who wrote : " Beyond a certain age, say 18, . . . the law has neither the right nor the duty to impugn immoral acts which are committed *inter mares, portis clausis, et consensu mutuo* ".[1]

(*c*) In a few of the modern Penal Codes some sort of compromise has been attempted between these two extremes. Homosexual acts have been made punishable, for instance, if committed for financial gain (Polish Penal Code, art. 207), or in addition, if the offender had exploited the difficult position of a person dependent on him for reasons of employment, etc. (Swiss Penal Code, art. 194). In Germany, the Draft Code of 1927 had made similar proposals, which were subsequently perverted by the Nazi Act of June 28, 1935. Under this latter Statute, homosexual acts—interpreted in the widest sense in which the term has ever been used in the practice of the German Supreme Court—have remained offences punishable with imprisonment, even in the absence of any aggravating circumstances (offenders under 21 may, in particularly slight cases, be discharged without penalty). If, however, any of the aggravating circumstances enumerated in the Draft Code of 1927 are present, the penalty may be increased up to ten years' penal servitude. As already indicated, this stiffening of the law has been followed by a further rise in convictions from 948 in 1934 to 5,321 in 1936. The increase in male prostitution among juveniles in cities like Hamburg seems to have been particularly alarming in spite of the risk of very severe penalties.[2]

In countries which still belong to group (*a*), the next step that can reasonably be expected is to adopt one of the systems in groups (*b*) and (*c*), i.e., to penalize homosexual acts only if committed either with young persons, say, of under 18, or habitually for financial reasons, or in exploitation of a person dependent on the offender. This would not only leave the legal position of the male prostitute unchanged, but would make it easier to prosecute him as his partners would be less afraid of giving information. It would also substantially reduce the

[1] Op. cit., page 580.

[2] On the position in Hamburg see the frank description given by the principal probation officer in *MSchrKr*, 1937, p. 512, and 1939, p. 94. Among juvenile offenders in Hamburg, the proportion of convictions for homosexual offences had risen from 1·6 per cent. of the total in 1933 to 11 per cent. On the psychological relationship between National Socialism and homosexuality see Peter Nathan, *The Psychology of Fascism* (1943), pp. 61 et seq.

prospects of the blackmailer. Bearing in mind the fact that in many cases homosexual offences are committed with boys under 18, it might be asked, however, whether the proposed change would perhaps be of practical value only in such a small proportion of cases as to make the reform not really worth while. Judging from available statistics, this criticism would not seem to be valid. In the East-de Hubert Report [1] it is stated, for instance, that " about half the homosexuals seen were interested in boys only, and another ten per cent. in boys and men ". This would leave a substantial proportion of homosexuals outside the scope of a reformed law, and it may be expected that this proportion will further increase as soon as the law distinguishes according to the age of the partner. For those who would still come under the scope of the law the question remains of how to deal with them. Whereas for male prostitutes and for those who exploit the dependent position of others severe sentences of imprisonment may be unavoidable, difficulties are likely to arise with regard to the treatment of persons who commit homosexual acts with boys under 18. For them, especially for those with incurable constitutional tendencies, the " penal institution of a special type ", as recommended in the East-de Hubert Report, or a " penal home ", as suggested by Dr. Clifford Allen,[2] will be the only solution. At present, terms of penal servitude imposed in such cases are sometimes excessively severe, and it is to be welcomed that the Court of Criminal Appeal in London has recently made it clear that " the habits of the age have led to a consideration of sentences of this severity " and that sentences of ten years' penal servitude should be very rarely passed.[3] In future, prolonged detention of a nature as little penal as possible may be unavoidable in really incorrigible cases of homosexual and other serious sexual offences. In a recent Report of the Committee for the Study of Sex Offences, appointed by the Mayor of New York, the first Recommendation is that

a law should be enacted which would make it possible to keep convicted psychopathic sex offenders who cannot be at large with reason-

[1] P. 152. [2] Op. cit., p. 189.

[3] R. v. Kirk, 28 Cr. App. R. 129 (1943) : a man of 31, convicted at Manchester Assizes of indecent assault on a boy of 7 and of committing an act of gross indecency with him, sentenced to ten years' penal servitude and two years' imprisonment, concurrently. Although he had served eighteen months' imprisonment for a similar offence only a few years before, the Court of Criminal Appeal regarded the ten years' sentence as excessive and reduced it to six years. A similar reduction was made by the same Court at the same time in a case of carnal knowledge of a girl of 12 : R. *v.* Duerden, 28 Cr. App. R. 128.

able safety to the public in institutional confinement even after the expiration of sentence.[1]

The choice will, therefore, be between three possibilities: prolonged detention of a throughout penal character; penal sentence of limited duration, followed by unlimited non-penal detention; unlimited non-penal detention without preceding penal sentence. The first course being ruled out in a progressive penal system, it is likely that either the second or the third system will have to be applied, according to the prevailing views on the need for a deterrent penal sentence.

Exhibitionism, though one of the most frequent sexual offences, need not concern us here. Considerable as may be the difficulties it presents to the medico-psychologist, there is but little in this offence to occupy the attention of the social and legal reformer. In the interests of public decency and order it cannot be removed from the statute book, nor will it be easy to find a clearer definition than that used in the present laws.[2] Even the most modern Codes have found nothing better than the old phrase " indecent (or obscene) act committed in public ", or " *actes impudiques commis publiquement* ", or " *outrage publique à la pudeur* ". What could, and should, be altered in English law is the antiquated incorporation of this offence in the Vagrancy Act, which means that the offender is treated as a " rogue and vagabond ". Needless to add that the equally unjustified threat of corporal punishment should be speedily removed and replaced by a provision requiring the Court to ask for a medico-psychological report in every case of this kind.

[1] *Journal of Criminal Law and Criminology*, Vol. XXXV, No. 5 (Jan.–Feb. 1944), p. 326.

[2] See Switzerland, art. 203; Italy, art. 527 (here punishable even in case of culpable negligence); China, art. 234; Egypt, art. 278. The English definition is somewhat more concrete: " every person who wilfully, openly, lewdly, and obscenely exposes his person in any street, road, or public highway, or in the view thereof . . . with intent to insult any female " (Vagrancy Act, 1824, sect. 4). The Russian Code contains nothing on the matter.

Chapter 5

OFFENCES AGAINST THE FAMILY

In spite of the enormous changes which the family has undergone within the past hundred years, in its functions as well as in social esteem, theoretically at least it is still regarded as one of the fundamental values of our civilization. How far is it desirable that it should be protected by the means at the disposal of the criminal law, and is the protection which it actually receives adequate to enable the family to play its proper part in communal life? It is obvious that, generally speaking, only the external structure and the material basis, not the spiritual side of family life, can be safeguarded by penalties. As a consequence, the defensive wall built around the family by the criminal law of most countries consists of four provisions only, dealing with bigamy, adultery, incest, and neglect to support. We are not here concerned with the much more numerous penal provisions for the protection of children, as most of them are equally applicable outside the family circle.

A. Bigamy.

With the exception of Mohammedan countries and, it seems, of Russia, *bigamy* is a crime everywhere. It is sometimes committed for gain or as a reaction against the narrowness of the divorce laws. As a mass phenomenon, however, it is a crime that grows whenever family life becomes disrupted through prolonged physical separation of husband and wife, particularly in times of war.[1] Apart from certain technical difficulties, mainly relating to the question of guilt,[2] the foremost task for the future will be the administrative one of how to devise some better methods to prevent the offence being committed. In some countries, especially in democracies with a strong dislike of anything that, however faintly, smells of state control and interference with individual liberties, it has been made much too easy for married persons to commit bigamy. This is one of the reasons why, in marked contrast to other offences of a sexual or semi-sexual character, the numbers of convictions for bigamy

[1] On the position in the last war, see the author's *War and Crime* (1941), pp. 101 et seq. Although the corresponding figures for the present war have not yet been published, it seems safe to say that the increase is at least as considerable.

[2] See Kenny, *Outlines of Criminal Law*, Chapter XX.

are much larger in England than in Germany with its stricter system of registration. For many years, English eugenists and lawyers have been pressing in vain for a system of registration and control, which would be useful in many other respects besides the prevention of bigamy.[1] In the course of a recent debate in the House of Lords, Lord Mottistone, urging the use of the war-time identity cards for the purpose, made, not without justification, the point that "when we rate monogamy so highly as to make a breach of it punishable by a sentence of seven years' penal servitude, and then take so few precautions to see that such breaches are not committed, we, as a State, render ourselves responsible for an untold amount of real suffering and distress of mind . . ."[2] As emphasized in the Government reply, the practical difficulties in establishing an effective system of control are probably insurmountable during war time. In peace time, however, everything will depend on the possibility of making citizens of a democracy realize that true liberty is not necessarily incompatible with a system of identity cards, designed not only for the prevention of crime but for a variety of scientific purposes as well. A more effective system of preventing bigamous marriages is needed, particularly in view of the unfortunate position of the offspring of such marriages.

B. ADULTERY.

Less clear from the legislative point of view is the case of *adultery*. Although it is at present an offence in most countries, except Great Britain and Russia, there is much to be said for the minority view that state interference is not really called for. Contrary to bigamy, where the external facts can be easily proved, the difficulties of evidence are often formidable. Moreover, whereas bigamy constitutes a permanent attack on the sanctity of marriage, adultery may be of momentary significance only. It is one of those anti-social acts which are better not made crimes.[3]

Those countries, however, which wish to retain adultery in their Penal Codes should at least abolish the discrimination between the sexes. Whereas Germany (art. 172) and Switzer-

[1] Leonard Darwin, *The Need for Eugenic Reform* (1926), p. 481; Heber Hart, *The Way to Justice*, p. 109; Cecil Whiteley, *Brief Life* (1942), p. 195.

[2] *Parliamentary Debates*, House of Lords, March 28, 1944, cols. 306 et seq.

[3] The matter is well discussed in T. H. Green's *Principles of Political Obligation* (*Works*, Vol. II, 1886), pp. 545 et seq. See also W. A. Bonger, *Criminality and Economic Conditions* (English translation, 1916), pp. 609 et seq.

land (art. 214), for instance, know of no such discrimination, the French Code Pénal (arts. 336 et seq.) and Codes based on it, such as the Italian (arts. 559 et seq.) and Egyptian (arts. 273 et seq.) Codes, treat adultery of the wife more harshly than that of the husband : the wife is punishable without any reservations, the husband only if he keeps a concubine in the conjugal home (" or notoriously elsewhere ", adds the Italian Code). Moreover, the maximum penalty is higher for the wife than for the husband. In China, a compromise has for the time being been reached in the new Code of 1935 between the claims of modern Chinese women, based on the doctrines of Kuo Min Tang and the constitution, for complete equality of the sexes, and the ancient idea that it is the paramount purpose of marriage to produce male children capable of continuing the cult of ancestors. In the interest of husbands who, in order to obtain male progeny, had to take resort to adultery men who were already keeping concubines before the Code came into force are not punishable. However, " *la difficulté demeure entière pour l'avenir* ".[1]

C. Incest.

Incest has probably aroused more interest and controversy among anthropologists, sociologists, and psychologists than any other crime. Every possible aspect of the matter has been scrutinized ; every possible theory has been put forward and disputed, and the peculiar significance which it has assumed for psycho-analysts has added to the heat of the discussion. All this, of course, refers mainly to the historical origin and the psychological and sociological factors responsible for the growth of the incest taboo, in other words, to the penological side of the matter (the word " penological " used in its widest sense).[2] The criminological side, i.e., the analysis of the causes not of the incest prohibition but of incest itself has been comparatively

[1] See Ho Tchong-Chan in his French edition of the *Chinese Penal Code* (1935), p. xvii and fn. 64.

[2] The literature is immense. Reference may be made to E. Westermarck, *The History of Human Marriage*, Vol. II, Chapters 18 to 20, and *Three Essays on Sex and Marriage* (1934) ; Freud, *Totem and Taboo* ; Sir James Frazer, *Totemism and Exogamy*, 4 volumes (1910) ; Brenda Z. Seligman, *Sociological Review*, Vol. 27 (1935) ; William I. Thomas, *Primitive Behaviour* (1937), Chapter VII. In Lord Raglan's provocative and stimulating study, *Jocasta's Crime* (1933), a critical survey of the principal theories is given, and in a recent paper by A. T. H. Jolly and F. G. G. Rose, " The Place of the Australian Aboriginal in the Evolution of Society," *Annals of Eugenics* (July 1943), pp. 44 et seq., the whole complexity of primitive kinship and taboos is again made clear.

neglected. Bearing in mind the very small numerical importance which the subject has in modern civilization, anything like a full discussion would be out of place in the present book. Nothing is needed but the briefest prognosis of the likely future development of this type of crime, together with a brief summary of the penal provisions relating to it.

In the world of to-day, incest has lost most of its mystical flavour. It is due to a variety of usually very prosaic and very obvious social and mental factors. Whereas bigamy is often caused by prolonged bodily separation, incest is largely the consequence of too much proximity between near relations. Overcrowding and lack of opportunity for social and sexual intercourse outside the family circle; alcoholism and low mentality; excessive sexual appetite of the husband and premature ageing of the wife—all of them play their part.[1] Moreover, the extremely strong religious taboos of primitive societies have been relaxed, and there are also lacking those manifold technical devices used by primitive man to prevent what seemed to him the greatest of all crimes.[2] Though for different reasons, the modern technique of prevention has been equally faulty here as in the case of bigamy.

Not without significance is the considerable increase in convictions in both England and Germany after the last war.[3] The explanation, it has been suggested,[4] may be that married soldiers, returning home, found their wives prematurely aged under the strain of the war years, while, on the other hand, after years of absence they were inclined to look at their daughters in a not purely fatherlike way. The overcrowded homes of the post-1918 period must have provided additional temptations. Impossible as it may be to eliminate the first of these factors, overcrowding should at least be reduced to the unavoidable minimum after the second world war.

For the law reformer, the principal task for the future is to keep the prohibition of incest within reasonable limits. The legal definitions of this crime, as in force to-day, show but little congruity with regard to the scope of the incest taboo. Some

[1] For an analysis of a few hundred cases of incest from inmates of the German convict prison at Ludwigsburg, see G. Schwab, *MSchrKr*, 1938, pp. 257–77.

[2] "Civilized man does not employ the same precautions against incest", Edward Glover, *The Danger of being Human*, p. 54 fn.

[3] England and Wales: annual averages (crimes known to the police): 1910–1914 = 71; 1915–19 = 57; 1920–4 = 89; 1925–9 = 101. Germany (convicted persons): 1910 = 487; 1917 = 235; 1921 = 760; 1925 = 1,010.

[4] Schwab, op. cit., pp. 263–4.

countries punish only sexual intercourse between near blood-relations, i.e., descendants and ascendants in the direct line and brothers and sisters, including half-brothers and half-sisters (England : Punishment of Incest Act, 1908 ; Switzerland, art. 213) ; others extend the prohibition to " relatives by marriage in the direct line " (Italy, art. 564) or to " *parents collatéraux du troisième degré ou au-dessous* " (China, art. 230), or to relatives by marriage, without any restriction (Germany, art. 173).[1] In several countries, notably Russia, France, India, Egypt, no special penalties for incest are provided. A choice between these different systems can be made only after due consideration of the reasons on which the legal prohibition should be based. Why do we now want to punish incest? Of all those aspects that have so far been ventilated,[2] probably only the following can be regarded as carrying some weight in modern society : popular disgust, the undermining of family life, and the dangers to progeny arising from inbreeding. None of them, however, can possibly justify the penalization of sexual intercourse outside the circle of blood relationship. Whatever may have remained of the true feeling of family cohesion, it hardly extends beyond the circle of blood relations. Again, how greatly popular feeling has changed in this respect is shown by the recent revision of the Church of England's " Table of Kindred and Affinity ", by which marriages between brothers and sisters-in-law, uncles and nieces-in-law, and aunts and nephews-in-law are made permissible from the point of view of the Church.[3] Lord Quickswood's violent protest against this change as " grievously injuring the reputation of the Church of England as a moral teacher . . . wrong has become right : black has become white ", far from arousing any popular outcry, was rejected by another correspondent of *The Times* as indicating " a grievous misunderstanding of the true character of the Church of England ".[4] On the other hand, the Italian system of making incest, even between near blood relations, punishable only if committed " in such a manner as to cause public scandal " (art. 564) does not recommend itself, partly because of the vagueness of this criterion, partly because the harm done through inbreeding should be prevented regardless

[1] The German Draft Codes before 1933 had proposed to restrict the prohibition to blood relations.

[2] See, for example, Lord Raglan's list of theories put forward to account for the prohibition of marriage between near relatives in *Jocaste's Crime*, Chapter XIV.

[3] *The Times*, May 25, 1944.

[4] *The Times*, May 31 and June 2, 1944. See also *Report on Sexual Offences against Young Persons* (1926, Cmd. 2561), p. 21.

of " public scandal ". It seems, therefore, that the Anglo-Swiss system deserves preference over any other.[1]

D. Neglect to Support the Family.

Apart from misbehaviour related to the sexual or semi-sexual sphere, the criminal law of most countries affords but little protection to the mutual claims of the members of a family. In the purely financial sphere, wilful *neglect to support one's family* is, as a rule, treated as an offence. The statutes defining it are, however, usually too antiquated and too much hedged in with impracticable provisos to be of any considerable practical value. It is, of course, quite true that, as Mr. Mullins says,[2] " the law does not, and cannot, object to married people leaving each other or going to live with somebody else.[3] All that the law can do is to enforce certain consequences in proper cases ". We are not here concerned with the civil consequences. On the criminal side, however, the consequences should be made more effective than they are now. This, in particular, in the following directions :

(*a*) At present, in the law of some countries, e.g., England (Vagrancy Act of 1824, sect. 3 ; similarly German Penal Code, art. 361, No. 10) neglect to maintain members of one's family is punishable only if, as a consequence, the relative concerned had to be supported by the community. This should no longer be a necessary condition, as there may be cases where, for technical or purely personal reasons, public assistance may not have been forthcoming, or not even been applied for. Why should this relieve the offender of his criminal responsibility ? The law is different already in Switzerland (art. 217), Poland (art. 201), Italy (art. 570), and Russia (art. 158), which latter country is, however, concerned only with the protection of children, not of other relatives.

(*b*) The circle of protected relatives should include illegitimate children. This does not seem so at present in English law, where only " the family " is referred to ; it is at least doubtful, for instance, in Italy and China, whereas explicit provision for illegitimates is made in the Swiss Code.

[1] Whereas in English law female persons involved in incestuous relations are exempt from punishment only if under the age of 16, the Swiss Code extends this immunity to the age of 21 provided the female has to be regarded not as the seducer but as seduced.

[2] Claud Mullins, *Wife and Husband in the Courts* (1935), p. 64.

[3] To this, by the way, as we have seen, the law in some countries does object.

(*c*) Another recommendable provision of the Swiss Code makes it an offence to desert and thereby expose to financial distress a woman who, as the offender knows, is pregnant by him.[1]

(*d*) At present many countries, e.g., England, Poland, Russia, punish only wilful misbehaviour, whereas the Swiss Code adds laziness and carelessness. This, too, should be seriously considered.

(*e*) " Failure to maintain " is altogether too narrow. There are other cases of misbehaviour which may have at least equally serious consequences for the family of the offender. In a letter to *The Times*, the Chairman of the Legal Committee of the Married Women's Association has drawn attention to " a large number of cases of hardship " coming before his Association where

> the husband has deserted his family, taking all the furniture and household belongings. Legally it is clearly his. In two recent cases young children were left without bedding. Even if a maintenance order can be obtained it does not remedy the loss of " the home ".[2]

Such cases are apparently provided for in the Italian Code (art. 570) with its extremely broad formulation :

> Any person who, by leaving the domestic fold or in any way pursuing conduct contrary to family order or decency, evades the obligations of assistance inherent in the paternal power, legal guardianship, or the capacity of married person, shall be punished . . .

The point has also received attention in the Nazi Draft Code which, regardless of any legal property rights, makes it an offence for a married person maliciously to sell or carry away the household goods and thereby seriously to imperil the domestic life of the other partner.[3] This, too, seems worthy of further consideration in spite of its tainted source.

(*f*) Finally, the maximum penalties are often inadequate. Criminal courts should be able to impose sentences which make it clear to the offender and the public at large that reckless conduct in the economic sphere of family life is an offence much more serious to the community than petty theft.[4] In the Soviet

[1] The Swiss example was followed by the Nazi Draft Code : Guertner, op. cit., pp. 112, 115.

[2] Mr. Ambrose Appelbe, *The Times*, Nov. 29, 1943.

[3] Guertner, op. cit. p. 115.

[4] It is hardly necessary to add, however, that the present treatment of this offence under the Vagrancy Act, whereby the offender is punishable as an " idle and disorderly person ", is out of date.

Union, according to the Webbs,[1] it was found ten years ago that the provisions requiring divorced parents to pay for the maintenance of their children were disregarded in thousands of cases because of the inadequacy of the penalties, among other reasons, and it was suggested to replace the maximum penalty of six months' imprisonment provided in art. 158 by a minimum of one year. Whether this has actually been done is not known to the writer ; it would, however, be in harmony with the recent tendency of the Soviet Government towards strengthening family life.[2]

It would go too far to examine in detail whether, apart from safeguarding the financial interests of members of the family, the criminal law might be able to contribute towards consolidating family life. Even a superficial consideration, however, leads to a number of interesting questions : Does the present criminal law really draw the logical consequences from the dogma of the unity of the family and the sanctity of family life, or is it mainly lip-service we have been paying to it ? When the young offender appears before a Juvenile Court, is he always treated there as a member of a family, or rather as an altogether separate unit ? Is the joint responsibility of the family throughout sufficiently taken into consideration ? Provisions such as sect. 55 of the Children and Young Persons Act of 1933 do not seem to go far enough in making parents realize their duty to prevent childish misbehaviour. The same might be said of the sections of the Act regarding the child who has become " beyond control ". Nor has the competence of the Juvenile Court as yet been extended far enough to establish it as a true " Family Court ". On the other hand, such attacks on family unity as were at one time to be found, but soon given up, in Soviet Russia, where children were encouraged to act as informers against their parents,[3] have not been imitated elsewhere, except in Nazi Germany. In probably every country, husband and wife enjoy some privileges with regard to having to give evidence against each other, and often this is extended to the parent-child relationship as well. These few examples may indicate that, while the importance of the family as a primary social group is generally recognized in criminal legislation, a consistent policy has yet to be evolved.

[1] *Soviet Communism*, Vol. II, p. 1058.

[2] See the recent accounts on the Soviet legislation of July 8, 1944, on marriage, divorce, and parenthood ; e.g. *New Statesman and Nation*, August 12, 1944.

[3] Sir John Maynard, *The Russian Peasant*, p. 463.

SECTION THREE. ECONOMIC CRIME—I

INTRODUCTORY REMARKS

At the beginning of these, possibly controversial, chapters it may be as well to ask the reader to keep in mind the special purpose of this book. We are not here concerned with the criminological question of the economic causes of crime, which will therefore be touched upon only occasionally. In accordance with the programme as set out in the Introduction, it is our primary object to examine the effect which contemporary changes in values have so far exerted on economic crime and its treatment by the law, and to point out the practical handicaps in the path of the legal machinery and the direction in which things are likely to move in the post-war period.

The term " economic crime " comprises a very great variety of offences and its scope is not easily definable. There is first the long list of traditional " offences against property ", with or without violence, as enumerated in *Criminal Statistics*, especially the many types of larceny and of breaking, embezzlement, robbery, extortion, fraud and false pretences, receiving, bankruptcy [1] ; the " malicious injuries to property " such as arson and the various forms of malicious damage. There are, moreover, all those economic offences which are usually regarded as of minor significance in English law, mostly " non-indictable " offences, such as adulterations, betting and gambling ; brothel keeping, prostitution, procuration ; offences against Shops Acts, Employment of Children Acts, Pawnbrokers and Moneylenders Acts, Poor Law, Revenue Acts, and scores of others. Most countries possess penal provisions against usury, and in the United States, the British Dominions and several other countries the criminal law is also used in the fight against restraint of trade and monopoly. And, finally, there is the immense and unwieldy mass of war-time Emergency Regulations which, backed by penal provisions, have fundamentally altered the economic structure of the country.[2]

[1] Continental jurisprudence and legislation have become accustomed to distinguish between offences against specific objects of property such as larceny, robbery, embezzlement, and offences against property as a whole, such as false pretences (see, for example, the Swiss Penal Code).

[2] Omitted from this list are offences such as forgery and coining which, though of an essentially economic flavour, are usually classified as offences against the State or against public faith, or for which no satisfactory classification can be found.

Quantitatively, the Tables of *Criminal Statistics* are completely dominated by economic crime. True, there are a few among the smaller countries where wounding seems to be more frequent than stealing (e.g., Austria, Belgium, Portugal, Sweden), and even among the principal countries considerable differences may be encountered: whereas economic offences numbered 3,440 out of a total of 7,370 per million of population in Germany in 1936 (= 46·6 per cent.),[1] they were 2,407 out of a total of 3,094 (indictable offences and non-indictable offences akin to indictable) in England and Wales in 1938 (= 77·7 per cent.).[2] Taken as a whole, however, and leaving out of consideration the recent mushroom growth of traffic offences, the administration of criminal justice all over the world has to devote probably three-quarters of its time and energy to economic offences.

Can it be maintained that legislators and courts have done their jobs in this field with fairness, common sense, and efficiency? Or have their energies and resources, to a considerable extent, been squandered on those who "steal the goose from the common", leaving "the greater villain loose who steals the common from the goose"? Has the first of these two categories, the petty economic offender of the familiar type, at least received a square deal?

In the following chapters, we propose to illustrate the problems involved by way of reference to some of the most important types of economic crime, especially theft, false pretences, and other offences against property, usury, taxation offences, and monopoly.

[1] *MSchrKr*, 1938, p. 338.

[2] *Criminal Statistics* for 1938, Table E. We omit the bulk of the non-indictable offences as their counterpart is not shown in the German *Kriminal-Statistik*. The numbers of economic offences against war-time regulations are unknown, even for the war of 1914–18, as separate figures for the different categories of offences against the Defence of the Realm Act have not been published (see the author's *War and Crime* (1940), p. 95).

Chapter 6

THE PROTECTION OF PROPERTY (I): CRITICISM OF THE TRADITIONAL APPROACH

The idea of property has, from times immemorial, occupied the minds of social and legal philosophers and reformers. Economists, sociologists and psychologists have pondered over its problems ever since these branches of human knowledge came into existence. One might have expected that the subject should have received similar attention on the part of criminal lawyers and the makers of penal legislation. At least, for the past hundred years, with the coming of a more scientifically minded age, one should have thought that the law of theft and those other inventions of the legal mind which aim at the protection of property should have been developed in close contact with the evolution of economic and sociological thought. In fact, very little of this kind has happened. If the law of sexual crime is sometimes called mediæval, that of economic crime has, to a considerable extent, remained archaic. In the survey of the "History of the Law relating to Theft and similar Offences" in which that great judge and scholar, Sir James Fitzjames Stephen, traces the development of the subject in his country before the passing of the Larceny Act of 1916,[1] the following adjectives occur, without a single word of praise interspersed among all this condemnation: "strange", "absurd", "peculiar", "intricate", "unsatisfactory", "inconsistent", "unintelligible", "capricious", "a mere incumbrance and source of intricacy and confusion".

Even the present Larceny Act of 1916 seems to have preserved far too many unnecessary or downright absurd relics of the past, and the law of foreign countries, though for the major part less antiquated and complicated, is, with few exceptions, also far from satisfactory.

A. Changes in the Economic and Social Structure of Property.

Without going into technical details that are of interest only to the lawyer, let us try to understand why it is that the criminal

[1] *A History of Criminal Law of England,* Vol. III (1883), Chapter XXVIII.

law should, so persistently, have fallen short of the requirements of economic and social life, and that it should have failed to adjust itself to the changes in the economic and social structure of property. What is, in the briefest outlines, the essence of these changes? The forces at work might perhaps be reduced to the following factors: [1]

(1) The gradual *shifting of the emphasis* from *agricultural* and mainly *immovable* to *commercial* and *industrial*, largely *movable* objects of property.

(2) The increasing *inequality* in the *distribution* of property; the amassing of great wealth, and consequently power, by the few and the impoverishment of the many.

(3) As a consequence of (1) and (2), the growing need to leave property, more and more, in the hands of *servants* or other persons.

(4) The transformation of an increasing proportion of wealth from property in visible and tangible goods into ownership in invisible and intangible *powers* and *rights*, such as insurance policies and especially, since the invention of the joint-stock company, in *shares*; moreover, since the coming into existence of the modern *social services*, for most working-class people the building up of a system of *social security* in place of ownership of goods.

(5) The passing of the most valuable objects of property from individuals to *big corporations*.

(6) The consequent large-scale *separation* between legal *ownership*, on the one hand, and *control* and *management*, on the other.

(7) As a further result, the *decline* in the feeling of *social responsibility* on the part of the owner of property. This in its turn provokes, as the inevitable reaction,

(8) a re-awakening of the ineradicable *belief* in the *social functions* and *obligations* of private ownership as its essence and only justification; a belief which is accompanied by

(9) a recognition of the fact that, from the point of view of social function, there are *different types of property*, with particular

[1] Only a few references to an immense literature can be given: Thorstein Veblen, *Absentee Ownership and Business Enterprise* (1924); Karl Renner, *Die Rechtsinstitute des Privatrechts und ihre soziale Funktion*, (1929) (English translation to be published in the International Library of Sociology and Social Reconstruction under the title "The Institutions of Civil Law and their Social Functions"); A. A. Berle and Gardiner C. Means, *The Modern Corporation and Private Property* (1935); Thurman W. Arnold, *The Folklore of Capitalism* (1937); Franz Neumann, *Behemoth* (1943); Peter Drucker, *The Future of Industrial Man* (1943).

distinction between property in the *means of production* and in other goods ; and

(10) by an increasing demand for the *nationalization*, or at least for *public management* or *public control*, either of all means of production or of some of them.

B. The Law of Theft.

What has been the attitude of the criminal law to the immense problems indicated in this list ? Are we entitled to claim that they, or at least some of them, are duly reflected in the history of criminal legislation ? Space forbids an analysis of all crimes against property, but as *theft* is still numerically by far the most common of them,[1] we may deal with it more fully. Looking back over the period of several thousand years which the modern law of theft has taken to develop, we find that the following factors have, at one time or another, been considered by various lawgivers [2]—when we say " considered " we mean that they have been deemed either essential elements of the legal concept of theft, or treated as aggravating or mitigating circumstances :

(*a*) The *object* of theft :
movable or immovable ; living or dead ; cattle—horses, foodstuffs, esp. grain—other merchandise—money ; sacred or profane ; specially protected or neglected ; value.

(*b*) The *place* of theft :
Church — graveyard — dwelling-house — warehouse — ship—dock—hotel—yard—railway—post office—shop.

(*c*) The *methods* employed :
open or secret ; by night or by day ; with or without violence (incl. breaking) ; armed or unarmed ; singly or with others ; use of false keys or other instruments ; picking pockets.

(*d*) The *person* of the *thief* :
social status ; in possession of stolen objects ; professional thief or other recidivist ; wealthy or poor.

[1] All but about 160 of the 2,407 (per million of population) persons tried for economic offences in England and Wales in 1938 (see above, p. 84) belong to this category. The 160 are cases of robbery, extortion, fraud and false pretences.

[2] For Anglo-American law, the following discussion is based, in addition to Stephen, *History*, Vol. III, and Kenny, *Outlines*, on Prof. Jerome Hall's book *Theft, Law and Society* (1935), one of the few really outstanding models of how successfully to combine legal history and analysis with the mastery of economic and sociological facts. See also Hall's article " Crime as Social Reality " in the *Annals of the American Academy of Political and Social Science*, Vol. 217 (Sept. 1941), esp. pp. 6 et seq.

(*e*) *Relationship* between *thief* and *owner* :
husband and wife ; parents and children, or other near relatives ; employer and employee ; *cestui que* trust and trustee.

(*f*) the *person* of the *owner* :
whether property of a private individual or property of the State, of a Corporation, etc. ; social status and economic position of owner.

(*g*) The social and economic *functions* of the stolen property :
use made of it by owner ; whether actually needed by him ; how difficult for him to replace it, and how much damage consequently caused to him through the theft ; on the other hand :
need for it on the part of the thief.

Most of these various factors might perhaps be summed up under three headings : danger, temptation, injury to owner and community ; and there will be universal agreement that the one or the other of them is likely to be of a special significance to the lawgiver at a certain stage of civilization, and also that different " vested interests " may place the emphasis on different points. Considering the paramount influence of magic and superstition, one must not, however, try to find too much rationality in earlier periods of the criminal law ; and, very often, a legal distinction for which there had been some good reasons when it was first applied has been quite unjustifiably preserved long after their disappearance. Moreover, naturally enough, it is rare for any of these special circumstances of theft to be of universal significance. Religious bodies may be particularly interested in the sacred character of the object ; the Police in the way the property is protected against theft ; the owner's chief interest may be in its monetary value, and the psychologist's in its symbolic meaning.

Reasons of space forbid to illustrate more than a few of these points by reference to certain features of the historical law of theft :

(*a*) regarding the *objects* of theft :

" Only movable articles can be stolen." Up to the present day, we have not succeeded in getting rid of this old tenet of Roman Law. In its origin, it was probably due to the absence of private property in land in early Roman society,[1] but the principle remained part of Roman and modern law long after

[1] Th. Mommsen, *Römisches Strafrecht* (1899), pp. 739 et seq. ; H. F. Jolowicz, *Historical Introduction to the Study of Roman Law* (1932), p. 140.

such property had become permissible. " It seems strange that land, by far the most important form of wealth in the Middle Ages, should have been left unprotected," says Kenny, though he agrees with Stephen that the omission had but little practical significance as it was " nearly impossible to misappropriate land permanently otherwise than by certain definite means which are usually crimes in themselves ". However, the principle did not only remain in force with regard to the land itself: to make things worse, trees and growing grain were treated as belonging to the land in matters not only of civil law, where it was justifiable, but of criminal law as well where it made no sense. To be the object of theft, a thing had to be movable already before it was stolen, which normally did not apply to trees or grain or sand, and it required " an amazingly long list of statutes " to fill this—from the economic point of view absurd—gap.[1] The real explanation has, of course, nothing to do with economics. It was the excessive severity of the ancient law of theft that induced the judges to narrow its scope as much as possible,[2] to cut off the trees from the conception of larceny, we might perhaps say. [3]

Cattle and *horse stealing*, in accordance with its reduced significance in economic life, has been somewhat dethroned from its elated position in recent times. In primitive societies this form of theft is usually the most common and most dangerous of all and therefore singled out for especially severe penalties—Pollock and Maitland go even so far as to say " If only cattle lifting could be suppressed, the legislators will have done all or almost all that they can hope to do for the protection of the owner of movables ".[4] Now this applies only to some mainly agricultural countries, such as Italy (art. 625), Russia (art. 166), and, with less justification, to twentieth-century England and Wales (Larceny Act, 1916, art. 3). The reason for this increased protection seems to have been not only the economic value of cattle but also the difficulty of protecting it from being stolen.[5]

[1] See Hall, *Theft, Law and Society*, pp. 40 et seq.; Stephen, *History*, III, pp. 134–5; Kenny, *Outlines*, pp. 200–1.

[2] See W. W. Buckland and Arnold D. McNair, *Roman Law and Common Law* (1936), pp. 281–2.

[3] In an article by Orvil C. Snyder, " Word-Magic and the Embezzlement of Real Property " (*Journal of Criminal Law and Criminology*, July–August 1937, pp. 164 et seq.), the Californian Penal Code, sect. 503, is mentioned as the only American Code which punishes the embezzlement of real property.

[4] *History of English Law* (1st ed., 1895), Vol. II, p. 155.

[5] Similarly for the theft of the harvest on the field, which was the only case of capital punishment in Roman Law as a public penalty, even where the thief was not caught in the act: Mommsen, op. cit., p. 272; F. Schulz, *Principles of Roman Law* (1936), p. 202.

In Blackstone,[1] we find a reference to the strange law of the Isle of Man where it was a felony to steal some small animal, a pig or a fowl, but a mere trespass to take a horse or an ox, because in that small island the fowl thief was more likely to get away with his booty than the horse thief. Under present conditions, however, the privileged position granted to cattle in the law of a not very large and mainly industrial country, such as England, with her highly efficient Police force, even making due allowance for any increased significance that cattle breeding may have as a result of the war, seems to be little more than an empty gesture. The legislator of the future may easily feel tempted to make special provision for theft of cars and bicycles, and to some extent this has already been done ; as a rule, however, it is unnecessary. If, however, considerations like those responsible in olden times for the increased protection of cattle should be applied to goods which are in equal need of protection to-day, surely, the bicycle should have been given a place of honour in the Larceny Act long ago. This has not been done, presumably because the average bicycle owner is a person of no account in present-day life, whereas the average cattle owner was a pillar of society.

One of the most embarrassing events in the history of the criminal law was the discovery of the use which can be made of electric power. Electricity was not regarded as a " thing " that could be stolen, and therefore, after a period of uncertainty, in most countries sooner or later some special provision had to be made to cover this unexpected contingency.[2] In view of the rapid development of the natural sciences this was, however, only the first step in the right direction.

From the very beginning the *value* of the object, and consequently the distinction between grand and petty larceny, has played a predominant part in criminal legislation, not only in the sense that, in order to be the object of theft, a thing must have some value, however small, but also that penalties have to be imposed in accordance with the value of the object. Already Plato had raised the question of " how far does the amount stolen modify the guilt ? ", but he wisely refrained from answer-

[1] Sir William Blackstone, *Commentaries on the Laws of England*, Book IV (7th ed., 1773), p. 16.

[2] England was, apparently, the first country to recover from this juristic shock : see the Electric Lighting Act, 1882, sect. 23, now Larceny Act, sect. 10 ; Russia, art. 163 ; Italy, art. 624 (2) ; China, art. 323 ; German Act of 1900.

ing.[1] The positive law, from its earliest beginnings, has shown less reluctance. This is so well known that detailed references may be unnecessary.[2] The point is important for us mainly for two reasons: First, because it is characteristic of the loving care which the criminal law, throughout its history, has bestowed upon the interests of the big property owner who alone can, as a rule, become the victim of grand larceny—unless this conception is watered down so as to comprise the theft of all and sundry. There is more in it than just another example of the general principle of criminal law that the damage done should be taken into account when meting out the penalty. If to kill a man was more expensive to the offender than to knock out a front tooth, this was justifiable as everyone had a life as well as (presumably) a front tooth, and everyone therefore enjoyed increased protection for the more important parts of his body. If, however, the thief was more severely punished if he stole a hundred sheep than if he took one or two, this, in most cases, favoured only the owner of a hundred. Sometimes, it is true, grand larceny may betray stronger criminal tendencies in the thief which justify a sterner sentence; often, however, this does not hold good and the thief may even be unaware of the high value of the stolen article. The second point of interest is that process of watering down, already referred to: it has in fact occurred, not, however, because legislators were anxious to afford the same protection to the small man as to the big one, but simply because the distinction between grand and petty larceny was often expressed in terms of money, and the money value of goods changed much faster than the law could follow suit. This inability of the makers of criminal law to adjust the creatures of their own ingenuity even to the least complicated changes in economic conditions, to changes which could be expressed in monetary terms, is one of the most depressing lessons of legal history. In the thirteenth century theft of property to the value of twelve pence (representing eight days' wages) was grand larceny and a capital offence in English law, but as a writer quoted by Hall[3] complains five hundred years later, although twelve pence at the time of Æthelstan had become

[1] *Laws*, Book XII, 857, b. 4.

[2] See, for example, L. v. Bar, *A History of Continental Criminal Law* (1916), pp. 138 and 287; H. Brunner, *Deutsche Rechtsgeschichte*, Vol. II (1892), p. 639; A. S. Diamond, *Primitive Law*, pp. 299, 329; Kenny, *Outlines*, p. 203; R. R. Cherry, *The Growth of Criminal Law* (1890), p. 50.

[3] Jerome Hall, *Theft, Law and Society*, pp. 302–3.

the equivalent of more than three pounds in the eighteenth century, the law had taken no cognizance of this change : larceny to the value of twelve pence remained " grand larceny " till 1827. In Massachusetts, according to Hall, the dividing line of fifteen dollars, fixed in 1867, is still in force, with tragic consequences regarding the minima penalties permissible.[1] The effects of this excessive conservatism of criminal legislation are widely known : judges and juries had to waste their energies to find ways and means to get round the law : juries by assessing, in the face of the facts, the value of stolen articles low enough to come under the scope of petty larceny, and judges by artificially excluding as many objects as possible altogether from the scope of the Larceny Acts.[2]

Even the present Larceny Act of 1916 has not yet entirely abandoned this idea that higher economic value should mean higher penalties.[3] On the other hand, such is the sacredness of property that even theft of an object which has no measurable value at all is treated like any other theft in English law and that of some other countries. " The principle is now distinctly laid down that although, to be the subject of a stealing, a thing must be of value to its owner, if not to other people, yet this need not amount to the value of the smallest coin known to the law, or of even ' the hundredth part of a farthing '." [4] This is a comparatively recent innovation, as " in earlier times it seems to have been thought that ' valuable ' implied serious practical importance as opposed to mere fancy or amusement ".[5] The Indian Penal Code, art. 95, has a useful provision that an act is not an offence if the harm done " is so slight that no person of ordinary sense and temper would complain of such harm ". The Polish Code, art. 272, makes the appropriation of objects without any material value a special offence, presumably in order to avoid in such cases the stigma of theft. In another respect, too, theft has lost its former character as an economic crime ; it is no longer necessary, as it used to be in Roman Law, that the offender should intend to make a profit out of his action.[6] This, on the surface purely technical point, has a considerable

[1] In some other States of the U.S.A. grand larceny means stealing to the value of over $200 ; see Barnes-Teeters, *New Horizons in Criminology*, p. 105.
[2] Kenny, *Outlines*, pp. 184 and 221. [3] Sects. 8, 13, 16.
[4] Kenny, Outlines, pp. 205–6.
[5] Stephen, op. cit., Vol. III, p. 143.
[6] Kenny, *Outlines*, p. 215 ; Germany, art. 242 ; Russia, art. 162 ; Poland, art. 257. Different : Italy, art. 624 ; Switzerland, art. 137 and some of the pre-Nazi German Draft Codes.

psychological significance. To omit the element of profit from the definition of theft means changing its psychological character. What remains is no longer an economic offence but an offence against public order.

(*b*) regarding the *place* of theft:

This has always been a particularly popular object of infantile criminal legislation. Apart from the Swiss Code, this model of wise legislative technique, there is hardly any criminal law without a number of special provisions offering increased penal protection to this or that type of building, especially to dwelling-houses. In a mature legal system, all this could safely be left to the discretion of the court. This would result in a considerable saving of brain-power, now unconstructively employed in trying to answer questions such as whether a certain building is a "dwelling-house" or a "wharf", and so on, within the meaning of the law. Moreover, the halo of increased protection against theft by which the "dwelling-house" used to be surrounded seems somewhat out of place as long as so little was done to make the dwellings of the masses really fit for human habitation.[1]

(*c*) regarding the *methods* employed by the thief:

Here the position is not much better, although some of the distinctions made in the present law may seem important enough to be preserved, as, for instance, between violent and non-violent methods; between night and day; between theft committed in gangs and singly. However, some of the laws still in force, in particular the French Code Pénal, overdo the matter in a ridiculous fashion. In some respects, a considerable change has taken place in the attitude of the law. In ancient Jewish law, for instance, theft which took place under conditions of secrecy was punished more severely than open robbery with violence, because "the thief committing this crime in secrecy believed himself not to be watched by God and hence should be reprimanded all the more".[2] Similarly, in mediæval English law, theft was regarded as far more dishonourable than robbery,[3] whereas it is much less severely punished to-day.

(*d*) regarding the *person* of the *thief*:

Penalties used to differ in olden times according to the social status of the thief. The Roman Twelve Tables provide scourging

[1] See *Our Towns. A Close-up* (1943.)

[2] M. May, "Jewish Criminal Law", *Journal of Criminal Law and Criminology* (Nov.–Dec. 1940), Vol. XXXI, p. 442.

[3] Pollock-Maitland, *History of English Law*, Vol. I, p. 492.

and enslavement for a freeman, but death for a slave.[1] Perhaps the most notorious instance, however, is the Benefit of Clergy, resulting in discriminations almost unparalleled in the history of criminal law—" a strange mixture of excessive severity and excessive laxity and inefficiency," according to Stephen's all too lenient verdict : [2]

> A man who could not read, and a woman whether she could read or not, must be hung for stealing 2 shillings. But a murderer of the worst kind who knew how to read escaped from nearly all punishment unless he had married a widow.

The fact that this institution which, in the words of Pike, " was not only one of the advantages enjoyed by a particular class of criminals and an inducement to break the law, but was also a cause of hatred between one class and another "—that this institution was not finally abolished before 1827 is indeed remarkable. Now, penalties differ mainly according to the thief's previous convictions [3] and his status as a professional thief or an amateur. Needless to say, this is, from the criminological point of view, one of the really vital aspects, and one which has received special consideration in most countries, not only in connection with theft but for crime, especially economic crime, in general. In this respect at least, modern legislation has made some determined efforts to keep abreast with the development of economic life and the results of criminological research. An analysis of the legislative problems involved would by far exceed the scope of this book, without substantially furthering our immediate purposes.[4]

The economic position of the thief and the purpose for which he has stolen are also sometimes taken into account by the law ; however, as these factors are too closely connected with the functional aspect (*g*), we may better postpone their discussion.

(*e*) regarding the *relationship* between *thief* and *owner* :

As far as family relationships are concerned, the history of the law of theft offers an illustration of the changes that have

[1] Mommsen, op. cit., p. 750 ; Diamond, op. cit., p. 329.

[2] *History of the Criminal Law in England*, Vol. II, p. 204 ; see also Vol. I, pp. 457 et seq. ; Holdsworth, *History of English Law*, Vol. III, pp. 293 et seq. ; Pollock-Maitland, *History of English Law*, Vol. I, pp. 441 et seq. ; Hall, *Theft, Law and Society*, pp. 68 et seq. ; Pike, *History of Crime in England*, Vol. I, p. 297.

[3] Larceny Act, sect. 37 ; Russia, art. 162 ; Italy, art. 99 et seq.

[4] Reference may be made to some of the more important Acts dealing with the problem of the professional criminal : English Prevention of Crime Act, 1908 ; New York Baumes Law, 1926 ; Swedish Habitual Criminals Act, 1927 ; Belgian Law of Social Defence, 1930 ; German Prevention of Crime Act, 1933.

taken place in the conception of marriage. Whereas, according to English law up to the Married Women's Property Act, 1882, husband and wife were held to be one person and could not, therefore, steal from each other, now, the economic bonds between them having become less intimate, their exemption from criminal liability for stealing each other's property has been abolished in two cases: (*a*) if they are not living together at the time of the theft, or (*b*) if the theft is committed by husband or wife when about to leave or desert the other partner.[1] Foreign Codes have adopted different systems: Germany (sect. 247), the French Code Pénal (art. 380), and Egypt (art. 312) entirely exempt from criminal liability; Russia, in accordance with her different conception of marriage, has no exemption whatsoever; Italy restricts the exemption to spouses not legally separated (art. 469); Switzerland and Poland punish only at the request of the other partner (arts. 137 and 257 resp.), and China leaves it to the discretion of the court (art. 324).

Theft by children from their parents may be of considerable psychological interest as indicating some serious maladjustment in the child's personality, and medico-psychologists have rightly stressed the need for a closer analysis of such cases.[2] It would be advisable to exempt such thefts, if committed by children under a certain age, from criminal liability, as has been done, for instance, in France and Italy. This, certainly, would not solve the psychological difficulties involved,[3] but it would keep out the legal atmosphere which may here do more harm than good.

Of vastly greater significance in the economic sphere is the relationship between master and servant in its manifold stratifications, and it is here that English criminal law, perhaps for the first time, has become conscious of its obligation to keep abreast of large-scale changes in the economic structure of the country. The factors referred to above (p. 86) under 1–3—the shifting of the main emphasis from agricultural to commercial and industrial property; the growing inequality in its distribution; the coming into existence of big fortunes and international trade;

[1] Larceny Act, sect. 36; Kenny, *Outlines*, p. 186.

[2] See, for example, Edward Glover, *The Diagnosis and Treatment of Delinquency*, pp. 13–14.

[3] The Ashanti, while regarding only theft outside the family group as a real crime—a person who took something from a kinsman was never termed a "thief"—nevertheless have a saying "I take something from father, I take something from mother, that is how one becomes a thief"; see R. S. Rattray, *Ashanti Law and Constitution* (1929), pp. 291 and 323.

and the consequent necessity for owners of property to entrust their goods to other persons—all such economic factors made it imperative to enlarge the original concept of theft so as to cover misappropriations on the part of these persons. Reduced to its barest outlines, the fundamental problem in all such cases is this : if property is voluntarily handed over by the owner himself to another person—which he may do for an infinite variety of economic reasons and in widely different legal and factual forms—and this other person, in one way or another, misappropriates the goods, or if he keeps for himself something which he has received for his master, is he guilty of an offence ? Economic needs clearly demand an affirmative answer. Normal business cannot be carried on if such relationships of trust should remain unprotected by the criminal law. Is it conceivable that there should be any legal difficulties in the way ? In fact, there have been not one but many of them, and in some countries it has taken courts and legislators the better part of a millennium to overcome them.[1] Theft requires a " taking " of the article, that is an infringement of possession, and in the cases described no such " taking " seems to have occurred as the owner himself seems to have voluntarily given up possession of the article. What else could be done, therefore, but either to stretch the conception of theft or to invent some new offences, such as embezzlement, or fraudulent conversion, or to try it both ways ? It has been done, but, as with most evolutions of the criminal law, it has been a slow process. One of the outstanding landmarks in the history of this process is the famous Carrier's Case of 1473, which has received its appropriate memorial in Professor Hall's *Theft, Law and Society*.[2] This is not the place to go into the extremely interesting and characteristic details of that case, or of any other historical landmark. Suffice it to say that the carrier who had misapproptiated some of the goods entrusted to him by a foreign merchant by taking the bales to a wrong place and breaking them open was convicted of theft. There seems to have been fairly strong pressure on the judges on the part of the King, as it would have been harmful to the needs of international trade and, consequently, to the economic policy of the Government, to let such things go unpunished. Sometimes, especially in later centuries, the legislative machinery acted very promptly to extricate big business from similarly

[1] For English law, see for example, Kenny, *Outlines*, pp. 187–94, 234–42.
[2] See also Stephen, *History*, Vol. III, p. 139 ; Kenny, *Outlines*, p. 191.

embarrassing situations. Already under Queen Anne and under George III special statutes had been passed which made it possible to punish servants of the Post Office and particular branches of trade for misappropriating things committed to their care. There was, however, no general enactment of this kind which could have been applied, for example, to a bank cashier misappropriating money he had received over the counter. When this gap was established beyond doubt in the Bazeley case in 1799, Parliament took immediate action.[1]

(*f*) regarding the *person* of the *owner* :

Again, the whole system of ancient and mediæval law is based on discriminations according to the social status of the injured party. On it, the amount not only of the *wergeld* for murder but also that of the fine for theft is dependent, and, under the law of Æthelbert, " if a freeman rob the King let him pay a forfeiture ninefold, but if a freeman rob a freeman let him make threefold satisfaction ".[2] What has become of this idea in modern criminal law? Obviously, the social status of the victim can no longer be officially recognized as an essential factor in theft. The property of a king no more enjoys increased protection. Social status, however, is no longer the problem. The interest centres round economic structure and economic power : is there, or should there be, any distinction on the part of the criminal law between the protection afforded to private and to State or communal property ; to property of the small man and to that of the millionaire or of the big Corporation? As the functions of property are very likely to be different in each of these cases, it seems to be appropriate to deal with the question together with the final point in our list on p. 88 :

(*g*) regarding the *social and economic functions* of the stolen property :

Beforehand, however, it may be well to pause for a moment and to look back. From our historical analysis of certain aspects of the law of theft, utterly scanty and inadequate as, for reasons of space, it had to be, this at least may perhaps have so far emerged : [3]

(*aa*) Economic needs, due to economic or technological

[1] Kenny, *Outlines*, p. 234 ; Stephen, *History*, Vol. III, p. 152.

[2] See George Ives, *History of Penal Methods* (1914), pp. 3–4.

[3] The interested reader who owing to the scarcity of our illustrative material may not yet have become convinced may be referred to the books quoted in the footnotes. Outside the scope of Anglo-American law, the position has been not much different.

changes, have no doubt often been the driving forces behind the evolution of the law of theft.

(*bb*) These economic needs have, as a rule, been the needs of the propertied classes—landowners, merchants, bankers, industrialists.

(*cc*) By over-emphasizing the element of value and by other methods, the law has further strengthened the protection given to the big property owner.

(*dd*) On the other hand, wherever the personal qualities of the thief have been taken into account, it has, more often than not, been done to the disadvantage of the small and uneducated man (Benefit of Clergy).

C. In Particular: the Neglect of Functional Aspects in the Law of Theft.

(*ee*) Changes in the law of theft, needed in consequence of far-reaching alterations in the economic and social structure of the country, have sometimes been exasperatingly slow in coming, because factors entirely divorced from, and alien to, such economic and social considerations have proved stronger: juristic hair-splitting and self-created "word-magic"; artificial difficulties due to unreasonably high minima penalties;[1] the traditional ultra-conservatism of the legal profession, and many more. All this has produced in the law of theft a state of what psychoanalysts would call a "fixation", an unduly protracted persistence in habits and attitudes which should have been abandoned long before. It is not that criminal lawyers, over the past thousand years, have not had any problems to occupy their minds in the field of economic crime, but their difficulties have, far too often, been of the wrong kind. Of the genuine problems caused by the transformation of the economic and social aspects of property—problems indicated in our list on pp. 86–87 and in the two final points of the list on p. 88—hardly a single one has so far been seriously tackled by the criminal law. In most legal systems of to-day, as a rule, neither the personal qualities of the owner of the stolen property nor the way in which he has acquired it, the use he has made of it, or the size of his property as a whole, are taken into account. Functional aspects are considered, if at all, only with regard

[1] Occasionally also unreasonably low maxima: the invention of "larceny by trick", for example, is said to have been due to such unduly low maximum penalties for false pretences (Hall, p. 18).

to the person of the thief. Many Penal Codes contain special provisions under which theft is treated with greater leniency or may even remain unpunished in the case of a poor offender who steals objects of little value, particularly food, in order to satisfy immediate personal needs of his own or his family.[1] No provision of this kind exists in English law. It might be argued that there is no practical need for it as, in the absence of any statutory minimum penalties, the courts can, and will, anyhow treat such offences with appropriate leniency, or even abstain from any punishment. This argument is, however, not entirely conclusive. In the first instance, as long as all those aggravating circumstances relating to value, time, place, and many others, are explicitly taken into account by the law to the disadvantage of the offender, the most elementary rules of fairness would seem to demand that certain extenuating factors should also find their place in the Larceny Act itself. Secondly, what is still more important, it makes a considerable difference in the criminal record of a person whether an offence is listed as " simple larceny " or whether a special name is found for it which, in one word, makes clear the existence of all those extenuating circumstances. The same is true of the general defence of necessity which has been treated with the greatest reserve in English law because, among other reasons, the judge would anyhow " take the extremity of the offender's situation into account by reducing the sentence to a nominal penalty ".[2] However, English law, as well as the Codes of most foreign countries, provides that in imposing a fine for any offence whatsoever the courts have to take into account the means of the offender.[3] On the other hand, recent legislation has fortunately taken pains to make sure that the offender derives no financial profit from his offence.[4]

Let us now, after this digression, return to the problem of the owner. It is no exaggeration to say that, for all practical purposes, the transformation of property as outlined on p. 86, has made this problem the pivotal point of the whole law of theft. If modern criminal law pretends to have as its object the same conception of property as its predecessor a thousand years ago, its whole basis must inevitably become fictitious.

[1] Germany, art. 370, No. 5 ; Switzerland, art. 138 ; Russia, art. 48 (*f*) and 162 ; Italy, art. 626, No. 2 ; Poland, art. 257 §2 and 262 §4.

[2] Kenny, *Outlines*, p. 78.

[3] Criminal Justice Administration Act, 1914, sect. 5 ; Russia, art. 42 ; Switzerland, art. 48 ; Italy, art. 26 ; Germany, art. 29b ; Poland, art. 56 ; China, art. 58.

[4] See, for example, Order in Council, March 19, 1942 (S.R. & O., 1942, No. 501) *re* stealing or receiving controlled goods and other black market offences.

The combined effect of the transformation outlined in our ten points above, p. 86, has been to stretch both the physical and the moral or social elements in the conception of property almost to breaking point.

(*a*) The *physical* element : We are not here concerned with any controversies about the historical origin and the legal definitions of property. One point, however, is clear beyond doubt : its close connection with the physical factor of possession, which makes property a relation between person and thing that is

> historically and essentially a local relation . . . the local situation of a thing is a prime factor in determining all the " rules of property " in regard to it . . . the history of the process of development of the idea of ownership is this that in the course of time the person or persons who hold a thing come to be considered to be entitled to hold it.[1]

There is, in other words, no absentee ownership in primitive societies ; " possession is the whole law ".[2] Although this stage has passed long ago,[3] nevertheless, the common man's respect for other people's property is still largely bound up with this tangible, visible, corporeal element. He is much more willing to keep away from it if he is physically aware of the owner's presence, and it would be mistaken to explain this willingness exclusively by fear of discovery. Modern economic developments have largely destroyed that physical basis by making for the most valuable objects of property absentee ownership and, in particular, ownership by impersonal agencies, corporations and the like, not the exception but the rule. As soon as this happens, as soon as ownership becomes divorced from possession, or legal possession from purely physical possession, or if there is nobody in possession, the position of the owner is bound to deteriorate. The criminal law can, of course, create new offences to protect him against the possessor ; it can even stretch the conception of legal possession so far as to make it an offence for the finder to keep the object he has found.[4] What the law cannot always do is to safeguard the respect for property which has no personal owner visibly behind it. This is one of the reasons why it has proved so difficult to stamp out those war-time epidemics of petty looting, in spite of heavy penalties. Looting is the typical crime against property behind which no owner can be seen, and,

[1] Diamond, *Primitive Law*, p. 262.
[2] William Seagle, *The Quest for Law* (1941), p. 55.
[3] Roscoe Pound, *An Introduction to the Philosophy of Law* (1922), p. 210.
[4] Larceny Act, sect. 1 (2).

as a consequence, the arguments used by persons charged with such offences have clearly shown that in many cases the feeling of moral wrongdoing was absent.[1] And this in spite of the fact that, more often than not, the looted objects were unmistakably the property of poor working-class people.

(*b*) The weakening of the *moral* and *social* elements in the institution of property, seen as a large-scale phenomenon, is the result of the growing inequality of its distribution and of the concentration of wealth in the hands of a comparatively small number of individuals and giant corporations. There is hardly any need to give chapter and verse for the facts as such, and even on their interpretation there is no longer any serious doubt.[2] As the result of the " corporate revolution ", two-thirds of the industrial wealth of the U.S.A. are said to have passed to ownership by large corporations.[3] Consequently, the property of individual persons, if of any size at all, consists now also very largely not of tangible goods but of contractual rights to money payments. Of the capital held by persons in Great Britain dying in 1935 and leaving more than £25,000, 77·4 per cent. consisted of Securities, Stocks and Shares, Mortgages and Insurance Policies, 6 per cent. in Land, Ground Rents and Mineral Rights, 1·3 per cent. in Trade Assets, and only 1 per cent. in Household Goods, 6·3 per cent. in House Property and Business Premises, and 8 per cent. in cash and " other Property ".[4]

Social scientists, different as may be the languages in which they have been preaching, have become almost unanimous in their conclusion : it is not one conception of property we are

[1] See the examples given by the author in *The Fortnightly* (Jan. 1942), p. 42.—The position is in some ways similar in the case of theft from automatic machines ; see the author's *Social Aspects of Crime in England between the Wars* (1940), p. 197.

[2] To give only a few references : see Josiah Wedgwood, *The Economics of Inheritance* (Pelican ed. 1939), Table IV, p. 71 : in 1924 adults over 25 in England and Wales with £0–100 property numbered 16,523,000, whereas the corresponding number of persons owning property of £250,000 and over, was 2,198. Table II, p. 65 : in 1919–20, 13,000,000 persons had incomes below £130, whereas 165 had incomes of over £100,000. See also Colin Clark, *The National Income, 1924–1931* (1932), p. 76. According to G. W. Daniels and H. Campion, *The Distribution of National Capital* (1936), p. 53, the distribution of capital between 1924 and 1930 was less unequal than before 1914. " 1 per cent. of the persons aged 25 and over in England and Wales owned 60 per cent. of the total capital in 1924–30 ; in 1911–13, 1 per cent. of the persons owned 70 per cent. of the total capital." As a result of the war, the proportion of higher incomes is now slightly larger than before : according to the fourth White Paper on the sources of War Finance and on National Income (Cmd. 6520, 1944) incomes of less than £250 have declined from 57·7 per cent. in 1938 to 51·3 per cent. in 1942 (after payment of tax).

[3] Berle and Means, op. cit., p. vii.

[4] Taken from a paper by Mr. H. Campion on " The Distribution of Property ", read at a Conference on the Social Sciences arranged by The Institute of Sociology in London, 1937.

confronted with to-day but a large variety of different types, each with its peculiar economic, social and moral merits or demerits. Whether we may distinguish, with Marxists, property in articles of consumption and property in the means of production or, with Hobhouse,[1] between property for use and property for power or, with Hobson,[2] between property and "improperty"—in theory at least the dividing line is clearly marked. And, as Tawney has so brilliantly pointed out, "it is idle, therefore, to present a case for or against private property without specifying the particular forms of property to which reference is made, and the journalist who says that 'private property is the foundation of civilization' agrees with Proudhon, who said that it was theft, in this respect at least that, without further definition, the words of both are meaningless".[3] That the distinction has to be made on the basis of function and according to the relation between property, on the one hand, and personal needs and work, on the other, is obvious. Tawney's list, consisting of four categories of property which are more or less closely related to work and needs and four others which are not,[4] may serve as a guide.

Among the many anti-social effects of these developments two are of paramount significance to us: the decline of the sense of social responsibility in the person of the owner of large property, and the undermining of the respect in which such property is held by the small man.

Sense of social responsibility on the part of the owner: the decline of this sense is not due to any absence of legal restrictions of property created in the public interest. The legal history of property is, perhaps more than anything else, the history of such restrictions.[5] Private property has, in fact, hardly ever been entirely free from them, and, especially in war time, the trend is strongly in favour of imposing even more. If Ely could write before the war of 1914[6]: "This same Moses who said 'Thou shall not steal' also laid down regulations for the use of private property which go a great deal further than any laws which have ever been passed or even proposed seriously in any American legislation", this may have become doubtful by now. Of the

[1] In *Property: its Duties and Rights* (new ed. 1922), p. 9.
[2] J. A. Hobson, *Property and Improperty* (1937).
[3] R. H. Tawney, *The Acquisitive Society* (1921), p. 57.
[4] Op. cit., p. 67.
[5] See esp. Richard T. Ely, *Property and Contract* (1914).
[6] Vol. I, p. 181.

Napoleonic Code Civil it could be said that it contained no obligation to dispose of property in a useful way.[1] Recent legislative trends, however, have been most forcibly expressed in the programmatical art. 153 of the Weimar Constitution: "*Eigentum verpflichtet. Sein Gebrauch soll zugleich Dienst sein für das gemeine Beste*" (Property creates obligations. Its use shall be devoted to public service, too). In spite of the stringent restrictions so far enacted, there is, however, still ample scope for the exercise of individual discretion and the practising of social responsibility on the part of the property owner, and here the tendency may not seldom be in the opposite direction. This partly because restrictive legislation which has not yet become a deep-rooted tradition easily produces a spirit of opposition, and partly because it is in the nature of many of these new types of property to destroy the sense of personal responsibility. It has an element of truth to say that the owner of a horse feels himself personally responsible for his property—as long as it is alive he has to feed it, and when it dies he must bury it, whereas the shareholder of a joint-stock company, who has probably never seen the factories owned by it, does not. "The spiritual values that formerly went with ownership have been separated from it."[2] In a thought-provoking essay on "Equality of Sacrifice", Mr. Francis Williams has commented on the, as he says, "very odd and, I think, important fact that there is a quite general agreement in all sections of the community that when the sacrifice of life is in question, then equality of sacrifice is the right and natural thing. But when it comes to the question of sacrificing possessions and power, the matter takes a different turn".[3]

Respect for property on the part of the small man: One explanation of its, at least partial, disappearance has already been suggested above: the loosening of the physical links between owner and thing. The other factors involved are the misuse that has only too frequently been made of property and the growing inequality of its distribution. This latter aspect of the matter has perhaps never received a more devastating criticism than from a writer of so moderate an attitude as T. H. Green:[4]

> The actual result of the development of rights of property in Europe, as part of its general political development, has so far been a state of things in which all indeed *may* have property, but great

[1] Harold J. Laski, *The Rise of European Liberalism* (1936), p. 228.
[2] Berle and Means, op. cit., p. 66.
[3] In *Victory or Vested Interest?* (1942) p. 23.
[4] *Principles of Political Obligation*, *Works*, Vol. II, pp. 525 et seq.

numbers in fact cannot have it in that sense in which alone it is of value, viz., as a permanent apparatus for carrying out a plan of life, for expressing ideas of what is beautiful, or giving effect to benevolent wishes. . . . A man who possesses nothing but his powers of labour and who has to sell these to a capitalist for bare daily maintenance, might as well, in respect of the ethical purposes which the possession of property should serve, be denied rights of property altogether. The rationale of property, in short, requires that everyone . . . should . . . be a possessor of property himself, and of such property as will at least enable him to develop a sense of responsibility, as distinct from mere property in the immediate necessaries of life.

To try to minimize the psychological effect of these two factors—misuse of property on the part of the owner and glaring inequality of its distribution—would be just as harmful as undue generalization. It cannot be taken too lightly when an experienced and cautious Prison Medical Officer, Dr. H. T. P. Young, from his observations in Borstal Institutions concludes : [1]

In the poorer districts, for instance, stealing from the home is regarded as a serious offence, while the appropriation of the property of other people, especially if it is apparently unwanted, may be connived at. The view that all stealing is unethical is regarded as a peculiarity of certain classes and outside everyday practice in their own.

Social psychologists are agreed that only those who have some property of their own can be taught to respect the property of others.[2] It is surprising that this particular weakness of institutional methods of rearing children has received so little attention in recent public discussions on " Children's Homes ".[3] Experiences with children evacuated from public institutions and billeted with private families have shown how difficult it is for many of them, unaccustomed to own anything individually, to get used to the idea of personal ownership, and as a remedy it has been suggested that each child should be given some small object of private property such as books, toys, or pets. With very young people this may work ; adults treated by analogous methods will be inclined to look at them as a pious swindle unless what they are offered is—to quote T. H. Green again—property " in that sense in which alone it is of value ".[4] It is for this

[1] *Journal of Mental Science*, May 1937, p. 286.

[2] Cyril Burt, *The Young Delinquent*, p. 496 ; Ernest Beaglehole, *Property* (1931), p. 304.

[3] See *The Times* of July and August, 1944.

[4] Industrial psychologists, it is true, regard it as important that factory workers should own at least their tools ; see H. E. Burtt, *Psychology and Industrial Efficiency* (1929), p. 288.

reason that the traditional argument: "the thief, though he violates the property of others, expects them to respect his own property" is bound to remain unconvincing in many cases. It is not property in abstracto that the thief attacks or wants to see protected.

As we have seen, the distinction between the big and the small owner of property is now, though by no means identical, at least closely related to that between the private individual and the corporation. Disregard of the claims of big property is therefore largely disregard of property owned by corporations. In a previous study [1] we have suggested that one of its roots may be that universal war-time inheritance: lack of respect for State property. The causal nexus may, however, as well be in the opposite direction: the suspicion and antipathy which the man in the street harbours against the big corporation because of its bigness, its invisibility and impersonality, its methods of exploitation and profit making—all this he unconsciously extends to the State because it, too, is big, invisible and impersonal and, he thinks, sometimes oppressive.

On the psychology of murder, as well as on that of the professional and the mentally abnormal thief, some valuable research has been done during the present century. Comparatively little is known, however, on the state of mind of the average, so-called normal, person who indulges in some occasional stealing. Yet this is probably the largest group of all. And because this group consists of quite ordinary people it would be revealing to analyse also the attitudes of non-delinquent or pre-delinquent individuals to economic crime in order to measure the width of the gap existing between their uncoloured views and the standards of morality which the law of the land seems, officially, to take for granted. Among the very few enquiries made in Great Britain into the attitude of average young people to pilfering, cheating and the like, that initiated by Mr. E. C. Gates and Professor T. H. Pear deserves mentioning, although their group of boys, aged 15 to 17, was too small and its social, educational and vocational background not made sufficiently clear. A few of the final conclusions reached by the investigators are worth quoting: [2]

[1] *Social Aspects of Crime*, pp. 112 et seq.

[2] See *Social Welfare* (published by The Manchester and Salford Council of Social Service), July 1941. Now also J. A. Waites, *Brit. J. of Psychol.* (Gen. Sect.), Sept. 1945.

It appears from a consideration of the attitude of these fifty boys to petty theft that their moral considerations are largely conditioned by the material consideration of the chances of escaping detection. Where the chances are great, the theft is condoned. . . . The only crime which earned universal censure was that of stealing from work-mates. . . . In general it would appear that the juvenile attitude to property is fundamentally not moral. . . . The other major consideration is that with increasing age and experience comes the realization of the necessity for some code of group behaviour, unless life is to become intolerable.

The demand for better "Education for Citizenship" has, rightly, become universal. For efforts in this direction to be successful it will be indispensable, however, to know much more about the actual patterns of thought as to the various types of anti-social behaviour prevailing in different strata of the community. Only on the basis of such knowledge can teaching of citizenship make practical sense.

What are the consequences to be drawn by the criminal law from this state of affairs? "There are lots of reptiles that God himself tells you to steal from, and there are others you simply mustn't steal from," said Mityagin, one of the inmates of that remarkable Russian experimental institution, the Gorki Colony.[1] Was this perhaps his way of interpreting Professor Tawney's lectures, published approximately at that time, especially his doctrine "Property is the most ambiguous of categories. . . . The course of wisdom is neither to attack private property in general nor to defend it in general"? He, Mityagin, might also have referred to a good many of the dicta of mediæval theologists. St. Thomas, for instance,

maintains that as human law cannot overturn natural and Divine law, and as material, or inferior, things were made to supply men's necessities, if there is evident and urgent need, a man may legitimately take either openly or by stealth what he needs, and it is even legitimate in such cases that one man should take another man's property to help him who is in want. In the case of extreme necessity, St. Thomas says, all things are common.[2]

Or Latimer in his *Sermons*:

If thy brother or neighbour therefore need, and thou have to help him, and yet showest no mercy, but withdrawest thy hands from him, then robbest thou him of his own, and art a thief.[3]

[1] Anton Makarenko, *The Road to Life*, p. 87.
[2] Dr. A. J. Carlyle in *Property, its Duties and Rights*, pp. 137–8.
[3] Tawney, *Religion and the Rise of Capitalism* (Pelican ed.), p. 292, note 117.

Or, not to mention Proudhon, Mityagin might have quoted from the writings of that " liberal anarchist ", Thomas Hodgskin :

> The whole of our penal legislation which relates to property is intended to protect the peculiar property of one portion of the community from the assaults of the other. . . . In other words, our penal jurisprudence, so far as property is concerned, is a species of class legislation,[1] [and] We may trace all the fraud and forgery in society, all the evils, in short, which call forth the exertions of vindictive law, and are embraced by the comprehensive term crime, up to the system of our artificial right of property which severs the mutual connection between labour and its rewards.[2]

Twentieth-century criminal law, of course, cannot leave it to the discretion of the individual to distinguish between property of the " reptiles " and that of the " others ". Already a hundred years ago, Friedrich Engels wrote :

> The workers soon realized that crime did not help matters. The criminal could protest against the existing order of society only singly, as one individual ; the whole might of society was brought to bear upon each criminal, and crushed him with its immense superiority. Besides, theft was the most primitive form of protest, and for this reason, if for no other, it never became the universal expression of the public opinion of the working men, however much they might approve of it in silence. . . . A new form of opposition had to be found.[3]

We find ourselves, it seems, somehow in the position of Professor Ely who, having at length expounded the social theory of property, takes great pains to make it clear that—

> it does not follow from the doctrine of property which we have laid down that a man who has ten thousand dollars should give even a cent to the man who has none. For whatever the sum may be that he has, so long as it is in his hands, it is a trust from society, and I cannot say to him " now you must divide with me " . . . he must be convinced before dividing with me that in so doing he is making a better use of his property than any other use he could make of it.[4]

We do not agree with this individualistic view ; we do not regard it as necessary to wait until the owner of the ten thousand dollars is " convinced "—but is there anything, apart from

[1] On Hodgskin see W. Stark, *The Ideal Foundations of Economic Thought* (1943), (International Library of Sociology and Social Reconstruction), esp. pp. 76 et seq.
[2] Hodgskin, *The Natural and Artificial Right of Property contrasted* (1832), p. 155.
[3] *The Condition of the Working Class in England, 1844* (English translation 1892), p. 214.
[4] *Property and Contract*, Vol. I, p. 244.

Mityagin's solution, the criminal law could possibly do to solve the dilemma? Granted that, to avoid chaos, even the most undeserving type of property has to be protected—does it follow that the criminal law has entirely to dissociate itself from contemporary views about "property and improperty"?

Chapter 7

THE PROTECTION OF PROPERTY (II): THE NEW APPROACH

A. Public and Private Property.

So far, as we have already indicated, the criminal law in most countries has done very little in this respect. It has made no distinction, for instance, between the man who steals my hundredth handkerchief and the man who makes away with my only one—to refer to Margery Fry's "Ancestral Child", that little masterpiece of wisdom and understanding.[1] Primitive people, in their peculiar ways, sometimes show a different attitude. Among the Eskimos of Bering Strait, "if a man borrows from another and fails to return the article, he is not held to account for it. This is because if a person has enough property to enable him to lend it, he has more than he needs".[2] Though the argument hardly holds water outside economic systems of the most primitive character, the idea itself is sound that the needs of the parties, the use which the owner has made of the stolen article and the damage inflicted on him should be taken into account. We find it expressed in a few modern Penal Codes: for instance, the Russian Code, art. 162, increases the penalty for theft if the article was known to be essential to the maintenance of the owner, and under the Italian Code, art. 133, the judge has to take into account the gravity of the injury. Cattle stealing, as we have seen, is especially provided for in the law of a number of countries, but only the Russian Code, art. 166, restricts the increased protection to cases where the animal is stolen "from an agricultural or animal-breeding population".

These are, however, only minor points compared with the fundamental distinction between public and private property made in the Russian Code. There is in Plato's *Laws* a famous inconsistency in this respect: whereas in one place the penalty for theft, whether of public or private property, is fixed equally at the double value of the goods, later the death penalty is provided for theft of state property "no matter whether of a

[1] The Fifth Clarke Hall Lecture (1940), p. 30.

[2] E. W. Nelson, *The Eskimos about Bering Strait*, quoted from E. Adamson Hoebel, *Journal of Criminal Law and Criminology*, Vol. XXXI, March–April, 1941, p. 667.

small or great amount, whether by guile or force ".[1] Some traces of this distinction can be found in modern Codes : The Italian Code, art. 625 No. 7, for instance, increases the maximum penalty for theft from three to six years' penal servitude if the object is " destined for public service or public use, protection or respect ". Soviet criminal law, however, uses this distinction throughout as one of the pivotal points of its system. In doing so, it follows closely the economic structure as laid down in arts. 4–10 of the Soviet Constitution of 1936, i.e., the distinction between personal property and socialist property, which latter is either State property or co-operative-collective property. Already under the Penal Code of 1926, the stealing of public property was more severely dealt with than the stealing of private property. Now, under the Decree of August 7, 1932,[2] which declares socialist property of any kind as " sacred and inviolable ", any pilferage of it is to be punished by death, or, in the case of extenuating circumstances, with deprivation of liberty for not less than ten years, with confiscation of property. The contrast to theft of private property, for which—in the absence of other aggravating factors—even in case of recidivism the penalty cannot exceed deprivation of liberty for six months, is extraordinary. When the American writer Mary Stevenson Callcott [3] expressed her surprise to find in a Russian Women's Prison a girl with nine previous prison sentences for theft serving a term of two years and another, a first offender who had stolen from a collective farm, with a sentence of ten years she was given to understand that " the word justice has another meaning in the U.S.S.R. than in the writings of bourgeois sociologists ".

This provision, as other similar articles in the Soviet Penal Code, is, of course, not much more than a symbolic gesture, but as such it has its political significance—just as the conspiracy of silence which surrounds crime against State property in most other legal systems has a symbolic and political meaning. There is no inherent reason why the law should make such friendly gestures exclusively in favour of the big private owner. Of greater practical interest, however, is the question whether those fundamental changes in the Soviet economic and legal system have produced a corresponding revolution in the social behaviour of the ordinary citizen ; in particular, whether State

[1] *Laws*, Book XII (transl. E. B. England), 857 a 2 as compared with 941.
[2] English translation in App. I of the official English Edition.
[3] See her excellent book *Russian Justice* (New York, 1935), Chapter XII.

property has become more immune in Soviet Russia than in capitalist countries and also more immune than the private property of the U.S.S.R. citizen. We are, unfortunately, unable to answer these questions from official Russian *Criminal Statistics*, and even if complete figures were available for a period of sufficient length, their interpretation might be misleading unless a large number of other factors were equally well known.[1] Certain conclusions can, however, with all due reservations, be drawn from the material presented by reliable writers on Soviet Russia. From such sources it appears that certain significant changes have indeed taken place, not immediately after the Revolution but slowly and almost imperceptibly, and more or less closely following the vicissitudes and convulsions of Soviet economic and social policy. Once, it is to be hoped, the time will come when, as part of the general history of the Soviet Revolution, the history of this criminological development will be written, fully and without bias, on the basis of the vast masses of material which must be in the hands of the Soviet Government. Here, for lack of such information, we can hardly expect to scratch the surface even of such a small section of the whole problem as theft of public property. Obviously, it must have taken some considerable time for any changes in the psychological attitude of the average Soviet citizen to become noticeable. We cannot expect that this should have happened during the first phase of the régime, that of "War-communism", sometimes called the "period of moneyless accounting".[2] In a period of starvation, when the peasants refused to supply the towns with their products and the urban population managed to keep alive only through illegally bartering their possessions against foodstuffs [3]; when in the words of the President of the State Planning Commission, "hoarding and smuggling were inevitable",[4] stealing must have been equally rife. Money was abolished as the instrument of exchange, and there was a complete prohibition of private trade. The State undertook to cater for the needs of the people in exchange for their labour. All articles of consumption became State property to be distributed by State organizations. However, as the system did not properly function, large

[1] Reference may be made to the detailed analysis of the difficulties in interpreting criminal statistics in Chapter 3 of the author's *Social Aspects of Crime in England between the Wars*.

[2] See in particular S. and B. Webb, *Soviet Communism*, Vol. II, pp. 540 et seq.; Barbara Wootton, *Plan or no Plan* (1934), Chapter II.

[3] Leonard E. Hubbard, *Soviet Trade and Distribution* (1938), p. 10.

[4] Quoted from Arthur Feiler, *The Experiment of Bolshevism* (1930), p. 54.

quantities were directed into private channels. "The State declared war against such defalcations. Prosecution followed prosecution, and those found guilty were shot, but it was all in vain. The theft of public property was a daily occurrence." [1]

The second phase, the New Economic Policy, lasting from 1921 to 1928, with its revival of many capitalist devices of private trade and profit-making, with its establishment of "innumerable small businesses of every kind" (Webb), can hardly have brought about any considerable improvement in this respect. General plans and individual responsibilities were still too inadequately worked out to foster the growth of a real community spirit, which requires at least a minimum of economic stability and legal security. Even where private enterprise was permitted, the private dealer was always in danger of being arrested or deported when a sudden change of policy seemed to require it. Under such conditions honesty can hardly be expected.[2]

> One revision of a scheme follows another, each of them taking from three to five months. In practice, however, there is a complete lack of proper supervision, so that funds are extensively misapplied, and the most unheard-of defalcations take place. . . . The legal proceedings against the management of the irrigation works in central Asia, those against the Sovkino Trust, against the Textile Trust, and, finally, the mining trial, give an alarming picture of bureaucracy, lack of a sense of responsibility, and official delinquency.[3]

One must not, of course, forget to take into account that writers with more or less pronounced anti-Soviet tendencies may unconsciously indulge in generalizations which cannot easily be checked.[4] However, the late Sir John Maynard, whose last book is no doubt one of the most impartial and informative works on the subject, has told a little story which also shows the failure of that period to create a new spirit [5]:

> From a co-operative inn, leased from a small dealer, plates, dishes, cups, even chairs disappeared in turn, till the society gave up the struggle. Now the kulak is installed in it once more, and making

[1] A. Yugoff, *Economic Trends in Soviet Russia* (1930), p. 38.

[2] Professor Samuel N. Harper, Chicago, has given a vivid picture of the unhappy plight of the private trader under N.E.P.; see his *Civic Training in Soviet Russia* (1929), p. 179.

[3] Yugoff, op. cit., pp. 76, 82, 102, 182.

[4] Yugoff is impartial enough, however, to admit that the existing troubles were by no means altogether due to incompetence, defalcations, and sabotage. "The real reason is to be found in the enormous extent of the task that has been undertaken" (p. 82).

[5] *The Russian Peasant and other Studies* (1942), pp. 170–1.

good money out of rubbish. Everybody's business has proved itself to be nobody's business.

He adds, however, the warning that such happenings are typical exclusively of the period of N.E.P.: "Lest the daughters of the Philistines rejoice, let us point out that the Socialists were still in quest of the right technique." At that time, before 1928, "rural Russia had preserved her ancient constitution in spite of all that had been done to alter it . . . the kulak was stronger than ever". However, even after the liquidation of the Nepmen and the kulaks,[1] and after the completion of the First Five-Year Plan (1928–32), which may be regarded as constituting the third stage, we still find that the rise of the Stakhanov Movement in 1935 is explained as a reaction against the mass-phenomenon of petty stealing. To judge from the descriptions given by Littlepage [2] and Sir John Maynard,[3] it was the essence of that movement to fight the universal shortage of tools in Soviet factories and mines. The general pilfering of tools had assumed such proportions that it seriously threatened production. Stakhanov insisted that not the individual worker but the engineers and foremen should be made personally responsible for a steady supply of tools.

When, in spite of such handicaps, the impression has gained ground among serious writers that, even before Hitler's attack on Russia in 1941, a new attitude towards public property had become visible in the Soviet Union this is mainly due to one factor: to the emphasis universally laid on the "we"-feeling, the sense of common ownership, to be found in particular among the younger generation in present-day Russia.

The sense of ownness goes deep [writes Sir John Maynard][4]; a seven-year-old boy visiting the Zoo was told that the elephant belonged to the State; and, after a few moments of thought, he said: "Then, a little bit of it belongs to me."

An American observer, more especially interested in the subject of juvenile delinquency, says [5]:

The "we"-feeling is constantly and generally emphasized. Thus, whereas, elsewhere, stealing generally means taking something from someone else, in the Soviet Union the impression the authorities

[1] See, for example, the impressive description in John D. Littlepage and Demarée Bess, *In Search of Soviet Gold* (1939), Chapter VII; moreover Yugoff, Chapter 10.

[2] Op. cit., p. 226.

[3] Op. cit. p. 277.

[4] Op. cit., p. 341.

[5] N. Berman, "Juvenile Delinquency under the Soviets," *Journal of Criminal Law and Criminology*, May–June 1939, Vol. XXX, p. 75.

try to give is that stealing is taking something that actually belongs to one's self. Considering the extent of opportunities for participation in communal life for all ages and sexes, this distinction is far from an illusion.

Even an expert so critical of Soviet achievements as Mr. Hubbard admitted, shortly before the war, that "very possibly quite a number of Soviet workers have a genuine feeling of collective proprietorship in their enterprises".[1] Should not all this remind us, again with all due reservations, of Plato's "The best ordered state will be one in which the largest number of persons use these terms (i.e., 'mine' and 'not mine', 'another's' and 'not another's') in the same sense".[2]

In countries which are expected to undergo, in the future, a process of gradual nationalization of "a limited number of key industries or services",[3] supplemented by a system of state supervision of privately owned industries and by growing equalization of incomes,[4] the resulting "we"-feeling may also eventually lead to a considerable decline of crimes of acquisitiveness, especially theft. This is probably the only way of how to get rid of the atmosphere of mistrust in everything, private or public, that is big and to liquidate stealing as a mass phenomenon. Such a view, which regards nationalization as a remedy for large-scale theft, will be severely criticized. People argue, for instance, that the employees of the London Passenger Transport Board are no more "socially-minded" than those of a private bus company.[5] Whether, as a statement of facts, this is true we do not know; no evidence has so far been produced. In any case, however, the argument overlooks that to bring about a real change of basic social attitudes, more is needed than to convert into Public Utility Companies or the like just a few industries as lonely islands in an ocean of private enterprise.

It is outside the scope of this book and the province of the author to express any views about the merits of nationalization as such. One thing, however, is certain, and it goes right to the roots of our specific problem: for nationalization and those other parts of the socialist plan for social reconstruction to have

[1] Hubbard, op. cit., p. 318.

[2] *Republic*, V, 462 (transl. Cornford), quoted by Sir Richard Livingstone, *Education for a World Adrift*, p. 148.

[3] Mr. Herbert Morrison, Preface to "Government and Industry" (Fabian Research Pamphlet No. 83, 1944).

[4] See, for example, the correspondence in *The Times* of Dec. 16 and 21, 1942, on the inequality of earnings in Soviet Russia, which has occasionally been exaggerated.

[5] Elliott Dodds, *Let's try Liberalism*, p. 14.

any substantial effect on petty economic crime it is essential not only that the programme should not be too much watered down, but also that the masses should know what is being done to reduce the present inequality in the distribution of wealth. In this respect as in others, it is not enough that justice is actually done—everybody must see that it is done. It is not enough, for instance, that Excess Profits Tax exists on the Statute Book, or even that it is actually paid, as long as references to it are " met with a roar of laughter " from working-class audiences.[1]

B. PROTECTION AGAINST DESTRUCTION OF PROPERTY.

There are other reasons as well why theft should not occupy in Soviet Russia that predominant position among economic crimes which, numerically at least, it possesses elsewhere. Soviet law is no longer exclusively interested in fighting such comparatively minor derangements in the *distribution* of goods ; its primary aim is to help to *extend production* and to *preserve existing* goods.[2] These latter aspects have so far been mostly neglected by the criminal law outside the U.S.S.R. This becomes particularly noticeable if we take the offence of wantonly or maliciously *destroying or damaging* property. The law in most countries punishes such acts, unless they involve cruelty to animals, only if the object damaged or destroyed belongs to somebody else, or if, though the property of the offender, it is directly devoted to public use, or if the very act of destroying or damaging the offender's own property at the same time endangers public safety or the property or life of others (e.g., arson).[3] The details are of little interest. The point we have to make is that, in time of peace at least, in most parts of the globe, with the exceptions just referred to, the owner was at liberty to destroy his property, although his action may have been greatly detrimental to the public. According to the German Code, art. 308, for instance, a person who maliciously sets fire to buildings, ships,

[1] *The Times*, January 2, 1942 ; "Brakes on Production." The explanation is given by N. Davenport, *Vested Interest or Common Pool ?* p. 103. See also below, pp. 146 et seq.

[2] It is significant that, as pointed out before, the type of theft which gave rise to the Stakhanov Movement was theft not of consumer goods but of means of production.

[3] See, for example in different variations, Italy, arts. 423 et seq., 635 et seq. ; Poland, arts. 215 et seq., 263 ; Germany, arts. 303 et seq. ; Switzerland, arts. 145, 221 et seq. ; China, arts. 193 et seq., 352 et seq. ; France, arts. 437, 445, 449. The English Malicious Injuries to Property Act, 1861, is, in spite of its clumsy draftsmanship, better in this respect than most Continental Codes, although in some of its many sections it is not altogether clear whether destruction of own property is also punishable.

stocks of commodities on public places, agricultural products, and so on, is punishable only if these objects belong to somebody else or if the fire is likely to endanger the property or life of another person. This attitude of peace-time law was entirely in harmony with the contemporary social philosophy and economic doctrine. Any concern they may have shown for the protection of existing goods was exclusively in the personal interest of the owner, not in that of the community at large. Any form of wastage, any device for getting rid of unprofitable "surplus" production was permissible. A change became noticeable in a few countries after the war of 1914–18: The Argentine Antitrust Act of August 23, 1923,[1] punishes "the intentional destruction of produce, in whatever form or stage of preparation, whether by producers, contractors, or merchants, with the object of causing price inflation". Similarly, under the Brazilian Monopoly Act of November 18, 1938, the "destruction or illegal use of raw material or products necessary for consumption of the people" have become a crime,[2] and in Mexico, too, the wilful destruction of products without the consent of the Government is punishable.[3] Under art. 499 of the Italian Code, "whoever, by destroying raw materials, or agricultural or industrial products or means of production, causes serious injury to the national production or a shortage to a notable extent of goods commonly or largely consumed" is punishable with penal servitude from three to twelve years and a fine. This, though on the right lines, is probably too narrow a definition to be applicable in other than the most serious cases. In other countries, however, a second world war was needed to restrict the arbitrary powers of the owner. Now, under the extreme pressure of shortage of food and raw materials of almost any description, the criminal law has been compelled to take part in the general battle for increased production and against wastage[4]:

If the crop harvested from any agricultural land is damaged or goes to waste as the result of any failure or delay of the occupier of that land in taking such steps as are reasonable to keep the crop in good condition, the occupier shall be guilty of an offence against

[1] See *Regulation of Economic Activities in Foreign Countries*, Monograph No. 40 published by the Temporary Economic National Economic Committee, 1941, p. 104.

[2] Monograph No. 40, p. 130. [3] Monograph No. 40, p. 154.

[4] For the war of 1914–18 see Sir William Beveridge, *British Food Control* (1928), p. 238.

this regulation and shall, on summary conviction, be liable to a fine not exceeding fifty pounds.[1] [and]

No person shall waste any food or cause or permit any food to be wasted [2] (with penalties as provided in Defence Reg. No. 92).

In a recent book,[3] Professor Hermann Levy has drawn attention to a " very remarkable figure " in the English book trade of the eighteenth century, James Lackington, who was bold enough to sell the remainder books at half-price in defiance of trade usage instead of destroying them, whereas the other publishers " had adopted a system which, in the corn trade, for instance, was branded in the same period as being the greatest possible crime that ' engrossers ' and ' forestallers ' could commit". He quotes from Lackington's *Memoirs* that " it was common for such as purchased remainders to destroy one-half or three-fourths of such books, and to charge the full publication price, or nearly that, for such as they kept on hand ".

Will war-time lessons again be lost on legislators ? Professor Hayek insists that there has never been in recent times any really large-scale destruction of stocks as a result of a faulty economic system.[4] All the better if this should be true ; other economists seem to hold different views, and, to be on the safe side, it may be better to guard against any such eventualities.[5] " ' Thou shalt not steal ' is replaced by ' Thou shalt not waste ' as property becomes socialized," writes Professor Haldane.[6] In a socialist society, the problem is, of course, much easier to solve as goods are, for the greater part, publicly owned, and the private citizen's opportunities of injuring the community by destroying his own

[1] Defence Regulation No. 62D, S.R. & O. 1940, No. 2115.

[2] The Waste of Food Order of Aug. 5, 1940, S.R. & O. 1940, No. 1424, where a comprehensive definition of " waste " is given. For paper, see for example, the Salvage of Waste Materials (No. 2) Order of Feb. 25, 1942, S.R. & O. 1942, No. 336 ; for rags, etc., the Order of July 9, 1942 (S.R. & O 1942, No. 1360) ; for fuel, the Control of Fuel (No. 3) Order of Dec. 8, 1942 (S.R. & O, 1942, No. 2510).

[3] *Retail Trade Associations* (1943, The Intern. Library of Sociology and Social Reconstruction), pp. 10–11.

[4] F. A. Hayek, *The Road to Serfdom* (1944), p. 150.

[5] In this respect, Professor W. H. Hutt, for example, seems to differ from Hayek ; see his *Plan for Reconstruction* (Intern. Library of Sociology and Social Reconstruction, 1943), pp. 65, 74. Hutt's " Resources Utilization Protection Bill " contains the following clause 59, p. 46 : " In any branch of industry, agriculture, fishing or transport, the Commission may instruct any or all corporations . . . that it shall be an offence to destroy or scrap, except through ordinary wear and tear and bona-fide utilization, any productive plant, equipment or like resources for which a bid greater than the net scrap value is obtainable, unless such plant equipment or like resources is immovable and orders have been given for its replacement within a reasonable period by plant, equipment or like resources on the same site of at least equal capacity."

[6] *Science and Ethics*, edited by C. H. Waddington (1943), p. 42.

property are therefore restricted. The Soviet Code, while containing the usual provisions against " wilful destruction of, or damage to, property belonging to a private person ", including arson (art. 175), punishes the wasting of State or public property (art. 130), the wilful destruction of or damage to public property (art. 79), and several more specific offences of wastage and destruction (art. 79, Nos. 1 and 3). It offers no solution, however, for the problem, which is so burning in capitalist or semi-capitalist communities, of how to deal with the private owner who wilfully destroys or damages his own property.[1] Should this be technically impossible? Ely, who was worried to see " the law taking no steps to prevent the apparent waste and misuse ", concluded that it was too difficult to frame a statute that would prevent misuse of property without at the same time hampering its proper use.[2] In the course of the discussions on a Nazi Penal Code it was regarded as a problem requiring solution how far damage to one's own property deserves punishment as an injury to the public[3]; but no answer seems to have been found. Recent war-time legislation has proved, however, that the technical difficulties are by no means unsurmountable. Probably one would have to choose between a considerable number of special provisions, each prohibiting, as at present, unjustified destruction or any other form of waste for a specific commodity, and one or two provisions of a very general character, more or less on the Russian model. As already indicated, in a national economy not run on Soviet lines, there would, however, arise the difficulty, which the U.S.S.R. has not to face, that most of the property would have to be protected not for, but against the owner. Consequently, minor acts of destruction or waste would have to be tolerated, if only in order not to put an unreasonable strain on the administration of criminal justice. The necessary exemptions in favour of the owner could be provided either by establishing minimum values in money where the principle *minima non curat praetor* would hold good, or by issuing suitable instructions to the prosecuting authorities.

[1] It can hardly be assumed that this is covered by art. 175 as its formulation is too general to include the property of the offender.

[2] *Property and Contract*, Vol. I, p. 143.

[3] Kohlrausch in F. Gürtner, *Das kommende deutsche Strafrecht, Besonderer Teil* (1935), p. 313.

C. Protection against Fraud.

(a) *The Conception of White-Collar Crime.*

Lack of space forbids to deal in detail with the offence of *fraud* or *false pretences*, the younger, much more refined and more dangerous brother of theft. As pointed out in an earlier book,[1] the increase in such offences in England and Wales from 4,447 in 1919 to 12,594 in 1938, though not alarming and nothing like the increase in certain other countries, is nevertheless serious enough, considering that the damage done by each fraud is, on the average, much higher than in the case of theft. For the U.S.A., it is estimated that the total losses from conventional robbery, burglary, thievery, pocket-picking, and the like, amount to something between two hundred and fifty and four hundred million dollars a year, whereas the damage inflicted to the American public by two types of fraud, i.e., bogus bankruptcies and the sale of worthless stocks and bonds, is estimated at about one billion dollars per year.[2] It was, as Thurman Arnold reminds us,[3] the financier, not the gangster, " Insull, not Capone, who wrecked the financial structure of Chicago ". American criminologists of to-day have done everything in their power to make it clear that at least in the U.S.A. the " white-collar " criminal, and not the bank-robber and pick-pocket, has to be regarded as Public Enemy Number One. Men like E. H. Sutherland and Frank Tannenbaum, H. E. Barnes and Negley K. Teeters, Morris Ploscowe, Donald R. Taft and many others, have pointed out, again and again, that all our traditional views about crime and its sociological and psychological causes are bound to remain one-sided, incomplete, and even distorted as long as white-collar crime is excluded from the picture. As long as the extreme dangers resulting from this type of anti-social behaviour are not clearly realized, and as long as legislators and administrators of criminal justice fail to take appropriate measures against white-collar crime, it is nonsensical to expect the penal system to be successful in its fight against the ordinary thief and burglar and other small fry.[4]

[1] *Social Aspects of Crime in England between the Wars* (1940), pp. 117–18, also 44.
[2] H. E. Barnes and Negley K. Teeters, *New Horizons in Criminology* (1943), p. 21.
[3] *Folklore of Capitalism*, p. 276.
[4] Reference may again be made to the masterly treatment of the problem in Barnes-Teeters, *New Horizons in Criminology* (1943), Chapters II to V ; and, for a brief but excellent exposition of the problem, to the articles by Sutherland, Ploscowe, Lindesmith and others in " Crime in the United States ", *Annals of the American Academy of Political and Social Science*, Vol. 217 (Sept. 1941).

What, then, is "white-collar crime"? According to Sutherland,[1] it is "a violation of the criminal law by a person of the upper socio-economic class in the course of his occupational activities". Its most general characteristic is violation of trust. It is, as Sutherland points out, more dangerous to society than crimes committed by members of the lower socio-economic class—not only because the financial losses are higher, but especially owing to the much greater damage it inflicts on public morale. When the community is threatened by a crime wave of the traditional type, "it usually gathers its forces under the leadership of men of the upper socio-economic class for more adequate enforcement of the criminal law according to conventional methods". Thus the morale of the community is strengthened. White-collar crime, however, destroys mutual trust and community morale. Since criminals of this type mostly belong to the leading class and since members of this class, even if they do not themselves participate in such crimes, are reluctant to attack other members, leadership is lacking in the fight, and there is no effective plan for the enforcement of the law. Because of their social prestige and political influence, white-collar criminals are but seldom prosecuted and even more rarely convicted. "When efforts have been made to perfect the implements for enforcement of the criminal law as it applies to white-collar offenders, the business interests which would be affected have been energetic in preventing such action." Equally difficult is it to study the genesis of white-collar crime and to invent suitable methods of dealing with it. The traditional theories on the causation of crime are beside the point in relation to white-collar crime, and the latter concept is, for the time being, "designed to reform the criminologists rather than the white-collar criminals".[2]

We have devoted so much space to this theory, as expounded by Professor Sutherland and his colleagues, because it is becoming clearer every day that social reconstruction and the future of crime are largely dependent on the attitude of society towards it.

So far, legislators have not always sufficiently grasped the danger involved in this type of offence and of fraud in general. Its legal definitions have, in a slow and roundabout way, grown out of the law of theft without so far reaching full maturity. Again, it was the social and economic philosopy of the *laissez-faire* age, slogans such as *caveat emptor* that prevented its evolution.

[1] *Annals*, loco cit., p. 112. [2] Sutherland, *Annals*, p. 115.

It is only natural that in the thirteenth century English courts should have provided in general " no remedy for the man who to his damage had trusted the word of a liar." [1] For the eighteenth century it is a little surprising, however, to read " When A got money from B by pretending that C had sent him for it, Chief Justice Holt grimly asked, ' Shall we indict one man for making a fool of another ? ' and bade the prosecutor to have recourse to a civil action." It was only in 1757 that " a statutory provision for the punishment of mere private cheating was made " in English law. [2] No wonder, then, that Holt's great contemporary Jonathan Swift thought it necessary to give his countrymen this reminder [3] :

> They (the Lilliputians) look upon fraud as a greater crime than theft, and therefore seldom fail to punish it with death ; for they allege that care and vigilance, with a very common understanding, may preserve a man's goods from theft, but honesty has no defence against superior cunning.

However, this otherwise useful reminder could be of but little assistance to English lawyers who were called upon to cope with the intricacies of early eighteenth-century trade and commerce.

> Probably both the Legislature and the lawyers were puzzled. The phenomenon of speculation in the shares of joint-stock companies was, as a commercial problem, new to the Legislature, and, as a legal problem, it was equally new to the lawyers. This fact we shall appreciate if we look at the extreme poverty of the ascertained rules of law applicable to commercial societies. . . . Obviously this state of the law tended to increase the risk of fraud, because it left the promoters, directors, or members of commercial societies, corporate or unincorporate, and the dealers in their shares, very free to act as they pleased.[4]

This description of a state of affairs prevailing shortly before the South Sea Bubble and the Bubble Act of 1720 might well serve as a motto for the legislative history of the efforts made over the subsequent two and a quarter centuries to fight commercial fraud by means of the criminal law. It has been a race

[1] Pollock-Maitland, *History of English Law*, Vol. II, p. 535.

[2] Kenny, *Outlines*, p. 246. Of Holt it has been said that he won his eminent position " by the zeal with which he gave legal force to the theories of *laissez-faire* " (Laski, *The Rise of European Liberalism*, p. 151). On Lord Mansfield, see C. H. S. Fifoot, *Lord Mansfield* (1936), p. 207.

[3] *Gulliver's Travels*, Chapter VI.

[4] W. Holdsworth, *A History of English Law*, Vol. VIII, pp. 213, 218.

between the crook and the lawmaker, in which the latter has mostly played the part of " also ran ". *Twentieth-Century Crime and Eighteenth-Century Methods of Control* is the apposite title of a recent book by an American lawyer.[1] The contrast between the attitude of the law towards fraud and that towards theft is most revealing. In the case of theft, as we have seen, the law can be fairly simple. Such legal problems as do exist have mostly been artificially created ; the real fight against theft is, apart from social and educational reform, a matter not for the legislator but for the Police, the courts and the administration of the penal system. Consequently, legislators have throughout been busy occupying themselves largely with the solution of non-existing problems. In the field of fraud, on the other hand, very genuine difficulties exist of how to define the offence so as to make it impossible for clever crooks to evade the law. In the words of a former Lord Chancellor (Lord Maugham), " nothing is harder in cases of this kind than to catch all ruffians and to let through honest men " (House of Lords' debate, February 28, 1939).

As far as England is concerned, it would be unjustified to give the impression that white-collar crime is as prevalent here as in the U.S.A. It would be equally wrong, however, to claim that it does not exist to any considerable extent. Direct evidence is scanty, and there has never been any comprehensive enquiry into the problem as a whole. Certain conclusions can be drawn, however, from the material available for two categories of white-collar crime : war-time profiteering in its various forms, on the one hand, and share-pushing, on the other. To give a full account of profiteering during the present war might require a comprehensive study in itself, which would far exceed the scope of this book and for which much of the essential information is not yet accessible. Moreover, as only a few types of profiteering are offences against property the matter is better discussed in another connection.[2] This, however, may be said already now : the existence of a considerable body of war-time profiteers is indicative of a substantial, though smaller, amount of peace-time white-collar crime. In other words, though many war-time profiteers become law-breakers because of the added temptations and opportunities provided by the war and because of the war-time prohibition of normally permitted business activities, for many others war-time profiteering is nothing but a continuation of unscrupulous and criminal peace-time practices.

[1] J. E. Hagerty, 1934.

[2] Below, pp. 136 et seq.

(*b*) *Share-pushing.*

However that may be, in order to illustrate our statement about the prevalence of white-collar crime and the comparative failure of the administration of criminal justice to check it, it is safer to choose a type of commercial fraud entirely unconnected with special war-time conditions: *Share-pushing.*[1] On this subject, we are in the fortunate position of having at our disposal the official material collected shortly before the present war by a body of experts and supplemented by very thorough debates in both Houses of Parliament.[2] In 1936, a Departmental Committee was appointed by the President of the Board of Trade—

> to consider the operations commonly known as share-pushing and share-hawking and similar activities, and to report which, if any, action is desirable.

The Committee reported in 1937.[3] Only a few of its many noteworthy observations can here be quoted:

> we are confident that the annual victimization of the public in connection with fraudulent dealings in stocks and shares involves a very large sum (p. 17);[4]
>
> . . . Section 356 (1), Companies Act, 1929, . . . provides that "It shall not be lawful for any person to go from house to house offering shares for subscription or purchase to the public or any member of the public" . . . Whatever the object may have been in prohibiting the going "from house to house", in preference to prohibiting the going to *any* house for the purposes mentioned, the phrase has had the effect of so limiting the practical application of the subsection as to have rendered it almost a "dead letter" (p. 18);
>
> . . . it has been suggested that some relaxation of the strictness with which the expression "false pretence" is interpreted might meet some of the difficulties not unusually occurring in cases in which a person has undoubtedly been "swindled", but the methods adopted preclude proceedings . . . (p. 23);
>
> there are certain difficulties with which the police are confronted in dealing with these cases. . . . The offences usually committed

[1] There are several types of Share-pushing. In its simplest form "the victim is persuaded to part with money or valuable securities in exchange for shares which prove to be worthless" (Report on Share-Pushing, p. 7).

[2] See House of Commons, Nov. 21, 1938, and Feb. 14, 1939 (Hansard, col. 1371–1428 and 1579–1657); House of Lords, Feb. 28, 1939 (Hansard, col. 970 et seq.).

[3] Report on Share-Pushing, Cmd. 5539 (1937).

[4] In the course of the evidence before the Committee, the annual losses caused by this one type of fraud were estimated at five million pounds (Hansard, 21.11.38), which was even regarded as an under-estimate by Mr. Bellenger, M.P. It was universally agreed that the victims were mostly small people. With this may be compared the figure of slightly over one million pounds, given in the Annual Report of the Commissioner of Police of the Metropolis for the year 1935, p. 46, as the value of property stolen in London during 1935.

in connection with share frauds are all misdemeanours, and there is no power of arrest without warrant, unless the offender is found committing the offence. The result is that there is delay involved. . . . If these offences were felonies, or the distinction between felony and misdemeanour ceased, we think the right of immediate arrest would be serviceable (p. 31) ;

it will thus be noticed that many continental governments have imposed control over and regulation of stockbrokers, whilst in the United Kingdom the only control is that exercised by the various stock exchanges over their members. The complexity of the financial system in this country no doubt in part accounts for this difference. . . . So long as anybody, however impecunious or inexperienced he may be, can call himself a " stockbroker ", there will be grave and obvious risk of losses inflicted on the ignorant public (p. 48) [1] ;

if he (the victim) should . . . endeavour to institute criminal proceedings, he, of course, may abandon any hope of recovering any part of his losses. He will incur heavy expenses, he has no facilities for making enquiries . . . and unless his case is taken up by some such authority as the police or Director of Public Prosecutions and properly investigated he may not succeed in securing a conviction, the defendant having the means out of the profits of his fraud to obtain adequate legal representation (p. 66).

The Report was made the subject of very valuable debates in both Houses of Parliament. With a number of important changes, its basic recommendations were approved, and as the result on April 28, 1939, the Prevention of Fraud (Investments) Act, 2 and 3 Geo. 6, ch. 16, was passed. When examining its principal provisions it may be useful to remember that, under the existing economic and legal system, there are, generally speaking, eight ways open to the State to arm itself more effectively in its struggle against commercial fraud :

(*a*) to clarify and to broaden the *definitions* of the kind of anti-social behaviour to be prohibited ;

(*b*) to relax the traditional requirements relating to the *internal side* of the crime, the *mens rea* ;

(*c*) to increase the *penalties* ;

(*d*) to facilitate the work of the *Police*, e.g., in such matters as arrests, search warrants, and the like ;

(*e*) to encourage *victims* to prosecute ;

(*f*) to make it easier for the *courts* to convict by shifting the burden of proof from the prosecution to the defendant ;

(*g*) to enlist the co-operation of *administrative authorities* outside the machinery of criminal justice ; especially

[1] *The Economist* was somewhat more outspoken : " The freedom enjoyed by rogues o set up as share dealers has too long been a public scandal " (July 30, 1938).

(*h*) to empower the competent ministry, by way of *delegated legislation*, to make the orders, with penal sanction, which are at any given time necessary to meet the situation.

Although some of these methods must be highly repugnant to traditional views, the Act of 1939 has adopted all of them, except that under (*f*). A review of its principal provisions, in connection with the corresponding sections of the Report, throws much light on the reasons why the administration of the criminal law, as a rule, cuts such a poor figure in its fight against commercial fraud.

(*a*) The *definitions* of prohibited activities have been in many ways improved. This was necessary in various ways. The faulty draftsmanship of the Companies Act, which made circumvention more than easy ("from house to house"), is not the only instance of clumsy formulations which had to be eliminated in favour of more general and elastic clauses. Of considerably wider interest is the improvement made in the conception of false pretences itself. In English law and a few Continental Codes a narrow conception of this offence is used: "The pretence must relate to some fact that is either past or present." Although the definition in art. 32 of the Larceny Act does not explicitly require a misstatement of "facts", it is commonly interpreted as if it did.[1] It is, therefore, as a rule, not punishable as false pretences to make wrong statements of opinion or forecasts, neither of which are "facts". This narrow interpretation, which must have been a real godsend to the share-pushing fraternity, is much more than a purely technical matter. Important questions of principle are involved. The reason why the law requires wrong statements of facts, past or present, is, on the one hand, that the untruth of mere statements of opinion may be difficult to prove; on the other, that "all future events are obviously matters of conjecture, upon which every person should exercise his own judgment".[2] Neither of these arguments is convincing. Difficulties of evidence are often likely to arise in connection with proceedings for commercial fraud; they cannot justify a defeatist attitude. The second argument is particularly characteristic of the old *laissez-faire* philosophy of

[1] Kenny, *Outlines*, p. 251. Switzerland, art. 148; Germany, art. 263; German Draft Code of 1930, art. 343, all require explicitly that the deception should be one about "facts". Not so Italy, art. 640; Poland, art. 264; Russia, art. 169; France, art. 405; China, art. 339; Egypt, art. 336; Guertner, *Das kommende deutsche Strafrecht, Besonderer Teil*, p. 346.

[2] Kenny, loco cit.

the liberalistic era of criminal law. It is, however, entirely out of place in an age when every conceivable device of mass propaganda and suggestion is employed to deceive and exploit the ignorance of the common man; in an age when commercial fraud has assumed dimensions altogether unforeseen by the originators of the restrictive formulation.[1] The Act of 1939, sect. 12, following the Report of 1937, has drawn the right conclusion from this state of affairs by providing penalties for a person who

> by any statement, *promise* or *forecast*, which he knows to be misleading, false or deceptive, or by any dishonest concealment of material facts, or by the reckless making of any statement, *promise* or *forecast* which is misleading, false or deceptive, induces or attempts to induce another person—(italics are mine).
>
> to enter into or offer to enter in
>
> (1) any agreement for, or with a view to, acquiring, disposing of, subscribing for or underwriting securities or lending or depositing money to or with any industrial or provident society or building society etc., etc.[2]

(*b*) As this quotation shows, the Act punishes not only deliberate lying but also the "reckless" making of untrue statements, etc., which probably means the making of such statements, etc., regardless of their truth or falsehood, at the risk that they may be untrue and that this may be harmful to others. Although this means a degree of guilt somewhat stronger than negligence, it is at least one step towards making grossly negligent behaviour an offence (see above, p. 57)—an indispensable device when the law has to deal with exceptionally dangerous and complicated business transactions.[3]

(*c*) The maximum penalty has been increased to seven years' penal servitude.

(*d*) Characteristic of the strangely benevolent attitude which even twentieth-century law likes to assume towards white-collar crime is the fact that, while the pettiest act of larceny still amounts to a "felony" in English law, false pretences, even if involving the ruin of thousands of families, is only a misdemea-

[1] In an earlier book, in which the relation between law and fact is discussed, the author was still too much under the influence of the traditional liberalistic doctrine: "*Beiträge zur Lehre von der Revision im Strafverfahren* (1925), pp. 52 et seq.

[2] See, moreover, the general provision in sect. 17.

[3] The Act has unfortunately watered down the useful provision contained in clause 9 of the Bill which proposed to penalize the making of promises or forecasts which the offender "has no reasonable ground for supposing to be fulfilled". This, however, was more than the City could stomach (see *The Economist*, 1938, pp. 231, 331, 385.

nour.[1] The practical consequence is that, as the Report complains, the Police have no power of arrest without warrant, unless the offender is caught in the very act.[2] This distinction shows particularly clearly how much modern criminal law has remained out of touch with the change in values brought about by the economic revolution of the last two centuries.

(*e*) The lack of a centralized office of Public Prosecutor in English criminal procedure and the reluctance of the local Police to prosecute at the public expense favour offenders who are able and willing to spend considerable amounts in order to frighten the victim. The Report of 1939 was fully justified in stressing that " share-pushing cases are of such importance that the Police or the Director of Public Prosecutions should where possible institute proceedings at the public expense, and that consideration of cost should not be allowed to prevent the operation of the criminal law " (p. 30).

(*f*) To shift the burden of proof in share-pushing trials from the prosecution to the defendant was neither recommended in the Report nor has it been done in the Act. It is a device that is certainly against the established principles of criminal procedure and does not easily recommend itself in normal times. Nevertheless, exceptions to the presumption of innocence cannot be altogether avoided. In the U.S.A., we are told, they are on the increase, and the New York Penal Code alone is said to contain at least forty such cases.[3] In English law, the number of exceptions is small but again characteristic of the traditional idea that theft and house-breaking are the most dangerous crimes where such an exception to the disadvantage of the accused is more needed and justified than anywhere else.[4] In war-time, however, a change has taken place and profiteering has, to some extent at least, been added to the list.[5]

(*g*) Perhaps the most important feature of the Act is the way in which the work of the Police and the criminal courts is linked up with, and facilitated by, administrative devices. Realizing that the punitive agencies of the State are incapable of mastering the evil unaided, the legislator has established a preventive system as the line of first defence. The Report of 1937, referring to the many precedents already in existence of legally recog-

[1] See Report on Share-Pushing, p. 31 ; Kenny, *Outlines*, p. 94.
[2] Kenny, pp. 460, 464.
[3] Barnes and Teeters, op. cit., p. 330.
[4] See the list given by Kenny, p. 364 ; Larceny Act, s. 28 (2) and Metropolitan Police Courts Act, 1839, s. 24.
[5] See below, p. 143.

nized control over professions and occupations, recommended a system of registration under which it should be unlawful for persons not registered or exempt from registration to transact business in stocks and shares.[1] The Government preferred a system of licensing to registration,[2] and this was enacted. Another interesting feature of the Act is the establishment of a special Tribunal, consisting of two lawyers and a financial expert, to hear appeals against the refusal or revocation of licences. There was some opposition to such a Tribunal in the House of Commons on the ground that no adequate reason seemed to exist why the matter should not be left to the ordinary courts and judges, to which the Government spokesman replied that, among other advantages, a Tribunal could be expected to act with greater speed.[3]

(*h*) Under sect. 7, the Board of Trade may make rules for the conduct of business by holders of licences (though a breach of these rules does not constitute a criminal offence). This, it has been objected, is "Legislation by Order" and, therefore, dangerous in the eyes of every upholder of individual liberty. On the other hand it provides "the essential flexibility of attack which has hitherto been lacking".[4]

From this brief and incomplete analysis of the principal features of the Act of 1939 it will have become apparent that, as far as can be judged from its mere wording, the Act, taken as a whole, seems to be an outstanding example of a new spirit in criminal legislation. From here to Chief Justice Holt it is a far cry. Holt refused to protect the fools against the rascals—Mr. Oliver Stanley, the then President of the Board of Trade, found it necessary to apologize to the House for introducing a Bill which aimed at "protecting the fool from his folly"[5]; yet he did introduce it. In some respects, it is true, the Act probably does not go far enough: it contains too many exemptions; the deposit of £500 may be too small; and the original drafting of sect. 12 ("reasonable ground") was preferable to the present ("reckless"). Nevertheless, the passing of this Act indicates a recognition on the part of the legislator of the changes in values that have taken place and of the exceptional dangerousness of

[1] Report, Parts V and VI.
[2] See the speech of Mr. Oliver Stanley in the House of Commons, Feb. 21, 1938.
[3] See the speeches by Messrs. Spens, Benson, Hely-Hutchinson, Nov. 21, 1938, Hansard, col. 1405 et seq., and the Government reply, col. 1424.
[4] *The Economist*, July 30, 1938, p. 231.
[5] See the speech of Feb. 21, 1938.

white-collar crime. It is a model Act, of course, only if looked at from the point of view of the present economic system : it tries to reduce some of its worst evils without attacking the structure itself. It makes it somewhat more difficult and risky to exploit the speculative instincts of other people, but it does not touch speculation as such. It protects private property against fraud, but it makes no attempt to guard the State and the community against the misuse of possibilities created by the laws of demand and supply. This has been left to war-time legislation (on which, see below, p. 136 et seq.).

There is yet another snag in the Act of 1939 : Although the penal provisions of sect. 12 came into force immediately, other important provisions, especially those relating to the licensing of dealers in shares, etc., were timed to come into force not immediately but on the day appointed by the Board of Trade, which has been as late as July, 1944. It is true that war-time conditions may have diverted a large body of share-pushers to other even more attractive business activities ; nevertheless, the long delay may have been detrimental.[1]

[1] It is significant to read in the Report of the Commissioner of the Police of the Metropolis for 1939 (p. 28) : "Eleven persons who might fairly be described as share-pushers have been arrested and twenty-five others summoned for kindred offences ; but there has only been one important share-pushing case before the courts. This related to a concern in which over half a million pounds had been obtained from the public". It may be noted that this Report does not refer to the area of the City of London Police Force in which most share-pushers operate (see Report of 1937, p. 27).

SECTION FOUR. ECONOMIC CRIME—II

Chapter 8

PROTECTION AGAINST PROPERTY

A. Usury.

In marked contrast to the abundance of devices which the criminal law has invented for the protection *of* property—antiquated and inefficient as many of them may be—stands its neglect to afford a corresponding protection *against* property. In a historical development of some thousands of years, there is indeed only one form of anti-social conduct by owners of property that has been persistently made an offence punishable by the law : *Usury*. No wonder that this illegitimate child of ecclesiastical, legal, and social thought has had to bear the brunt of the most vehement attacks of which the defenders of " Improperty " have been capable. Fortunately, it has survived in many parts of the world, though the loss of many of its teeth is somewhat deplorable.[1] Granted that the Middle Ages had greatly overdone the matter. The prohibition of usury had, in the words of Tawney,[2] become the kernel of its doctrines of economic ethics, and the money-lender the most conspicuous species of unpopular character. Even when Thomas Wilson wrote his famous *Discourse* of 1572, this was still, " after the land question, the most burning social problem of the day ", " too scandalous to be tolerated and too convenient to be altogether suppressed ".[3] Clearly the

[1] The history of the offence of usury forms an important part of the general economic history. No references to works of such general character are, therefore, needed. For the history of criminal legislation in particular see, for example, Th. Mommsen, *Römisches Strafrecht*, pp. 849 et seq. ; Stephen, History III, p. 198 ; Isopescul-Grecul, *Wucher-Strafrecht* (1906) ; Richard Schmidt, *Rechtsvergleichende Darstellung des deutschen Strafrechts, Besonderer Teil*, Vol. VIII (1906) ; F. W. Ryan, *Usury and Usury Laws* (Boston, 1924) ; W. Holdsworth, *History of English Law*, Vol. VIII, pp. 100–113 ; *Encycl. of Social Science*, art. " Usury ". Much valuable historical material also in R. H. Tawney's *Religion and the Rise of Capitalism*, and in his Introduction to *Thomas Wilson, A Discourse upon Usury (1572), with an Historical Introduction by R. H. Tawney* (1925).

[2] *Religion and the Rise of Capitalism* (Pelican ed.), p. 144 ; see also pp. 49 et seq., and passim. Mosaic law also forbade usury. It is sometimes assumed that this prohibition referred only to loans between Jews (e.g. Archbishop Dr. Temple, *Christianity and Social Order*, Penguin Special, 1942, p. 31). However, as Chief Rabbi Hertz explains, the words in Deuteronomy xxiii. 20, " unto a foreigner thou mayest lend upon usury " permitted the taking of interest only for commercial loans to non-Jews, not for loans needed for subsistence (*The Times*, Feb. 6, 1943).

[3] Tawney, Introduction, pp. 2 and 20.

wholesale penalization of any form of interest for loans of money was, already then, both unjustified and impracticable. One concession after the other had to be made, till Bentham's " Letters in Defence of Usury " of 1787 succeeded, at least for a while, in altogether destroying the last remaining vestiges of faith in the criminal law of usury. Apparently, it seemed impossible to dispose of Bentham's argument [1] :

> For him who takes as much as he can get for the use of any other sort of thing, a house, for instance, there is no particular appellation, nor any mark of disrepute : nobody is ashamed of doing so, nor is it usual so much as to profess to do otherwise. Why a man who takes as much as he can get . . . for the use of a sum of money should be called usurer . . . any more than if he had bought a house with it and made a proportionable profit by the house, is more than I can see.

There was no answer to this as nobody wanted to give the only possible answer, namely, that those other forms of usury, not connected with money-lending, should likewise be punishable.[2] It is, however, characteristic of the slowness with which the criminal law adapts itself to changes in economic thought that it took about two-thirds of a century for Bentham's ideas to be transformed into the small coin of legislation. It was, in fact, only between 1854 and 1867 that usury laws were repealed in most European countries, as well as in the States of the U.S.A., i.e., at a time when, as Dicey has pointed out,[3] Benthamism represented already only public opinion of yesterday.

The history of criminal law shows two different lines of approach to the problem : Either the law fixes certain maximum rates of interest and punishes any excess ; or no such maxima are fixed and it is left to the courts to decide what, according to a general definition, is excessive. The first method, which is the older of the two, is sometimes, following Bentham's example,[4] called the *legal*, the other the *moral* conception of usury. Under the first, the charging of rates above the general maximum prescribed by the law is an offence even if, under the special circumstances of the individual case, they should not be excessive. The second method, which fixes no such legal maximum, has the

[1] *Works of Jeremy Bentham*, Vol. III, p. 4. As a deterrent, these Letters are still worth reading and may be particularly recommended to our individualists.

[2] See also p. 9 : " while, out of loving kindness or whatsoever other motive, the law precludes a man from *borrowing* upon terms which it deems too disadvantageous, it does not preclude him from *selling*, upon any terms, however, disadvantageous ".

[3] *Law and Opinion*, p. 33.

[4] Op. cit., p. 4.

disadvantage that a very considerable amount of discretion has to be left to the criminal courts. The task of the latter may be made easier either by establishing for professional money-lenders a licensing system under the administrative authorities, or by giving the civil courts far-reaching powers, for instance, of declaring void, or even of remaking, oppressive agreements.

In England, for many centuries, the first method was used. In 1545, a statute of Henry VIII "saved the face of the older doctrine by a condemnation of usury in the old terms, but at the same time recognized the new conditions by repealing all the former statutes and by permitting persons to lend money at a rate of interest not exceeding 10 per cent".[1] This was repealed in 1551, but revived in 1571, and in the course of subsequent centuries the maximum rate was gradually lowered to 5 per cent.; in 1854, however, any legal restrictions of interest were abolished. The Continent, with a few exceptions, followed suit: Denmark 1855, Sweden 1864, Belgium 1865, Germany 1867, and Austria 1868. The consequence was a tremendous expansion of usury, and, therefore, the last quarter of the nineteenth century witnessed a new wave of criminal legislation: Germany 1880, Austria 1881, Russia 1894, Norway 1902. In England, a belated and tardy confession of failure was made through the passing of the Money-lenders Act of 1900, amended by the Money-lenders Act of 1927. Its principal features are:

(*a*) Wide powers for the civil courts, if proceedings are taken by a money-lender for the recovery of money, to give relief by re-opening the transaction, relieving the debtor and setting aside and re-making the whole agreement, if the amount charged is held excessive and the transaction "harsh and unconscionable" or against the rules of equity. Under the Act of 1927, sect. 10, where it is found that the interest charged exceeds 48 per cent. per annum, the court has, unless the contrary is proved, to presume that the rate is excessive and the transaction harsh and unconscionable. This means a combination of the moral and the legal method, limited, however, to the civil side of the matter.

(*b*) An administrative system of registration, since 1927 of licensing, for professional money-lenders, the licence to be granted on the basis of a certificate by Petty Sessional Courts. The latter may refuse to certify persons who cannot produce evidence of good character, or are not regarded as fit and proper persons, etc.

[1] Holdsworth, op. cit., Vol. VIII, p. 108.

(*c*) Penalties are provided only for violations of the licensing system, for false statements or promises in order to induce a person to borrow money, not, however, for charging excessive rates of interest. In other words, the criminal law is used to buttress only the administrative, not the civil structure of the Act. The court may, however, endorse the certificate if excessive rates are charged.

Continental criminal legislation is on different lines. Most Penal Codes contain provisions against " moral " usury, i.e., no maximum rates of interest are fixed but the charging of rates which the criminal court regards as excessive is an offence. More or less detailed definitions are given of the types of contract which come under the scope of the law, and of the factors which the courts have to consider when deciding whether a certain agreement is usurious. Both aspects of the matter have caused plenty of headache to legislation, as this is an offence where it is particularly difficult to prevent evasions of the law. Codes of the older type, notably the German Code, dealt originally only with usury relating to loans of money and similar financial transactions (Germany, arts. 302*a* to *d*). It was only later that the equally dangerous potentialities of other contracts, especially the selling and lending of goods, were recognized. At present, some Continental Codes make no longer any distinction in this respect ; they provide penalties for anybody who enters into a contract whereby the partner has to undertake a financial obligation of whatever kind, if the economic value of this obligation is disproportionally higher than the value of the offender's performance, and provided the offender, in order to get the contract, has taken advantage of the bad position, or lack of experience, carelessness, or low intelligence, of his victim.[1] The Soviet Code (art. 173) tries to combine both methods : it provides penalties for " the taking of interest in respect of a loan of money or property at a rate higher than the maximum interest on loans prescribed by law ", but also for " the lending of means of production or cattle, for a consideration in money or in kind or in labour, at a rate flagrantly higher than that customary in the locality ".

It goes without saying that all these penal provisions of Continental law are supplemented by the usual provisions of

[1] Switzerland, art. 157 ; Poland, art. 268 ; Germany, arts. 302*a* to *e*. Also China, art. 344. Italy, art. 644, is limited to " loans of money or other movable objects ".

civil law which, as a rule, declare usurious contracts null and void.

The characteristic feature of the U.S.A. legislation is its distinction between large and small loans.[1] For the latter, i.e., loans of usually no more than 300 dollars, in an increasing measure so-called Small Loan Laws have been passed on a uniform model, based on the old " legal " method of fixing maximum rates of interest. Massachusetts was the first State to legislate on such lines (1916), and in 1924 only five States possessed no such statute.[2] The tendency has, therefore, been entirely different from that of Continental legislation. On the other hand, these laws are not simply a new edition of those old European statutes which also used fixed maximum rates. There are very important differences : First, the maximum rates have become much higher, 3 to 3½ per cent. per month instead of the former 5 or 10 per cent. per year, as the modern legislator has come to realize that maxima which do not compensate for the trouble and risk of the small loan business inevitably lead to evasions. The second characteristic of American legislation is the remarkable way in which it uses the social services and the idea of family case work in order to make the abstract provisions of the statute really living law. It has been recognized in the U.S.A. that it is not enough to provide the usual framework of licensing money-lenders, fixing maximum rates of interest, and empowering civil courts to interfere with oppressive agreements if it is left to the personal initiative of the victim to obtain relief from the court. A system of social services has been set up, administered by Small Loan Supervisors, appointed by the State, who have to investigate complaints, inform borrowers of their rights and duties, prosecute violators, and are generally responsible for the smooth working of the Act.[3] This stress laid on the social case work side of Small Loan legislation shows the guiding hand of the Russell Sage Foundation which has, from the beginning, played the leading part in the drafting of the Uniform Small Loan Law and supervised the way in which it has been put into practice by the individual States. Most of these Small Loan Laws provide imprisonment and fines for violations of

[1] On the position in the U.S.A., see in particular, Ryan (above, p. 130 fn. 1) and articles in the *Annals of the American Academy of Political and Social Science*, Vol. 196 (March 1938), esp. by John S. Bradway, Reginald Heber Smith, Rolf Nugent, Earl E. Davidson, and Charles A. Gates.

[2] Ryan, op. cit., p. 6.

[3] See esp. the articles by Rolf Nugent, Charles A. Gates and Earl E. Davidson, loco. cit.

the maxima. American views about their merits seem to be very favourable, and it is stressed that, in view of the similarity of the economic problems present in most small loan cases, it is possible for experts successfully to fix general maxima of interest.[1] There has, however, been a tendency in recent years, instead of fixing the maximum in the Act itself, to leave this task to special fact-finding Commissions in order to make it easier to adapt the rates to changing economic conditions without legislative interference.[2]

American usury legislation for loans which exceed the limits set by the Small Loan Laws is of little interest to us. Its maximum rates are much lower, and the penalty is usually only forfeiture of interest or avoidance of contract.[3]

The question arises whether certain features of the American Small Loan legislation may recommend themselves for introduction in other countries. When the English Money-lenders Act of 1927 was under discussion,[4] only scanty attention seems to have been paid to that piece of social reform, and it may then perhaps have been too early to form an accurate opinion of its value.[5] In the intervening twenty years, however, a wealth of experience has been collected in the U.S.A. which other countries can afford to ignore only if they are fully satisfied with their own usury laws. Conditions in England have recently been severely criticized in that remarkable study *Our Towns*,[6] and its disclosures must have come as a shock to those who may have regarded the Act of 1927 as a success.

> Illegal money-lending by unregistered persons still prevalent in defiance of the law . . . One of the authors of this book wrote in 1932 : " I know of no other law which is broken so often and so openly. The recognized rate of interest for weekly loans is 1*s* 8*d*. in the £, or 1*d*. in the shilling, i.e., 433 per cent. per annum. This rate is paid as a matter of course. It is never questioned ".

Instances of hair-raising exploitation are quoted ; however, the money-lender, it is stated, is never brought before the court

[1] Ryan, op. cit., pp. 142 et seq.

[2] This was already recommended by Ryan, op. cit., p. 165, and has now been done by Wisconsin, Indiana, New Hampshire, and Iowa ; see Bradway, loco cit., p. 183.

[3] See Ryan, pp. 25 et seq.

[4] See in particular the *Proceedings* of the Joint Select Committee of the House of Lords and House of Commons on the Money-lenders Bill, 1925.

[5] A summary of American methods was presented to the Committee by Miss D. Keeling (see *Proceedings*, p. 77).

[6] *Our Towns, A Close-up*. A study made in 1939–42 with certain recommendations by the Hygiene Committee of the Women's Group on Public Welfare (in association with the National Council of Social Service), 1943, esp. pp. 18 et seq.

because his victims are afraid or ashamed. As long as widespread poverty exists, this witness concludes, the evil will continue, but it could be lessened if illegal actions were more often prosecuted. Other remedies indicated by the Study Group are the setting up of, presumably official or semi-official, schemes as part of the social services to satisfy the needs of the small man for loans of money and better education of the masses in the law and economics of money-lending. Both these suggestions are admirable. In addition, the following aspects of the American system seem worthy of further consideration :

(*a*) Its distinction between the small loan of the poor working-class man, needed mainly for purposes of consumption, and larger loans for productive or speculative purposes. This enables the legislator to work out a Small Loan Law especially adapted to the needs of the former class, without having to make concessions in the interest of the second group.

(*b*) The fixing of maximum rates of interest—preferably not in the Act itself but by some administrative body—is thereby made possible. Without such maxima the courts are burdened with the, for them, too difficult task of determining in each individual case what is " excessive ".

(*c*) The closest co-operation between civil and criminal courts and administrative agencies. This means, among others, penalties for money-lenders guilty of exceeding the maxima fixed by the administration, and a network of statutory social services on American lines. In the U.S.A., it also means permanent contact with a social research body, the Russell Sage Foundation, which can be relied upon to keep the whole problem under constant review and to insist on changes in the law as soon as the need becomes apparent.

B. Economic Crime against the State.

(*a*) *Profiteering.*

Under a capitalist economy, in time of peace, the individual has but little opportunity of committing economic crime against the State. In a total war, the wholesale change in values necessarily produces a different type of criminal legislation and, consequently, of crime. Economic crime, as a rule, becomes crime against the State. The same is true in a militant socialist State, regardless of war or peace. One aspect of this revolution has already been discussed : its effect on the treatment of theft of State property and of waste.[1] This is, however, only one particle in the vast network of criminal legislation designed to protect the whole system of State regulated production, distribution, and consumption. It may be useful to compare the impact on criminal legislation of such a system as it exists in two countries, the U.S.S.R. and war-time England. Even leaving aside those spectacular sabotage trials which were more of a purely political than of an economic character,[2] Soviet methods of dealing with economic crime differ strikingly from those of capitalist countries and have, perhaps more than anything else, been responsible for the distrust of the U.S.S.R. so frequently to be encountered in the outside world. Foreign critics may well have thought the penalties for stealing State property disproportionally high, but it was at least stealing, a universally recognized and detested offence. Many other forms of economic behaviour, however, which make the offender liable to the most severe penalties in the U.S.S.R. are, elsewhere, not regarded as crimes, or even as anti-social, at all. Here, as in the matter of theft, the criminal law closely reflects the economic and political system of its country and its ideology of economic and political behaviour. In a country whose whole existence depends on the success of the " Plan ", economic misbehaviour is bound to be regarded as a political crime of the first order.

The principal characteristics of the Soviet conception of economic crime can be summed up under five headings :[3]

(1) It includes activities which are, as a rule, not punishable elsewhere ; for instance :

" Speculation ", i.e., " the purchase or sale by private persons, for gain, of any agricultural produce or of any article of mass-consumption " (art. 107). " Gain " is by no means identical with " excessive profit ". Sentences of up to ten years' imprisonment are said to have been imposed, for instance, on women who sold at " what we would consider a very modest profit " goods they had bought in Government stores after much queueing.[4] Although this appears excessively harsh, it may be necessary for a period of transition in order to stamp out centuries-old habits and to build up a new, anti-profitmaking mentality.

[1] Above, pp. 109 and 115.
[2] For brief accounts of them with literature see S. and B. Webb, op. cit., II, pp. 550–60, 1152 et seq.
[3] See now also Rudolf Schlesinger, *Soviet Legal Theory*, 1945 (Internal. Libr. of Sociology and Social Reconstruction).
[4] Littlepage-Bess, op. cit., p. 130.

Or the employment of labour for private gain: Pat Sloan[1] tells this story:

Some time ago, when a certain well-known American business man was visiting the Soviet Union, he happened to boast to his guide that he employed several thousand of men in his various enterprises. The guide . . . was unable to hide her dismay. "People get ten years for that in this country," she said.

"The delivery by any industrial or commercial enterprise, systematically or on a large scale, of goods of bad quality" (art. 128*a*).[2]

The making of "disadvantageous contracts" by managers of State or public institutions (art. 129).

"Any obstruction of the lawful activities of any factory or works committee, or trade union, or of any authorized representative of any of them" (art. 135).

During the world war, officials have received sentences of imprisonment up to five years for undue delays in considering applications for allowances and for failing to show a "receptive and sympathetic attitude towards relatives of men in the Forces".[3]

(2) The vagueness and the sweeping character of many of the definitions used in the Penal Code; for instance:

"The undermining of State industry, transport, trade, currency, or system of credit, or of the co-operative system with counter-revolutionary intent, by utilizing the State institutions or enterprises concerned or by working against their normal activities . . ." (art. 58, No. 7).

"Maladministration by any person in control of any State or public institution or enterprise . . . if it results in waste or in irreparable damage to the property of the institution or enterprise . . ." (art. 128).

Or the already quoted arts. 135 and 130, the latter punishing "waste" without defining its meaning.

(3) The frequent changes and reversals of policy, in accord-

[1] *Soviet Democracy* (1937), p. 43. See also S. and B. Webb, op. cit., Vol. II, p. 1122: "Instead of rewarding or honouring those who engage others at wages in order to make a profit out of the product of their labour, Soviet Communism punishes them as criminals, guilty, irrespective of the amount of the wages that they pay, of the crime of 'exploitation'."

[2] Under a decree of July 10, 1940, penalties for this offence have been further increased, and a number of trials for producing goods of poor quality have been reported; see Hubbard, *Soviet Labour and Industry* (1942), p. 100.

[3] *The Times*, Feb. 24, 1942.

ance with varying needs in the economic and political sphere. On this, we have already commented in connection with the treatment of abortion (above, p. 44). This feature has been particularly pronounced in the field of economic crime where the private enterpreneur, tolerated or even encouraged at one stage of the N.E.P., had to face deportation or execution immediately after.

(4) The open discrimination by the law to the disadvantage of *Kulaks*, of the "*intelligentsia*" and other anti-Soviet elements, e.g., in case of non-payment of tax, or refusal to perform work for the State, or illegal slaughter of horses, or use of violence against collective farm workers aggravated penalties if committed by *Kulaks* (arts. 60, 61, 79, Decree of August 7, 1932).

Such methods of discrimination had particularly unfortunate results because of the vagueness of the term *Kulak*.

> The line drawn between a *Kulak* and a middle peasant is so hazy [says Mr. Yugoff with reference to the anti-*Kulak* campaign of 1928], that the repressive measures everywhere affected the peasant as a whole. According to the reports of the People's Commissariat for Justice, among the peasants who were arrested and tried for refusing to sell grain to the State authorities at the officially fixed prices, there were only 66 per cent. of *Kulaks*.[1]

(5) The peculiar treatment of the internal side of the crime, the guilty mind. In the case of economic offences against the State it is rare for the Soviet Code to require the highest degree of guilt, i.e., malice, intent, or at least knowledge of the harmful consequences. Often negligence is enough (e.g., arts. 111, 112, 128), and even more frequently the requirement of guilt is altogether omitted (e.g., arts. 87, 87*a*, 97, 99, 105, 107, 113, 128*a* and *b*, 129, 133).

It is this last-mentioned feature that used to be criticized perhaps more severely than anything else even by otherwise benevolent foreign observers. Some of them were open-minded enough to realize that an entirely new economic and social system must inevitably lead to an equally unorthodox system of criminal law which treats as crime actions perfectly legitimate in a capitalist society; which cannot invariably use the clear-cut definitions aimed at—though not always actually employed—in bourgeois law; which has to be altered with every new turn of general policy. What, to them, seemed really intolerable was the practice of using the machinery of criminal law to make

[1] A. Yugoff, *Economic Trends in Soviet Russia* (1930), p. 139.

scapegoats of men who had been guilty, at most, of errors of judgement, or whose economic activities had, even without any fault of theirs, turned out to the disadvantage of the community.

Every period of stress in the U.S.S.R. [writes Sir John Maynard [1]], claims its sacrifices or scapegoats. In March, 1933, thirty-five persons were executed for so-called sabotage in connection with the agrarian difficulties. All were officials of the Agricultural Commissariat and of the farms . . . I think that failure is often treated as a deliberate offence.

And:

No less than 132,000 shop-assistants were in disgrace (in 1937) for alleged peculation and waste till higher authority stepped in and reinstated them.

Or, as Mr. Hubbard puts it,[2]

Imprisonment for mistakes innocent of any suggestion of deliberate misdoing, in factory or office, can befall anyone.

He explains, however, that this meant, in many cases, only short terms in prison during which the offender may have been offered another job at a higher salary, though probably with the disadvantage of having to live somewhere far from Moscow.

When passing verdict on this new brand of criminal law one has to admit that what the Soviet Union has done amounts to no more than a reversal of tendencies which have characterized certain preceding epochs in the history of criminal law: In a feudal society, the Benefit of Clergy created two categories of criminal law, one for the educated and well-to-do, another for the illiterate and the poor. Under the capitalist system, exaggerated attention has been paid to, and unduly harsh punishment meted out for, theft and other petty offences of the small man, whereas white-collar crime has been treated with undue leniency, or altogether condoned. In Soviet Russia, the turn of the *intelligentsia* and of the well-to-do classes has come. It is of no use complaining that two wrongs do not make one right. "*Tu l'as voulu, George Dandin.*" Once, somewhere, this process of undoing old wrongs has had to take its course in the interest of social justice, and Western democracies may be thankful to Russia that she has done the job for them. All one can hope for is that, this time, it will not take centuries to restore

[1] *The Russian Peasant and other Studies*, pp. 297 and 469; see also pp. 19 et seq. on the "Terror".

[2] Leonard E. Hubbard, *Soviet Labour and Industry* (1942), p. 6.

the right balance. There are already signs of a reversal of policy. Since 1931, a marked improvement in the position of the *intelligentsia* has been noticed by various writers, and, in particular, " punishment for ' production risks ' is now frowned upon ".[1] In this respect as in so many others, in spite of occasional relapses, a gradual assimilation to Western standards is likely to occur. On the other hand, recent developments in the economic structure of most capitalist countries will also inevitably reduce the hitherto existing gap between their and the Soviet conception of economic crime. As long as property, control, and management were together in one hand, the fiction—it often was no more than a fiction—could be upheld that there was no need to control the activities of the owner through the criminal law—in his own interest he would do the right thing anyhow. Now, with ownership getting more and more divorced from control and management, the need to control managers and other leading employees has become more apparent, and, as will be shown immediately, the possibility is not to be excluded that, to an ever-increasing extent, even negligence will have to be treated as an offence.

From our point of view, the principal weakness of Soviet methods of dealing with economic crime is this : exaggerated reliance is placed on the possibilities of the machinery of criminal justice, and, as a consequence, the criminal courts, perhaps insufficiently aided by the administrative branch of Government, are allowed to play an over-great part in the shaping of the country's economic policy. From the purely negative and protective side their functions have been too much expanded so as to aim at performing positively constructive tasks as well. This, as we have already seen [2], is dangerous unless perfect co-operation and division of labour exists between courts and administration. Under the Soviet Penal Code, the criminal courts have to decide such intricate questions as, for instance, whether the accused is guilty of " maladministration " (art. 128), " making disadvantageous contracts " (art. 129), causing " disorganization " of the State administration (art. 112), " undermining of State industry, transport ", etc. (art. 58, No. 7). As repeatedly pointed out, to answer such questions is beyond the capacity of the average criminal court ; they should be left to

[1] Louis Fischer, *Machines and Men in Russia* (1932), pp. 288–9, quoted from S. and B. Webb, op. cit., p. 556. See also Ella Winter, *Red Virtue*, p. 76.

[2] Above, pp. 50, 54.

administrative boards, with the criminal courts in the background to control the procedure and to impose penalties on violators. The Soviet legislator, in other words, has apparently not yet been able to work out an effective system of distribution of powers. This becomes particularly clear by a comparison with certain sections of English law which deal with similar problems. One has, of course, to resort to English war-time and immediate post-war emergency legislation in order to obtain material which is in any way comparable. In some cases, it is true, because of differences in the economic system, the problem which the Soviet legislator had to solve was so much simpler than that before his English colleague that no elaborate machinery was required.

Let us take the case of *profiteering* as dealt with in art. 107 of the Soviet Penal Code and in recent English war-time legislation : Whereas the Soviet Code is content to prohibit any kind of " purchase or resale for gain, i.e., as a speculation ", English law is compelled to distinguish between lawful and illicit gain, and, for that purpose, an elaborate and complicated structure is needed of partly administrative, partly judicial character. Under the Prices of Goods Act, 1939, for instance, it has become unlawful to sell any price-regulated goods at a price which exceeds the permitted price, that is to say, the basic price together with the amount of the permitted increase (sect. 1). As a rule, the " basic price " is the price on the 21st of August, 1939 (sect. 3), whereas the " permitted increase " is tantamount to the increase " reasonably justified in view of changes in the business " (sect. 4). In order to relieve the criminal courts of the task to determine what is " reasonably justified ", the Board of Trade has been given power " to specify basic price, permitted increase or permitted price " (sect. 5). There are also the Price-regulating Committees to advise the Board of Trade and, in suitable cases, to request it to institute criminal proceedings (sect. 8). The civil law, too, may play its part, as the buyer has the right to avoid the transaction or to recover the excess price paid (sect. 10). Moreover, in order further to facilitate the work of the criminal courts, the burden of proof has, in two ways, been shifted from the prosecution to the accused. First, if it has been established that the price charged was higher than the basic price, it is for the accused to prove that the price did not exceed the permitted price (sect. 9). Secondly, if the offence was committed by a corporation, every director or officer is deemed to be guilty unless he proves that the offence was committed without his consent or connivance and that he had exercised all such diligence to prevent the contravention as he ought to have exercised, having regard to the nature of his functions and to all the circumstances. Thus, we find here employed many of the technical devices already known from our discussion of the Prevention of Fraud (Investment) Act of 1939, and, in addition, one for which the time was not yet ripe before the war; the shifting of the burden of proof. In spite of this, the Prices of Goods Act was, for various reasons, not a success: The power to control prices did not go far enough [1]; the Committees set up under it had no power over foodstuffs [2]; the duty of reporting transgressions was left to the private citizen, "with highly unsatisfactory results" [3]; there were loopholes in the Act which enabled unscrupulous middlemen to make high profits without performing any useful services in the distribution of goods [4]; the licensing system was inadequate; the penalties provided by the Act, and, even more, those actually imposed by the magistrates were often ridiculously low. In spring 1941, the disclosures of the North Midlands Price Regulation Committee, in particular, led to a public outcry, and, as a result, the Goods and Services (Price Control) Act of the 22nd July, 1941, and the Food (Restriction on Dealings) Order of the 20th August, 1941,[5] were passed. Among other provisions, they extended the licensing system, especially for middlemen, provided for the appointment of Inspectors to enforce the law, and, for a while at least, they were generally regarded as effective.[6] Very soon, however, the alarm was sounded again. In March, 1942, *The Economist* wrote:

> There are indications that the control of prices of civilian goods is not so effective as the public was led to expect at the time of the passing of the Goods and Services (Price Control) Act 1941 . . . the public cannot be blamed for holding the view that (these Acts) are just another example of legislation ostensibly passed to meet an urgent need, but never properly enforced.[7]

Consequently, new legislation became necessary, this time mainly aiming at a considerable stiffening of the penalties and with the particular object that convicted profiteers should not be allowed to keep their illicit gains. The utter inadequacy of

[1] *The Economist*, March 29, 1941. [2] *The Economist*, April 20, 1940.
[3] *The Economist*, August 2, 1941.
[4] *The Economist*, May 3, 1941; *The Times*, May 1, 2, 5, 16, 1941, and often.
[5] S.R & O., 1941, No. 1234 (p. 563). [6] Davenport, op. cit., p. 107.
[7] *The Economist*, March 21, 1942, p. 405.

most fines so far imposed was too glaring to be any longer ignored. Instances were quoted as typical of fines of £50 for selling goods above the maximum price, leaving the offender with a profit of more than £1,000.[1] Two Orders in Council made it possible, or even imperative, to impose greatly increased penalties for black market offences and more adequate sentences of imprisonment in default of payment of large fines and contained provisions for the enforcement of large fines by bankruptcy proceedings.[2] The position seems to have improved since that time, and the imposition of very considerable fines has become fairly frequent. While we are not here concerned with any statistical or other technical detail, certain general impressions arising from this brief historical survey may be added. To anyone familiar with corresponding happenings in the war of 1914–18—happenings which have been described in detail for at least three of the belligerent countries [3]—the likely course of events in the field of black market and similar offences in the second world war must have been fairly clear from the very beginning. It is somewhat difficult to understand, therefore, why effective legislation against profiteering, which ought to have been introduced in 1939, had to wait till 1941 and 1942. Admittedly, to produce watertight definitions of the manifold profiteering offences so as to leave the smallest conceivable number of loopholes at any given time, is the most difficult task which the legal draftsman has to face,[4] and, in rapidly changing economic conditions, legislative history may not be able to teach very much. However, such indispensable pillars of the whole structure of war-time control as an elaborate system of licensing, effective provisions against parasitic middlemen, and, above all, really deterrent penalties ought to have been established without delay. Sir William Beveridge [5] reports that in the 1914–18 war in Britain " trivial fines were not the order of the day ", quoting two cases of fines amounting to several thousands of pounds. However,

[1] *The Magistrate*, Jan.–Feb., 1942, p. 79. See also the whole daily Press in the months preceding the passing of the Orders quoted below.

[2] Orders in Council of March 19, 1942 (S.R. & O. 1942, No. 501), and of May 22, 1942.

[3] Sir William Beveridge, *British Food Control* (1928) ; Moritz Liepmann, *Krieg und Kriminalität in Deutschland* (1930) ; Franz Exner, *Krieg und Kriminalität in Österreich* (1927)—all three published as parts of the " Economic and Social History of the World War " of the Carnegie Endowment for International Peace.

[4] Sir William Beveridge, op. cit., p. 288, quotes evidence given before the Select Committee on High Prices and Profits, 1919, regarding " the extreme difficulty of defining ' profiteering ' ".

[5] Sir William Beveridge, op. cit., p. 237.

" the fine ", he adds, " did little more than take away the illicit profits made. Statutory provision for this was made later by the Defence of the Realm (Food Profits) Act, which became law on May 16, 1918 ; under this Act every person convicted . . . was to forfeit twice the amount of any illegal profits that he had made ". The late date of this Act might have served as a warning to the legislator of 1939.

In another direction, too, the anti-profiteering campaign arising out of the last war might provide useful lessons : The reasons why the short-lived Profiteering Act of 1919 proved a failure have been indicated by Sir William Beveridge [1] ; it made " unreasonable " profits an offence, but failed to provide the courts with a workable definition of " reasonable " or with effective assistance on the part of administrative authorities.

In conclusion, one may say that, in theory, the English legislator has at last been successful in dealing with a situation in many ways more complicated than that confronting his Soviet colleague. In practice, the principal weakness of the English system, contrary to that of the U.S.S.R., has been occasional failure to pass effective legislation in time and to impose adequate penalties.

(*b*) *Taxation Fraud.*

For several reasons, taxation frauds are of considerable interest to us : First, they are, for all practical purposes, among the most important white-collar crimes. Second, the well-known phenomenon of a nucleus of downright criminal behaviour surrounded by a much larger area of anti-social but not illegal, or illegal but not criminal, actions can be studied here perhaps more clearly than anywhere else. And, thirdly, a crisis in values has recently become apparent in this field which may be symptomatic of a general change in socio-legal attitudes.

The criminal law of taxation is based upon the distinction between *tax evasion* and *tax avoidance*. In theory, this distinction is simple and straightforward : evasion constitutes a violation of the criminal law with all its consequences, whereas mere avoidance means some more or less artful juggling which, though in all probability very anti-social, still manages to keep within the letter of the law. Sometimes, the distinction is made between evasion and the " minimizing " of taxes, which latter is defined as " the reduction of legal tax liability to the lowest possible

[1] Op. cit., pp. 287 et seq.

amount through the skilful utilization of every legitimate method ".[1] We do not intend here to deal with tax evasion proper. Its legal problems present no particular difficulties, except such of evidence, and in *Criminal Statistics* offences of this type appear as an inconspicuous appendix to the much more impressive figures of motor-car and dog licence offences. The really dangerous tax offender does not evade; he avoids. Unfortunately, it is very difficult in practice to discover the right line of demarcation, and, as Judge Ferdinand Pecora has pointed out in his remarkable study of American conditions,[2] it is often only the outcome of legal proceedings which makes it retrospectively clear whether in an individual case the accused has been guilty of the offence of tax evasion or whether he has merely made use of his solemn right as a citizen to " avoid " the unnecessary payment of taxes. This state of uncertainty is no doubt undesirable and should be remedied. The task before the legislator, however, is not solely one of clarification and definition. He has, above all, to consider whether the domain of mere tax " avoidance " has not in recent times been too much extended at the expense of " evasion ". The drawing of the right line of demarcation is, of course, largely dependent upon the spirit of social philosophy in which the task is approached. Only recently, we have been provided with a public re-statement of the old philosophy, formulated more pithily and uncompromisingly than one might have expected in these days : " Taxation ", writes Lord Quickswood,[3]

> is *prima facie* a wrong, for it consists in taking from the taxpayer what belongs to him ; and that is *prima facie* wrong. Taxation is justified only by the authority of the State, which is expressed in the law. The taxpayer is morally bound to obey the law, but is not bound beyond the law ; for apart from the law taxation would be blackmail or racketeering. There is not behind taxing laws, as there is behind laws against crime, an independent moral obligation. When therefore the taxpayer has obeyed the law he has done all that morality requires.
>
> It is said that by avoiding a tax he throws a load on to some other taxpayer. But this is not quite accurate ; for the deficiency might be met by reducing expenditure . . . is it not a good thing that there should be this last lawful remedy against oppressive taxation by a majority, that human ingenuity can always find a way by which the minority can escape from tyrannical imposts ?

[1] R. M. Haig, *Encycl. of Social Science*, art. " Taxation ", p. 535. On the whole subject see also Josiah Wedgwood, *The Economics of Inheritance*, Chapter X.

[2] *Wall-Street under Oath*, Cresset Press (London, 1939), p. 191.

[3] Letter to *The Times*, Feb. 20, 1943.

What was the immediate occasion for this amusing attempt to raise the art of tax avoidance to the moral level of political martyrdom, or as another correspondent in *The Times* put it,[1] "to make Hampdens of our modern tax dodgers"? Lord Quickswood's letter was written as a protest against certain noteworthy and widely discussed remarks of the Lord Chancellor, Viscount Simon, in the case Latilla *v.* Inland Revenue Commissioners[2]:

> My Lords, of recent years much ingenuity has been expended in certain quarters in attempting to devise methods of disposition of income by which those who were prepared to adopt them might enjoy the benefits of residence in this country while receiving the equivalent of such income, without sharing in the appropriate burden of British taxation. Judicial dicta may be cited which point out that, however elaborate and artificial such methods may be, those who adopt them are "entitled" to do so. There is, of course, no doubt that they are within their legal rights, but that is no reason why their efforts or those of the professional gentlemen who assist them in the matter, should be regarded as a commendable exercise of ingenuity or as a discharge of the duties of good citizenship. On the contrary, one result of such methods, if they succeed, is, of course, to increase *pro tanto* the load of tax on the shoulders of the great body of good citizens who do not desire, or do not know how, to adopt these manœuvres. Another consequence is that the Legislature has made amendments to our Income Tax Code which aim at nullifying the effectiveness of such schemes.

Plain and self-evident as the truth of these words must appear, they constitute nevertheless a complete break with the traditional attitude of the Judiciary. In comments appearing in legal journals reference was made to Lord Sumner's dictum of 1928 in Levene *v.* Inland Revenue that

> the subject is entitled to so arrange his affairs as not to attract taxation enforced by the Crown, so far as he can legitimately do so[3]—a dictum that, it was said in the House of Commons,[4] has been condemned and held up to contempt in this House every time it has been quoted;

or to Lord Tomlin's similar but even more recent formula in Duke of Westminster *v.* Inland Rev., 1934. Lord Sankey's "it is perfectly open for persons to evade income tax if they can

[1] *The Times*, Feb. 23, 1943.
[2] House of Lords, Feb. 11, 1943, *Tax Cases*, Vol. XXV, p. 107; also *The Law Reports*, *1943*, Part V, pp. 377 et seq.
[3] See *Law Notes*, Vol. LXII (March 1943), p. 37, and (April 1943), p. 56.
[4] Mr. Benson, June, 3, 1943, Hansard, col. 420.

do so legally" (Hawker *v.* Compton, 8 T.C. 306) proved also very useful.[1]

The "first dawn of a social conscience on the part of the Judiciary as respects the evils of 'legal avoidance' of taxation", as Mr. A. Farnsworth has pointed out in one of his admirable Notes on the subject,[2] is to be found in the judgement of Lord Greene, M.R., in Howard de Walden *v.* Inland Rev. (1942), 193 L.T. 42, and in certain recent decisions of the Supreme Court of the United States, all of which are more or less on the lines of the Lord Chancellor's statement. A similar stiffening has become noticeable in recent English tax legislation, alluded to by him. Its history over the past ten or twenty years, especially during the 1939–45 war, seen against the background of the parliamentary debates, is extremely illuminating and should be carefully studied by all those interested in the struggle between legislators and white-collar crime. With taxation becoming increasingly heavy and tax dodging correspondingly frequent, the legislator has found it more and more imperative to include in his annual Finance Acts special provisions for the prevention of "avoidance". In the Finance Act of 1936, sect. 18, we see him struggling with "avoidance of income tax by transactions resulting in the transfer of income to persons abroad"; in the Act of 1937, sect. 12, with "certain transactions in securities", particularly the popular "agreements to buy back or re-acquire"; in that of 1939, sect. 17, with "interconnected companies". It is in 1941, however, after the coming of Excess Profits Tax, that the battle is joined in earnest: The Finance Act of that year, sect. 35 (1) contains the interesting general clause:

> Where the Commissioners are of opinion that the main purpose for which any transaction or transactions was or were effected . . . was avoidance of or reduction of liability to excess profits tax, they may, if they think fit, direct that such adjustments shall be made as respects liability to excess profits tax as they consider appropriate so as to counteract the avoidance or the reduction . . .

It fell to the Finance Act of 1943, apart from increasing the penalties for certain forms of evasion, to deal with cases of the

[1] See Jasper More, *The Saving of Income Tax, Surtax and Death Duties* (1935), p. 5: "There is nothing illegal, before a particular liability has arisen, in disposing property in such a way that the liability, when it does arise, will arise in less oppressive form, or in disposing it in such a way that liability will not arise at all. This principle has been recognized by the highest judicial authorities." See also Laski, *Parliamentary Government in England*, p. 366.

[2] *Modern Law Review*, Vol. VI, Dec. 1943, p. 243; see the same writer in *M.L.R.*, 1942, p. 75, and 1944, p. 84; *Law Quarterly Journal*, 1942, p. 168.

notorious "Whisky Deal" type.[1] The result was the complicated sect. 24, directed against "Disposal of Company's Stock at under Value", which, it was hoped, would kill this type of transaction by making it unprofitable. As a by-product, it was enacted that certain categories of professional advisers of business men, barristers, solicitors, accountants, bankers, should not suffer because of their having assisted in devising such schemes, provided they had received only the customary remuneration for their services. "Strong objection was rightly raised in Parliament to the relief thus given to the very persons without whose help these 'evasion' schemes could not be effected."[2]

The climax has so far been reached with the Finance Act of 1944, which was preceded by what must have been one of the most illuminating House of Commons Debates on matters of tax avoidance. When introducing the Bill, the Government had to confess to Parliament that, in thousands of cases, the general clause in sect. 35 of the Finance Act 1941 (see above) had failed to achieve its purpose: tax dodgers had shown no hesitation to give the most solemn assurances that the "main purpose" of their transactions had not been tax avoidance, and, as a consequence, the Special Commissioners, "being scrupulously fair to the taxpayer," had not been prepared to regard the contrary as proved.[3] This came in no way as a surprise as already in the course of the 1941 debates the apprehension had been expressed by some members that the word "main" would completely vitiate the effect of the Act.[4] Now, the phrase "the main purpose" had to be replaced by "the main purpose or one of the main purposes" (Finance Act 1944, sect. 33 (1)). As it had been rightly argued, however, that a purely subjective test using "purpose" or "motive" as the key word was altogether unsuitable,[5] in sect. 33 (3) an attempt was made to introduce an objective criterion as well by providing that, if tax avoidance or reduction is the main benefit to be expected from the transaction, it shall be deemed to have been the main purpose or one of the main purposes of the transaction. In spite of some criticism alleging that this was a violation of

[1] For the details of this ingenious and, apparently, highly successful scheme of "avoiding" Excess Profits Tax see Hansard, June 2, 1943, col. 307 et seq.; *The Times*, June 3, 1943; *Daily Telegraph*, June 30, 1943.

[2] A. Farnsworth, *Modern Law Review*, Dec. 1943, p. 229.

[3] The Solicitor-General, Hansard, June 14, 1944, col. 2053.

[4] Mr. Benson, Hansard, July 1, 1941, col. 1274.

[5] In particular Mr. Benson, loco cit. and Hansard, June 14, 1944, col. 2073.

fundamental legal principles,[1] sect 35 of the Act of 1941 was explicitly made retrospective, as it was recognized that only by doing so could the legislator hope to cope with tax avoidance. As outside the penal law—and no penal clauses were attached to that section—retrospective legislation is, in fact, a perfectly legitimate and often indispensable instrument, such criticism appears to have been unfounded.

Considering these brave efforts to deal with one of the most intricate problems of modern legislation, one might feel tempted, with the greatest diffidence, to offer a few observations of a general character :

(*a*) Might not the time have arrived for the working out of a new philosophy of tax paying to be set against the old one represented by Lord Quickswood ? Its essence would be a recognition of the simple fact, expressly disputed by the latter, that there is indeed behind taxation laws just as much, or just as little, " moral obligation " as there is behind other laws against economic crime. As soon as it is realized that the financial needs of the State, if backed by the law, have to be respected just as much as individual property,[2] it will have to be admitted that taxation fraud stands in no way on a moral level superior to that of stealing and looting.

(*b*) The backing of the law is, of course, indispensable, and it is here that the difference between " evasion " and " avoidance " will have to be re-examined in the light of recent developments. Should it really be beyond the wits of men to conquer the seemingly impregnable fortress of what is now called " avoidance " by splitting it up into two parts : the one consisting of acts which are in conformity not only with the letter but also with the spirit of the law ; the other " tax-dodging " pure and simple, and distinct from " evasion " only by its lack of straightforwardness ? Unless a general formula is found to carry through this distinction, the legislator will have to continue to tread the wearisome path of casuistry, exemplified by those sections of the Finance Acts which try to deal with specific forms of avoidance.[3] The more closely the various types of tax-dodging are scrutinized that have in recent times come to the notice of the public the more clearly seem to stand out the

[1] See, for example, Hansard, June 14, 1944, col. 2040 et seq., and often.
[2] See above, Chapter 7.
[3] " It is a weariness to us year after year to have to try to find fresh words to meet some fresh ingenuity of the tax-dodging fraternity " (Mr. Denman, M.P., Hansard, July 1, 1941, col. 1273).

criteria which distinguish them from perfectly legitimate economic behaviour : first, they are characterized by activity as contrasted with mere omission ; and, secondly, from an objective point of view no economic reasons other than tax avoidance are visible behind such activity or, if they are, their weight is disproportionally small. General formulations on similar lines are already to be found in previous statutes, as, for instance, sect. 132 of the Income Tax Act of 1918 or sect. 33 of the Finance Act of 1927, the latter treating as avoidance " any fictitious or artificial transaction ".[1]

To make the distinction dependent upon subjective criteria such as " purpose " or " motive " seems to be out of place in a provision aiming merely at the nullification of economic effects which are contrary to the aims of taxation laws. The exclusive test should be the objective one of economic effect or benefit.

(*c*) It is difficult to see, however, why the legislator has so far abstained from making even the most drastic cases of tax avoidance criminal offences. In the scale of anti-social activities they rank very high. Certain remarks of the then Chancellor of the Exchequer, the late Sir Kingsley Wood, made during the Committee stage of the Finance Bill of 1943, are well worth remembering :

> I am surprised that more Members of the Committee have not got up to suggest that instead of a civil penalty some criminal penalty should be imposed. There is a great deal to be said for that, because this is very much akin to a black market offence. It is an endeavour to make money in a way that I think must be abhorrent to all.[2]

Similarly Mr. (now Lord) Pethick-Lawrence :

> The time may come when we ought to be in a position to consider the extension of fraud from merely defrauding individuals to defrauding the State . . .[3]

If this should be done and the worst cases of tax avoidance made criminal offences, the subjective test of purpose or motive would, of course, become indispensable in addition to the objective one.

(*d*) Such a tripartite scheme : legal in every respect—illegal with no other consequences than nullity of the transaction for

[1] Attention to this phrase was drawn by Mr. Benson, Hansard, July 7, 1943, col. 2165.

[2] Hansard, June 2, 1943, col. 321. See also Earl Winterton, June 29, 1943, col. 1499.

[3] Hansard, June 29, 1943, col. 1512.

taxation purposes—illegal and criminal, whether as evasion proper or as criminal avoidance—clearly requires a well-thought-out system of distribution of powers between administrative authorities and criminal courts. Should it be left to the former to deal with the objective criteria, i.e., the factual side and the economic implications of the transaction, and the latter to decide the subjective test of purpose or motive? Occasionally, magistrates might find it impossible to discover any disreputable motive in cases concerning "respectable" people; the majority of them, however, will probably be able to draw the right conclusions from the economic situation as elucidated in the findings of the administration—findings which should be binding with regard to the external facts. The task of the courts would be easier here than in monopoly cases where verdicts would have to be passed not merely on one single transaction or chain of transactions but on the whole economic policy of the firm or trade association concerned. The other alternative would be to confine the criminal courts to control of procedure and imposition of sentence.

(*c*) *Monopoly.*[1]

I. Whereas usury may be regarded as the small property owner's method of exploitation, the abuse of monopolistic power is the corresponding crime of big business. As in the case of usury, it is a highly controversial matter whether, and how, such abuses of property should be brought under the scope of the criminal law. Because of the infinitely greater significance and complexity of the problem of monopoly the question is, however, incomparably more difficult here than it is there, and the interests of the State itself are much more vitally affected. To the criminal lawyer and criminologist the matter provides an almost ideal opportunity of examining the much wider problem as to whether the criminal branch of the law is capable of dealing with large-scale economic and social issues, or whether its scope should rather be confined to the protection of property in its simplest forms and of similar more tangible and altogether less complex values. Should the criminal law, in the economic field, be content to penalize anti-social actions of a comparatively primitive character, mostly those types of offences committed by the poorer classes of the community, or is it equally well equipped

[1] By permission of the publishers, a shorter version of this chapter was published in advance in the *Modern Law Review*, Vol. VII, April 1944.

to contribute to the solution of even the most complicated issues of modern economic policy? And if the answer should largely be in the negative, what are the consequences to be drawn for the future of criminal legislation?

Early English law is remarkable for its insistence upon the criminal character of combinations in restraint of trade. There would be little point in re-telling this often told history.[1] In recent times, however, this country has turned away from the criminal to the civil law in its attempts to balance the claims of combination, monopoly, and free competition. To many English lawyers and business men of to-day, any legal system that would try to solve these problems by means of penal legislation would appear foredoomed to failure. The Report on Trusts of 1919, whose members were "unanimously of the opinion that it would be desirable to institute in the United Kingdom machinery for the investigation of the operation of monopolies, trusts, and combines", did, apart from a few minor suggestions by Sir John Macdonell, recommend no penal legislation, and Professor John Hilton, whose "Study of Trade Organizations and Combinations in the United Kingdom" was appended to the Report, found it unnecessary to devote to the American Anti-Trust laws more than a few uncomplimentary remarks.[2] Even now, a quarter of a century later, however, it has been said that "few British people know much about these laws; and what they have been taught through occasional and almost always hostile references in the Press is mostly quite misleading".[3] On the European Continent, too, anti-trust legislation of a penal character is very rare. In Soviet Russia, of course, whose whole economic structure is, at least since 1928, based on State monopoly to the exclusion of almost any private competition,[4] no such legislation is needed, and the Penal Code of 1926 contains merely certain provisions for the safeguarding of State monopoly, as, for instance, arts. 58(7), 59(11), 107, 111, 129*a*. It is noteworthy, however, that the Penal Code of Tsarist Russia of 1903 provided that "A merchant or manufacturer who increases the prices of

[1] See for example, the brief survey by Sir John Macdonell in the Report on Trusts (1919, Cmd. 9236), pp. 31 et seq., and from the point of view of the economist E. A. G. Robinson, *Monopoly* (1941), pp. 256 et seq.; for combinations of workmen Sir Henry Slesser and Charles Baker, *Trade Union Law*, (3rd edition, 1927), pp. 178 et seq.

[2] See also the Final Report of the Committee on Industry and Trade (1929, Cmd. 3782), p. 191.

[3] Hutt, *Plan for Reconstruction*, p. 221 fn. 1.

[4] See for example, Leonard E. Hubbard, *Soviet Labour and Industry* (1942), p. 126.

victuals or other articles of prime necessity in an extraordinary degree, in accord with other merchants or manufacturers dealing in the same articles, shall be punished with imprisonment ".[1] No provision of this kind exists in German criminal law, which is not surprising in view of the favourable attitude German legislation and court practice has always assumed towards cartels and other industrial combinations.[2] France, on the other hand, has inherited from the Code Pénal of 1810 the following art. 419 (as amended by an Act of Dec. 3, 1926)[3]:

All persons : (1) Who, by wrongful or calumnious reports deliberately disseminated among the public, by market bids made for the purpose of upsetting quotations, by offering better prices than those asked by the sellers, or by any fraudulent means or devices whatsoever ;

(2) Or, who, by exercising or attempting to exercise, either by individual or collective action, any influence on the market for the purpose of acquiring profit other than that derived from the natural operation of the law of supply and demand ;

Directly or through a third person promote or attempt to promote an artificial rise or fall in the prices of foodstuffs and other commodities or negotiable securities, either public or private :

Shall be punished with a term of imprisonment varying from two months to two years and a fine varying from 2,000 to 100,000 francs.

The Court may also forbid the offender to reside in a certain place for not less than two and not more than five years.

Since the end of the nineteenth century criminal prosecutions under this article are, however, said to have been rare in France, and the distinction, which was soon to become popular in the U.S.A., between "good" and "bad" combinations began to dominate the picture.

The position is different in the United States, Argentine, Brazil, Mexico, and in the British Dominions where it is rather the rule than the exception to find anti-trust laws containing penal provisions.

[1] Quoted from the Report on Trusts (1919), p. 11.

[2] See the brief survey of the economic and legal position in Germany by Dr. Rudolf Callmann in *Regulation of Economic Activities in Foreign Countries* (Monograph No. 40, published by the American Temporary National Economic Committee, 1941), Part II, Chapter 1, esp. pp. 47 et seq.

[3] See on the situation in France Part III of the Monograph quoted in the foregoing footnote, by Dr. Agnes Roman and others. The translation of art. 419 is taken from the Report on Review of the Legal Aspects of Industrial Agreements, prepared for the Economic Committee of the League of Nations (Economic and Financial Section), 1930, p. 42, as quoted on p. 88 of Monograph No. 40. The translations of Latin American Acts reproduced in the text are taken from Monograph No. 40.

Under the Argentine Anti-Trust Act of August 23, 1923, it is a criminal offence " to make an agreement, pact, combination, amalgamation, or fusion of capital which tends to establish or sustain a monopoly for the sake of profit in one or more branches of production . . ." As acts tending to establish a monopoly are regarded " those which, without representing technical or economic progress, arbitrarily increase the personal profit of persons practising them out of proportion to the capital actually involved, and those which make it difficult for other persons, natural or corporate, to compete freely in production and in domestic or foreign trade ".[1] Other acts of monopoly, as, for instance, " cornering, withdrawal from consumption, or agreeing not to sell, with the object of raising the prices of articles of prime necessity " are also punishable.

Under the Monopoly Act of Brazil of November 18, 1938,[2] the " promotion or participation in combinations or agreements to restrain competitors " and the " retaining or monopolizing of raw material, means of production, or products necessary for the consumption of the people, for the purpose of dominating the market and causing increase in prices " are crimes against the public, to be tried before the Tribunal of National Safety.

The Mexican Anti-Trust Act of August 22, 1931,[3] based on art. 28 of the Constitution, defines as a punishable monopoly " any industrial or mercantile condition in which free competition is suppressed with injury to the general public or to any class of society ", and in a second Act of August 24, 1931, a number of activities are specified as tending to create monopoly. This Act has already been succeeded by another of August 24, 1934.

The Sherman Act of 1890 of the U.S.A., the various Canadian Anti-Trust Acts, and the Australian Industries Preservation Act of 1906–10 are the most remarkable examples of this kind.[4] The present chapter is mainly concerned with the Sherman Act because the abundance of factual and critical material which exists regarding this Act—court decisions, books, articles, and

[1] Monograph No. 40, p. 104. An official English translation of the Argentine Act is given in the *Board of Trade Journal*, 1923, p. 530.

[2] Monograph No. 40, p. 130. [3] Monograph No. 40, p. 152.

[4] The earlier Dominion Anti-Trust legislation is reproduced in the Report on Anti-Trust Legislation in the British Self-Governing Dominions (1912–13, Cmd. 6439). Some later Statutes, together with an admirable discussion of the whole legislation, can be found in Philip Strickland's study, *Journal of Comparative Legislation and International Law*, 3rd Series, Vol. XVIII, 1936, p. 240, and Vol. XIX, 1937, p. 52. Moreover, the Australian Act is dealt with in an article by D. B. Copland and J. G. Norris, *Annals of the American Academy of Political and Social Science*, Vol. 147, (Jan. 1930), p. 117.

reports by official, semi-official, and non-official writers—makes it possible to form an independent view, whereas for all the other statutes quoted the material at our disposal seems too scanty as a basis for critical analysis.

II. In the U.S.A., it is the penal side that has been the most controversial in this hotly disputed field of legislation, and the tendency to turn away from penal to civil and, in particular, to administrative methods has found its expression in subsequent enactments such as the Clayton Act and the Federal Trade Commission Act, both of 1914, which contain no penal provisions. According to the interesting statistics given by Hamilton-Till,[1] there have been, in the first fifty years of its existence, altogether no more than 252 criminal actions under the Sherman Act, only 24 of which, involving 96 individual persons, resulted in sentences of imprisonment. During the same period, the number of cases in which fines were imposed was 97, involving about 1,500 individuals and corporations. In spite of these not very impressive figures, it would be a mistake to assume that the attempt to fight the evils of restraint of trade and of monopoly by penal legislation has been universally regarded as a failure by American expert and public opinion. A thorough analysis of the vast and extremely informative literature on the subject—up to the present day has the Sherman Act been living up to its early acquired reputation as " the most discussed statute of our time " [2]—shows, in spite of much criticism of detail, a not entirely negligible amount of support for the fundamental idea of the Act. And this support has come not only from those who, like Thurman Arnold,[3] Robert H. Jackson,[4] and Corwin D. Edwards,[5] have been playing a leading part in the official administration of the Anti-Trust laws, but also from independent lawyers, economists, and even business men.[6] However, granted

[1] Walton Hamilton and Irene Till, *Antitrust in Action* (No. 16 of Monographs published by the Temporary National Economic Committee, 1940), pp. 78–9 and App. A and B.

[2] Robert L. Raymond, *Journal of Political Economy*, Vol. XX, 1912, p. 315.

[3] *The Folklore of Capitalism* (1937) ; *The Bottlenecks of Business* (1940).

[4] *The Struggle for Judicial Supremacy* (1941).

[5] " Can the Antitrust Laws preserve Competition ? " (*American Economic Review*, Vol. XXX, Part 2 (March 1940), p. 164), and his recent paper " Thurman Arnold and the Antitrust Laws " (*Pol. Science Quarterly*, Vol. LVIII (Sept. 1943), p. 338), which gives an interesting survey of the five years of Thurman Arnold's leadership of the Antitrust Division of the Fed. Department of Justice. There is no doubt that during that period the criminal sections of the Sherman Act have been applied more energetically than ever before.

[6] See, for example, J. Harvey Williams, *Annals of the American Academy of Political and Social Science*, Vol. 165 (Jan. 1933), p. 72.

even that the penal side of the Sherman Act should have to be regarded as a complete practical failure, the mere fact, as such, would help but little to answer the crucial question put at the beginning of this discussion. It has, moreover, to be admitted that the practical effect of a penal statute does not wholly depend upon the number of convictions registered under it. Though never applied a statute may have considerable value as a deterrent.[1] Everything will therefore turn upon a detailed analysis of the various criticisms that have been made of the Sherman Act and its practical application. Do these criticisms touch something inherent in the very nature of the criminal law or are they concerned merely with weaknesses of a casual character which might be cleared away in the light of the experiences of the past fifty years?

A great many factors have been held responsible by American writers for the somewhat disappointing results of the Sherman Act.

(*a*) Faulty draftsmanship: Gerald C. Henderson, the historian of the Federal Trade Commission, even goes so far as to call the Statute against Forestallers, Regraters, and Engrossers of 1552 (5 and 6 Edw. VI, Chap. 14) "from the juristic viewpoint a much more highly developed product than the Sherman Act of 1890".[2] This verdict seems to be amply borne out by the wording of the relevant sections which make an offence "every contract, combination in the form of trust or otherwise, or conspiracy, in restraint of trade or commerce among the several States . . ." (sect. 1) and penalize "every person who shall monopolize, or attempt to monopolize, or combine or conspire with any other person or persons, to monopolize any part of the trade or commerce among the several States . . ." (sect. 2). No doubt, these are formulations which seem to go against all the old-established rules of legal draftsmanship in criminal legislation, handed over from generation to generation ever since the age of enlightenment. Instead of describing in simple terms the prohibited action, they penalize certain effects

[1] That the Sherman Act possesses some deterrent effect was not very long ago testified by a member of the New York Bar, W. G. Merritt, *Annals of the American Academy of Political and Social Science*, Vol. 147, Jan. 1930, p. 197. Hamilton-Till, op. cit., p. 80, and Thurman Arnold, *Bottlenecks of Business*, p. 209, have emphasized that a considerable stigma is attached in the American business world, not so much to actual convictions and sentences, which are rare, but to an indictment under the Sherman Act, a state of affairs which is, generally speaking, of course, far from desirable.

[2] *The Federal Trade Commission* (1924), p. 4.

of undefined actions, using antiquated legal conceptions of an ambiguous character and leaving almost everything to the discretion of the courts. Did not already Jeremy Bentham know that " Thou shalt not steal " could " never sufficiently answer the purpose of a law. A word of so vague and unexplicit a meaning can no otherwise perform this office, than by giving a general intimation of a variety of propositions each requiring, to convey it to the apprehension, a more particular and ample assemblage of terms ".[1] Penal legislation framed in too general terms, it has been said,[2] will necessarily include actions which should not be punishable and which the legislator himself never intended to include. It is for this reason that not only the Larceny Act of 1916 but probably every modern definition of theft dissolves the term " stealing " into a considerable number of components. In the Sherman Act, however, not the slightest attempt is made to define what constitutes a combination, a conspiracy, restraint of trade, or monopoly, although these terms appear to be much more difficult and in need of an authentic interpretation than words such as stealing, robbery, and perhaps even fraud. It is certainly strange that the non-penal Clayton Act should have been framed in far more explicit and definite terms than the essentially penal Sherman Act.[3] In one case, before the U.S. Supreme Court, the argument was indeed, unsuccessfully, brought forward by the defence that the Act was " so indefinite and vague as to be inoperative on its criminal side and against the requirement of due process of law ".[4] In short, in the words of an American writer, " a tale of little meaning, though the words are strong " [5] and, to quote one of its most eminent English critics, " a queer piece of drafting ".[6]

Or perhaps not quite so queer and devoid of meaning? A satisfactory answer to this question would, in fact, require a discussion of the whole problem of legislative technique in criminal matters as it appears to-day. The defence of the Sherman Act

[1] *Introduction to the Principles of Morals and of Legislation* (reprint of 1823 edition, Oxford), p. 331.

[2] Jerome Hall, *Theft, Law and Society* (1935), p. 67. See also Stephen, *History of Criminal Law*, Vol. III, p. 355.

[3] Compare, for example, the extremely vague terms of sect. 1 of the German *Reichsgesetz gegen den unlautern Wettbewerb* of June 7, 1909, which is concerned with damages, with the much more precise language of the penal section, sect. 4, of the same statute.

[4] Nash *v.* United States, 229 U.S. 373 (1913). See W. H. Taft, *The Anti-Trust Act and the Supreme Court* (1914), p. 109.

[5] H. Parker Willis, *Journal of Political Economy*, Vol. XX (1912), p. 590.

[6] Sir Frederick Pollock in the *Pollock-Holmes Letters*, Vol. I, p. 164.

has been conducted on the following lines : In the first instance, it has been said, the terms " restraint of trade " and, to a smaller extent, " monopoly " are old common law conceptions with a long history of judicial precedents behind them, and, as a consequence, the Act—" our economic common law ", as it has indeed been called [1]—if read " in the light of this body of authority, possessed a concreteness of meaning not otherwise apparent on its face ".[2] From this point of view, the Sherman Act was necessary only because it was believed that there was no " Federal common law ". However, even if this common law of restraint of trade would have been less ambiguous than it actually is,[3] it might be argued that it should not be the function of criminal legislation to preserve common law conceptions with all their vagueness. On the other hand, it is precisely that vagueness of the Sherman Act which has frequently been hailed as its greatest merit. When President Wilson, in 1914, recommended an " item-by-item " definition of the actions prohibited under the Act, this was rejected by Congress because of its " strait-jacketing effect ".[4] And all the principal spokesmen of the Anti-Trust Division have, again and again, emphasized the need for the greatest elasticity, without which the objects of the law would, it seems, have been altogether unattainable.[5] " Industry is on the move and restraint moves with it ".[6] As economic conditions and the organization and technique of industry and commerce undergo incessant transformations, the organization and technique of restraint and monopoly have to change as well. Moreover, every single branch of industry and commerce may require its own peculiar forms of restraint. From this, it follows that there are three courses open to the legislator who wants to employ the weapon of the criminal law in fighting restraint of trade and monopoly : either to frame his statute in the broadest and most general terms available, wide enough to cover any conceivable abuse that might in future arise, but at the same time flexible enough to make restrictive interpretation possible ; or, if it should be regarded as impera-

[1] Thurman Arnold, *The Bottlenecks of Business*, pp. 105 and 270.

[2] Milton Handler, *A Study of the Construction and Enforcement of the Federal Anti-Trust Laws* (No. 38 of the Monographs published by the Temporary Economic Committee, 1941), pp. 2 and 76.

[3] Milton Handler, p. 4. See also Wyndham White, *Journal of Comp. Legislation and International Law*, 3rd Series, Vol. XX (1938), p. 35.

[4] Milton Handler, p. 96.

[5] Thurman Arnold, *The Bottlenecks of Business*, pp. 132 et seq.

[6] Hamilton-Till, op. cit., p. 15.

tive to use specific and concrete terms, at least to make it permissible for the courts to extend the scope of the statute by means of analogy ; or, lastly, to change the wording of the statute at frequent intervals so as to keep up with changing economic conditions and techniques. The third method is likely to prove ineffective since economic conditions and techniques will usually move much faster than the pace of the law. Again, analogy to the disadvantage of the accused is, no less than the use of general terms, against the traditional principles of criminal law.[1] What else does, therefore, remain but the method used in the Sherman Act ? After all, it may be said, nobody takes exception to a statute which makes it a crime to " kill " without enumerating the various methods of killing.[2] There is, of course, the difference that, while there are no degrees of killing, restraint of trade and monopoly may appear in innumerable shades. With regard to monopoly, in particular, " the Supreme Court, unaided by history and unschooled by experience, was called upon to draw the line somewhere in the scale from 0 to 100 ".[3] One of the many problems which the Sherman Act forces upon us is the place within penal legislation of conceptions that are not only of a general character but require also an evaluation, as contrasted with purely factual conceptions. In some ways, the Sherman Act marks the beginning of a movement which has reached its peak in the National Socialist legislative technique of systematically permeating the whole body of the criminal law with conceptions of this type.[4] The suggestion has been made that the general clause of the Act should be supplemented by more specific prohibitions of particularly harmful trade practices.[5] While this may be useful as more clearly indicating the course the legislator wants to be taken, it cannot solve the problem itself.

No wonder, then, that soon after the passing of the Act certain important adjustments should have become necessary in the general policy of the courts.

[1] Analogy, *nullum crimen sine lege*, the creation of new common law offences on the model of Rex *v.* Manley (1933) 1 K.B. 529, and similar problems which loom in the background will be discussed below, Part II.

[2] See, however, Stephen, *History of the Criminal Law*, III, p. 3.

[3] Handler, op. cit., p. 76.

[4] See, for example, Freisler in Guertner, *Das kommende Deutsche Strafrecht, Bes. Teil*, pp. 52 et seq. Stephen, Vol. III, pp. 357–8, however, has also emphasized the need for such terms as " reasonably ", " manifestly ", " for the public good ", " in excess ". It may be noted that his *History* was published some years before the Sherman Act.

[5] Handler, p. 97.

(*b*) The Act, it was said, went too far. Under its general terms could be brought any kind of combination in restraint of trade, regardless of its merits and even when altogether inevitable. In one of the first cases decided by the Supreme Court [1] competing Railway Companies were prosecuted, in non-criminal proceedings, for having agreed to charge the same freight rates. " The layman naturally asks : what else could they do ? " [2] The Supreme Court, too, after a brief period of confusion, abandoned the " absolute " in favour of the " functional " interpretation of the Act, confining its prohibitions to " unreasonable " acts of restraint and monopoly. This functional test was applied, in particular, in the following directions [3] : Did the combination, etc., lead to a raising of consumer prices ?, to a limitation of production ?, to a deterioration in the quality of the product ?, to a decline in wages ?, to a lowering of the prices of raw materials ?, to unfair or oppressive treatment of competitors ? The change from the absolute to the functional interpretation, which took about twenty years,[4] was performed in spite of the refusal of Congress to introduce the test of reasonableness by way of legislation. While making the Sherman Act somewhat more concrete and meaningful, it still enabled the judges to apply the statute in the light of their own ideas, prejudices and experiences, and of their understanding of social and economic questions. The step taken by the Supreme Court has sometimes been attacked as an example of arbitrary and inadmissible " judicial legislation ", and in the face of the refusal of Congress to change the law it may have looked like it. In fact, however, it seems to have been nothing but a legitimate attempt to make the best of an otherwise unworkable statute. Of special interest is the defence of the rule of reason by William H. Taft, later Chief Justice of the Supreme Court and President of the United States :

> If the Court would have said : There are good trusts and bad trusts, and we have the power to say what are the good and the bad ones, according to our economic and political views . . . that would be legislation, not judicial power. The Court has only said that according to common law, which has to be used to interpret the statute, reasonable restraint was not intended to be included.[5]

[1] U.S. *v.* Trans-Missouri Freight Ass., 166 U.S. 290 (1897).

[2] James T. Young, *Annals of the Amer. Academy*, Vol. 147 (Jan. 1930), p. 171.

[3] For a detailed description of this change in judicial policy see Carl F. Taeusch, *Policy and Ethics in Business* (1931), pp. 113 et seq. Also Handler, op. cit., p. 3.

[4] Handler, p. 71.

[5] William H. Taft, *The Anti-Trust Act and the Supreme Court* (1914), p. 114. See also Allyn A. Young, *Journal of Political Economy*, Vol. XXIII (1915), p. 209.

On the other hand, Taft criticized the Australian Industries Preservation Act of 1906–10 for " conferring on the judges and courts a power which ought never to be entrusted to them. It is submitting not to their legal, but to their economic and business judgement questions for decision that are really legislative in character ".[1] It may be noted that under the Australian Act the courts have to decide, among other points, whether an action is intended to be " to the detriment of the public ", whether the preservation of a certain industry is " advantageous to the Commonwealth, having due regard to the interest of producers, workers, and consumers ". Having lived through the Thirty Years' War of the " *Freirechts-Schule* " since Taft's book was written, we have become more conscious of the artificial character of his distinctions. We now know that, however carefully we may draft our statutes, we shall never be able altogether to avoid " judicial legislation ". Nor can recourse to common law precedents secure for us absolution from this " sin ". Any differences that may exist in this respect between the Australian Act and the " rule of reason " will, at most, be differences in degree.

The critics of the Supreme Court may also have overlooked that a restrictive interpretation of a criminal statute is always permissible in favour of the accused, provided there are adequate reasons for it. The history of the administration of criminal justice shows an abundance of instances of this kind.[2] The real criticism which might justly be levelled against the Supreme Court is not that it introduced the test of reasonableness, but that it did not throughout apply it in an equitable manner. Proof of this, among others, the inclusion among the prohibited types of combinations of labour organizations without any test of reasonableness.[3] On the other hand, the initial exclusion of combinations of manufacturing firms from the scope of the Sherman Act[4] had the effect upon the public mind as well as upon Congress of discouraging hope " that the statute could be used to accomplish its manifest purpose and curb the great

[1] Taft, op. cit., p. 115.

[2] See also Stephen, *History*, Vol. III, p. 360 : " It is one thing to say that no one shall be convicted of a crime unless his conduct is explicitly condemned by a written law. It is another thing to say that no excuse for what would otherwise be a crime shall be admitted unless it is explicitly provided for by a written law."

[3] Thurman Arnold, *Folklore of Capitalism*, p. 212 ; Robert H. Jackson, *The Struggle for Judicial Supremacy*, p. 63 ; J. A. Emery, " Labour Organizations and the Sherman Law ", *Journal of Political Economy*, Vol. XX (1912), p. 899. On the present position Th. Arnold, *Bottlenecks of Business*, p. 249 ; moreover, the Apex Hosiery case, 60 Supr. Court 982 (1940) and the comment on it by R. Steffen, *50 Yale Law Journal* (1941), p. 787.

[4] United States *v.* Knight, 156 U.S.1 (1895).

industrial trusts ".[1] This initial mistake, though later reversed, presented the manufacturing trusts with sufficient breathing space for further growth until they had become too powerful for judicial interference.

(*c*) In other respects, too, the Act did not seem to go far enough in spite of its general terms. It prohibited combinations in restraint of trade, but was silent about complete mergers. The acquisition of a competitor was not regarded as restraint of trade by the courts, and only in exceptional cases was it treated as an attempt to establish a monopoly. This encouraged the growth of that very type of giant corporation which the Act had set out to prevent.[2] " Faced with the Sherman law against trusts, the promoters, who saw rich rewards to be obtained by the fusion of interests of a number of businesses, were forced to consider some such subterfuge as Holding Companies, and the expedient thus adopted has worked very well in practice ",[3]— " well " from the point of view of the promoters, of course. Another gap in the Sherman Act resulted from its insistence upon the existence of a " contract, combination, or conspiracy " as the only object of attack. Where price leadership was achieved by other means, i.e., by mutual imitation rather than by explicit agreement, the Act was powerless.[4] It is difficult to see, however, how this could be altogether avoided by a different formulation of the statute, although something might be achieved by way of a presumption that price leadership indicates agreement or monopoly.[5]

(*d*) So far attention has been drawn to some—by no means to all—of the weaknesses in the formulation of the Sherman Act and in its application by the Supreme Court of the U.S.A. It is, however, not only the drafting of the Act and its handling by the professional judges that are to blame. Other branches of the legal profession as well as a number of other legislative and administrative acts and omissions have to bear their fair share for any disappointment that may have occurred. There

[1] William H. Taft, op. cit., p. 60.

[2] Th. Arnold, *Folklore*, p. 276 ; *Bottlenecks*, p. 262 ; Corwin D. Edwards, *Am. Econ. Rev.* XXX, p. 178 ; Handler, op. cit., p. 85 ; Peter Drucker, *The Future of Industrial Man* (1943), p. 58 ; Hermann Levy, *The New Industrial System* (1936), p. 167 ; W. Arthur Lewis, *Modern Law Review*, Vol. VI (1943), p. 108 ; W. H. Hutt, *Plan for Reconstruction* (1943), p. 287.

[3] A. J. Simons, *Holding Companies* (1927), p. 4.

[4] See Note in *49 Yale Law Journal* (1940), p. 761 ; Handler, op. cit., p. 43. Lewis, p. 110.

[5] This is suggested by Handler, pp. 44–5.

seems to be general agreement, for instance, that the temporary sabotaging of the Anti-Trust laws by the National Recovery Act of 1933, declared null and void by the Supreme Court in 1935, has had an unfortunate effect. N.R.A. provided that the individual branches of industry could set up their own codes of business ethics, with the effect that actions which conformed to such codes were exempt from the Anti-Trust laws. This undermining of the authority of the Acts must have fostered among wide circles of the American people the view that the future belonged to unrestricted private monopoly anyhow.[1] There was, moreover, the complete failure of the Government to provide the necessary funds for the proper application of the Sherman Act. Dr. W. Arthur Lewis has already stressed the numerical inadequacy of the Anti-Trust Division's staff at the earlier stages of its history.[2] No less inferior seems to have been in former days their quality, at least if we are to judge from descriptions given by such writers as Professor Taeusch. Whereas, according to him, the ablest lawyers were employed by the trusts to defend them against charges under the Anti-Trust laws, muddle-headedness and inefficiency were the characteristics of many government lawyers.[3] As a result, even long before the passing of N.R.A., already under Harding, Coolidge, and Hoover, " industry enjoyed a moratorium from the Sherman Act ", and only the most flagrant violations were taken up.[4] The evils of this system of sporadic prosecution, of " token " or " ritual " enforcement,[5] have been exposed by many writers.[6] Even if a case was taken up, however, the Division had largely to rely upon the assistance of F.B.I. men, more or less unsuited for this special task.[7] On the other hand, the defence had at its disposal the biggest battalions and entered the battlefield fully equipped with the most modern and most expensive armament. In the Madison Oil case, we are told, there were for the defence no less than a hundred and one lawyers who had leased an entire hotel for the duration of the trial,[8] whereas the Anti-Trust Division had to be content with

[1] On N.R.A., see F. Zweig, *The Planning of Free Societies* (1942), p. 203 ; E. A. G. Robinson, *Monopoly*, p. 218 ; Robert H. Jackson, *The Struggle for Judicial Supremacy*, p. 109 ; Corwin D. Edwards, *Am. Econ. Rev.* XXX, p. 166 ; Wyndham White, loco cit., p. 40.

[2] *Modern Law Review*, Vol. VI, p. 107.

[3] Taeusch, op. cit., p. 110. Also Robinson, op. cit., p. 210.

[4] Robinson, quoting from Paul T. Homan, *Quarterly Journal of Economics*, Vol. 54 (1939–40), p. 222.

[5] Homan, loco cit., p. 90.

[6] E.g., Th. Arnold, *Bottlenecks of Business*, p. 191 ; Hamilton-Till, p. 41.

[7] Hamilton-Till, p. 40.

[8] Th. Arnold, *Bottlenecks*, p. 208.

seven lawyers.[1] Even in cases against small industries, however, the financial resources of the defendants greatly exceeded those of the prosecution.[2] Facts of this kind must necessarily give rise to the gravest doubts whether it is not an altogether hopeless undertaking to administer Anti-Trust laws of the Sherman Act type in a country otherwise dominated by big business.

Such doubts are still further confirmed by what we hear about the attitude of juries who, in the lower courts, had to deal with criminal charges under the Sherman Act. On their part, too, the administration of the law seems to have encountered certain obstacles which, on account of their typical character, are worthy of our attention. Considering that the Sherman Act owed its existence to the vague but very strong and widespread feeling of alarm and indignation at the unprecedented growth of the trust movement and the consequent concentration of power and wealth in the hands of a small number of individuals who exploited them mainly in their own selfish interests,[3] one should have expected that the man in the street of the type usually found on jury benches should have seized with perhaps even over-great zeal this opportunity of destroying that mortal enemy of his economic and political liberties. Nothing of this kind has happened. Observers are unanimous in complaining how difficult it proved to secure convictions under the Sherman Act. " In theory," writes William H. Taft,[4] " members of the public wish to draw blood, but when they are in a jury box they do not like to send their fellow-citizens to jail for doing what some years ago was only regarded as shrewd business." Even in cases where the evidence had been conclusive, the jury sometimes found the charges not proved, or, if they returned a verdict of guilty against the corporation, they acquitted its leading officials who had done all the actual work. A proposal to abolish the choice between imprisonment and fines was regarded as endangering the very existence of the Act, since juries would have never convicted if the only possible consequence of a verdict of guilty would have been prison.[5] As a result of his traditional upbringing and also of the political and economic pressure to which he was subjected, the average juryman regarded a violation of the Sherman Act as " an offence

[1] Hamilton-Till, p. 42. [2] Hamilton-Till, p. 44.

[3] See the now classical account of this development in Adolf A. Berle and Gardiner C. Means, *The Modern Corporation and Private Property* (1935).

[4] Op. cit., p. 131. Also Corwin D. Edwards, *Am. Econ. Rev.*, XXX, p. 174.

[5] Taft, p. 131.

so general, so abstract, so little tainted with a general and customary imputation of immorality " [1] as to have no proper place in a Penal Code. Occasional escapades such as the earlier English laws against engrossing and the like have never been really successful and are now long forgotten.

Nor have superstitions of this kind been confined to the average juryman. The most ardent and enlightened supporter of Anti-Trust legislation, Thurman Arnold himself, occasionally drops the remark that violations of the Sherman Act are no " ordinary crime " but are committed by " respectable people ".[2] In other words, the tradition, now dating back over some thousands of years, which attaches the stigma of crime exclusively to stealing and similarly primitive attacks on the economic system, cannot speedily be transformed so as to cover monopolistic tendencies as well. Modern criminal legislation has, within limits, and so far mainly confined to times of war and the immediate post-war periods, succeeded in building up a corresponding stigma for actions such as " profiteering ", which are now regarded as " just as bad as stealing ", probably because their ill effects are more directly felt by the man in the street. The evils of monopoly are usually too cleverly hidden to be realized by him. It is only in a Soviet State and through a legal system on the lines of the Soviet Penal Code, which deliberately uses the political weapon of criminal prosecution to shape the economic system according to its ideology, that old traditions of such strength can be comparatively quickly destroyed. In a capitalist democracy, it will inevitably take longer than half a century and require a much greater measure of moral and material support on the part of the community than has so far been forthcoming in the U.S.A. to make a statute of the Sherman Act type a success.

Among many other, more technical but nevertheless highly significant, points the unsuitability of the rules of criminal procedure and of the law of evidence for proceedings of this kind has to be particularly stressed. These rules have been evolved as the best method to discover the truth with regard to criminal behaviour consisting of comparatively simple acts such as killing, stealing, rape, arson, and the like, where most of the evidence can be supplied by witnesses. One of their objects is to keep the scope of the proceedings within narrow limits and to avoid any complication that might cause bewilderment to the un-

[1] Allyn A. Young, loco cit., p. 218.
[2] *Bottlenecks of Business*, pp. 135 and 97. Also Hamilton-Till, p. 78.

trained minds of the jury. In Anti-Trust prosecutions, the most important evidence may consist of documents, statistics, general trends of economic policy; and it is, as a rule, not one single act but a network of trade practices, involving perhaps the whole history of the building up of a giant company, that has to be presented to a court often unfamiliar with such topics and at every step hampered by the rules of evidence.[1] Those who have some personal experience of the technical problems involved in the disentanglement of big bankruptcy and fraud cases may be inclined to think that there is nothing out of the ordinary in this respect about Sherman Act prosecutions. There is, however, at least this additional difficulty: Whereas bankruptcy and fraud charges are usually directed against defendants who, after initial successes, have made a mess of things, prosecutions under the Sherman Act have to deal with the most prosperous adversaries at the height of their powers.

No wonder, then, that the tendency in the U.S.A. has been more and more in favour of administrative measures instead of criminal procedure, whether they may assume the official form of proceedings by the Federal Trade Commission or the unofficially developed form of an advisory opinion [2] or of the particularly interesting "consent decree",[3] none of which have so far proved entirely satisfactory.

III. *Conclusions.* The lessons to be drawn from this survey are fairly obvious. A few of them are mainly technical in character; others involve questions of principle and general policy; many of them, however, belong to both categories at the same time. Certain of the difficulties arise from the attempt to solve problems of high economic policy by means of the criminal law; others are common to any legal machinery in this field.

Emile Durkheim [4] has pointed out that "the only common characteristic of all crimes is that they consist . . . in acts universally disapproved of by members of each society . . . crime shocks sentiments which, for a given social system, are found in all healthy consciences". Although this requirement of universal disapproval may appear somewhat exaggerated, there can be no doubt that without the backing of at least the

[1] See for example, Hamilton-Till, pp. 41, 51, 58, and passim; Corwin D. Edwards, *Am. Econ. Rev.*, XXX, p. 172.

[2] Hamilton-Till, p. 86.

[3] Thurman Arnold, *Bottlenecks of Business*, p. 141; Hamilton-Till, p. 88.

[4] *Division of Labor in Society* (English translation by George Simpson, 1933), pp. 70 et seq.

major part of the community criminal legislation, in a democracy, must fail. Such support will be forthcoming only if individual members are conscious of the real meaning of the law, its objects, and its necessity. Closely connected with this is the other requirement that each single piece of criminal legislation should be in harmony with the social and economic structure and the whole ideology of the community in which it is expected to function. That structure and ideology cannot be changed by means of haphazard and sporadic legislative titbits.

How far does the Sherman Act comply with these basic requirements? At the time when it was passed the Act might have been regarded as the incarnation and logical fulfilment of that philosophy of *laissez-faire* and free competition which dominated American life. Now, that idol has irretrievably lost its former splendour and its absolute character, and nothing is any more taken for granted in this sphere. Free competition, just as monopoly, may be good or bad according to circumstances, and, to a large extent, the real issue is no longer between these two alternatives but between private or public monopoly. Sherman Act enthusiasts, no less than the Supreme Court, have, of course, not failed to realize these complications. Proof of this is not only the introduction of the rule of reason but also the repeated assurance that it is not "bigness as such", not "mere size", but bigness leading to inefficiency that has to be fought.[1] This tactical change of front, however, was bound to deprive the Act of most of its emotional appeal to the man in the street. To stamp out murder, kidnapping, robbery, rape, and profiteering may have a magic of its own. There is little glamour in charges of "restraint" and "monopoly" as soon as they are diluted with the "rule of reason" and the test of inefficiency. If efficiency is the keynote, the whole struggle may lose its moral background, and, after all, there are other values besides efficiency worth fighting for. Again, is it practicable to select for criminal prosecution just one isolated type of abuse of economic power in a social, economic, legal, and political system otherwise based upon the principle, and imbued with the spirit, of private profit-making? It is neither particularly fair nor is it likely to succeed. Business men, it has been said, are torn between the desire to have all the advantages of monopoly for themselves and all the disadvantages of free competition for their competitors, and, at last, racketeering has presented a

[1] Thurman Arnold, *Bottlenecks of Business*, pp. 3–4 and passim.

temporary, though not altogether desirable, solution by offering that protection against the abuses of competition which monopoly could no longer give.[1]

All this justifies Laski's verdict that " the scale of the problem is beyond the power of a government that is subject to the normal pressure politics of capitalist democracy ".[2] And there is in this respect but a difference in degree between the criminal, the civil, and the administrative side of Anti-Trust legislation. Such a difference does, however, exist. The criminal law has, quite definitely, to play an important part in the matter, but, here as in so many other branches of modern legislation, it cannot fulfil its task unaided. A good deal of the failure of the Sherman Act has been due, it seems, to two legislative mistakes : first, to the placing of an over-great burden on the criminal sections of the statute and, secondly, to the absence of any organic link between them and the existing administrative machinery.

Monopoly legislation, one is tempted to say, can properly work only if that pressure to which Laski refers is removed or, at least, considerably relaxed. However, as such relaxation of the " normal pressure politics of capitalist democracy " is itself one of the principal purposes of monopoly legislation, it is difficult to avoid the awkward feeling that one may be constantly moving in a vicious circle. This point, as one of high policy, is outside the scope of the present discussion, and, though for different reasons, the same is true of the required reform of Patent Law and Company Law. A further *conditio sine qua* would seem to be the stiffening of the criminal law concerning white-collar crime in general so as to provide a suitable background for the inclusion of monopoly offences. All this done, four problems of a slightly more technical character remain for the legislator. Naturally, above anything else the question will require a clear answer whether one wants to prohibit monopoly as such or only " bad " monopoly. This implies, second, some knowledge as to what constitutes " badness " in this field, and, third, the ability to express such knowledge in terms suitable for application by courts or administrative boards. Finally, there is the task of drawing the right line of demarcation between civil, criminal, and administrative law, and between courts and administration.

From our summary of existing Anti-Trust Laws it seems that, apart from the Sherman Act, no statute prohibits " monopoly "

[1] See the interesting remarks by Donald R. Taft, *Criminology* (1942), p. 188.
[2] Harold J. Laski, *Reflections on the Revolution of our Time* (1943), p. 325.

as such. Unless industry should become altogether nationalized, which is for the time being beyond the reach of practical politics, the existence of private monopolies on a fairly big scale is inevitable.[1] They have received too much encouragement, official and non-official, and become too convenient and too powerful to be abolished at a stroke. Legislation can, therefore, be directed only against certain exaggerations and abuses. These dangers of monopoly may be summed up, in the words of Mr. Herbert Morrison's brilliant Fabian lecture,[2] as inefficiency, exploitation, and, greatest of all, the political menace: the " peril of the Over-Mighty Subject ". The first two may be not altogether out of reach for ordinary legislative technique. An attempt will have to be made either to define a number of prohibited practices, such as the unjustifiable raising of prices, arbitrary restriction of output, and many others, or to find a general formula to characterize " badness " in terms of inefficiency and exploitation. Some of the foreign laws referred to above try to combine both methods, and, as we have seen, this has also been recommended by American writers (above, p. 160). A " general " formula may be truly general, i.e., it may characterize " badness " simply as something which is " against the public interest " (e.g., Australia) ; or it may try to explain what, in the view of the legislator, goes against the public interest (e.g., France : " profit other than that derived from the natural operations of the law of supply and demand ", which is plainly unworkable, or Argentine : " acts which, without representing technical or economic progress, arbitrarily increase the personal profit . . ."). All such explanatory phrases ran the risk of remaining either useless commonplaces or dangerous half-truths taken from out-of-date economic textbooks. The choice, therefore, seems to be between a truly general formula (" against the public interest ") and a detailed description of specific activities, or a combination of both. " The law ", it has recently been argued by Mr. E. F. Schumacher in a well-balanced and thoughtful paper,[3] " cannot easily go beyond illegalizing actions that can

[1] The reasons given by Elliott Dodds (*Let's Try Liberalism*, p. 64) for his view that most monopolies are not inevitable are convincing probably only for a small minority of industries.

[2] " The State and Industry," in *Can Planning be Democratic?* (1944), pp. 15–16.

[3] " An Essay on State Control of Business," *Agenda*, Vol. III (Feb. 1944), p. 50. In this essay, a distinction is made between State control by legislation, administration, representation, and participation. The author, who is particularly in favour of control by " participation ", regards control by legislation as the least effective form. " If it is extended into too much detail and spread over too wide a field, it runs the risk of compromising the very idea of law and legality" (p. 52).

be proved to be against 'the public interest'. Yet what is for or against the public interest is just one of the most tricky questions imaginable". And, indeed, as indicated above, each of the possible methods of drafting, the general as well as the specific one, has its weaknesses. It can hardly be said that the one is always superior to the other. Where a strong and homogeneous body of experience and tradition has been built up in a prolonged struggle with certain practical problems, a general clause may be all that is needed. In the case of a Statute destined to operate on virgin soil, however, phrases like "reasonable", "public interest", and the like, have too little meaning,[1] and it will be wise to supplement that clause by a catalogue enumerating the principal types of prohibited activities. A catalogue which, on the model of the Finance Acts in their fight against tax avoidance,[2] may have to be annually revised. On a few outstanding types of prohibited practices, a certain amount of agreement seems already to exist among experts from outside the Trusts themselves. *The Economist*[3] suggests a law:

> to make it definitely illegal for associations or agreements to fix minimum prices or maximum quotas of output without specific permission from some public authority . . .

and Professor Hutt's "Resources Utilization Protection Bill" contains a somewhat similar clause.[4] The question of drafting is, moreover, also closely bound up with that of distribution of powers between judiciary and administration. If the application of the Anti-Trust Act is in the hands of administrative authorities a general clause may be preferable, to be interpreted, whenever the need arises, by ministerial regulations. In the case of a court, however, more details will have to be included in the statute.

This leads to the final question posed above: Where is the right line of demarcation between civil and administrative law, on the one hand, and criminal law, on the other? Is it indispensable to buttress an Anti-Trust Act by penal provisions, and of what kind? Looking at the matter in isolation, one might feel inclined, as much as possible, to dispense with penal protection in dealing with a problem of general economic policy. On the other hand, the close affinity which, in its economic, social and psychological implications, it bears to other forms of abuse

[1] Stephen (see above, p. 160 fn. 4) could not anticipate the vast complexity of the problems that might lurk behind such phrases.

[2] See Chapter 8 B (*b*).

[3] June 24, 1944, p. 834.

[4] *Plan for Reconstruction*, p. 32.

of financial power now commonly treated as criminal offences makes it imperative to use the resources of the criminal law in the fight against " bad " monopoly. Being not less but in many instances even more anti-social in their consequences and constituting a greater, though less open, menace to the community than profiteering, share-pushing, usury, and the like—not to mention theft and other small fry—, it would be too much against the idea of social justice to leave abuses of monopoly altogether outside the criminal law. In future, we shall have to get used to the idea that not only the protection *of* property but also the protection *against* property falls under the scope of the criminal law. In spite of his practical failure, the American legislator can at least claim to have drawn the consequences from this truth. It is for his successors to avoid his mistakes.

The first lesson to be learnt is that criminal courts should never be asked to apply an Anti-Trust Act framed in general terms, such as " against the public interest ", or the like [1]—not because this would mean " judicial legislation ", but because it would, almost inevitably, mean *bad* judicial legislation. Second, as proved by the fate of the Sherman Act, to have monopoly charges tried by juries as at present constituted is expecting the impossible. Even courts consisting entirely of professional judges, whatever may be their legal qualifications, are however likely to fail. In the U.S.A. as well as under English common law " the judges were forced . . . not so much to interpret the law as to act as social philosophers, political scientists and economists. . . . In this rôle the judges were far from expert ".[2] Nor would it substantially improve matters if, instead of a general formula or combined with it, a catalogue of strictly defined offences were to be worked out in what may appear to the legislator unequivocal terms, such as " fixing minima prices " or " restricting output "—even if, as suggested above, this catalogue would be annually revised. Changing conditions may make any definition assume a different meaning, and, above all, nothing could prevent the courts from introducing, not *contra* but *praeter legem*, a " rule of reason ", as they understand it, in favour of the accused. For the time being, it may, therefore, be necessary to make the findings of those administrative bodies which will be dealing with the non-penal side of monopoly binding on the criminal court. Judicial discretion will have to be limited,

[1] See also Elliott Dodds, *Let's Try Liberalism*, p. 70.
[2] Hutt, *Plan for Reconstruction*, p. 223.

apart from control of procedure, to strictly individual aspects, i.e., the question of subjective guilt, and to the finding of the sentence, and even here it may have to be curtailed by high statutory minimum penalties on the model of recent war-time profiteering legislation. This would mean an amount of interference with the powers of the courts as great, or even greater than, for instance, that suggested in the case of tax avoidance.[1] Its justification is the, for the outsider, unusually complicated nature of monopoly disputes. Tax avoidance, though it may also appear in a great variety of disguises, has at least only one single purpose which runs through the whole structure, determines the activities of the dodger, and can, as a rule, be laid bare by any capable accountant. In profiteering cases, there exists at least the normal price policy of the honest trader as a basis for comparison with that of the profiteer. Problems of monopoly, however, may touch not only one set of transactions of one firm—they may affect the life of an entire industry or branch of industries.

As Anti-Trust Acts of the future may be expected to contain a considerable number of purely technical provisions requiring public registration of associations and their agreements and many other forms of publicity,[2] the assistance of the criminal law will have to be invoked to safeguard their observance. This second set of penal provisions may, in the course of time, even assume a greater practical significance than the first-mentioned catalogue of prohibited trade practices.

There may, however, still be a third task awaiting the criminal law. It is the task, alluded to by Mr. Herbert Morrison, of dealing with " the peril of the Over-Mighty Subject ". In its domestic as well as in its international aspects, which latter have recently gained so much publicity through the various steps taken by the U.S.A. Attorney General, this can truly be regarded as one of the most dangerous modern forms of high treason. It is for the penal law reformer to adapt the law of high treason to these new requirements.

To sum up, three sets of penal provisions will be required to deal with the problem of Monopoly : a catalogue of prohibited practices ; provisions to enforce publicity and other technical safeguards ; and, finally, a revised law of industrial high treason.

[1] See Chapter 8 B (*b*).

[2] A few details are given, with further references, by Mr. Schumacher, loco cit., p. 48, who describes them as " mostly admirable in themselves " but falling short of State control proper. See also *The Times*, June 16, 1944, on " Trade Associations."

Chapter 9

THE PROTECTION OF LABOUR AND THE PROTECTION AGAINST LABOUR

The large body of modern legislation for the protection of labour which exists in every civilized country to-day clearly needs enforcement through penal provisions. Apart from the usual points of legislative technique, no questions of principle seem to arise with regard to any of them. In practice, most complaints are directed against the frequent inadequacy of the penalties provided by the law and actually imposed by the courts on employers for violation of statutes which are of vital importance for life and health of workers.[1] Moreover, it has been stressed in certain quarters that the ability to work, as the principal, or even only, asset of most people, should be afforded at least the same protection by the criminal law as property. It is in particular Nazi propaganda that has exploited this popular idea in order to put forward a number of far-reaching but rather nebulous proposals : it has been suggested, for instance, to make it a criminal offence to cause an industrial stoppage and long-term unemployment through " frivolous squandering of the means of production ".[2]

Much more complex and controversial is the question of how the resources of the criminal law should be used to protect the community against possible abuses on the part of labour. There is no need for us to deal with the history of that extremely intricate part of English law which makes the very existence of combinations of workers a criminal offence. Its details have been told in several excellent treatises,[3] and it is unlikely to present any practical problems for the future. Social values and policies have so unmistakably changed that there is little danger of the criminal law once more becoming a weapon against Trade Unionism as such. For all practical purposes, it is exclusively against strikes, absenteeism, and actions connected

[1] See *Social Aspects of Crime in England*, p. 61.
[2] Grau in Guertner, *Das kommende deutsche Strafrecht, Besonderer Teil*, pp. 231 et seq.
[3] See, for example, Sir Henry Slesser and Charles Baker, *Trade Union Law* (3rd ed., 1927) ; W. Milne-Bailey, *Trade Unions and the State* (1934) ; C. M. Lloyd, *Trade Unionism* (3rd ed., 1928). On the law of conspiracy : Holdsworth, op. cit., Vol. VIII, pp. 378 et seq. ; Kenny, *Outlines*, Chapter XVIII ; Stephen, *History*, Vol. III, pp. 206 et seq. ; Dicey, *Law and Opinion*.

with them, that its protection is being and will be sought. To treat strikes as an offence was flagrantly illogical and unfair in the days of the *laissez-faire* economy of the past. In a planned society things may be different. If the law punishes the owner who fails to use his property to the best advantage of the community or resorts to unjustified lock-outs it is at least arguable that the worker who, without adequate reasons, withholds his labour should not take his immunity any longer for granted. Provided both sides—employer and employee—are treated on an equal footing, or if the State becomes the employer, the whole question, it might be said, is transformed from one of social justice into one of mere expediency. This is, of course, a fairly big proviso. And, even so, the argument may overlook the fundamental psychological and economic differences in the relationship between man and his property, on the one hand, and man and his labour, on the other.

I. Strikes and the Criminal Law.

In accordance with the general plan of this book, it is the main object of the following discussion to find an answer to the question whether the criminal law is a suitable machinery of dealing with strikes as such. It is not intended, therefore, to give anything like a complete picture of the existing law on the subject. We are, in particular, not here concerned with the wider criminological implications of strikes,[1] i.e., with ordinary crime committed in the course of a strike, nor even with specific aspects such as picketing.

Roughly speaking, the following basic types of legislation can be distinguished regarding the use of the criminal law in dealing with strikes : [2]

(*a*) Criminal legislation is not concerned with strikes as such. The State provides some legal machinery to promote voluntary arbitration and peaceful settlement of industrial disputes, without using compulsion or attaching any penalties to strikes entered into in disregard of such machinery.

(*b*) Even in countries where this principle of voluntary arbitration and absence of penalties is generally upheld, exceptions are sometimes made either for industries which are regarded as of vital importance for the community ; or for certain categories

[1] On this, see Edwin E. Witte, *The Government in Labor Disputes* (1932), Chapters VIII and IX, and the present author's, *Social Aspects of Crime in England between the Wars* (1940), pp. 153 et seq.

[2] See *Encycl. of the Social Sciences*, art. " Strikes and Lockouts ".

of strikes, as, for example, so-called general or political, or sympathetic, or "closed shop" strikes: in such cases, striking as such may become a criminal offence. The same may happen in time of war to strikes which fall under none of these special categories. Also fairly frequent is, in peace and in war, penal legislation restricted to instigators or leaders of strikes.

(*c*) Countries belonging to the third group have in common that, under their laws, strikes are treated as criminal offences not only in exceptional circumstances but as a matter of principle, and not only with regard to instigators and leaders but also with regard to the rank and file.

This tripartite scheme provides, however, only the framework within which there is room for so many shades that it is sometimes difficult to determine to which group a country actually belongs. This applies in particular to the line of demarcation between groups (*b*) and (*c*), i.e., by far the strongest and most important categories. Great Britain, before the war an example of group (*b*), may now have to be regarded as a member of group (*c*) although in theory the possibility is not entirely ruled out that a strike may be legal. Whereas Germany, Russia, and Fascist Italy were clear examples of group (*c*), the case of Australia, whose history of federal strike legislation has seen many changes, is at least doubtful.[1] Up to 1930, in the event of a strike, fines could be imposed by the Commonwealth Arbitration Court under the Commonwealth Conciliation and Arbitration Acts, 1904–28; but in 1930 this was repealed except for the power of the Court to insert in an award a clause prohibiting a strike under threat of penalties.[2] Though war-time legislation (Regulations of February, 1942) has restored the previous power of the Arbitration Court to impose penalties,[3] it is unlikely that any considerable use has been made of it as, in the view of the Australian legislature and judiciary, "it is not desirable that the Court should impose penalties for breaches of the Act, since it is essentially an arbitrator".[4]

Equally difficult is it, because of considerable differences according to time and place, to define the proper place of the U.S.A. in the tripartite scheme. Apart from extreme cases such as Kansas, where, under a short-lived Act of 1920, every

[1] See on it the two books by Orwell de R. Foenander, *Towards Industrial Peace in Australia* (1937) and *Wartime Labour Developments in Australia* (1943).
[2] de Foenander, *Towards Industrial Peace*, p. 58.
[3] de Foenander, *Wartime Labour Developments*, p. 27.
[4] Ibidem, p. 25.

strike constituted an offence,[1] and California where it was entirely lawful, State legislation and jurisdiction up to 1932 used to distinguish according to the motives and purposes behind the strike. In practice, the American scene was dominated by the Labour Injunction,[2] which was largely regarded as a preventive machinery designed to strengthen the power of the criminal law. While such injunctions often prohibited only the use of violence in labour disputes, sometimes they went further and forbade workers to go on strike.[3] Violations could be dealt with as contempt of court, either by civil or by criminal proceedings,[4] and in the latter case punished by fines or imprisonment. This state of the law seems to have brought the U.S.A. under group (*b*) or even group (*c*). The Clayton Act of 1914 did not greatly improve matters, and it was left to the Norris-La Guardia Act of 1932 to disallow in labour disputes the issuing of injunctions which prohibit workers to strike. Soon afterwards the necessary arbitration machinery was created under the New Deal by the National Industrial Recovery Act, 1933, and after its repeal by the National Labour Relations Act, 1935.[5] The war brought several restrictions of the right to strike : first, under President Roosevelt's Proclamation of May 27, 1941, the right of the Government to take over the operation of plant and to break strikes by the use of regular troops, and, after the U.S.A. had entered the war, the Smith-Conally Act of 1943. Even the latter, however, does not go so far as to threaten penalties on individual strikers.

We may now pass to recent English strike legislation. Although as a result of the coexistence of a great mass of complicated statutes, many questions of detail are still open to doubt, this at least seems to be beyond dispute : The Conspiracy and Protection of Property Act, 1875, sect. 3, in spite of its extremely vague and cautious language, is said to have

> freed strikes and other combinations from criminality . . . provided that they were in contemplation or furtherance of a trade dispute between employers and workmen, that they were for the commission

[1] Witte, pp. 255 et seq.

[2] The literature on the subject is enormous ; the following books deserve special mention : Felix Frankfurter and Nathan Greene, *The Labour Injunction* (1930) ; Duane McCracken, *Strike Injunctions in the New South* (1931) ; Gordon S. Watkins, *Labour Problems* (rev. ed. 1929) ; Edwin E. Witte, op. cit., with comprehensive bibliography.

[3] Witte, p. 97.

[4] Witte, p. 99.

[5] On this development see Florence Peterson, Chief, Industrial Relations Division, Bureau of Labor Statistics, Washington, in *Intern. Labour Review*, Vol. 41 (1940), pp. 479 et seq.

of some act which would not be a crime apart from the combination, that they did not involve a conspiracy punishable by statute, and that they were not breaches of the law relating to riot, unlawful assembly, breach of the peace, sedition, or any offence against the State or the Sovereign.[1]

It is, however, an offence for persons employed in gas or water supply services wilfully and maliciously to break their contracts, knowing the probable consequences of such action (sect. 4), and this was extended to electricity workers by the Electricity (Supply) Act, 1919, sect. 31. Moreover, malicious breach of contract was made an offence if the worker had reasonable cause to believe that it would involve serious injury to persons or property (sect. 5). Finally, after the General Strike of 1926 several penal provisions were added by the Trade Disputes and Trade Unions Act of 1927, notably against sympathetic and political strikes,[2] and to sect. 4 of the Act of 1875 a provision was added prohibiting corresponding breaches of contract by persons employed by local or other public authorities.

The two world wars brought further important restrictions of the right to strike and penal provisions for strikers. The Munitions of War Act, 1915,[3] rendered strikes and lockouts illegal and subject to fines for each day of contravention unless the Board of Trade had failed to refer the dispute for settlement to the appropriate authority within 21 days after the matter had been referred to the Board. The Act provided machinery for the settlement of industrial differences by compulsory arbitration through the Board of Trade and established Munition Tribunals which were competent, among other matters, to punish offenders. These Tribunals, which " represented a new departure in the English system of judiciary ", were held to be more suitable than the criminal courts to deal with a lawbreaker whom it would have been " both absurd and unfair to regard as in the ordinary sense a criminal ".[4] Two other provisions of the Act are also characteristic of its spirit : According to sect. 15 (4), imprisonment in default of fines imposed by the Tribunals was not permissible ; it was the intention of the legislator to achieve his object without resorting to imprisonment.

[1] This is how sect. 3 is summarized by Mr. Milne-Bailey, op. cit., p. 182.

[2] Neither the word " sympathetic " nor the words " political " or " general " strike are used in the Act.

[3] An admirable account of the working of this Act is given in Humbert Wolfe's *Labour Supply and Regulation* (Economic and Social History of the World War, British Series, 1923).

[4] Humbert Wolfe, op. cit., p. 110.

Instead, the Tribunal was entitled to order deductions to be made from the offender's wages. This prohibition, which at first applied only to minor offences, was made general in 1916 as certain cases in which imprisonment had actually been employed had led to profound dissatisfaction. On the other hand, the Act did not apply to incitement to strike, which could be dealt with much more severely under Defence Regulations.[1]

It is difficult retrospectively to assess the effect of these penal sanctions on the frequency of strikes in England during the first world war. The material which Humbert Wolfe produces[2] " in the hope of throwing some light on the question whether the prohibition of strikes and compulsory arbitration are in fact a means of securing industrial harmony " cannot, in the nature of things, be altogether conclusive. On the one hand, only a fortnight after the coming into force of the Act, 200,000 Welsh miners went on strike " in defiance of the Munitions Act and, instead of being punished, won practically the whole of their claims ".[3] Illegal strikes continued to occur on a fairly large scale in 1916 and particularly in 1917. In comparatively few cases the men were prosecuted and fined. As already mentioned, the power of the Tribunals, reluctantly used in a few cases, to inflict imprisonment for non-payment of fines, had soon to be abolished, and before its abolition very strong pressure was exerted on the Government for the release of the imprisoned men. In the Clydeside strike, out of a large number of strikers only seventeen men had been prosecuted and fined ; of the total fine of £170 not a penny had been paid by the men themselves, and it was argued that the proceedings had disturbed production almost as much as the strike. In another case, too, none of the twenty-eight men tried paid their fines, nor was any attempt made to compel them to pay. On the other hand, it has to be stressed that the total figures of working days lost through strikes and of workers involved were considerably lower during the war than before, and also that in certain particularly serious cases it was actually possible to carry out fairly long prison sentences or deportation orders on a number of leaders without provoking protest strikes of any dimensions in reply.[4]. It is difficult, however, to say whether this favourable result was due to the existence of penal provisions or rather to the patriotic

[1] Wolfe, pp. 123–4. [2] See his Chapter VIII.

[3] G. D. H. Cole and others, *British Trade Unionism To-day* (1939), p. 61 ; see also Wolfe, p. 126.

[4] Milne-Bailey, p. 42 ; Wolfe, pp. 132–3.

feeling of the workers or perhaps to the threat, used by the Government in the later stages of the war, to call up strikers for military service. Although in all probability these two last-mentioned factors were stronger, the fact that a strike constituted an offence, and even more perhaps its mere illegality, may also have contributed to the eventual success.

In the 1939–45 war, the legal position of strikes [1] was not altogether identical with what it was in 1914–18. In both cases, strikes became criminal offences within the first year of the hostilities, and special machinery had to be established for compulsory arbitration. In 1940, the legal basis was provided by the Emergency Powers (Defence) Act, 1940, and Defence Regulation 58AA, which came into force on July 7, 1940.[2] Under powers given to him by the latter, the Minister of Labour made the " Conditions of Employment and National Arbitration Order " of July 18, 1940.[3] It established the National Arbitration Tribunal and, following in the footsteps of the Munition Act of 1915, provided in art. 4 that—

> An employer shall not declare or take part in a lockout and a worker shall not take part in a strike in connection with any trade dispute unless the dispute has been reported to the Minister in accordance with art. 2 of this Order and twenty-one days have elapsed since the date of the report and the dispute has not during that time been referred by the Minister for settlement in accordance with the provisions of that Article.

Any contraventions of this art. 4 are punishable under Defence Regulation 92, on summary conviction by imprisonment up to three months or a fine up to £100 or both, and on indictment by imprisonment up to two years or a fine up to £500 or both, whereas in the case of a body corporate the maximum amount of the fine is unlimited.

The effect of art. 4 has been to make any strike in connection with a trade dispute illegal for the first twenty-one days after the dispute was reported to the Minister of Labour and for an indefinite time afterwards, provided the Minister refers the matter within that period to the National Arbitration Tribunal, which he will do in the case of any major dispute. In theory, it is

[1] See on it in particular the illuminating analysis by Mr. D. N. Pritt, K.C., M.P., " Defence Regulation 1AA " (published by the National Council for Civil Liberties, 1944) and his speech of April 28, 1944, in the House of Commons (Hansard, cols. 1099–1111) ; moreover, Dr. O. Kahn-Freund's valuable paper, " Collective Agreements under War Legislation " in *Modern Law Review*, April, 1943, pp. 125 et seq.

[2] S.R. & O. 1940, No. 1217.

[3] S.R. & O. 1940, No. 1305.

therefore true to say that, here as in the war of 1914, the prohibition of strikes is only conditional; it is equally true, however, that in practice "it is almost impossible for any strike to be legal".[1]

It is of considerable interest to examine the actual part played by the criminal law in the suppression of strikes during the second world war.

	Number of Strikes.	Number of Workers Involved.	Number of Working Days Lost.
1938	875	275,300	1,334,000
1939	940	337,300	1,356,000
1940	922	299,000	940,000
1941	1,251	360,000	1,080,000
1942	1,303	456,000	1,527,000
1943	1,785	559,000	1,810,000
1944	2,194	826,000	3,710,000

(Taken from the Ministry of Labour Gazette.)

The corresponding figures of prosecutions are less easily obtainable. On April 20, 1944, the following information was given in the House of Commons by the Minister of Labour on the number of employers and workers prosecuted and imprisoned for "offences against the industrial code which were not punishable before the outbreak of the present war": [2]

> Up to February 29, 1944, 127 employers and 23,517 workers prosecuted in England and Wales for the offences mentioned, 1,807 workers and no employers sentenced to imprisonment.

As these figures include other industrial offences, particularly absenteeism, besides strikes, it is impossible from the information given to draw any conclusions as to the exact figures. It is obvious, however, that the total of workers prosecuted for illegal strikes must have remained substantially below 23,517. Nevertheless, it can be inferred from press reports that not infrequently prosecutions have actually taken place against fairly considerable numbers of working people. The following instances may be quoted: [3]

[1] Pritt, Hansard, col. 1103.
[2] *The Times*, April 21, 1944; Hansard, vol. 399, col. 343.
[3] Taken from *The Times*.

Date.	Place.	Number of Workers Prosecuted.	Penalties Imposed.	Total of Workers Involved.
Jan. 1942 :	Betteshanger Colliery, Deal, Kent	1,017	3 prison sentences of up to 2 months; the others fined £1 to £3 each [1]	"Over 1,000"
April 1942 :	Blairhall Colliery, Dunfermline, Scotland	24	Fined £5 each	Unknown
Oct. 1942 :	Lincolnshire Road Car Comp., Lincoln	135	Fined 15s. each	Unknown
May 1943 :	Hatfield Main Colliery, near Doncaster	67	Fined £3 each for each shift lost	Unknown
May 1943 :	Radiator & Press Work Company, Coventry	93	Fined £25 each	Unknown
Aug. 1943 :	Hatton Garden Industry, London	73	Fined £2 to £35 each	Unknown
Oct. 1943 :	Western Auchengeich Colliery, near Glasgow	72	Fined £3 each	Unknown
Feb. 1944 :	Waleswood Colliery, Rotherham	700	Case dismissed on technical grounds	Unknown
Feb. 1944 :	Glapwell Colliery, Chesterfield	157	"Decision reserved for 6 months to see how the men worked"	1,500
Nov. 1944 :	Bradford Road Gas-works, Manchester	36	Fined £10 each (under Act of 1875)	Unknown
Dec. 1944–Jan. 1945	Walker-on-Tyne Naval Yard, Vickers-Armstrong	125 [2]	Fined £10 each	550
Nov. 1944–Jan. 1945	Manchester (Bradford Rd.) Gas-works	36	Fined £10 each [3]	At one time apparently more than 300

[1] The greater part of the prison sentences was apparently remitted after a few weeks had been served.
[2] These 125 men seem to have been on work of particular urgency.
[3] The strike spread when the men were committed to prison in default and ended when the fines were paid by the manager.

In other cases, the complaint has been made in the Press and elsewhere that the total of penalties has been negligible in relation to the numbers of strikers or that no prosecutions have taken place at all even in the case of strikes involving considerable numbers of men and causing great loss of output.[1] Mrs. Barbara Wootton, on the other hand, regards it as "a charming piece of illogicality, and one on which we might do well to build", that so many illegal strikes have taken place "without any penalties apparently being imposed on anybody".[2] This somehow reminds us of Oliver Goldsmith's "cosmopolitan Chinaman who maintained, among other fanciful actions, the paradox that it was the height of wisdom to fill the statute book with laws threatening offenders with most severe penalties which were rarely or never exacted".[3]

An important feature has been the tendency of large bodies of workers to go on strike in order to enforce the release from prison or to prevent the prosecution or imprisonment of some of their mates dealt with for offences against the anti-strike Regulations. A few such cases may be quoted:

> Some 20,000 shipyard workers in Belfast on strike as a protest against the refusal of the Northern Ireland Minister of Home Affairs to release five men imprisoned for taking part in a strike of aircraft workers.[4]
>
> Nearly 3,000 miners in Lanarkshire on strike as a protest against the arrest of six miners who failed to pay fines of £5 each, imposed in connection with a previous unofficial strike.[5]
>
> Round 15,000 Nottinghamshire miners, more than half the miners in the county, on strike because of the imprisonment of an 18-year-old surface worker who had refused to work underground. After serving one week of his one month's sentence the lad changed his mind and was released, whereupon the men returned to work.[6]
>
> About 1,000 Northumberland miners also decided to strike if an 18-year-old surface worker were sent to prison for the same reason.[7]

The most outstanding example of this kind is the case of the Manchester gasworkers referred to above for whom the works' manager paid the fines in order to prevent a prolongation and further spreading of the strike.

This brief summary of some of the outstanding features arising from the war-time penalization of strikes is not intended as a criticism of the methods employed by either party. Its

[1] See the data given by Mr. J. C. Johnstone in the *Daily Telegraph and Morning Post*, Aug. 5, 1943, who speaks of "an abdication of the authority of the State". A similar complaint is made in the Mass-Observation Enquiry, *People in Production* (Penguin ed.), p. 246.

[2] See her brilliant Fabian lecture "Freedom under Planning" in *Can Planning be Democratic?* (1944), p. 49.

[3] *Citizen of the World* (Works, III, 194), quoted from Dicey, *Law and Opinion*, p. 74.

[4] *The Times*, April 6, 1944.

[5] *The Times*, Sept. 27 and 28, 1943.

[6] *The Times*, Sept. 15 to 18, 1943.

[7] *The Times*, Sept. 16, 1943.

only purpose, to repeat it once more, is to contribute in a small way to the solution of the crucial problem : Is it in the best interests of the community to use the criminal law for the prevention and suppression of strikes ? Though the answer cannot be entirely conclusive, the following facts seem to be indisputable : For strikes involving only small numbers of workers the use of penal sanctions is not required, unless key men are concerned who are able to bring whole industries or vital public services to a standstill. If this is the case, penal sanctions can usually be employed without difficulty. For large-scale strikes of many hundreds or thousands of workers, however, the machinery of the criminal law is clearly unsuitable. Not only because of the difficulty, encountered in New Zealand and elsewhere, of collecting fines from large bodies of men, but for other reasons of far greater weight as well : Heavy penalties, which might act as a deterrent, can be imposed against members of the rank and file only if there is, among the community at large, a very strong and fairly unanimous feeling of indignation at that particular strike action. This will usually be found where a particular strike is morally and socially unjustifiable, and, where it exists, it will provide social pressure effective enough to enable the community to deal with the matter without penal sanctions. Where it is absent, only trifling penalties can be imposed which are practically useless or positively harmful.

In some ways, the problem is similar to that which confronts the legislator in the case of Monopoly.[1] There it is the financial and social power of the " Over-mighty Subject " that threatens to defy the law ; here it is numerical strength, the " mass factor ", that may have the same effect. The analogy is, however, far from perfect. In cases of monopoly and similar abuses of economic power, social pressure of a non-penal character is, as experience has shown, either entirely absent or too weak to have any practical effect. The reason is that the economic consequences of monopolistic practices are too complex, and too difficult to grasp, to evoke any large-scale social counter-action on the part of the public, whereas the harm done by strikes is obvious even to the man in the street.

Our reference to the " mass factor " should not be understood as meaning that wherever large numbers of law-breakers are involved penal action becomes automatically impossible. Although the Motor Traffic Acts, too, have to deal with masses

[1] Chapter 8 B (*c*).

of offenders—nearly half a million persons found guilty of traffic offences in 1938—nobody advocates their abolition. It is not the mass factor in itself: it is only where there is the additional element of internal social cohesion to bind these masses together that the machinery of the criminal law becomes unworkable. There is no social cohesion among motorists as a class comparable to that among workers. On the other hand, non-penal social pressure from outside can be relied upon to prevent anti-social behaviour to much less an extent among motorists than among workers.[1]

One of the most popular ways out of the impasse into which penal anti-strike legislation is likely to drift is to concentrate on strike leaders and instigators. This is the method underlying the much-discussed Defence Regulation 1AA of April 17, 1944 (now repealed).[2] Although in spite of Clause 1 (*a*) not only the instigator but also the ordinary worker might conceivably be prosecuted under the Regulation, this was neither its real object nor would it have been practical politics.[3] Other difficulties which might possibly arise from its formulation or that of the even more complicated and controversial Trade Disputes and Trade Unions Act of 1927 need not concern us here. It is interesting to note, though, that there is still a great deal of uncertainty about the interpretation of some of the most fundamental conceptions used in the Act of 1927, some of which may also apply to the administration of Regulation 1AA. It is only now, for instance, that the phrase " in furtherance of a strike " has been interpreted by the Court of Criminal Appeal as being restricted to acts committed after the strike had already broken out.[4] Other terms employed in the Act, as that of " hardship upon the community ", are almost as vague as the notorious sections 1 and 2 of the Sherman Act.[5] The chief difficulty to be faced by all such attempts to concentrate upon the leaders and instigators is, however, not the legal but the factual one of how to deal with thousands of workers who go on strike in protest against heavy sentences passed on such leaders and instigators.

[1] Other socio-psychological arguments against the use of compulsion in labour disputes are well brought out by M. Jørgen S. Dich, Econ. Adviser to the Danish Minister of Social Affairs, in *International Labour Review*, 38 (1938), pp. 575 et seq.

[2] It is also employed in the U.S.A. Smith-Connally Act of 1943 and in several other countries, such as pre-war Poland (*Industrial and Labour Information* (1939), p. 292), Chile (*International Labour Review*, Vol. 43, p. 426).

[3] See Pritt, *Defence Regulation 1AA*, p. 15.

[4] Rex *v.* Tearse and others, *The Times*, Sept. 26, 1944.

[5] See the remarks by W. H. Thompson in Cole, *Trade Unionism To-day*, p. 125.

It is mainly for this reason that legislation on the lines of Regulation 1AA is likely to end in a *cul-de-sac*. If the leaders have no strong following they are not dangerous and no special legislation is needed for them ; if they are dangerous such legislation may do more harm than good.

Another possible solution is the setting up of a special Tribunal in the place of the ordinary criminal court to deal with strikers. It may be remembered that in Australia it is the Commonwealth Court of Conciliation and Arbitration, not a criminal court, that has power to impose penalties. However, this idea found no favour with the English legislator in the last war. The hope expressed by Mr. Humbert Wolfe [1] that the Munitions Tribunals of 1915–18 would become a permanent part of the English judicial system has not been realized. The Pit Tribunals established in Durham and Yorkshire to deal with absenteeism, which will be discussed below, are of a different character.[2]

After the completion of this chapter, similar conclusions have been drawn in an admirable letter to *The Times* [3] by Sir Lynden Macassey, whose outstanding contributions to the settlement of labour questions during the 1914–18 war are well known :

> You cannot imprison the whole of a large body of strikers. Alternatively, to pick out a selected few and make examples of them only elevates them into popular martyrs. When proceedings are taken, courts of summary jurisdiction hesitate to convict, knowing that, if imprisonment does result, things will happen as in Manchester. So the rule of law . . . is brought into public disrepute and undermined.

II. Absenteeism and other Offences under the Essential Work Order.[4]

Under the Essential Work (General Provisions) Order, 1941, and Defence Regulation 58AA various powers of great importance are given to the Minister of Labour and National Service and his officials. They may direct workers to take up a particular job with a particular employer or they may refuse permis-

[1] Op. cit. p. 111.

[2] The suggestion has been made that the National Service Officers should be given the right and the duty to fine strikers automatically according to a fixed scale for every day of an illegal strike ; see J. C. Johnstone, *Daily Telegraph and Morning Post*, Aug. 5, 1943.

[3] *The Times*, Jan. 27, 1945.

[4] On the contents of this Order and the way it works see *Worker's Pocket Series No. 10* (3rd ed., May 1943) ; Gertrude Williams, *The Price of Social Security* (1944), pp. 96 et seq. ; *People in Production, by Mass-Observation*, Chapters XVI and XXXIV.

sion to a worker to leave his job or to exchange it for another. In cases of absenteeism and persistent lateness at work they may give written directions. Failure to comply with any such directions constitutes an offence under Defence Regulation 92. The right to impose penalties is, however, reserved to the criminal courts. On the other hand, the power of the latter to go into the merits of the individual case has been seriously curtailed, if not altogether eliminated, and it is this point that has aroused widespread misgivings. As the law stands, the distribution of powers is as follows : A number of safety valves have been included in the law, to be administered, however, not by the magistrates but by the officials of the Ministry of Labour : for instance, a person shall be directed to perform only such services as he is, in the opinion of the Minister, " capable of performing " ; or a worker may be prosecuted only if he is absent from work " without leave or reasonable excuse ", or if he is " persistently late ". Various decisions of the High Court of Justice, King's Bench Division, have made it clear that the criminal courts are not competent to question the correctness of the interpretation given to these elastic terms by the administrative authorities. All they are called upon to do is to impose suitable penalties, even if in their view the Ministry of Labour official has made wrong use of his powers.[1] Nor is the right of appeal to the local Appeal Boards created by the Essential Work Order of much value as their functions are, as a rule, purely advisory. The position is, thus, somewhat analogous to that created for Regulation 18B cases by the widely criticized decision in Liversidge *v.* Anderson :[2] here, too, the Advisory Committee has no real power, and the right to question the reasonableness of a Detention Order made by the Home Secretary has been denied to the courts ; the fact that the Minister honestly believes to have " reasonable cause " to make an Order is sufficient justification. Criticism of the corresponding decisions under the Essential Work Order has been no less strong than that of Liversidge *v.* Anderson. Under the heading " The Seeds of Dictatorship ", *The Justice of the Peace* writes, " We suggest that such a position is contrary to the fundamental conceptions of English law ",[3] and comments in

[1] See, for example, Horton *v.* Owen, *The Times*, November 5, 1942 ; Davies *v.* Smith, *The Times*, January 13, 1944.

[2] (1942), 110 L.J.K.B. 724. On the constitutional background of this case see G. W. Keeton, *5 Modern Law Review* (1942), p. 162 ; C. K. Allen, *Law and Orders* (1944), App. 3 and 5.

[3] Vol. CVII, p. 459, of Sept. 25, 1943.

The Magistrate have been, if anything, even more outspoken.[1] In an interesting and restrained Note in the *Modern Law Review*, the General Editor, Professor R. S. T. Chorley, comments : [2]

> We thus have the beginnings of what may be described as administrative criminal law. . . . The function of the regular Court is in effect reduced to, first, that of ensuring that the administrative tribunal has reached its decision in a regular way and in accordance with the authority conferred upon it, and secondly, that of determining the punishment to be awarded. This may turn out to be an innovation of great importance.

Indeed, it may. It is, however, proposed to deal with these wider aspects of the matter in another connection.[3] There is only one question of considerable interest which may suitably be discussed at once : Why is it that criticisms of the kind levelled against certain features of the Essential Work Order and of Regulation 18B have not been made against the Defence Regulations which restrict the right to strike ? Is not the position here fundamentally the same ? Strikes may be illegal solely because they are declared to be illegal by the established administrative machinery regardless of the true merits of the workers' case. In such cases, criminal courts are, consequently, called upon to impose penalties without being able to enquire whether the strike may perhaps have been due to justified grievances. As far as one can see, there are between this and the other categories of cases the following three differences which may go a long way to explain the different attitude of the critics : first, that safety valves of the kind included in the Essential Work Order and in Regulation 18B (" reasonable excuse ", " capable of performing ", etc.) are absent in the provisions dealing with strikes, i.e. Regulation 58AA and the Conditions of Employment Order of 18.7.1940, and that their place is taken by arbitration machinery. This means that no elastic terms which could possibly be left to interpretation by the magistrates are provided in the case of strikes. It is doubtful, however, whether this difference in legislative technique should in fairness be used to the advantage of persons charged under the Essential Work Order. Second, in the case of strikes, which as collective disputes are of greater practical importance than individual charges under the Essential Work Order, arbitration will usually be in the hands of officials of experience and standing superior to that

[1] Nov.–Dec., 1942, p. 148 ; Jan.–Feb. 1944, p. 3 ; and passim.
[2] 5 *Modern Law Review*, p. 235.
[3] Below, pp. 215, 218.

of National Service Officers. This is an important consideration, but one that affects only the technical working of the present distribution of powers, not the principle as such. Third, and perhaps most important, persons charged under the Essential Work Order may often belong to a social class different from that of those charged under the anti-strike Regulations. It is significant that the opposition to the present system is mainly, if not exclusively, concerned with cases of failure to comply with directions to take up a certain employment. This is often an expression of middle-class or upper working-class attitudes, and therefore more likely to find a sympathetic hearing on the part of lay magistrates, whereas the mentality of strikers is more characteristic of the average working-class attitude.[1]

However that may be, there is, it seems, a widespread feeling that the system of prosecuting cases under the Essential Work Order before the criminal courts has largely failed. The imposition of prison sentences is particularly resented, especially in the case of young people.[2] From various quarters, the proposal has been made to substitute industrial Tribunals for the criminal courts.[3] In response to such suggestions, voluntary Pit Tribunals have been established by the Ministry of Fuel and Power in the Durham District, one for each colliery, composed of an official of the Ministry as chairman and two assessors representing the management and the miners. They deal with cases of absenteeism and indiscipline and can impose fines up to £1, which are refunded if the offence is not repeated within six weeks. It is stated that these Tribunals, though lacking in legal status and powers of compulsion, have been working well; that up to July, 1944, more than 12,600 cases had been dealt with by them in the Durham coalfields, of which only 34 per cent. had resulted in recidivism.[4]

[1] This should not be misunderstood. It is not argued here that *only* middle-class people have been affected by the Essential Work Order, which would be flagrantly untrue (see, for example, Hansard, 1942, Vol. 377, cols. 1849 et seq.), but that they have *also* been affected by it, not however by the Anti-Strike Regulations.

[2] According to a statement by the Minister of Labour in the House of Commons, up to the end of Aug. 1942, 609 miners had been prosecuted for absenteeism, lateness, or leaving without permission, of whom 128 had been sentenced to imprisonment (*The Times*, Oct. 16, 1942); according to a later statement, 143 "Bevin Boys" had been imprisoned (*The Times*, Dec. 15, 1944). *The Magistrate*, May–June, 1944, estimates the number of young women sent to prison for offences against industrial legislation at "well over 200".

[3] Mr. Keeling, M.P., in the House of Commons, Oct. 12, 1943 (*The Times*, Oct. 14, 1943; *The Magistrate*, Jan.–Feb 1944, p. 3).

[4] Thomas Hornby, Regional Controller Northern B Region, in a letter to *The Times*, July 15, 1944.

EPILOGUE TO PART I

There is no need for us to remind the reader of the many gaps in our survey. To the expert, the history of the prolonged but largely unsuccessful struggle to bring the criminal law into line with modern requirements is only too familiar. In this book, which is concerned more with general principles than with points of detail, no completeness can be achieved. Universal agreement does seem to exist, however, about the need to abolish antiquated distinctions such as those between indictable and non-indictable offences, and between felony and misdemeanour with their important but no longer justifiable repercussions in the field of criminal procedure.[1] It is here that an all too faithful adherence to an obsolete scale of values has produced anomalies of a most striking character. The distribution of the various types of offences among the different categories of criminal courts, for example, has become thoroughly out of date.

> . . . the larceny of the finest car ever made can be tried summarily, but the theft of the sorriest nag must go to the sessions. The most intricate charge of false pretences can be dealt with by the magistrates, but the extraction of a packet of cigarettes from a shop window by cutting away a piece of cardboard is a matter for judge and jury.[2]

Only recently attention has been drawn by Dr. C. K. Allen [3] to the fact that " it is still an offence, punishable by ecclesiastical censures, for a member of the Church of England not to attend his parish church on Sunday ", and that it is not only an ecclesiastical but also a criminal offence for any person educated in, or professing, the Christian religion to deny this religion to be true or the Holy Scripture to be of Divine authority. Mainly with regard to sexual misbehaviour, Mr. George Ives has complained of " The continued Extension of the Criminal Law ".[4] The overstrict law of libel is a very serious impediment to honest criticism and the publication of scientific research, although it

[1] See also Margery Fry, *The Treatment of the Adult Offender* (1944), p. 14. J. Whiteside, *The Justice of the Peace and Local Government Review*, Dec. 7, 1940 (Vol. CIV), p. 682.

[2] *The Justice of the Peace and Local Government Review*, Aug. 28, 1943 (Vol. CVII), pp. 411–12.

[3] *Democracy and the Individual* (1943), pp. 55 and 86. See also H. Bradlough Bonner, *Penalties upon Opinion* (Thinker's Library No. 39).

[4] Privately printed, no date (1922).

is here more the civil than the criminal side of the law that is in need of reform.

On the other hand, the question arises whether it might not be desirable to invoke the protection of the criminal law to enforce respect for the dignity of the human personality against attacks made not in the interest of bona fide criticism or of scientific research but as an expression of unjustifiable prejudices and fear of competition. In view of recent occurrences such as the Constantine case and similar manifestations of colour prejudice [1] it may be not altogether inappropriate to examine the advisability of making any manifestation of this kind a criminal offence. This has been done, apparently with outstanding success, in the Soviet Union. " Since 1928, the Soviet Government has rigorously enforced the laws making the slightest demonstrations of race prejudice criminal offences . . . no offence was likely to be punished more swiftly ".[2] It is, not least of all, this attitude of the law that seems to have led to the disappearance of any form of colour bar and similar discriminations, thus securing that happy co-operation between the many races represented in the U.S.S.R. which has so greatly contributed to the success of the present régime.[3] To find a suitable formula for a penal statute of this kind will, of course, be no easy task.

Summary of Principal Recommendations made in Part I

Section One : 1. *Suicide* (Chapter 1 B) : Suicide should not be treated as an offence. Other persons who have participated in the act of suicide or attempted suicide, or who have committed homicide at the serious request of the killed person should not be indiscriminately treated as guilty of murder. The same applies to partners in death-pacts.

2. *Euthanasia* (Chapter 1 C) should, with suitable safeguards, be made lawful.

3. *Murder and Manslaughter* (Chapter 1 and Appendix) : Different degrees of murder should be recognized by the law, and intentional manslaughter should be clearly distinguished from killing by negligence.

4. *Sterilization* (Chapter 2 B) should be permitted on a voluntary basis and for narrowly defined categories of cases, as suggested in the " Report on Sterilization ", 1934.

[1] See the reports in *The Times* of June 20, 22 and 29, 1944, Aug. 2 and 10, 1944, and the debate in the House of Commons, Sept. 23, 1943.

[2] Littlepage and Bess, *In Search of Soviet Gold*, p. 237.

[3] See also the discussion of the problem in Leonard Barnes, *Soviet Light on the Colonies* (Penguin Special, 1944) Chapter VII, and the excellent analysis by K. L. Little, " The Psychological Background of White-Coloured Contacts in Britain ", *Sociological Review* (Jan.–April 1943).

5. *Birth Control* (Chapter 3 C), instead of being hampered by penal provisions or administrative regulations, should be given its proper place within the educational system and the social and health services.

6. *Abortion* (Chapter 3 D) should be legalized on clearly defined therapeutic, eugenic, ethical, socio-economic or personal grounds, and special Boards should be established to permit abortion on such grounds and to educate the public. Abortion not permitted by these Boards should be punished by the criminal court. A central Board should supervise and co-ordinate the work of the local Boards and be responsible for their general policy.

7. The law of *Criminal Negligence* (Appendix) should be further developed so as to make it possible to impose adequate penalties for negligence causing death or injuries or serious danger to life or health of human beings.

Section Two : 8. Antiquated statutes penalizing *sexual misbehaviour* (Chapter 4) not harmful to society should be repealed. The exploitation for sexual purposes of a woman's economic dependence should become an offence. *Homosexual activities* should not be punishable unless carried on for financial gain or involving the corruption of young persons. Corporal punishment for *exhibitionism* should be abolished.

9. The whole body of criminal law relating to the *Family* (Chapter 5) should be made more consistent. There should be a more efficient system of preventing bigamous marriages. The prohibition of incest should not extend beyond the narrow circle of near blood relations. Neglect to support one's family should be more effectively dealt with by the criminal law.

Section Three : For the branches of the criminal law dealing with *economic crime*, closer contact with contemporary changes in the economic and social structure of society is required. *This will mean :*

10. The disappearance of those provisions of the present law of *theft* which contain technical detail unnecessary or obsolete in present-day society, or which are unfair to the poorer classes of the community ; increased protection for public property and that of the small property owner (Chapters 6 and 7 A).

11. The malicious or wanton *destruction* of, or damage to, property committed by the *owner himself* should, if necessary in the public interest, within reasonable limits be punishable on the lines of war-time legislation (Chapter 7 B).

12. A wholesale shifting of the main emphasis from theft and other forms of comparatively petty economic crime to the various more complicated and more dangerous types of *white-collar crime.* In future legislation, criminal fraud will have to be treated on the lines of the English Prevention of Fraud (Investments) Act of 1939 and of war-time profiteering statutes and regulations (Chapter 7 C).

Section Four : 13. *Usury* (Chapter 8 A) should be attacked with greater energy by the criminal law. In the case of small loans it should be an offence to exceed the maximum rate of interest fixed by an administrative body (further suggestions at the end of Chapter 8 A).

14. *Taxation Frauds* (Chapter 8 B b) should be treated in no way more favourably than stealing and other economic offences; and active "tax avoidance" should become punishable. The factual findings of the competent administrative authorities should be binding on the criminal courts.

15. *Monopolistic Activities* (Chapter 8 B *c*) should be made punishable if against the interest of the community at large, and the factual findings of the competent administrative bodies should be binding on the criminal courts.

16. *Strikes* (Chapter 9) should not be punishable. Absenteeism and similar offences, should be dealt with by industrial Tribunals rather than by criminal courts.

PART II. CRIMINAL JUSTICE AND SOCIAL RECONSTRUCTION

RE-PLANNING CRIMINAL JUSTICE

Chapter 10

I. SUMMING UP

A stage has now been reached where it may be advisable to sum up our principal results and to draw certain conclusions :

The crisis in values makes it imperative to remodel large sections of the criminal law. Certain activities which are at present criminal offences should cease to be punishable, as, for example, attempted suicide, euthanasia, and, with the necessary provisos, sterilization, strikes, selected forms of abortion and homosexual activities. On the other hand, anti-social behaviour such as the breaking up of the family home, usury, tax avoidance, dangerous monopolistic policies, and certain cases of negligence should be brought under the scope of the criminal law. In a third group, existing criminal legislation should be either relaxed and brought into line with modern psychological and sociological knowledge, as in the case of murder and theft ; or strengthened, as for frauds, profiteering, and similar more refined forms of economic offences.

Such a wholesale shifting of emphasis from simpler to more complicated types of anti-social behaviour will be practical politics only if accompanied by an equally determined re-thinking of a number of problems which could be shelved only as long as criminal legislation either remained altogether static or had to live a bare " hand to mouth " existence.

Of what kind, then, are these new problems ? They are concerned partly with the functions of the criminal law itself, and partly with its relations to kindred branches of the law :

(1) The function of the criminal law is no longer primarily to protect individual rights and interests, but at least as much to protect the rights and interests of the community at large.

(2) This can be achieved better by large-scale preventive action than by punishing individuals after the event.

(3) Large-scale preventive action is necessarily of an administrative rather than of a judicial character. It requires expert knowledge of a great variety of subjects, and it often means the transfer of the initiative from the individual to the State. Apart from Police action, it implies such devices as the issuing of licences and permits, fixing of prices and rates of interest, giving advice in advance on matters of economic policy—in a word: *Planning*.

(4) All this is bound fundamentally to affect the relationship between the criminal courts, on the one hand, and administrative bodies and experts on the other, and to restrict the courts, in many fields, to the formal side of the question at issue. To one of these problems, the redistribution of powers between criminal courts and administrative bodies, attention has already been drawn in the course of the previous chapters. Such redistribution may assume two different forms: either wholesale transfer to agencies outside the criminal courts, or division of functions between administrative bodies and courts. We propose to deal with the second type first. In various connections, the point has been stressed that the criminal courts cannot be expected to cope with their new responsibilities unless they are relieved by the administration of some of their functions. Without such a division of labour, the judge is bound to remain a helpless amateur.

The analysis of the various practical questions which we have undertaken has shown that this relief action cannot follow the same pattern everywhere, regardless of the specific situation in which it is required. This refers to the character and composition of the administrative body as well as to the scope of its duties. Sometimes it will be the competent Minister himself (e.g., the Minister of Health in the case of sterilization, or the President of the Board of Trade in the case of price fixing), sometimes a Board or Tribunal set up by him (e.g., in the case of abortion, or of dealing in shares, or fixing of rates of interest, or of taxation, monopoly, etc.). Their function may be either to issue a special permit (for sterilization or abortion) or a general licence to carry on business (as a stockbroker or money-lender or wholesaler); to settle certain questions of policy (e.g., to fix the rate of interest permitted) or to decide individual cases (e.g., of monopolistic activities or violation of taxation laws or labour disputes). By such methods, the task of the criminal courts will be in many ways facilitated: The policy of extending the licensing system to a growing number of occupations has a considerable crime-preventing effect, or, at least, it makes it easier to deal with such acts of law-breaking as may, in spite of it, occur. It reduces the potential number of law-breakers and it substitutes, in many cases, the formal offence of acting without a licence, which is easy to prove, for the more complicated offence of wrongdoing in a material sense. The setting up of administrative Boards or Tribunals to decide such issues, as, for instance, whether euthanasia, sterilization or abortion should be permitted in an individual case ; or to decide whether certain business practices constitute a violation of the taxation or monopoly laws, or whether the behaviour of certain workers amounts to a breach of labour legislation, or to fix maximum prices or rates of interest—innovations of this kind greatly simplify the task of the criminal courts. As we have seen, the latter would thereby be confined mainly to questions of subjective guilt and to the finding of a suitable sentence.

All this refers to the stage before conviction, to what might perhaps be called the *criminological* stage of the work of the courts ; and the overriding justification for those restrictive tendencies is the fact that too many and too different aspects of human life are involved to be mastered by one and the same agency, the criminal court. This is the consequence of the complexity of modern civilization and of the crisis in values which has shattered our belief in the ability of criminal courts to do full justice to the social and economic issues at stake. This development has, in fact, already gone so far that, with the exception of comparatively few, though of course very important, types of crime such as murder and theft, the whole future work of the criminal courts will depend on their satisfactory collaboration with administrative bodies.

The second great advantage of such a transfer of functions from the courts to the administration is that it enables the individual to find out in advance whether his intended action, may it be sterilization, abortion, or the charging of a certain price or rate of interest, the " minimizing " of tax or the " reorganizing " of an industry, is lawful or not.

In recent years, however, two additional movements have made their appearance, which tend either to oust the criminal courts from the *penological* sphere of their activities or to replace them *altogether* by other agencies. The first movement has produced the American idea of the *Treatment Tribunal* ; the second favours the establishment of *Youth Welfare Councils* in the place of Juvenile Courts, and of *Comrades Courts*, *Pit Tribunals*, etc., in the place of the ordinary criminal courts.

The discussion of these tendencies may be left for a later stage.[1]

[1] See also below pp. 223 et seq. and p. 245.

II. POSSIBLE OBJECTIONS: SEPARATION OF POWERS—"ADMINISTRATIVE LAW"—THE RULE OF LAW

The difficulties which stand in the way of the changes so far outlined are too obvious to be overlooked. There is a formidable array of ideological "vested interests", ready to prevent any further expansion of the administration at the expense of the judiciary. The arguments may have slightly changed in the period from Dicey to Lord Hewart and Professor Hayek, but all of them have already been adequately disposed of in the brilliant writings of Sir Cecil Carr,[1] Dr. W. A. Robson,[2] Dr. Ivor Jennings,[3] Dr. E. C. S. Wade,[4] and of many American students of the subject,[5] and, with certain reservations, in the Report on Ministers' Powers of 1932. There is still the doctrine of the Separation of Powers; there is the distrust, still fairly widespread, of anything in the way of "Administrative Law" that has to be overcome; and there is, of course, the Rule of Law itself.

However, Separation of Powers—"to the English it is a respectable ideal, not even a legal fiction: the multitude of exceptions disproves the rule",[6] and in the words of a great American judge,[7] "it is not meant to affirm that they must be kept wholly and entirely separate and distinct. . . . The true meaning is that the *whole* of one of these departments should not be exercised by the same hands that possess the *whole* power of either of the other departments." It is difficult to believe that a different interpretation should be seriously upheld in a country

[1] *Concerning English Administrative Law* (1941); *Law Quarterly Review*, Vol. 51 (1935), pp. 58 et seq. and Vol. 58 (1942), pp. 487 et seq.
[2] *Justice and Administrative Law* (1928); *Public Enterprise* (1937).
[3] Especially *The Law and the Constitution* (2nd ed., 1938).
[4] Introduction and Appendix to the Ninth Ed. of Dicey's *Law of the Constitution* (1939).
[5] See, for example, James Roland Pennock, *Administration and the Rule of Law* (1941): Joseph P. Chamberlain, Noel T. Dowling, Paul R. Hays, *The Judicial Function of Federal Administrative Agencies* (New York, The Commonwealth Fund, 1942); James M. Landis, *The Administrative Process* (1938); Ernst Freund, *Administrative Powers over Persons and Property* (1928).
[6] Sir Cecil T. Carr, *Concerning English Administrative Law* (1941), p. 17.
[7] From Judge Story's *Commentaries on the American Constitution*, quoted in James Roland Pennock, *Administration and the Rule of Law* (1941), p. 158 fn. 14.

whose magistrates are so widely engaged in the discharge of administrative duties.[1]

Mistrust of " Administrative Law " ? Even so determined an opponent of the whole conception as the late Lord Hewart took some pains to distinguish between what he called " administrative lawlessness " and the Continental system which " profoundly repugnant as it is to English ideas, is at least a system. It has its courts, its law, its hearings and adjudications, its regular and accepted procedure." [2] The question arises whether the first of these elements, the existence of proper administrative courts, might safely be waived in favour of Boards, particularly if some form of judicial control, exercised by criminal courts, is established.

With regard to the *Rule of Law*, too, a growing body of responsible opinion is willing to recognize that the principle, though indispensable in itself, can no longer be maintained in its full rigidity. " The criticism of Dicey . . . is not that the Rule of Law is undesirable, but that it was not correct analysis of the British Constitution of 1885 and has become even more incorrect since," writes Dr. Ivor Jennings,[3] and Mr. Rowse, writing as a non-lawyer, even went so far as to claim that " among ordinary people there is a general feeling that they would prefer despotism of the civil service to a despotism of the law any day . . .".[4] As defined by the Dicey-Hewart school of thought, " Rule of Law " means, apart from other aspects which do not concern us here, that in England " no man is punishable or can be lawfully made to suffer in body or goods, except for a distinct breach of law established in the ordinary legal manner before the ordinary courts of the land ".[5] In this definition, the accent is clearly laid on two factors : one relating to the substantive law (" distinct breach of the law ") and another relating to the law of procedure (ordinary proceedings before ordinary courts of law). With regard to the latter, Dicey's formula is now widely regarded as so out of date that in 1936 an eminent member of the U.S.A. Supreme Court, Mr. Justice Brandeis, tried to

[1] On the history of the " legendary Separation of Powers," see William A. Robson, *Justice and Administrative Law* (1928), pp. 12 et seq. ; Report on Ministers' Powers, pp. 9 and 94.

[2] *The New Despotism* (1929), pp. 13 and 45.

[3] *Modern Law Review*, Vol. III (1940), p. 322. See also Harold J. Laski, *Will Planning Restrict Freedom ?*, p. 32.

[4] A. L. Rowse, *Politics and the Younger Generation* (1932), p. 155.

[5] A. V. Dicey, *Introduction to the Study of the Law of the Constitution*, 8th ed., p. 183 ; Lord Hewart, op. cit., pp. 24 et seq.

restate the principle in the following terms : "The supremacy of the law demands that there shall be opportunity to have some court decide whether an erroneous rule of law was applied and whether the proceeding in which the facts were adjudicated was conducted regularly ".[1] This means that, whereas, according to the old view, proceedings leading to the imposition of a penalty had to take place before the ordinary court from beginning to end, the new version requires no more than an adequate measure of judicial control over proceedings conducted outside the court.

The second, substantive element of Dicey's definition is so closely related to the question of "Certainty and Predictability" that it may be treated in connection with it. It is mainly this idea that has recently been taken up by Professor Hayek in support of his general attack on "socialist planning": in addition to the exclusion of "arbitrariness, prerogative, or even of wide discretionary authority on the part of the Government", it is in particular the idea of predictability that occupies a central position in his argument. Rule of Law means, above all, that

> government in all its actions is bound by rules fixed and announced beforehand—rules which make it possible to foresee with fair certainty how the authority will use its coercive powers in given circumstances. . . . Within the known rules of the game the individual is free to pursue his personal ends and desires, certain that the powers of government will not be used deliberately to frustrate his efforts.[2]

On the other hand, these rules of law should be of a merely formal, not of a substantive, character in the sense that they must never contain any concrete prescription of how people should actually behave in a given situation. They should only lay down a "Rule of the Road", not "order people where to go". Because of their purely formal character it is impossible to foresee who will actually come under their scope, and at what time and place. In other words, everything should be dependent upon the action of the individual, he alone should be able to foresee the legal consequences of his behaviour, whereas from the point of view of the State these consequences should be unforeseeable in order to preserve the impartiality of the legislator. The requirement of predictability rules entirely out the use of elastic terms such as "fair" or "reasonable".[3] To their increasing application in modern statutes, favoured by the teach-

[1] In St. Joseph Stock Yards Co. *v.* United States, 298 U.S. 38, 84 (1936).
[2] F. A. Hayek, *The Road to Serfdom* (1943), p. 54 and the whole of Chapter VI.
[3] On the distinction between "legal rules" and "legal standards of conduct" see also F. Neumann, *Behemoth* (1942), p. 360.

ings of the "*Freirechtsschule*", the recent decline of the Rule of Law is, according to Hayek, largely to be ascribed.

Professor Hayek's book is, of course, primarily directed against the establishment of suitable legal and administrative machinery for economic planning in the socialist sense. Problems of criminal justice are only at the periphery of his attack. Nevertheless, the reader of our previous chapters will be aware of the deep antagonism between his line of thought and the main thesis of this book. The practical consequence for the administration of criminal justice of Hayek's teachings would be to secure all possible advantages for the individual or rather for one class of individuals, none for the community. The individual alone should be able to foresee not only the economic but also the legal implications of his actions, whereas the organs of the State should always remain in the dark. This makes the Rule of Law a perpetual game of "Heads I win, tails you lose" in favour of the individual—the ideal of an age that has definitely passed. It remains for us to consider the problem of "Certainty and Predictability" as it actually presents itself to-day.

III. IN PARTICULAR: CERTAINTY AND PREDICTABILITY

This is no doubt one of the highest ideals of any legal system.[1] If it had to be expected that such changes in the criminal law as are here suggested would make the administration of justice considerably less certain and predictable this would indeed be a serious matter. Is it, however, true that there is necessarily a marked difference in this respect between criminal courts and administrative bodies?

Certainty and predictability depend on a number of factors. One of them is the legislative technique used for drafting criminal statutes, which in its turn is at least partly dependent on the nature of the problems to be solved by a particular statute; another, the method of interpretation to be employed by those entrusted with the administration of the law; a third, the character and training of these administrators; and a fourth, the nature of the legal remedies provided for the purpose of securing uniformity in the administration of criminal justice. Obviously, Points One and Two belong together as questions of substantive law, whereas Points Three and Four are essentially questions of procedure.

(1) The Technique of Legal Draftsmanship.

Points of legislative technique have repeatedly arisen in the course of our previous discussions. Difficulties have been encountered in determining the best method of defining, for instance, the legal requirements of sterilization, or the offences of breaking up the family, or share-pushing, profiteering, or certain acts of "tax avoidance", or monopolistic activities.[2] It has been shown that no universal recipe exists in matters of criminal legislation. The Soviet legislator has had to be criticized because of his predilection for all too general and vague terms. On the other hand, we have come to realize that the opposite extreme of making the definitions in criminal statutes as detailed and as narrow as possible has had very disappointing results and has in fact only encouraged evasions of one kind or another. The technically most accomplished

[1] To some extent this was admitted even by leading Nazi lawyers; see E. Fraenkel, *The Dual State*, p. 62, on the legal theory of the Gestapo.

[2] See above, pp. 33, 81, 125, 142, 149, 157.

Penal Codes of to-day, as in particular the Swiss Federal Code of 1937, have chosen a middle way, with a slight bias towards the use of general terms and elimination of avoidable detail. One fact has, however, distinctly emerged from our discussion of a number of concrete legislative tasks which State and Society of to-morrow will have to tackle : In an age chiefly characterized by rapid change in the political, economic, and social spheres, the criminal law can fulfil its functions only if some mechanism is devised to make it more readily adaptable than it has been so far. As already indicated in connection with the question of Monopoly,[1] there are only three debatable alternatives in which this can be achieved : first, by the use of general terms ; second, by the admission of analogy in the interpretation of criminal statutes ; and, third, by a complete revision of the main body of criminal law at regular intervals of, say, one year in order to keep up with any economic and other changes that may have occurred. Each of these alternatives is bound to come into conflict with at least one of the old-established principles of traditional law and jurisprudence.

The technique to be used for the drafting of criminal statutes has been a favourite subject of discussion among legal philosophers, at least since Beccaria, Montesquieu, and Bentham. According to them, the terms employed have to be so clear and unambiguous that the decision to be given by the judge should appear as the only possible conclusion, and the judge himself be reduced to an automatic machine. This alone, it was believed, could safeguard the liberty of the citizen. Government by the law, not by man, was the keynote. It is essential, writes Montesquieu,[2] that only such words should be used by the lawgiver as are bound to produce the same notions in the minds of all men ; and, as a model not to be followed, he refers to an enactment by Richelieu which permitted the impeachment of a minister, with the proviso, however, that the accuser was to suffer heavy punishment unless the proceedings brought to light some " serious " misconduct on the part of the minister.

The use of wide and ambiguous terms, as we have seen, might also be regarded as incompatible with the Rule of Law which requires a " distinct breach of the law ". If the law is formulated in very broad and nebulous terms, who can convinc-

[1] See above, p. 159.

[2] *Esprit des lois*, livre XXIX, chapitre XVI. See also H. Drost, *Das Ermessen des Strafrichters* (1930), p. 86.

ingly maintain that a certain type of behaviour is contrary to that law? Nevertheless, who will throw the first stone when everyone seems to be sitting in a glass-house? In English law, the most conspicuous example is the conception of Conspiracy, i.e., " the agreement of two or more persons to effect any unlawful purpose ", which includes " agreements to do certain (other) acts which are not breaches of law at all, but which nevertheless are outrageously immoral or else are, in some way, extremely injurious to the public ".[1] Even so moderate a critic as Kenny, though defending the vagueness of this definition as at least " historically intelligible ", has to admit that it " renders it possible for judges to treat all combinations to effect any purpose which happens to be distasteful to them as indictable crimes ". Is there any real difference between this and the provisions of the Soviet Penal Code discussed above? One feels that this might have been a suitable object of criticism for the distinguished author of *The New Despotism* who wrote that

> nothing perhaps is more profoundly repugnant to the English mind than that authority should be irresponsible or uncontrolled, that it should operate at pleasure or in the dark, that men should live in an atmosphere of uncertainty as to the nature of the rights they enjoy or the penalties to which they are exposed, or that among fellow-citizens there should be one code for one class of persons, and a different code for others.[2]

The law of Conspiracy, though probably the most notorious, is, however, by no means the only part of English criminal law framed in terms so general and vague that the decisions of the court can hardly be regarded as predictable. The whole law of Treason and kindred offences against the safety of the State shows the same tendency.[3] Similarly, under the Trade Disputes Act, 1927, a strike is an offence if it is " designed or calculated to coerce the Government either directly or by inflicting hardship upon the community ". It is clearly impossible to foresee how these terms might be interpreted by the courts in an individual case, and the same applies to the term " intimidation " used in the Act.[4]

[1] Kenny, *Outlines of Criminal Law* (14th ed., 1933), pp. 296 et seq. Also Holdsworth, *History*, Vol. VIII, pp. 378 et seq.; Stephen, *History*, Vol. III, pp. 191 et seq., 267, 467 et passim.

[2] Lord Hewart, *The New Despotism*, p. 25.

[3] See the details in Kenny, *Outlines*, Chapter XVII.

[4] See W. H. Thompson in G. D. H. Cole, *British Trade Unionism To-day* (1939), p. 125. See also for further instances Laski, *Parliamentary Government in England*, pp. 379–80.

There are, however, in the criminal legislation of practically every country, without exception, a number of offences defined in terms so vague as to defy any possibility of foreseeing the outcome of an individual case. What constitutes " *un attentat à la pudeur* ", or " *eine unzüchtige Handlung* ", or " indecent assault ", or " obscene exposure ", depends largely on the personal views of the individual judge.[1] Only where a large body of precedents has been built up can there be, at least in theory, anything approaching predictability.[2] It is becoming increasingly clear, however, that under modern conditions elastic terms (the much-discussed " *Generalklauseln* ") are indispensable. The perplexity and tempo of modern life can no longer be mastered by conceptions of a purely factual and descriptive character alone—a certain dose of " normative " terms has to be added in spite of the embarrassment they are bound to create for the work of the courts. True as it is that, in the words of Professor Jerome Hall,[3] " such notions as ' welfare ', ' the public good ', ' the protection of society ', and so forth . . . include nothing of value in social problem solving ", it is nevertheless equally true that legislators have not yet worked out a technique of draftsmanship that would enable them satisfactorily to solve the problems of modern society entirely without the aid of such general formulæ. It was for very good reasons that the *Freirechtsschule* favoured the use of elastic terms. This school, far from being responsible for the decline of certainty, only drew the inevitable consequences from developments which could not be prevented.

There is, however, in the suggestions made in some of our previous chapters one feature which may largely compensate for the lack of predictability implied in the use of elastic terms in criminal statutes : If for a growing number of typical situations some administrative machinery is set up to enable the individual to ascertain the legality or otherwise of an intended action this may be preferable to any apparent predictability achieved

[1] Nathaniel F. Cantor, *Crime and Society* (1939), p. 264, refers to those U.S.A. juvenile delinquency laws which admit a charge of " juvenile delinquency " against juveniles, instead of a charge of a specific offence. However, these statutes are of a non-penal character.

[2] It would go too far here to argue the difficult question whether, and to what extent, precedents can really produce predictability, and which of the two systems—the English or the Continental—is more likely to achieve this result. See, for example, A. L. Goodhart, *Law Quarterly Review*, Vol. 50 (1934), pp. 40 et seq., esp. 58 ; Edward Jenks, *The New Jurisprudence*, pp. 99–108 ; E. J. Cohn, *Cambridge Law Journal*, Vol. 5 (1935), pp. 366 et seq.

[3] *Readings in Jurisprudence* (1935), p. 1075.

by the use of more definite terms. *Decision before action, instead of action before decision*, should be the motto.

(2) *Nullum crimen sine lege.* Delegated Legislation.

Legislative technique, however, is, not everything. Criminal statutes, however formulated, have still to be interpreted, and, although this is a judicial function that naturally increases in difficulty with the growing vagueness of the terms used by the law, it is never easy. As Jawaharlal Nehru has said,[1] "even the most exact and explicit statements are likely to be misunderstood by people whose way of thinking is entirely different". Apart from the ordinary rules of interpretation common to all branches of the law, two special principles have been evolved regarding the interpretation of criminal statutes, or rather two different formulations of the same idea: the rule of strict construction in Anglo-American law, meaning that "penal statutes are to be construed strictly, enabling statutes liberally"; and in Continental law the prohibition of analogy to the disadvantage of the accused, usually expressed as "*nullum crimen sine lege*" and "*nulla poena sine lege*". In spite of its Latin dress, the idea was unknown to Roman law and probably incompatible with its totalitarian character.[2] Attempts to trace its origin back to old English law, particularly to Magna Carta, art. 39, are equally unconvincing, because the principle is obviously in the first place designed for written law. It was essentially a child of the eighteenth century and of the age of enlightenment. Among the first European legislative documents to raise it to the status of positive law were the *Déclaration des droits de l'homme et du citoyen* of August 26, 1789, and the Penal Code of Joseph II of Austria of 1787. Most Continental and many non-European Penal Codes followed suit in the course of the nineteenth century, and under the Weimar Republic the principle, so far expressed only in the German Penal Code (sect. 2), was even made part of the Constitution (art. 116). It has indeed become, in the words of Franz von Liszt, the Magna Carta of the law-breaker, and its abolition by the Act of June 28, 1935, was commonly regarded as one of the most outrageous expressions of the legal philosophy of National Socialism. Under that Act, a person is punishable not only if he commits an action explicitly declared to be an offence by the law, but also "if his action deserves punishment according to the fundamental idea of a penal statute and to the

[1] *Autobiography*, p. 227.   [2] F. Schulz, *Principles of Roman Law*, p. 173.

sound sense of justice of the people. If no statute is directly applicable to such an action, it has to be punished under the statute the fundamental conception of which comes nearest to it". It is our object not to defend this change but to examine its meaning and background, as a problem of legal technique and legal philosophy.

First, it has to be stressed that punishment by analogy seems to constitute no essential characteristic of totalitarian legal systems. The Penal Code of Fascist Italy of 1930 prohibits it explicitly, whereas a democratic country like Denmark admits analogy.[1] The attitude of the Danish legislator was originally traced back to the lack of a complete and coherent system of Danish criminal law, but even under the Penal Codes of 1866 and 1930 a person may be punished who has committed an act which is "entirely comparable" to an act expressly declared to be an offence. This means the admission of the so-called "*Gesetzesanalogie*" (i.e., the application of the legal idea underlying a specific statutory provision to analogous cases), not however of the "*Rechtsanalogie*" (i.e., the application of a principle underlying the entire legal system). It is an offence under sect. 179, for example, for a man wrongly to describe himself as the father of a child. By way of analogy, a man was punished for having declared his illegitimate children to be the offspring of his deceased wife. Moreover, in Denmark persons who misappropriated electricity were punished for larceny, whereas in most other countries special legislation was needed.[2] It is, therefore, not entirely true to say, with Hayek, Ashton, and others, that *nullum crimen sine lege* is "an essential part of criminal procedure in all liberal countries",[3] whereas *nullum crimen sine poene is* "the logical basic maxim of Fascist criminal law".

Next to the National Socialist Act of 1935, it is, however, art. 16 of the Soviet Penal Code that has become the most widely known provision in favour of punishment by analogy:

> Where a socially dangerous act has not been expressly dealt with in the present code, the basis and limits of responsibility in respect thereof shall be determined in conformity with those articles of the code which deal with the crimes most closely resembling it.

It was only natural that Nazi lawyers should describe this

[1] Landsdommer F. Lucas, Copenhagen, in *MSchrKr*, 1937, pp. 231 et seq.

[2] See above, p. 90; these examples are taken from Lucas, loco cit.

[3] Hayek, p. 63 fn. 2; A. B. Ashton, *The Fascist, his State and his Mind* (1937), p. 119 fn. 1.

article as much more extreme, vague and dangerous than the German Act of 1935.[1] How can it be explained, however, that distinguished non-German experts should have shared this view? [2] There are, it has been said, three limitations of punishment by analogy inherent in the German Act: first, it must never be applied against the expressed intention of the lawgiver, otherwise the judge would be able to overrule the will of the Führer; second, application by analogy must be in accordance with the "fundamental idea" of an existing penal statute, which probably means that only "*Gesetzesanalogie*," not, however, "*Rechtsanalogie*" is permitted; and third, it must conform to "the sound sense of justice of the people". In the eyes of certain critics, these were substantial safeguards, only the third of which is present in Soviet law, in so far as the requirement of a "socially dangerous" act seems roughly to correspond to an act which is, in Nazi language, against "the sound sense of justice of the people". There is, they argue, in art. 16 no reference to the "fundamental idea" of a specific penal statute (and therefore not only "*Gesetzesanalogie*" but also "*Rechtsanalogie*" is permitted). Consequently, Soviet courts, it is believed, are in no way bound to restrict their adventures in analogy to the "Special Section" of the Penal Code; nor are they prevented from punishing even acts which the Soviet legislator has deliberately left outside the Penal Code.[3]

Granted that the Russian formula is much clumsier and more straightforward than that used in the German Act, and that it has but little of that Goebbelsian smoke-screen so successfully used by Nazi lawyers for the deception of those who were only too willing to be deceived. Let us, however, at least now drop those mere technicalities and legal quibbles and get down to fundamentals. It is not the formula that decides the issue but the men who have to apply the formula. The truth is that Nazi lawyers, with their narrower formula, have gone at least as far as Soviet courts with their wider one. Whereas in the Soviet Code, arts. 1 and 6, the aim of Soviet criminal law is frankly described as "protection of the socialist State of the

[1] E.g., Freisler in Guertner, *Besonderer Teil des deutschen Strafrechts*, p. 48. See also Erich Schinnerer, *German Law and Legislation* (Terramare Office, Berlin, 1938), p. 18.

[2] See, for example, Prof. Donnedieu de Vabres, *La crise moderne du droit pénal. La Politique criminelle des états autoritaires* (Paris, 1938), pp. 135–6, 159.

[3] Donnedieu de Vabres, p. 159. Freisler in Güertner, *Der Besondere Teil des Strafrechts*, p. 48. On analogy in Soviet Criminal law see now R. Schlesinger, op. cit., pp. 107 and 225.

workers and peasants", with the consequence that every act directed against that State and its order of things may be punished, in Nazi Germany the corresponding effect was achieved by roundabout routes and underhand methods. The final exploit in this direction seems to have been the use of phenomenological ideas[1]: a burglar is one who is "a burglar in essence", not one who commits burglary. It is characteristic of such tendencies that those "safeguards" referred to above are not, as in Soviet law, framed in objective ("socially dangerous", etc.), but in subjective terms ("sound sense of justice").

There is, however, an important consideration in favour of the Nazi Act of 1935, of greater weight than the merits of the formula employed, but surprisingly little noticed: Criminal justice under the Nazi régime has been administered, for the bulk of non-political offences at least, under the old Penal Code of 1871 with its comparatively narrow conceptions, framed in accordance with the teachings of the Classical School. Consequently the need for extension by analogy has been far greater than in the U.S.S.R., where an entirely new system of criminal law had been created, using a different technique and the widest and most elastic terms imaginable.

The unfettered admission of analogy, it cannot be disputed, is incompatible with the ideal of certainty and predictability which figures so predominantly in the arguments of the Dicey-Hewart-Hayek school of thought. What the adherents of this school are too readily inclined to assume is, however, that the prohibiton of analogy is in itself capable of maintaining those safeguards of civil liberty. Actually, as no lawyer with inside knowledge of the work of criminal courts in whatever country can honestly deny, this is nothing but an illusion. Where statutes have to be interpreted, a considerable margin of uncertainty is, and will always be, inevitable.[2] Even the line of demarcation between what is still permissible as "extensive interpretation" and what becomes prohibited "analogy" is only too often shrouded in darkness.[3] The practical difference between the

[1] F. Neumann, *Behemoth* (1943), p. 370.

[2] It is not without interest to read the remarks of an experienced K.C., Dr. Heber Hart, on this point: *The Way to Justice* (1941), pp. 13 and 20.

[3] In 1942, a householder was charged before the Derbyshire Justices under Reg. 22 (11) Defence (General) Regulations, 1939, with failure to care to the best of his ability for a "child" billeted on him. The "child" was a girl of 14. According to sect. 107 of the Children and Young Persons Act, 1933, "child" in this Act means a person under the age of 14. The Justices held that the girl was not a child for the purpose of the Defence Regulation and dismissed the charge. The King's Bench Division sent the case back to them, the Lord Chief Justice pointing out that

two systems is, therefore, far less important than often claimed by many theorists and outsiders, and there is no reason to believe that the interpretation of statutes by administrative bodies is inherently bound to be less certain and predictable than that by criminal courts.

This is a consideration of legal technique. There are, however, yet other arguments, mostly belonging to the sphere of legal and social history and philosophy, that should make us hesitate in our wholesale condemnation of analogy. First, the prohibition of analogy came into being as one item in a programme of reforms directed against excessive and arbitrary powers of the judges and against over-harsh penalties. It was intended sometimes to protect the public against the judges, and sometimes to assist the judges in their efforts to restrict as much as possible the scope of capital punishment. In pre-revolutionary France, for example, the judges were almost completely free to impose any penalties they wanted to. In addition to the *peines légales*, they had at their disposal *peines en usage* and *peines arbitraires*.

> *Les juges sont tellement maîtres d'arbitrer la peine suivant l'atrocité du crime qu'il peuvent prononcer la peine de mort, si ce crime est de nature à mériter cette peine, quoiqu'elle n'est pas établie par la loi.*[1]

Under such circumstances, it was the protection against the imposition of arbitrary penalties (*nulla poena sine lege*) even more perhaps than against an extension of the scope of offences that was in the minds of reformers. This aspect of the matter has now become comparatively insignificant because of the extremely wide margin of discretion given to the courts in most modern penal laws. Again, judges need no longer rely on the prohibition of analogy in their fight against capital punishment.

Another point of at least equal importance and one that has so far been persistently overlooked : As a child of the French Revolution, the principle *nullum crimen sine lege* was mainly designed to favour the *tiers état* as the social class which was the principal usufructuary of the Revolution. It has retained this

" no definition (of the term ' child ') was necessary to cover such a case as this. In the ordinary use of the English language, a person of 14 years of age is a child. . . . A girl of 14 is so plainly, in my opinion, a child that it is not open to Justices to hold otherwise " (Rodger *v.* Varey, *Magisterial Cases*, July–Sept. 1942, p. 73). This decision was no doubt perfectly justified, but was it based on " extensive interpretation " or on analogy ? The different terminology of the Act of 1933, though in no way binding outside that Act, cannot be entirely overlooked.

[1] Jousse, *Traité de la justice criminelle de France* (Paris, 1771), partie III, titre 25, p. 603, quoted from R. Hoehn, *Die Stellung des Strafrichters in den Gesetzen der französischen Revolutionszeit* (Berlin, Leipzig, 1929), p. 22.

characteristic ever since. As a rule, it is the bourgeois, the business man, the *entrepreneur*, who profits by it, as the member of the community more likely than anybody else to know the law and, with the support of his legal advisers, to find ways and means of getting round it. The bulk of offences most commonly committed by the small man, thefts, burglaries, drunkenness, and the like, will but rarely give rise to any difficult questions of interpretation by analogy, and even his gambling usually takes some straightforward form of law-breaking. It is mostly when big business interests become involved that systematic efforts are made to devise ways and means of committing anti-social acts still left free by the criminal law. This can be observed particularly in those sections of the criminal law where organized business interests are active, such as the betting and gambling laws, the commercial exploitation of sex, Drug Acts, taxation laws, and profiteering. There exists a striking parallelism in this respect between the principle *nullum crimen sine lege* and the ideal of equality as understood by the French Revolution. It, too, is the typically bourgeois product of an essentially bourgeois Revolution. As Tawney has shown,

> the form which the equalitarian programme assumed in France was dictated by the character of the inequalities which existed. Since the most conspicuous of them were juristic, not economic, it was, in the first place, legal privilege, not inequality of wealth, which was the object of attack. . . . The burning problem was that, not of the propertyless wage-worker, but of the property owners.[1]

And just as little as that purely legalistic brand of " Equality " has secured real equality for the common people, just as little has *nullum crimen sine lege* established the ideal of certainty in the administration of criminal justice. To the common man who commits an anti-social act it is, much more than the question of guilt which is comparatively easy to answer, the selection of the sentence that matters, and here judicial discretion is becoming more and more unfettered.

It is not our purpose to advocate the unrestricted admission of analogy—this would indeed be tolerable only in a perfectly homogeneous society where law and social morality have become

[1] R. H. Tawney, *Equality*, pp. 124–5. See, moreover, in particular Harold J. Laski, *The Socialist Tradition in the French Revolution* (1930).—In his otherwise admirably well-balanced article in *Journal of Comparative Legisl. and Intern. Law*, Third Series, Vol. XXIV (Feb. 1942), p. 36, Prof. Stefan Glaser expresses the view that " all attacks against the principle are inspired by political motives and aims ". Is this however, not equally true of the defence ?

identical[1]—but merely to show the problem in its proper perspective. The fate of civil liberty depends on the men who have to administer criminal justice much more than on this or any other legal formula.

English law has shown a better balanced attitude in the matter than the Continent. Its rule of strict interpretation of penal statutes, though duly respected, is hardly regarded as one of the most sacred guardians of civil liberty, and it has even been said that "the tendency of modern decisions, upon the whole, is to narrow materially the difference between what is called a strict and a beneficial construction".[2] On the other hand, when in 1933 the King's Bench Division established a new type of offence by extending the Common Law offence of "public mischief" to a new type of human behaviour, the judges had to face the strongest and the most unanimous criticism on the part of legal writers.[3]

For the law-maker who wants to have the best of both worlds —i.e., to avoid the use of elastic terms; to impose the strictest ban on the use of analogy; and, in spite of such handicaps, to get the better of white-collar criminals—the only way out would be constant revision of the wording of criminal statutes.[4] Even this, however, could not work without greatly extending the scope of *delegated legislation.* At a time when the stream of delegated legislation has anyhow overflowed its banks and played havoc among the guardians of tradition, this is bound to be an unpopular idea. However, the very extensive debates in and outside the House of Commons—culminating in 1944 in the setting up by the Home Secretary of a Select Committee of the House to carry out a continuous examination of all Statutory Rules and Orders[5] —have shown that delegated legislation, on a very large scale,

[1] F. Neumann, op. cit., p. 362.

[2] Sir Peter Benson Maxwell, *On the Interpretation of Statutes* (7th ed. 1929), p. 244. See also the sceptical remarks by Prof. Edward Jenks, *The New Jurisprudence* (1933), p. 94. Mr. J. W. C. Turner, writes, *Law Quarterly Review*, Vol. 58 (1942), pp. 348 et seq.: "The natural reluctance of judges to allow an obviously dishonest man to escape criminal punishment has often led them to proclaim as established principles of law doctrines which were in fact not only quite new, but which have sometimes had the unfortunate result of rendering the law itself more indistinct and uncertain." The famous Carrier's case—see above, p. 96—is already "an illuminating example of legislation by judges who assert that they are applying the principle of *stare decisis* in all its rigor" (Jerome Hall, *Theft, Law and Society*, p. 323).

[3] See for example, Dr. W. T. S. Stallybrass, *Law Quarterly Review*, Vol. 49, pp. 183 et seq.; *Cambridge Law Journal*, Note in Vol. V, p. 263; on the historical development, Percy H. Winfield, *The Province of the Law of Tort* (1931), p. 190.

[4] See for example, above p. 204.

[5] See Hansard of May 17, 1944; *The Times* of May 18, 1944. The scope of the Committee's functions is set out in *The Times*, June 16, 1944.

has to be accepted as inevitable and that there are ways and means of making it comparatively innocuous through appropriate control. As Sir Cecil Carr, the legal adviser to the Committee and probably the greatest authority on the subject, has pointed out, there are three chief justifications for delegated legislation: "first, the limits of the *time* of the legislators; secondly, the limits of the *aptitude* of the legislature . . .; and, thirdly, the need of some weapon for coping with situations created by emergency".[1] Surely, the anti-social activities of citizens who try to exploit gaps in criminal statutes as described in previous chapters are well able to create a state of emergency. The criminal law may therefore have to continue, even in peace-time, to claim its proper share in delegated legislation of a technical character, i.e., in matters where the general trend of policy is clear but the formula has to be persistently kept up to date.[2]

Professor Jerome Hall has rightly drawn attention[3] to the Swedish system—which is used in the U.S.A. and Soviet Russia as well—of deliberately legislating for short periods of time only and keeping the results constantly under scientific review with the assistance of suitable research organizations. In England, similar tendencies have also become apparent, under the pressure of war-time needs or in order to frustrate attempts to evade the law.

(3) Character and Procedure of the Administrative Agencies to be Employed.

So far, it has here been argued that at least some of the much-vaunted pillars of the liberal era of criminal justice are less solid than we have been taught to believe. There is but little inherent virtue in the technique of draftsmanship peculiar to the criminal law, or in the rules of interpretation applied by the criminal courts. Where certain functions of the courts have been left to administrative agencies, or should be transferred to them in future, the latter would, however, be expected to comply with the traditional methods of interpretation. To refer to

[1] Sir Cecil Thomas Carr, *Concerning English Administrative Law*, p. 37. See also Report on Ministers' Powers, 1932.

[2] We do not propose to go so far as Prof. J. Schumpeter who, in *Capitalism, Socialism, Democracy* (1942), p. 292, wants, in a democracy, to limit the share of Parliament in this field to the question whether or not the country is to have a Criminal Code at all, and to the framing of a few issues that "the Government may choose to select for political decision which is more than formal", whereas for the rest the specialist's advice should be unreservedly accepted.

[3] *Readings in Jurisprudence*, p. 1081, fn. 8.

one of the most striking cases in our collection, the National Service Officer who has to decide what is a " reasonable excuse ", or whether a worker is " capable of performing " a certain job, will, in view of the penal consequences that loom in the background, have to apply the rules of " strict construction ", for what they are worth. This, however, is not enough to make " administrative criminal law " palatable to a democratic country. It is clear that instances of law-making such as represented by the Essential Work Order are open to criticism mainly for three reasons : first, because of the character of the administrative agency employed ; second, because of the absence of adequate rules of procedure ; and, third, because of the exclusion of the criminal courts from almost the whole field of criminal proceedings except the selection of the sentence.

(*a*) First, if administrative agencies are entrusted with decisions of great, often even of vital, importance for the life of the individual citizen, they have to be of an adequate calibre and standing. Its members must be suitably trained for their specific jobs and enjoy reasonable security of tenure of office. It is, as a rule, unwise to leave such decisions, as has been done in the Essential Work Order, in the hands of a single official, especially if this official enjoys no superior standing in the world of bureaucracy. Such a monocratic system is not only in itself incapable of inspiring confidence ; it also lends itself to various abuses, the most frequent of which is the tendency for prosecutor and judge becoming one person. If the same National Service Officer who receives and investigates complaints has also to decide the case, his impartiality will be questioned by those affected by his decision. At least within the administrative agency, there should be a separation of the investigating and prosecuting from the quasi-judicial function.[1]

(*b*) There is, secondly, the need for an adequate *procedure*. Nobody will wish for a complete imitation of the rules of procedure evolved in the ordinary courts of law. The comparative simplicity of administrative procedure is, on the contrary, one of the reasons why it is so widely preferred. There are, however, certain fundamental principles of " natural justice " which have to be honoured in whatever kind of procedure.[2] The gradual working out of such principles has been one of the most encouraging features of the theory and practice of Anglo-American

[1] See also Chamberlain-Dowling-Hays, op. cit., p. 210.
[2] See Report on Ministers' Powers, pp. 75 et seq.

administrative law in recent decades. In the U.S.A. this has been done in compliance with the "Due Process of Law" clause of the Constitution. This is not the place for a comprehensive review of the subject as a whole [1]; a few essential features may, however, be briefly referred to: there are the rules established in this country in R. *v.* Arlidge,[2] 1915, A.C. p. 120, and other famous cases; for instance, that administrative tribunals must not listen to evidence from one side only; that no party must be condemned unheard; that no one must be judge in his own cause [3]; that, except in trifling cases, reasons for the decision must be given. Whether the hearing must be in public may be questionable, particularly in view of the existence of a new category of ordinary courts where the proceedings are not openly conducted: the Juvenile Courts. There is no reason, however, why the scope of publicity before administrative boards should not be widened.[4] Adequate records should always be kept, and the more important decisions of the higher administrative Tribunals should be published in order to make their policy widely known and to build up a uniform tradition.[5] It is hardly necessary to stress the significance of this point in matters such as are discussed in previou schapters of this book, e.g., sterilization, abortion, usury, share-pushing, taxation, monopoly.

Special difficulties are presented by the law of evidence.[6] Many of the cumbersome rules which have been developed merely in view of the special needs of a lay jury can be discarded in proceedings conducted by and before a body of experts. Hearsay evidence may, therefore, not have to be rigidly excluded, provided it is used not as a basis for the decision but only as a guide to first-hand evidence.

If these rules of the judicial game are faithfully observed

[1] See especially the detailed discussion in W. A. Robson, *Justice and Administrative Law*.

[2] Robson, pp. 143 et seq.; Report on Ministers' Powers, p. 107.

[3] This has to be stressed not only with reference to administrative justice. The principle may also give rise to particular difficulties in Courts of Summary Jurisdiction manned with lay justices who, very frequently, are at the same time members of local authorities, e.g., in cases of non-payment of local rates, or cases under the Education Act. Difficulties of this kind are continuously discussed in professional journals like *The Magistrate*. In a letter to *The Times* of May 25, 1944, the correspondent stated that out of a total of forty-seven magistrates on a local Bench twenty were members of local authorities.

[4] W. A. Robson, op. cit., p. 276.

[5] Chamberlain-Dowling-Hays, op. cit., p. 61.

[6] See, for example, Pennock, op. cit., pp. 78, 155 et seq.; Chamberlain-Dowling-Hays, pp. 22 et seq.

Sir Cecil Carr's word may become true that " it is not at all certain that administrative tribunals are unpopular in England ".[1]

(c) Perhaps the most crucial question is that of *Court Control* over decisions of administrative bodies. The dilemma is obvious : if Court Control is too much restricted or altogether excluded, explosions on the part of public opinion or certain sections of it may easily occur. The dissatisfaction with the working of the Essential Work Order shows where the danger lies. On the other hand, if Court Control is too much extended, the administrative agency loses its *raison d'être* as a semi-judicial body. It is essential, therefore, to steer a middle course.

> When the executive itself exercises quasi-judicial functions, the judiciary should have such power of scrutiny as will enable it to see that the rules adopted by the executive are such as are likely to result in justice.[2]

From this principle the following deductions can be made : Court Control should be essentially restricted to questions of law. It is mainly because of their superior knowledge of the factual side of the problems involved that the participation of administrative bodies is regarded as indispensable, and it would be very odd if findings of facts which are treated as conclusive and final even when made by inexperienced lay jurors should be open to judicial revision if made by specially qualified administrators.[3] In view of the intrinsic difficulties of separating the sphere of law from that of facts it is, however, far from simple to apply this formula in practice. Moreover, in both directions a number of exceptions has been established in the course of time. In U.S.A. court practice,[4] for example, the interpretation of technical terms of which the administrative agency is supposed to have specialized expert knowledge is entirely left to the latter ; on the other hand, the courts claim control over so-called " jurisdictional facts ", i.e., facts on the existence of which the competence of the administration depends.[5]

With regard to matters of procedure, the courts will claim

[1] *Concerning English Administrative Law*, p. 100.

[2] Harold J. Laski, *A Grammar of Politics* (4th ed. 1938), p. 307.

[3] See James M. Landis, *The Administrative Process* (1938), p. 124 ; Report on Ministers' Powers, p. 108.

[4] See the details in Pennock, op. cit., esp. pp. 152 et seq., 210 et seq., and passim ; Chamberlain-Dowling-Hays, op. cit., pp. 202 et seq. ; James M. Landis, op. cit., pp. 136 et seq.

[5] The French Conseil d'Etat has the right, in matters of *excès de pouvoir*, to examine the facts in so far as this is necessary for the discovery of an illegality ; see Raphael Alibert, *Modern Law Review*, Vol. III (1940), p. 269.

the right to examine whether the administrative findings of facts are supported by evidence collected in an orderly and fair manner, i.e., by observing the rules referred to above under (*b*).[1] In a recent non-criminal case, the House of Lords confirmed the right of the courts to examine whether a non-judicial body, in exercising jurisdiction entrusted to it by statute, has reached its decision " after due inquiry ".[2]

One aspect of judicial control which is of special importance for the relation between administrative agencies and criminal courts is the question of individual guilt, *mens rea*, in particular of insanity and kindred aspects. It might be argued that they should always be left to the criminal courts which are, or should be, better equipped to deal with them.

From this, it becomes clear, that the procedure adopted under the Essential Work Order falls short of the requirements of judicial control. Though it should not be open to the courts to oppose the interpretation by the National Service Officer of such terms as " capable of performing ", " reasonable excuse " —technical terms on which the Officer must be expected to have expert knowledge—the courts which are asked to impose penalties should have the right to examine the fairness of the procedure used for the collection of the basic facts.[3] This, however, will inevitably lead to difficulties in the case of criminal courts manned exclusively by lay justices. Courts for which the right is claimed to control the administration in questions of law and procedure need at least a professional lawyer of sufficient standing as chairman.

[1] Sometimes the courts have gone even further in their claims ; see Landis, pp. 128–9.

[2] General Medical Council *v.* Spackman, *The Times*, Aug. 6, 1943. The decision is based on Sect. 29 of the Medical Act 1858, which empowers the Council to order the erasion from the medical register of the name of a medical practitioner found guilty, " after due inquiry ", of infamous conduct in any professional respect.

[3] How far this principle should be stretched must remain doubtful in individual cases. In Conway *v.* Stocks, *The Times*, April 9, 1943, the King's Bench Division decided that it was only for the National Service Officer to say whether a " Works Committee " in the meaning of sect. 6 (3) of the Essential Work (Gen. Provisions) (No. 2) Order, 1942, existed, whereas Rylands *v.* Nutter, K.B.D., Jan. 27, 1944 (*Min. of Lab. Gaz.*, 1944, p. 44) seems to point in the opposite direction.

Chapter 11

IV. MAKING THE ADMINISTRATION OF CRIMINAL JUSTICE MORE SCIENTIFIC

(1) The Place of the Expert.

It is the question of how to make the best use of the *expert* that constitutes one of the crucial issues for the administration of criminal justice to-day. So far, criminal courts have not been altogether fortunate in their handling of this intricate matter. Their difficulties are of a twofold character: there is, first, the general mistrust of the expert which many a magistrate shares with the man in the street.[1] Both are equally apt to regard the " rule of the expert " as the mortal danger to the rule of law and to democracy. They refuse to see that most of the ills from which modern society suffers are due not to an excessive but to an insufficient or at least one-sided use of expert knowledge. It is perhaps not out of place at this time of the day to quote Professor Webster's recent description of peace-making after the last war,

> how men, who came entirely new to diplomatic problems, grasped at solutions of whose imperfection they were dimly aware. The experts were often thrust on one side when they produced inconvenient conclusions, and amateur schemes were hastily adopted. Some of the worst points in the treaties came without intention by the use of such methods.[2]

Little wonder, then, that the expert has so far not received in criminal courts the treatment due to him; that his work has not become sufficiently integrated and valued as an essential part of criminal justice, and that the interests of the latter have thereby suffered. While the complexity and variety of problems would require an ever-growing amount of close co-operation, experts are still often regarded more as intruders than as collaborators. This may partly be due to the historic fact that psychiatric experts were among the first to appear in criminal courts in any considerable number, only to be regarded by the judges with particular suspicion as usurpers of judicial prerog-

[1] Characteristic Dicey, *Law and Opinion*, p. lxxvi.
[2] C. K. Webster, " Peace-Making: Vienna, Paris, and To-day ", *Agenda*, Vol. II (May 1943), p. 105.

atives. In fact, the psychiatrist has neither shown himself inclined to assume the rôle of the judge, nor is he the only type of expert needed for the proper administration of criminal justice.

Under the Anglo-American law of criminal procedure a second, more specific, technical difficulty arises. This system, based on the accusatorial principle which leaves it, as a rule, to the parties to shape the features of criminal proceedings, has only reluctantly granted to the judge the right to call expert witnesses of his own accord. In the higher criminal courts, experts are usually selected and called not by the judge but by one of the parties, and therefore apt to be regarded as expert witnesses for either the prosecution or the defence. This leads to two grave dangers : the psychological of partisanship, and the social of establishing a privilege for the rich at the expense of the poor defendent. With regard to the former danger, it has recently been stated that—

> Perhaps the greatest objection to accepting the opinion of such a medical witness is that, under the present system in England, he is usually partisan ; the judge does not control the experts, he acts rather as an umpire than as a judge. Were the judge to be allowed to call an impartial expert witness, at the public expense, it would do much towards restoring confidence in expert testimony.[1]

As to the second danger, in connection with the use of the electro-encephalograph for the diagnosis of epilepsy, especially in murder trials, reference has been made to [2]

> the obvious disadvantage of the defence in the cases of poor defendants in securing expert evidence of equal weight to that of the prosecution with all the resources of the State behind it. . . . The solution of the difficulty, and this applies not only to medical, but to *all* technical matters, would be to make expert opinion, and all necessary apparatus, available for the Court independently of both prosecution and defence. This proposal is not new, it has been made often before and it is

[1] H. Barnes, " A Century of the McNaghten Rules ", in the *Cambridge Law Journal*, 1944, p. 306. See also Dr. W. Norwood East, *Medical Aspects of Crime*, p. 409.

[2] Nat. Council for the Abolition of the Death Penalty, *Wartime Bulletin No. 9*, Jan. 1943 (reproduced by permission of the Secretary, Mr. John Paton, M.P.). See also the letters to *The Times* of Sept. 16 and 25, 1942, where a distinguished medico-psychologist, Dr. H. Crichton Miller writes : " The situation will not improve until a radical change is made in the status of the medical expert ". In the Report of the Committee on Insanity and Crime (1924, Cmd. 2005), pp. 10 and 21, it was recommended that " Provision should be made, under departmental regulations, for examination of an accused person by an expert medical adviser at the request of the prosecution, the defence, or the committing magistrate ".

already the practice in technical Courts like those dealing with Admiralty matters . . . the provision of expert evidence would be a function of the Court alone.

These statements have been reproduced here at such length because of the obvious importance of the matter. Under the Continental system of criminal procedure with its strongly inquisitorial tendencies, it is exclusively a matter for the judge to decide whether he requires the assistance of expert witnesses, and if so whom he should call. Suggestions on the part of the prosecution and the defence, though permissible, are usually received with the utmost reserve and therefore rarely made. The expenses are borne by the State and, in case of conviction, later debited to the accused. For the U.S.A., the law of criminal procedure has been strongly blamed for the partial failure of psychiatry to exert the desirable influence on court practice.[1] Recently, however, it has been stated that Rule 26 of the proposed Federal Rules of Criminal Procedure, " providing for the calling of expert witnesses by the court, as well as by the parties, should enable the court to correct many current abuses and ensure less partisan expert testimony ". [2]

In English Magistrates Courts and Juvenile Courts, there is fortunately little left of these drawbacks of the accusatorial system. Regardless of the initiative and financial resources of the accused, magistrates are now making fairly wide use of medico-psychological expert knowledge before sentencing. Remands are freely made in order to obtain psychological Reports from experts selected by the magistrates, and occasionally it has even been suggested that there should always be a medical psychologist on the Bench to make sure that no cases in need of psychiatric examination should be overlooked.[3] The process of integration has therefore made fairly satisfactory progress in these courts, although even here many problems have still to be solved.

It has to be stressed, however, that all this refers to one type of expert only, the medico-psychologist, whose services may possibly be needed in any type of criminal case. The position is bound to be much more difficult in criminal cases where expert

[1] See Barnes and Teeters, *New Horizons in Criminology*, p. 319.

[2] Wendell Berge, Ass. Attorney General of the U.S.A., in *Journal of Criminal Law and Criminology*, Nov.–Dec., 1943, p. 223.

[3] In Italy (Juvenile Court Act of 1934, art. 2) one of the three judges of the Juvenile Court has to be a citizen who has distinguished himself in social welfare work and is experienced in questions of biology, psychiatry, crimino-anthropology and pædagogics, whereas the two others are professional judges. The supply of such citizens is not likely to be ample.

knowledge of a varied character is required, for the collection and digestion of which the ordinary criminal court cannot be equally well equipped. Administrative agencies which specialize in one single category of case, or in a few of them, can usually provide such knowledge from within the ranks of their own officials. To guard against the danger of partisanship they may have to establish permanent Advisory Committees or Appeal Boards composed of experts from outside.[1]

The more thoroughly this danger and the dependence on the financial resources of the parties are removed, the better the work of the expert becomes integrated as an essential part of the proceedings, the greater will also be the likelihood of achieving a higher degree of certainty and predictability in criminal cases. This does not mean that the individual should be handed over, tied hand and foot, to the tender mercies of the experts. In a democracy, their rule will have to be carefully circumscribed. " Decisions on values ought never to be in the hands of experts ", " the fundamental issues of society are not the kind of problem the expert is accustomed to handle ", says Laski,[2] which, if we understand him rightly, means that decisions on leading principles of more than purely technical character should always rest with Parliament and Government. Here, however, we are throughout concerned with the technique of administration, especially that of justice, which has become much too complicated to be mastered by laymen.[3] In the often quoted words of Lawrence Lowell, the late President of Harvard, the test of democracy is in its ability to use experts. Below, this test will be applied to certain

[1] Sometimes these Appeal Boards consist not of experts, but of representatives of public opinion, and in this case their task is usually restricted to questions which require no expert knowledge. A case in point is the Appeals Board set up under the National Service (2) Act of December, 1941, which is competent to decide not on the relative importance of the worker's previous job and the job to which she has been directed, but only on questions arising from her personal circumstances. Consequently, we find here a tripartition of functions between Employment Exchange, Appeals Board, and criminal courts. See Gertrude Williams, *The Price of Social Security*, p. 93.

[2] " Choosing the Planners " in *Plan for Britain* (Fabian Lectures, 1943), p. 118, and in particular *Democracy in Crisis* (1933), p. 171. See also A. D. Lindsay, *The Modern Democratic State*, Vol. I (1943), pp. 242 and 268 ; and Karl Mannheim, *Man and Society*, pp. 193 and 294.

[3] Admittedly the line of demarcation between high policy and mere technical administration is sometimes difficult to draw in practice, especially where the highest human values are involved in the decision of individual cases. Mr. Alec Craig, for example, is strongly opposed to the setting up of boards or committees to take the place of criminal courts in cases of " obscene publications " because of the unsuitability of the " eminent literary men and women of incredible respectability " who would sit on such committees. Consequently, " Bad as the Courts are, such a body certainly would be worse ", *The Banned Books of England* (1937), p. 173.

specific problems such as that of the Treatment Tribunal and of the Lay Magistrate.

(2) THE TREATMENT TRIBUNAL.

As already indicated, there is a strong movement at present afoot to restrict the powers and responsibilities of the criminal courts, not, as suggested above for certain categories of offences, for the stage *before*, but for that *after* conviction. During the five years' period since the matter was briefly discussed in an earlier book of the author,[1] its development has been so rapid and momentous that a re-examination may not be out of place. In the U.S.A., in particular, the idea has now passed from the stage of mere theoretical speculation to that of serious legislative drafts or even enactments. We have witnessed the publication in 1940 of the American Law Institute's Draft of a model " Youth Correction Authority Act " ; [2] followed by highly informative and at times controversial debates among U.S.A. experts, and culminating in the passing of the California Youth Correction Authority Act of 1941 and drafts submitted in subsequent years to the Legislatures of New York, Rhode Island, and other States. Of equal significance are the " Report to the Judicial Conference of the Committee on Punishment for Crime ", made by a Committee of Federal Senior Circuit Judges,[3] and the illuminating *Hearings* before a Committee of the House of Representatives on a " Bill to provide a Correctional System for Adult and Youth Offenders convicted in Courts of the United States ",[4] drafted in accordance with the Report of the Judges.

In this country, the idea has been in principle approved by Miss Margery Fry [5] and Professor D. K. Henderson,[6] but

[1] *The Dilemma of Penal Reform* (1939), pp. 201 et seq. The author is greatly indebted to Director William Draper Lewis and Mr. John R. Ellingston, of the American Law Institute ; to Mr. Benedict S. Alper, now in the U.S. Army, to Director Karl Holton of the Californian Youth Authority, Sacramento, and to Mr. Leland L. Tolman, of the Staff of the Administrative Office of the United States Courts, Reporter to the Judicial Conference on Punishment for Crime, for the material on which the following is based. Apart from the original documents quoted below, and the material issued by the A.L.I., the best information on the matter is to be found in the symposium on " The Correction of Youthful Offenders ", in *Law and Contemporary Problems*, Vol. IX, No. 4 (Autumn 1942), issued by the School of Law, Duke University.

[2] See the article by the present writer in the *Howard Journal* (1941), pp. 70 et seq.

[3] Washington, D.C., June 1942.

[4] Federal Corrections Act and Improvement in Parole. Hearings before Subcommittee No. 3 of the Committee on the Judiciary ; House of Representatives, 78th Congress, First Session, H.R. 2139 and 2140 (May 18 and 19 and June 10, 1943), Government Printing Office, Washington, 1943.

[5] See her admirable pamphlet, " The Future Treatment of the Adult Offender " (1944), pp. 21 et seq.

[6] *Psychopathic States* (1939), p. 164.

rejected by Mr. Claud Mullins.[1] In view of the not inconsiderable differences between the recommendations of the American Law Institute (A.L.I.) and those of the Circuit Judges, it is essential to keep them separate when examining the matter. Both Drafts have in common the proposal to set up a special board with the duty, among others, to relieve the judges of certain parts of their sentencing functions. Even leaving out all points of merely technical interest or peculiar to the American legal system,[2] there is, however, but little common ground with regard to details :

Whereas the A.L.I.'s Draft is restricted to adolescent offenders between 16 and 21, the Judges' Report deals with adults as well. On the other hand, the A.L.I. is much more radical than the Judges. It leaves untouched only the power of the criminal courts to deal with offences of the most serious character, i.e., mainly those for which the penalty, in the case of an adult, would be death or life imprisonment, and with very petty transgressions. For the bulk of offences, the A.L.I. scheme proposes the complete transfer of the right to select a suitable sentence from the courts to the "Youth Correction Authority" (Y.C.A.). In other words, the judges shall no longer have power to send an adolescent offender to prison, except for life, or even to place him on probation. The California Act does not go quite as far. Under it, the courts are free to grant probation and to impose short prison sentences up to ninety days. On the other hand, the age limit of that Act is much wider as the Authority may accept for treatment any boy or girl of Juvenile Court age up to the age of 23.[3]

The Judges' Bill distinguishes between adults and "youth offenders", i.e., male persons under 24. For adults, the present system of making probation orders and imposing death sentences or prison sentences of no more than one year shall remain unchanged. If, however, the judge regards a sentence of more than one year as necessary he has to impose the maximum term permitted by the statute, and it is only then that the administrative body which corresponds to the Y.C.A., here called Board of Corrections, comes into operation. Within a period of no

[1] *Crime and Psychology* (1943), pp. 213, 219.

[2] The Judges' Scheme, for example, aims at Federal, the A.L.I.'s at State legislation.

[3] For reasons of expediency this was later reduced to 21. On the work of the California Youth Correction Authority during the first year of its existence, see Karl Holton in *The Correction of Youthful Offenders*, pp. 655 et seq. and for the subsequent period the Report of the Assembly Fact-finding Committee on Correctional Problems to California Legislature (1945).

more than six months since the prisoner has begun to serve his sentence, the Board, after close study of all aspects of the case, has to submit to the court its recommendations as to the length of the sentence to be finally imposed. It is then left to the judge to accept or reject this recommendation, though in the latter case he has to state his reasons. The principle of judicial review of administrative action, characteristic of American legislation in general,[1] is therefore upheld. " The Judge reviews the Board ", whereas under the A.L.I.'s draft " the Board reviews the Judge ".[2] This and the retention of the power of the court to order probation are the most important differences between the A.L.I. and the Judges' Bill, and the reader of the *Hearings* gains the impression that without the concession of judicial review the chances of the Bill to pass Congress would be very small indeed.

In cases of " Youth Offenders ", too, the proposals of the Judges leave this fundamental principle of judicial review untouched. The judge is free to proceed as in the case of an adult ; i.e., if he finds that the offender is not in need of " treatment ", he may place him on probation ; if he finds that the offender will derive no benefit from " treatment ", he may impose a prison sentence, with the only proviso that if this sentence is for more than one year the same procedure has to be adopted as in the case of adults. The judge is, however, free to take an entirely different course, and it is here that the Judges' Bill comes nearest to the A.L.I.'s draft : he may " sentence the youth offender to the custody of the Authority (i.e., Youth Authority Division of the Board of Correction) for treatment and supervision until discharged by the Authority as provided in this Title ". This gives the Authority power either to place the offender under probation or to arrange for him the appropriate institutional treatment. After a maximum of four years he has to be released conditionally under supervision and after another two years unconditionally.

Is there anything in the nature of these proposals, we may ask, to make them appear strikingly new and revolutionary ? What are the advantages which would justify the setting up of a new administrative Board ? Generally speaking, to restrict the sentencing power of the judges is a step in some ways less, and in others more, drastic than a restriction of their competence at

[1] See above, p. 217.
[2] Report to the Judicial Conference, p. 8 ; *Hearings*, p. 10.

the guilt-finding stage. Less drastic, as it affects only individuals who have already been found guilty of an offence by the court; and more drastic as it means interfering with that judicial function on which the judges themselves should be experts, whereas for the finding of guilt answers may be required to a great many questions from the most diverse branches of knowledge on which nobody can expect the judges to be experts. Whatever may be our attitude in this respect, the Judges' Bill cannot well be regarded as over-revolutionary considering that the restriction it proposes on the sentencing function of the court is merely compulsion, in certain cases, to call in the expert penologist, not compulsion to accept the expert's advice. Some ardent reformer might even be inclined to find the Bill slightly too timid and conservative and to ask whether the proposed changes are really worth while. That this would certainly mean taking too narrow a view of this significant scheme becomes clear from an analysis of the chief advantages to be expected from it. They are, as has been pointed out in the *Hearings*, threefold:[1] to remedy the lack of sufficient knowledge on the part of the sentencing judge; to produce greater uniformity of sentences; and to facilitate better co-ordination between the sentencing and the paroling authorities.

(*a*) *Lack of knowledge*: There are two sides to this which have to be kept apart; on the one hand:

> No judge, however learned, however wise [says Judge Parker], can acquire in the short period he devotes to sentencing sufficient knowledge of the defendant and his surroundings to be sure that he imposes the sort of sentence that is best in the premises.

This is inevitable and indisputable. There is, however, an additional reason;

> Then, we have this fact that we might as well face: Some of the judges in the Federal Courts are not men who have given their lives to the practice of criminal law, and are not at all expert in the matters of criminology. They are the successful civil lawyers, and they come to this problem of crime late in life with little knowledge of its background . . . that, I think, has been recognized by every Attorney-General of the United States for the last twenty years.

One has only to compare this statement with the recent criticisms by Mr. Claud Mullins,[2] himself one of the shining

[1] See Judge John J. Parker, Chairman of the Judges' Committee, *Hearings*, pp. 6 et seq.

[2] *Crime and Psychology*, pp. 205 et seq.

exceptions, to realize how widespread this ignorance of the tools of their trade is even among professional judges, to say nothing about lay magistrates. To improve matters nothing short of a profound change in the training of young lawyers, combined with a different system of judicial appointments, would do. For England, in addition, a considerable restriction of the competence of lay magistrates, as outlined below, would be needed in order to secure sufficient elbow-room for the better-trained lawyer. All these changes are desirable in themselves, even if no Treatment Tribunals should be established. On the other hand, they would but little affect the truth that no judge can be expected to find the best method of treatment after a brief hearing ; and even the most thoroughly conducted preliminary enquiries by probation officers plus observation in special observation centres, indispensable as they are, will never entirely exclude the possibility of errors which have to be put right in the course of the sentence. In short, the ideal solution seems to be to increase the supply of lawyers with adequate training ; to make such training a *conditio sine qua non* of judicial appointments ; to put at the disposal of the judge the necessary equipment such as experts, observation centres, etc. ; and, finally, to make much wider use of the *indeterminate* sentence to compensate for the initial lack of knowledge on the part of the authorities. Confining the argument to this one aspect—lack of adequate knowledge on the part of judges—the conclusion seems therefore this : only if all attempts satisfactorily to solve the question of judicial training should fail, or if they should have to be regarded in advance as futile, only then would the proposal of a Treatment Tribunal seem to be justified as a second best. Whether such a pessimistic view is in fact justified, it is not for the author to decide, though the symptoms have so far not been altogether encouraging. Concerning the choice between the compulsory system of the A.L.I. and the non-compulsory system of the Judges, the former might perhaps seem more logical because, if there is really no hope of securing more competent judges, the fear might not be entirely unfounded that judges would not avail themselves of the advice offered to them by experts. On the other hand, the A.L.I. system might discourage individual judges from privately securing better penological training.

(*b*) There remains, however, still the second argument : the need for *greater uniformity of sentences*. It is on this point that the greatest emphasis has been laid by the supporters of the Judges'

Bill, and it is here that we are approaching one of the most difficult problems to be faced by modern penal philosophy : first, in what sense is uniformity of sentences desirable at all ; and, secondly, how can it be achieved ? It is no use denying that, in its practical consequences, individualization of treatment, that dominating principle of modern penology, is bound to clash with the traditional requirements of justice as understood by the man in the street. To him, justice still too often means mechanical equality, equality at any price, equal treatment not only of equals but also of unequals. His conception of equality still remains largely the old one of the Classical School of making the punishment fit the crime, i.e., fit the characteristics of the offence, not of the offender—the number of previous convictions being the only exception. As experience in courts of appeal shows, it is one of the most frequent grievances of an appellant that he has been given a longer term than his friend who " has done exactly the same ". The meaning of individualization according to personality and personal circumstances of the offender is but rarely grasped ; and as long as punishment still implies not only treatment but also stigma, this feeling cannot be entirely neglected. If of two boys who have jointly stolen, the one is put on probation and the other sent to an approved school because of different home conditions, the latter will inevitably develop a strong grievance against the court and society in general.[1] There are, it seems, only two alternatives : either the old policy of making the punishment fit the crime, which is compatible with a stigmatizing penal system, or the new idea of individualization according to personal needs with corresponding " de-stigmatization " of treatment wherever justified. The present system of connecting the social stigma with the penalty imposed rather than with the crime is unfair and illogical.[2] Apart from this question of stigma, however, a partial solution of the problem lies in the working out of really scientific principles of individualization which will make it possible at least roughly to re-establish the rule of equal treatment of equals.

[1] Within the institution, the same problem exists, of course. " The greatest difficulty in treating aggression in a group ", writes Dr. S. R. Slavson (*American Journal of Orthopsychiatry*, July 1943, p. 430), " is the danger of losing status with the entire group by individualizing the management of any one child in the group ; for it is expected by the children that equal treatment of all members . . . will be accorded." See also S. R. Slavson, *An Introduction to Group Therapy* (New York, The Commonwealth Fund, 1943), pp. 33 and 48.

[2] The point has been argued at length in the author's, *The Dilemma of Penal Reform*, Chapter IV, esp. pp. 117–18.

It is in this connection, too, that the Prediction Tables worked out by the Gluecks will be valuable.[1] As soon as these new principles become known and accepted, beyond a small circle of experts, by the community at large, individualization will no longer be suspected as injustice.[2]

For the time being, this is still a very distant goal. Not for a moment do we overlook the tremendous difficulty of defining the meaning of " equal " in this connection. There is, however, as yet far too much unequal treatment of equal cases, even in violation of the most elementary rules of the game. Recent studies of the sentencing policy of American criminal courts [3] have revealed a striking lack of uniformity between district and district as well as between judge and judge, and the discussions on the Judges' Bill before the House of Representatives have added further illuminating material on this point. " A man in the middle district in one State will receive 6 months for a particular kind of crime and a man in the western district, in the same State, will receive 5 years, where there is no justification for the difference ".[4] The particularly interesting material presented by Mr. James V. Bennett, Director of the Federal Bureau of Prisons, shows that in 1941 local variations in the use of probation for male offenders by Federal Courts ranged from 5·5 per cent. in western Tennessee to 73·3 per cent. in middle Pennsylvania, and that liquor law offenders in northern Alabama received sentences of more than 2 years in 86·2 per cent., in southern Alabama, however, only in 3·8 per cent.[5] It is difficult to believe that such differences were simply due to an application of the principles of individualization and unequal treatment of unequals. In any case, Mr. Bennett's conclusion is likely to be correct that such conspicuous lack of uniformity is bound to create very awkward problems for the rehabilitation of offenders, particularly in institutions where inmates have ample opportunities of comparing their respective offences and sentences.

[1] On this subject see the author's review articles in *The Sociological Review*, Vol. XXXIV (1942), pp. 226 et seq., and *Modern Law Review*, Vol. V (1942), pp. 273 et seq.

[2] In *Jail Journey* (1940), Mr. Jim Phelan, who served twelve years in English prisons under a life sentence, writes " A Governor should be 100 per cent. sympathetic, intelligent, progressive and informed, or as mechanical as an adding machine ", p. 92.

[3] See the useful summary in Barnes and Teeters, *New Horizons in Criminology*, pp. 332 et seq., and the literature quoted.

[4] Judge Parker, *Hearings*, p. 7.

[5] *Hearings*, pp. 94 et seq., 116–17, 125 et seq. In Germany, too, it was claimed that in some districts prison sentences were, on an average, eight to ten times longer than in others ; see the author's, *Revision im Strafverfahren* (1925), p. 176.

Similarly striking regional variations in the use of the different methods of treatment are shown in the material available on the sentencing policy of English criminal courts. The following table gives the maximum and minimum percentage figures for the most important methods of treatment as used in 1933 by Courts of Summary Jurisdiction, excluding Juvenile Courts (indictable offences only) : [1]

	Imprisonment without Option of a Fine.	Fines.	Probation.	Binding Over without Supervision.	Dismissed after Charge Proved.
Average for England and Wales . .	24·7	31·1	19·1	15·3	7·8
Maxima . .	36·8 (Bristol)	73·6 (Glamorgan County)	43·8 (Nottingham)	27·1 (Manchester)	31·6 (Leeds)
Minima . .	5·1 (Glamorgan County)	12·4 (Portsmouth)	5·0 (Glamorgan County)	4·9 (Leeds)	2·7 (Birmingham)

The picture was only slightly more uniform for Juvenile Courts in the same year : [2]

	Committals to Home Office Schools.	Fines.	Probation.	Binding Over without Supervision.	Dismissed after Charge Proved.
Averages for England and Wales	9·5	3·1	53·9	9·5	22·5
Maxima . . .	22·1 (Newcastle)	6·2 (Durham County)	78·1 (Birmingham)	23·9 (Bristol)	54·4 (Liverpool)
Minima . . .	3·5 (Glamorgan County)	1·0 (Birkenhead)	29·4 (Bristol)	— (Several Courts)	2·9 (Newcastle)

In 1938, the average percentage of adult offenders placed on probation by Courts of Summary Jurisdiction was 15, whereas

[1] Compiled from the Report on the Social Services in Courts of Summary Jurisdiction (1936, Cmd. 5122), p. 175. Although Glamorgan County happens to be more often than any other district at one end of the scale, it is by no means an isolated instance. Other districts show deviations from the average which are only slightly less considerable.

[2] Ibid., p. 176.

the figures for London were 24, for Bradford 35, for Wakefield 42, for Liverpool 3, and in several districts none.[1]

Obviously, under a system where 1,044 Courts of Summary Jurisdiction manned with about 20,000 lay magistrates, not counting the comparatively insignificant number of stipendiaries, administer criminal justice, local differences in sentencing policy are bound to be greater than in countries where the bulk of criminal court work is done by a smaller number of professional magistrates. In the absence of a Ministry of Justice, "no authority is charged to consider how a Court of Summary Jurisdiction does its work or what defects may exist in its organization or methods . . . there is no central source from which authoritative information can be obtained about the methods adopted by the numerous courts up and down the country . . .".[2]

Appeal courts can, no doubt, make important contributions towards greater uniformity.[3] This has been experienced in England, particularly since the Court of Criminal Appeal was established in 1907.[4] The usefulness of appeal courts in this direction is, however, inevitably limited, not so much to the cases brought before them—the individual case can often be used to establish general principles [5]—but to the problems with which they are concerned. It is more or less left to chance, and to the means of the offender, what kind of problem and of miscarriage of justice comes to the notice of the Court of Appeal. In countries where only the prisoner has the right to appeal against the sentence, this, too, is likely to create serious gaps. Moreover, appeal courts are naturally disinclined to interfere with any but the most flagrant mistakes in sentencing. As far as lower appeal courts, such as Quarter Sessions, are concerned, their districts are too small and their sentences receive too little publicity to make them factors of real significance in producing greater uniformity. Last, not least, even appeal court judges may lack the necessary training for the task which requires not only legal but penological experience.

The existence of a centralized office of public prosecutor, to

[1] *Criminal Statistics* for 1938, p. xiv. In previous years, similar differences could be observed.

[2] Report on Imprisonment by Courts of Summary Jurisdiction in default of Payment of Fines and other Sums of Money (1934, Cmd. 4649), p. 5. See also Laski, *Parliamentary Government in England*, p. 369.

[3] *Hearings*, p. 131.

[4] D. Seaborne Davies, *Nineteenth Century and After*, April 1937, p. 537.

[5] See, for example, the decisions of the Court of Criminal Appeal referred to above, p. 73.

be found probably everywhere outside England, is also likely to produce greater uniformity. These officials, who usually attend a number of courts and thereby get an opportunity of observing the sentencing practices of many judges, can use their legal right to make suggestions as to the proper sentence in order to draw attention to existing differences. They have, however, no actual power to enforce their views, and their training may show the same deficiencies as that of the judges.

The system proposed in the Judges' Bill and the more radical one of the A.L.I. would certainly do much more than appeal courts or public prosecutors to produce greater uniformity. Even with its limited competence in cases of adults, the new authority, operating over a wide area and staffed with specialists, would at least serve as a unifying agency and constitute the hitherto missing link between the various courts. In cases of adolescents, it would be able to work out its own treatment policy.

Another consideration may be added : when analysing the records of recidivist offenders for an earlier work,[1] the author was often struck by the apparent inconsistency in the length of sentences imposed upon the same person within a short period. To take one typical instance : if an offender, aged 24, receives as his tenth sentence 1 month's imprisonment for stealing a watch, and two years later, as his twelfth sentence, for the same offence, 3 years' penal servitude, and again five years later, as his fifteenth sentence, 6 months for stealing a gramophone, it is difficult to believe that there had been any sufficiently cogent reasons to justify so different sentences in a case where the age factor was hardly involved. This does not mean that such reasons might not have existed—on the contrary, there may be all the difference in the world between stealing a watch and stealing a watch. It would be most unfortunate indeed if the former rigid tariffs, based upon the value of the stolen goods, etc., were reintroduced. It is now the personality of the offender that matters much more than his particular offence. Is it, however, likely that the offender should have changed his character so completely to warrant this zig-zag course of justice ? In former years such differentiations in the length of prison sentences might have been justified by the fact that prison conditions varied greatly from one part of the country to another.[2] This consideration, how-

[1] *Social Aspects of Crime in England between the Wars*, Chapter 12 : " Recidivism ".

[2] See, for example, *Sir Evelyn Ruggles-Brise, A Memory of the Founder of Borstal*, compiled by Shane Leslie (1938), p. 98.

ever, no longer holds good. The truth is that fluctuations of this kind, which are at present of common occurrence in the criminal courts of probably all countries in the world, will be unavoidable as long as uniform and scientific principles for the treatment of recidivists are lacking. If a person has to undergo medical treatment twenty times in the course of his life, it is bad enough for him to have to use the services of twenty different doctors. If each of these in addition applies different methods, the patient will hardly manage to survive. What often happens now in the administration of criminal justice for adult offenders is that one doctor prescribes hot baths and the other cold ones, the third a tonic and the fourth a sedative. If the one does not cure, the opposite method may have a better effect. The whole treatment is purely empirical, and its inconsistencies are aggravated by the fact that the doctor who prescribes it is never identical with the one who carries it out. Such differences of policy are, of course, to a certain degree inevitable in human judgements. They may, nevertheless, be considerably diminished through the establishment of a common background of scientific training and the setting up of a Treatment Tribunal which is likely to reduce the number of different individuals who have to prescribe treatment for the same offender in the course of comparatively short periods of time. Regional differences, in particular, would probably lose much of their present significance.

(*c*) There is yet a third argument that has been used in the American debates : the need for greater co-ordination between the sentencing and the paroling authorities :

> A judge sentences a man to, say, two years in prison. The paroling authority can release him when he has served eight months. The paroling authority is not advised as to the judge's views with respect to this particular prisoner. The judge is not advised as to what action the paroling authority may take. We felt that there should be some unification . . .".[1]

Surely, this is a most important point, and one to which close attention should be paid outside the U.S.A. as well. The Borstal system, which has received much well-deserved praise throughout the American debates on the Treatment Tribunal idea,[2] may serve as an illustration. Though rightly regarded

[1] *Hearings*, p. 7.

[2] See especially Report to the Judicial Conference of the Committee on Punishment for Crime, App. II ; *Hearings*, pp. 33–4 and passim ; Healy and Alper, *Criminal Youth and the Borstal System* (1941) ; William Healy in *The Correction of Youthful Offenders*, pp. 687 et seq.

as one of the outstanding successes in the treatment of adolescent offenders, complete integration and co-ordination between the executive authorities and the judiciary are hardly among its many achievements. The respective rights and duties of judiciary and administration are clearly defined by statute: it is in the discretion of the court whether an offender should be sentenced to Borstal detention; once, however, such an Order is made it means, with one exception, detention for a maximum period of three years, and it is now entirely left to the Prison Commission to decide when (after a minimum of six months for boys or three months for girls) the offender should be released on licence.[1] In spite of this state of the law, the Prison Commission has repeatedly been criticized, in open court, by the learned Recorders of Liverpool and Manchester for prematurely licensing boys sentenced by them to Borstal Detention.[2] This can only be interpreted as indicating that, almost forty years after the passing of the Prevention of Crime Act of 1908, distinguished members of the judiciary are not yet prepared to concede to the Prison Commission that indispensable freedom of discretion entrusted to it by statute. It may also show that there is a strong case for a further widening of the powers of the administration on the lines of some of the American proposals. A comparison of the present functions of the Home Secretary or the Prison Commissioners with those of the Board of Correction as envisaged in the Judges' Report—not to speak of the much more radical proposals of the A.L.I.—reveals certain important differences: as already stated, for offenders of Borstal age it is in the discretion of the court whether or not an Order of Borstal Detention should be made. Although the courts, before making such an order, have to ask for a report from the Prison Commission as to the offender's suitability for Borstal treatment,[3] they are not obliged to accept the Commissioners' views. On the other hand, once a Detention Order is made it is entirely for the Prison Commission, within the limits set by the law, to fix the date of licensing and also to transfer to prison cases found unsuitable for Borstal. Under the Judges' scheme, the courts would be equally free to choose between the various methods of treat-

[1] Prevention of Crime Act, 1908, sects. 1 and 5.

[2] *The Times*, April 7, 1941; Aug. 1 and 10, 1944. On the other hand, Borstal governors and heads of Approved Schools have occasionally complained that recorders and chairmen of Juvenile Courts, when committing young offenders to institutions of this kind, sometimes hold out unwarranted prospects of an early release, a procedure which is bound to cause disappointment and bitterness to the offender.

[3] Prevention of Crime Act, sect. 1 (1).

ment; for offenders under the age of 24, however, they could as well take the plunge and give the Board a free hand. Moreover, as the courts would be compelled to obtain the opinion of the Board in all cases of juveniles and adults where a sentence of more than one year is contemplated, co-operation between judiciary and administration would become not, as at present, a rare exception but an event of almost daily occurrence.

Many of the details of the Judges' scheme are, no doubt, open to criticism: it might be preferable, for instance, to make it compulsory for the courts to obtain the views of the Board even in a number of cases where a sentence of less than one year is contemplated. The present scheme may not sufficiently take into account the danger that, with the proposed line of demarcation, many cases which are in urgent need of expert advice may never get it. The crucial question which it is now suggested to leave to the judges, whether a "youth offender" is in need of treatment or will not derive benefit from treatment, might better be decided by the experts of the Board, or it should at least be made mandatory on the courts to hear the Board's views on it. Sceptics may, moreover, be inclined to doubt whether the courts will be prepared to listen to the voice of the penologists of the Board and, consequently, whether men of first-rate ability will be found willing to accept office in the face of such limitations; many of them may therefore be altogether in favour of the A.L.I.'s system of compulsion. While the latter will stand a poor chance, in most countries, of overcoming traditional prejudices, it is worthy of note that so well informed and moderate a reformer as Miss Margery Fry[1] recommends, for England, the setting up of a Treatment Authority,

> preferably other than the Prison Commission, to whom should be handed over the duty of prescribing and supervising treatment, whether institutional or other, of defined classes of persons, and in particular of young persons, whom the Courts would otherwise sentence to prison or Borstal.

This would apparently leave the courts free to use probation; on the other hand, Miss Fry proposes no limitation of the discretion of the Authority in their choice of methods.

This is not the place to draw up a detailed scheme for a Treatment Tribunal. The point we wish to argue is that, for the reasons given above, the setting up of an administrative

[1] Op. cit., p. 24.

authority of this kind, endowed with wide powers, will sooner or later become imperative in most countries who wish to make the sentencing policy of criminal courts both more scientific and more uniform and to produce closer co-operation between courts and the penal system. As far as the present English system is concerned, the powers enjoyed by the Prison Commission in cases of Borstal Detention are the first step in the right direction. There is no reason why, as a further instalment, they should not be extended to all sentences of imprisonment, in the sense that the Commissioners' opinion would have to be asked for and considered by the courts as to whether the imposition of such a sentence was advisable. Already this would so considerably add to the extent and responsibility of their work that a reconstitution and expansion of the Prison Commission would become indispensable.[1] The expenses incurred would be insignificant, however, compared with the savings to be made by the considerable reduction in the number of unnecessary prison sentences which is likely to occur. This reform would, moreover, have to be accompanied by a complete prohibition of all prison sentences of less than, say, three or six months [2] and by the introduction of a system of indeterminate sentence under which the court fixes only the minimum and the maximum of the sentence to be served, whereas the actual length is determined by the Prison Commission or its successor.[3] There are already, outside the Borstal System, important precedents of this kind in the Children and Young Persons Act, 1933, for committals to Approved Schools, and for adults in sect. 14 of the Prevention of Crime Act, 1908, for habitual criminals sentenced to preventive detention. For the ordinary local and convict prisoner, the existing powers of granting remission of part of the sentence are too limited and applied with too little discrimination to be of much real use. The Criminal Justice Bill of 1939, sects. 37–40, proposed to extend not only the scope of "corrective training" and preventive detention but also the duty of the courts to consider reports by the Prison Commissioners. It also tried to widen the margin between the minimum and maximum terms of the sentence (from two to four, and in exceptional cases even

[1] The abolition of the Prison Commission and the transfer of its functions to the Home Secretary was proposed by the Criminal Justice Bill, 1939.

[2] See *The Dilemma of Penal Reform*, pp. 133 et seq.

[3] On the bewildering variety of systems at present in force in the U.S.A. see the survey of "State Sentencing Practices and Penal Systems", by Ronald H. Beattie and Leland L. Tolman in the Report to the Judicial Conference (Washington, 1942), pp. 81 et seq.

to ten years). On the other hand, it greatly limited the discretion of the courts by making such indeterminate sentences dependent on the type of offence and the number of previous convictions. This was an attempt to reconcile the old ideals of the Classical School with modern penological requirements. Post-war developments will probably tend still more to underline the latter at the expense of the former.

To sum up the main suggestions made in this section: In order to achieve a more scientific and more uniform system of sentencing and better co-ordination between criminal courts and the authorities in charge of the penal system, as a first step,

(*a*) a central Board should be established to advise the courts before the passing of a prison sentence and to administer the whole institutional side of the penal system;

(*b*) the scope of the indeterminate sentence should be widened, even beyond the limits proposed in the Criminal Justice Bill;

(*c*) short prison sentences should be prohibited by the law, with a consequent strengthening of the Probation Service.

After an experimental period, it might be provided that the advice of the Board should be sought even before a Probation Order is made. Even so, this scheme would fall short of the proposals of the American Law Institute. Sooner or later, the Board will probably have to be given power to determine the method of treatment to be employed.

Chapter 12

V. MAKING THE ADMINISTRATION OF CRIMINAL JUSTICE MORE DEMOCRATIC

One of the principal objects of the measures so far recommended in this book is to make the administration of criminal justice *more scientific*. This, however, is only one side of the problem. It is equally important to make criminal justice *more democratic*. This would require a discussion of the following questions : the part to be played by the *lay magistrate* and the *juror* ; the employment of, and co-operation between, *laymen* and *trained workers* in other sections of the penal system ; the position of the *professional judge* and *magistrate*, and of the *lawyer as advocate* ; *legal aid for the poor defendant* ; the question of *public* versus *private enterprise* in penal administration ; the introduction of *more democratic methods*, especially of suitable forms of inmate participation (" shared responsibility "), *in the management of penal and reformatory institutions* ; and, finally, the significance of *international co-operation*. For reasons of space, not all of these problems can, however, be discussed in the present book.

(1) Lay Magistrates.

" The English system horrifies foreigners by its use of lay magistrates," writes Miss Fry.[1] This is not quite true. What actually horrifies foreign observers, or at least some of them, is not the use of lay magistrates as such but the specific way of using their services, which has hardly any counterpart in other countries. How to distribute powers and responsibilities,—this is the real problem. The whole question, it seems to the author, is frequently debated on wrong lines and, therefore, with much unnecessary heat. This applies in two directions : first, supporters and critics of the present system too often take it for granted that the choice can only lie between lay *or* professional magistracy ; and, second, they are too much inclined to conduct their argument on the basis of comparisons between an ideal type of stipendiary and the worst type of lay magistrate conceivable, or vice versa. Both lines of approach are mistaken. It should, in particular, be beyond dispute that professional and

[1] *The Future Treatment of the Adult Offender* (1944), p. 15.

lay magistracy are equally indispensable. Very few critics will probably, on second thoughts, wish to see the layman driven out of the criminal courts and, as a result of a "managerial revolution", altogether replaced by stipendiaries, as was done in Nazi Germany at the beginning of the 1939–45 war.[1] A system of criminal justice administered entirely by professional lawyers stands condemned in the light of history as well as in that of practical experience. Too exclusive and prolonged an occupation with criminal cases tends to make any man a slave of his routine and comparatively indifferent to human suffering, except those few endowed with a philosophical mind and uncommon independence of character. To the layman, on the other hand, every case appears to be unique and deserving his special attention. Torture could flourish only in countries without lay magistrates; in England, its use was mainly confined to the Court of Star Chamber and its professional judges.[2] It is, however, not only his tendency towards excessive severity, it is also his frequent lack of familiarity with the ways of living and thinking of people in other walks of life that may hamper the work of the professional magistrate. The lay magistrate, on the other hand, is the indispensable middleman who alone can make the general public familiar with the work of the courts. Without him, no really democratic system of criminal justice is conceivable.

Equally obvious, however, are the shortcomings of the lay magistrate, if he is left to himself. Presumably without any legal knowledge, he is nevertheless expected to apply the law. To acquire any real judicial experience his opportunities of sitting on the bench may be much too rare. However, even if the extent of his work should be fairly considerable this may lead to nothing but a more frequent repetition of the same mistakes.[3] Being familiar, as a rule, only with the routine of his own court, he is not in a position to make comparisons, whereas the previous

[1] Mr. Cecil Whiteley, K.C., the late Common Serjeant, it is true, writes (*Brief Life*, 1942, p. 120) that "there is a growing body of opinion that the 'great unpaid' . . . should be abolished and all the judicial work of the Summary Courts should be done by stipendiary magistrates". Similarly, the President of the Associated Law Societies of Wales in a letter to *The Times* (Jan. 15, 1944).

[2] W. Holdsworth, *History of English Law*, Vol. V, pp. 173 and 185; E. Jenks, *The New Jurisprudence*, p. 233.

[3] For an eloquent and convincing "Plea for Trained Magistrates in the Juvenile Court" see Mr. W. J. H. Sprott in the *Howard Journal* (Autumn 1942). The whole problem of the lay justices is now admirably treated in Prof. R. S. T. Chorley's paper, "The Unpaid Magistrate and His Future", *The Modern Law Review*, Vol. VIII, (March 1945), pp. 1 et seq.

training of the professional magistrate makes him conversant with the methods of many experienced judges.[1] Real impartiality of judgement is a quality to be acquired not as a by-product of the mere process of sitting on the Bench, but only through systematic training.

Nor can the assistance of the clerk to the justices fully compensate for such shortcomings as are inherent in the very system. The introduction of the reforms recently recommended by the Departmental Committee on Justices' Clerks,[2] though of very great value, would not affect the fundamental weakness which lies in the peculiar relationship between clerk and justices. Being a clerk, not a magistrate, he can act only in an advisory capacity ; he has considerable power but comparatively little or no responsibility.

> The responsibility for the decision given whether dependent upon fact or law ought to remain the responsibility of the justices and not of the clerk ; any part taken by the clerk in the conduct of a case ought to be taken at the request of the justices ; [and] he should not, unless consulted, advise as to the course to be adopted.[3]

In short, this is a case of inadequate integration of the services of the expert. Power without corresponding responsibility is undesirable. Purely advisory functions will, moreover, as a rule not easily attract men of really first-rate ability ; a comparison between a Cabinet Minister in this country and a member of the President's Cabinet in the U.S.A. may serve as an illustration.[4] Nor are such functions strong enough to prevent mistaken decisions on the part of the justices. Who would be willing to entrust a difficult surgical operation to a medical layman solely because there is an expert standing at his elbow ready to advise him as to how to use the knife ? Surely, the analogy, though far from perfect, is not entirely beside the point. How can the clerk be expected, for example, to dispel mistaken views of the justices which may emerge during their deliberations, or to prevent them from overlooking certain legal problems if he does not even retire with them ?

[1] " Those who think experience makes magistrates wise are misled by proverbial analogy," writes that stern but apparently well-informed critic, " Solicitor ", *English Justice* (Pelican ed. 1941), p. 31.

[2] 1944 (Cmd. 6507).

[3] Report on Justices' Clerks, Nos. 55, 64, 66.

[4] See Harold J. Laski, *The American Presidency* (1940), Chapter II. The fact that " the office of justices' clerk is held during pleasure, and consequently the clerk can be dismissed at any time " (Report, Nos. 25 and 101) is not likely to make it more attractive.

The system, familiar to the Continent but occasionally also used in this country,[1] of a judicial bench consisting of a professional chairman and two lay magistrates, is sometimes rejected as undemocratic.[2] It is feared that in such a combination of lawyer and laymen acting as one body the influence of the trained mind might be overwhelmingly strong and the lay assessors nothing but puppets. This danger, though undeniable, can be eliminated, however, by proper selection and training of both parties concerned, and where this is achieved the advantages of the system are very considerable.[3] It is the only type of criminal court based not upon the principles of mutual suspicion, separation and control, but upon the ideals of trust, integration, and co-operation between the man in the street and the professional. Trial by jury and the lay bench advised by the clerk are perfect symbols of an atmosphere of splendid isolation and mutual distrust between the different social classes, the characteristic legacy of the French Revolution. The jury court with its two separate Benches, having hardly any contact with each other except for the Judge's summing up ; and the lay magistrates' court with the clerk " advising them only when consulted " and " retiring with them only at their request " —is this really the most accomplished expression of democracy? If democracy means something at least ideologically aiming at the gradual effacement of class distinctions, including those resulting from professional qualifications, and at the establishment of a " classless society ", surely the co-operation between expert and layman should assume a different form. It is only when these two elements have a chance of meeting on common ground and on equal terms that they can fully display their most valuable qualities and learn from each other more than a few technicalities and peculiar habits of thought.

Justices of the Peace are often attacked on account of personal shortcomings, as being too old and infirm or ignorant even of the most elementary principles of the criminal law and of the actual working of the penal system ; as being appointed for political services (meaning services to a political party) ; as

[1] For example, sometimes in Juvenile Courts, according to the Children and Young Persons Act, 1933, Second Schedule.

[2] The merits and weaknesses of this system are discussed in the author's paper, " Trial by Jury in Continental Law ", *Law Quarterly Review*, Vol. LIII (1937), pp. 408 et seq. On Soviet Russia see Ralph Millner, *Soviet Justice*, p. 12.

[3] It is now regarded as " the ideal Court " in *Administration of Justice*, a Report of a Sub-Committee set up by the Conservative and Unionist Party Organization, Feb. 1945, p. 20, and is also strongly recommended by Prof. Chorley, loco cit.

exhibiting strong class prejudices and lack of social understanding; or as too closely connected with local interests of one kind or another.[1] Criticism of stipendiary magistrates, though less frequent and vocal, is not entirely absent either.[2] It is not our intention to take any part in these discussions. It is only the system as such, not its representatives, we are here concerned with, and we have been trying to show that a decision on this vexed question can be reached independent of such personal considerations. One of the most frequent criticisms of the stipendiary magistrate, i.e., that he is the only person who has, as a one-man bench, power over liberty and property of his fellow citizens, would disappear with the introduction of the combined system recommended above.

There are only a few more observations that might usefully be added. The first is the internal change which is bound to come about in the composition of the lay magistracy as a consequence of the gradual disappearance of the leisured middle and upper classes. While the full significance of this development cannot yet be foreseen, it seems likely that the average Justice of the Peace of the future will have less time to spare for court work than his predecessor. This will make closer co-operation with professional magistrates and an extension of the sphere of activities of the latter all the more imperative. The growing complexity of criminal court work, to which frequent reference has been made throughout the course of this book, will have the same result. There can be little doubt that as long as the lay magistrate dominates the scene no effective machinery will be available to deal with "white-collar" criminals. Moreover, the tendency in favour of the professional magistrate will receive a further stimulus through the coming into existence of the new science of Criminology. Mr Claud Mullins has recently made the interesting remark that "more sympathy with progressive ideas, and in particular with the psychological treatment of delinquency, has hitherto been shown by lay justices than by

[1] See already above, p. 216. In the Report on Justices' Clerks (No. 217), it is regarded as generally undesirable that the Mayor should be chairman of the borough bench before which the local authority has frequently to appear—a practice which, according to the same Report (No. 216), is used in a large majority of boroughs. For other criticisms see *The Pub and the People, by Mass Observation*, p. 333, and esp. R. S. T. Chorley, loco cit., pp. 7 et seq.

[2] See, for example, "Solicitor", *English Justice*, p. 37; "Simple Simon", *Howard Journal* (1943), p. 149. Mr. John A. F. Watson, *The Child and the Magistrate* (1942), pp. 197 et seq., tries impartially to discuss the question with special reference to Juvenile Courts.

professional magistrates and judges ".[1] True as this may be if the comparison is based on absolute figures, it may become more doubtful when the great numerical inferiority of the professional element within the English judiciary is taken into account. That 20,000 lay magistrates should have in their midst more " white sheep " than a hundred stipendiaries is not surprising. In any case, however, the state of affairs as described by Mr. Mullins would only mean an additional reason for thorough reforms in the training of the legal profession. Such reforms should be much easier to carry through than an improved training scheme for lay magistrates. Praiseworthy and indispensable as the recent educational courses of The Magistrates' Association no doubt are, it seems hardly possible to raise the general standard of knowledge above a certain level which, for the great majority of magistrates, is bound to remain comparatively low. The various branches of scientific knowledge which have to be mastered require a much more prolonged and systematic study than can in fairness be expected from the average layman. The idea that the latter can be adequately trained to make, even unaided, the best possible use of scientific research shows a regrettable failure to grasp the meaning of such research in the fields of Criminology and Penology. To repeat it once more, here as in other branches of knowledge, it requires many years of full-time theoretical and practical study to master the subject.[2] It should at long last be recognized that the treatment of crime does not differ in this respect from that of disease. Granted that there are at present some lay magistrates who conform to such requirements and are in no way inferior to the type of professional magistrate envisaged, they serve only to confirm the rule, and even they are likely to die out.

Miss Margery Fry [3] fears that the substitution of a large body of stipendiary magistrates may involve the loss of independence and " destroy a way of justice which has the advantage of keeping the courts free from direct governmental control ". While it may be true that a Government will find it easier to exercise a certain amount of supervision over a small number of professional than over a large body of lay magistrates, it cannot possibly be taken for granted that the latter are, as a rule, more independent of outside influences than the former. On the

[1] *Crime and Psychology*, p. 206.

[2] See also R. S. T. Chorley, loco cit., p. 12 : " ' A little learning is a dangerous thing ', and perhaps nowhere more so than in the realm of law."

[3] *The Future Treatment of the Adult Offender*, p. 15.

contrary, the social, economic, and political forces which tend to impair the judicial integrity of lay magistrates may be by far the stronger, if only because they are brought to bear on untrained minds.

One of the fundamental reasons for the popularity of the lay magistrate is his apparent cheapness. Even this, however, is deceptive. If the salaries of the justices' clerks are adequately raised in accordance with the recommendations of the Report of 1944, the difference in expenditure between the present system and one in which a considerable part of the work of the clerk is done by the stipendiary will probably become almost negligible.[1]

After this had been written, an interesting correspondence on the problem of "lay and professional magistrates" was published in *The Times*, in which distinguished members of the English judiciary expressed themselves in favour of appointing legally qualified and paid chairmen in magistrates' courts.[2] Particular stress was laid on the danger inherent in the present separation of power and responsibility. Of the arguments produced by supporters of the opposite view only the following, used by Sir George Jessel, seems to require some comment:[3]

> An accountant or an engineer may be called in to advise a board of directors, but is not often asked to become a director, still less chairman. A general is not often made Secretary of State for War, but a civilian with power of judgement and an acute mind.

Here it is overlooked that accountancy and engineering for a Board of Directors, or military science for a Secretary of War, important though they may be, are not the principal branches of knowledge required. Financial ability in the case of the former, and parliamentary skill for the latter, may be regarded as even more useful. A judge, however, is helpless without legal training, and "power of judgement and an acute mind" are no monopoly of the legal layman.

Reference has already been made to the tendency to transfer certain categories of cases entirely from the criminal courts to other tribunals.[4] The most important of these categories are

[1] See also R. S. T. Chorley, loco cit., pp. 5 and 11.
[2] Sir Henry Slesser, Feb. 28, 1944; Sir Edward Marlay Samson, March 3, 1945; Mr. J. P. Eddy, K.C., March 2, 1945.
[3] March 6, 1945; other letters March 3 and 8.
[4] See above, p. 197, and p. 189 (Pit Tribunals).

offences committed by children under fourteen. In the United States and Great Britain, such offences are dealt with by juvenile courts which are chancery courts in the former country, whereas in Great Britain they are modified criminal courts, in various ways adapted to the specific needs of the young offender. In recent years the conviction seem to have been growing in this country that no such adaptation can possibly be adequate because there are inherent in the idea of court procedure elements entirely unsuitable for a child. As a consequence, certain suggestions have been put forward to the effect that, for cases concerning children under fourteen, the present juvenile courts should be either converted into chancery courts on the American model, or replaced by administrative bodies on the lines of the Scandinavian Child Welfare Councils. Such replacement could be either unconditional or, at least for certain cases, subject to the right of the accused to ask for committal to the juvenile court. Space forbids to go into the details of this difficult and highly controversial problem.[1]

In the Soviet Union, another group of cases has been taken away from the competence of the criminal courts. So-called "*Comradely Courts*" have been established, consisting of ordinary citizens, to deal with the following offences:[2] minor quarrels between neighbours and other petty offences which constitute the "remnants of the old way of living", such as libel or slander, petty assault, theft by workers within their factory up to the value of 50 roubles, and similar actions which disturb "the normal development of socialist production". The idea behind these courts is, according to Laski, to bring the pressure of public opinion to bear upon anti-social individuals; to teach the art of reconciliation; and to put into operation Lenin's principle that "as large a proportion of the population as possible should be related directly to the business of government". These courts have power to impose fines up to about 10 per cent. of the monthly wages of the lowest-paid worker; where they regard this as inadequate, they have to pass the case on to the ordinary court. This system, which seems to be a more general application of the idea behind war-time Pit Tribunals or Munition

[1] See on it the author's, *The Dilemma of Penal Reform* (1939), Chapter VI, esp. pp. 194 et seq.; *The Times Educational Supplement*, Aug. 30 and Sept. 6, 1941; and on the Scandinavian System, the League of Nations' Report on Child Welfare Councils, Geneva, 1937; Ragna Hagen, *The Howard Journal*, *1944–45*.

[2] The following text is based on the descriptions given in Harold J. Laski, *Law and Justice in Soviet Russia*, pp. 36 et seq.; S. and B. Webb, *Soviet Communism*, Vol. II, pp. 1085 et seq.; Pat Sloan, *Soviet Democracy*, p. 109.

Tribunals in Great Britain,[1] has the advantage over the lay magistrates' courts in this country that their competence is much more restricted and that they are expected to administer justice not according to the strict rules of law, an impossible task for laymen, but rather according to rules of natural law, or "justice without law".

THE JURY.

Trial by jury has but few supporters among lawyers to-day, and it is indeed difficult for those familiar with its weak spots to say much in its favour.[2] Almost its only consoling feature is the thoroughness of its decline. This process of displacing the jury by other types of criminal courts, the so-called "*correctionalization*", has gone so far that in most of the larger countries only a tiny percentage of all offences are actually tried by a jury.[3]

The whole idea of trial by jury has become obsolete to-day. Its main object was to protect the individual against arbitrary action on the part of the State and, in particular, of the judges in an age when no other protection was available. Whether trial by jury has ever been able to fulfil this function may be open to doubt. What it has actually done is to replace the tyranny of the judge by that of the juror. In English law, the powers of the jury are in certain respects more restricted and those of the judge wider than on the Continent, and the opinion has been expressed that it is mainly this restriction that makes trial by jury tolerable in England.[4] Even so, however, flagrant mistakes, in particular unjustifiable verdicts of "not guilty", are bound to occur only too often. The layman may be inclined to regard this as one of the chief advantages of the system that it can act as an unofficial pardoning agency—"an act of conscience under the covenant of grace", this is how Bernard Shaw has recently described the verdict.[5] However, if this is the idea it should be clearly expressed, instead of being disguised as justice.

[1] See above, pp. 178, 189.

[2] Reference may be made to a few striking verdicts by distinguished lawyers: Mr. Justice Holmes in the *Holmes-Pollock Letters*, Vol. I, p. 74; Cecil Whiteley, *Brief Life*, Chapter IX; Claud Mullins, *Crime and Psychology*, pp. 35, 186 et seq.; Heber Hart, *The Way to Justice*, p. 88; "Solicitor", *English Justice*, Chapter VIII.

[3] See the author's, "Trial by Jury in Continental Law", *Law Quarterly Review*, Vol. 53 (1937), p. 404. In England and Wales, only 1·1 per cent. of all offences, indictable and non-indictable, were tried by Jury in 1938 (*Criminal Statistics* for 1938, p. VI). Similarly low figures are reported for the U.S.A.; see Barnes and Teeters, *New Horizons in Criminology*, p. 364.

[4] See the material presented in the *Law Quarterly Review*, 1937, pp. 394 et seq.

[5] *Everybody's Political What's What* (1944).

Another important object of trial by jury is to associate as many citizens as possible with the administration of justice.[1] This can, however, as well be attained by reforming the magistrates' courts.

The application of scientific methods is gravely handicapped in criminal courts dominated by the jury, and its place is often taken by sophistry and humbug. To make problems of modern psychiatry clear to the average juror is impossible if presentation and discussion have to take place in the strait-jacket form of jury proceedings. The same is true of questions of evidence, whether the difficulties may be of a legal or of a psychological character. No real progress can be made in evolving a scientific system of forensic psychology, in particular that of the witness, as long as the most complicated and serious cases have to be tried before a jury. Where laymen and professional magistrate have a chance of deliberating together, doubtful points of law or psychology can be brought out, discussed, and clarified. Although the establishment of a Treatment Tribunal would provide a solution for the sentencing stage, a more scientific handling of the legal and psychological issues involved is almost equally needed for the pre-conviction stage.

A forceful and convincing plea has recently been made by Mr. Claud Mullins [2] for the abolition of trial by jury in cases of juveniles charged with offences and in cases of a sexual character against adults where children have to appear as witnesses. Instead, he suggests the setting up of a special court, consisting of a High Court Judge as chairman and two lay magistrates, for the trial of such cases. The present writer can wholeheartedly subscribe to his criticism as well as to his proposals. It is not trial by jury that is needed in such cases for the protection of the accused, but knowledge of the many psychological problems involved. The remedy for the shortcomings of the present lay magistrates' court is not the jury but a differently constituted, a more knowledgeable and efficient magistrates' court and, for very serious or very complicated cases, a court consisting of one or more High Court Judges and a suitable number of lay assessors. In the case of sexual offences against children, in particular, preliminary enquiries by well-trained officers capable of securing reliable evidence without endangering the interests of

[1] Chorley, loco cit., p. 17; Laski, *Will Planning Restrict Freedom?* (1944), pp. 7 and 16.

[2] Op. cit., pp. 186–200.

justice or causing psychological injuries to child witnesses are essential.[1]

The only type of offence for which trial by jury may still be justifiable is political crime.

In the past twenty-five years, many attempts have been made in Continental countries, notably in France, Belgium, Poland, and Austria, to reform trial by jury by narrowing the existing gap between judge and jury. In some instances, the jurors have been given the right fully to participate in the determination of the sentence; in others, the judges have been admitted to the deliberations of the jury; and sometimes even both steps have been taken. For reasons indicated by the author elsewhere,[2] none of these innovations can be regarded as successful.

The judicial bench is, of course, by no means the only sector of penal administration where the question amateur *versus* professional worker may have to be reconsidered. As it is not intended in this book to deal in any detail with the reform of the Penal System itself, the matter can only very briefly be touched upon. The principal fact which seems to emerge from a casual survey of present penal administration is the apparent lack of any system in this respect. Whereas certain sections of it have largely been handed over to the trained worker, others have been entrusted entirely to amateurs. The Probation Service has in recent years become the most outstanding example of the first category,[3] whereas education in prison and prison visiting belong to the second group. There are, apart from trade instructors, no paid professional teachers in the English Prison Service (outside the Borstal system), and hardly any trained social workers. While it would be distinctly unwise to exclude otherwise suitable amateurs from educational or social work in prison and in particular from prison visiting—apart from anything else, the very fact that their work is voluntary makes it valuable—the organization and supervision of these

[1] Some of the questions touched upon above were discussed in the Report of the Departmental Committee on Sexual Offences against Young Persons (1926, Cmd. 2561). In view of the great progress made within the past twenty years in subjects such as Child Psychology, the establishment of Child Guidance Clinics, the training of psychiatric social workers and the Women Police, the findings and recommendations of the Report can in some respects no longer be regarded as up to date.

[2] *Law Quarterly Review*, Vol. 53, 1937, pp. 400 et seq.

[3] Even here, progress has been slow, however, particularly as a result of the war. The highest figure of appointments in the Probation Service filled with trained candidates was 70 per cent. in 1939; in other years it went down even to 44 per cent. See *Probation*, Sept. 1942.

most important services should, it is submitted, be entrusted to professionally trained and paid workers. "It is essential to any sound democracy to recognize what part the ordinary public can take in the government of the State and what it cannot," writes Dr. A. D. Lindsay.[1] In other words, not that system can claim to be the most democratic one that places the heaviest burden on the shoulders of its citizens, but that system which employs each individual so that he can be of the greatest benefit to the community. To overstrain the responsibilities of the ordinary public is not democratic and can only lead to a general lowering of standards.

(2) Legal Aid for the Defendant.

To achieve a more democratic machinery of criminal justice nothing is more essential than an efficient system of legal aid for the poor person charged with an offence. By the time this book will appear in print the Report of the Committee appointed in May, 1944, by the Lord Chancellor, sitting under the chairmanship of Lord Rushcliffe, will no doubt have been published.[2] As we do not intend to speculate on its probable findings and recommendations, the following remarks will be of a general character only.

Nobody with even the slightest knowledge of the criminal law and criminal proceedings can possibly dispute that, apart from habitual criminals, only very few accused persons can be expected efficiently to conduct their own defence. A certain standard of education; the ability to think logically and to express oneself clearly; equanimity and presence of mind in face of unexpected situations; and even some degree of familiarity with the atmosphere of a law court are the minimum requirements. In somewhat more complicated cases knowledge of the substantive criminal law and the law of procedure, especially the rules of evidence, and a thorough preparation of the defence before the trial are essential. That this is generally recognized in well-informed circles is conclusively proved by the fact that, except in trivial cases, no layman who can pay for legal aid

[1] *The Modern Democratic State*, Vol. I, p. 282.

[2] The Report "on Legal Aid and Legal Advice in England and Wales" (Cmd. 6641), published in May 1945, is generally regarded as a most valuable document. See now also Robert Egerton, *Legal Aid* (1945, Intern. Libr. of Sociology and Social Reconstruction).

ever takes the risk of facing a criminal charge without such assistance. It is only the poor who, more often than not, have to rely on their own resources. Even if there were no other justification for the common saying that " there is one law for the rich and one for the poor ", this fact alone would suffice. It has always been one of the most revolting experiences of the present writer, from the Bench or from other observation posts, to watch the tremendous difference between the prospects of properly defended prisoners and those of their less fortunate fellow-sufferers. Judges do what they can to bridge the gap ; but only the most inexperienced among lay magistrates are able to deceive themselves by thinking that their well-intentioned efforts can compensate for the lack of a skilled defender. In an age which has become resolved to build up a system of medical assistance for all, the corresponding development of legal aid should not be entirely neglected. " Justice ", as Sir Ernest Barker has recently said,[1] " should be a matter of social (or public) service, and not of private purchase."

In many countries, among others in England, existing provisions have so far been seriously inadequate. In the years 1935 to 1938, the number of legal aid certificates granted by the 1,044 English Courts of Summary Jurisdiction (excluding cases committed by them for trial to higher courts) never exceeded 400 per year.[2] Persons found guilty of offences of all kinds by these courts during the same period numbered between 700,000 and 800,000 annually, and 19,079 prison sentences were imposed upon them. " Is crime a monopoly of the well-to-do ? ", asks " Solicitor ", " the Poor Prisoners' Defence Act is a farce so far as the police courts are concerned ".[3] And it has to be borne in mind that these courts, with very few exceptions, are manned by lay magistrates ; that their competence has been greatly extended by recent legislation ; that the system of a formal " plea of guilty " and of cross-examination tends to make an effective defence particularly difficult to the uninitiated ; and that legal assistance is particularly expensive in a country where the legal profession is divided into two separate branches.

What is the explanation for this state of affairs ? It is in

[1] Letter to *The Times*, Sept. 15, 1944. See also the excellent comparative study by Dr. E. J. Cohn, " Legal Aid for the Poor ", *Law Quarterly Review*, 1943, which, though dealing only with civil cases, throws much light on the problem as a whole.

[2] See the annual *Criminal Statistics* and App. II of the Report of 1945.

[3] *English Justice*, p. 52 fn. ; see also pp. 38, 72, and Chapter XII.

part due to certain shortcomings of the Poor Prisoners' Defence Act of 1930, and in part to the manner in which it is applied. The following are, as commonly agreed, the principal defects of the Act :

(1) Even in case of inadequacy of means, the granting of free legal aid is compulsory only for charges of murder. For other charges, no matter how serious they may be, the decision is left to the discretion of the court. This is inadequate and out of harmony with modern legislation in other countries. For all charges of a more serious character it should be mandatory upon the court, given inadequacy of the defendant's means, to issue a legal aid certificate.

(2) The same applies to cases where, although the charge may not be one of particular gravity, the defendant is more than usually handicapped in his defence, for instance, by physical or mental disabilities such as blindness, deafness, stammering, subnormal intelligence, or by ignorance of the language in which the proceedings are conducted. The phrase "exceptional circumstances" in sect. 2 of the Act is too vague.

(3) Defendants and even lay magistrates are said to be often ignorant of the existence and the working of the Act of 1930. Special information on the matter should therefore be given to every newly appointed magistrate, and to every defendant at the earliest possible stage of the proceedings.[1]

(4) Payment for legal aid has at present to be made out of local funds (sect. 3), which makes magistrates even more reluctant to grant a certificate. The administration of justice being not a local but a national concern, these expenses should be borne by the Exchequer.

(5) Legal aid is frequently granted at too late a stage of the proceedings, and, as a consequence, the defence cannot be properly prepared. The matter should have to be considered as early as possible and, in particular, if the accused is arrested, immediately after his arrest.

(6) Under the present law, legal aid has to be either fully granted or altogether refused. This ignores the existence of a large number of defendants of small means who, though able to make a modest contribution towards the expenses, are not in a position to bear the full amount.

[1] According to the Report on Justices' Clerks (1944), No. 62, "it may well be considered to be the duty of the clerk to remind the Court of its provisions in suitable cases, particularly where the prosecution has the benefit of legal assistance".

(7) The present machinery for the assessment of means of the accused is said to be inadequate. Such assessments should be made by persons trained for this task.

The suggested reforms would probably do much to eliminate the worst deficiencies of the present system. Whether their effect would be altogether to wipe out the great advantages which the rich defendant now possesses over the poor is, however, more than doubtful. Even an improved machinery of this kind would too much depend on the enthusiasm and the spirit of social service of the legal profession. The tariffs fixed by the State are not always likely to attract able and experienced lawyers who have become accustomed to very high fees. No discussion of the problem would be complete, therefore, without at least a brief reference to those two systems which have gone far beyond any mere patching up of the usual machinery: the American "Public Defender" and the socialized legal profession of the Soviet Union. It is significant that in both the U.S.A. and the U.S.S.R. the right of the citizen to be properly defended is expressly guaranteed by the Constitution.[1]

In an earlier chapter,[2] reference had to be made to the dangerous excesses which had become prevalent in the U.S.A. in the conduct of the defence of persons prosecuted under the Sherman Act. It is common knowledge that these evils have by no means been limited to monopoly cases. The sinister figure and infamous practices of the "shyster" lawyer, though in no way peculiar to that country, have nowhere become so familiar as in the U.S.A.[3] On the other side, however, it is one of the proudest achievements of the American legal profession to have created the institution of the Public Defender—not for the first time in history but for the first time successfully and on a large scale.[4] The outstanding characteristic of the Public Defender is that he is an official, appointed and paid by the State or a local authority, whose duty it is to defend those who

[1] VI. Amendment to the U.S.A. Constitution and art. 111 of the Soviet Constitution.

[2] Part I, Chapter 8B(*c*): Monopoly, esp. p. 164.

[3] See the vivid description of this type in Barnes and Teeters, *New Horizons in Criminology*, pp. 49 et seq.

[4] A fairly large and extremely interesting literature exists on the Public Defender in the U.S.A. See, for example, Reginald Heber Smith and John S. Bradway, *Growth of Legal Aid Work in the U.S.A.* (Dept. of Labor, Bulletin 607, revised ed. 1936); "Frontiers of Legal Aid Work", *Annals of the American Academy of Political and Social Science*, Vol. 205 (Sept. 1939); Barnes and Teeters, *New Horizons in Criminology*, pp. 367 et seq.; Charles T. Mishkin, *Journal of Criminal Law and Criminology*, Vol. 22 (1931), pp. 488 et seq.

are in need of legal assistance. This system, which originated in Los Angeles in 1914, has spread to San Francisco, Chicago, New Haven, Hartford (Connecticut), St. Louis, Cook County (Illinois), and a number of other districts, and it seems to have given general satisfaction. The Public Defender, who is usually selected by, or on the advice of, high judicial authority, gets his clients from the court after arraignment if the accused cannot afford to pay for legal assistance.

In addition, a system of Voluntary Defender exists in a number of States of the U.S.A., especially in New York City, under which legal aid is supplied through private organizations of lawyers. In New York, a Senior and a Junior Panel of attorneys have been formed who are willing to offer their services in a number of criminal cases without a fee.[1] In Chicago, public and voluntary machinery exist side by side. Both systems have their merits as well as their shortcomings, and without first-hand knowledge of their actual working in the U.S.A. it is impossible to choose between them. It seems to be one of the weaknesses of the voluntary type of organization as experienced in America that, even if capable and honest lawyers are available in sufficient numbers, adequate funds are lacking to enable them properly to prepare the defence in all but the simplest cases. Moreover, it is questionable whether important public functions should have to depend entirely on voluntary effort. It has been said [2] that, in capital cases, where the publicity effect compensates the defender for his immediate financial loss, the voluntary system works well, not however for the masses of less sensational cases. On the other hand, the supporters of the public system assert that not a single one of the many criticisms directed against it—no fewer than twenty-three have been registered—has proved to be justified. In particular, neither the expected collusion between Public Defender and Public Prosecutor nor any increase in expenditure are reported. On the contrary, special emphasis is laid on the considerable savings in time and money effected by this system, and, in addition, it is claimed [3] that "public

[1] Great improvements in the New York organization of voluntary aid appear to have been due to the efforts of Thomas E. Dewey as District Attorney : see Rupert Hughes, *Thomas E. Dewey, Attorney for the People* (1940), pp. 195 et seq.

[2] Smith and Bradway, op. cit., p. 77.

[3] Kimpton Ellis, Member of the Board of Directors of the Los Angeles Legal Aid Foundation, in *Federal Probation* (Oct.–Dec. 1942), p. 40. "The ancient Italian institution of Advocate of the Poor," writes Enrico Ferri, "if substituted for the present illusory assistance by the courts, would prevent many acts of revenge" (*Criminal Sociology*, p. 128).

defenders prevent much bitterness. They correct much of the anti-social attitude that predominates the thinking of many persons who commit crime."

The American Public Defender movement has, moreover, as a useful by-product, facilitated the collaboration between criminal courts and University Law Schools.[1] In several districts, law students act as temporary assistants to the Public Defender, relieving him of much donkey work and acquiring a better understanding of the practical administration of the law and of the social factors leading to crime. Under both the public and the voluntary systems sometimes social workers are employed in addition to lawyers to enable the defendant to contact other social services as required.

More radical is the Soviet system,[2] under which " lawyers no longer practise individually except in districts where there is not enough work to justify the establishment of a set of Chambers ". The work is, not only in cases of poor persons but in general, distributed among the members of the Chamber by a senior lawyer appointed by the Collegium of Advocates. All fees are paid not to an individual lawyer but to his Chamber according to a scale with maxima prescribed by the State. Although the client is entitled to ask for the services of a particular lawyer, such cases " must be included in determining the share of work to be distributed to him, so that no one is overloaded with work " ; and the practice of " devilling " for other lawyers who have more cases than they can personally handle is forbidden. If it is found in the course of preliminary proceedings that the accused is not defended by counsel, a lawyer is assigned to him. This nomination has to be made at least three days before the trial to ensure the adequate preparation of the defence. At the conclusion of the case the defendant, according to his means, is ordered to pay the prescribed or a smaller fee, or nothing at all. In the latter case, the lawyer receives no remuneration whatsoever.

Whereas the American institution of Public Defenders implies the preservation of the dual system—private enterprise and free competition in the case of accused persons able to look after

[1] See various articles in " Frontiers of Legal Aid Work ", *Annals*, 1939.

[2] See the detailed description in Ralph Millner, *Soviet Justice*, Chapter III, from where the quotations in the following text are taken ; and for the history since the Revolution, J. Zelitch, *Soviet Administration of Criminal Law* (1931), pp. 139 et seq.

themselves, and State provision for the others—the U.S.S.R. has socialized the whole machinery of legal aid regardless of the means of the accused.[1]

[1] The question of nationalizing the Bar has recently been discussed in this country by Mr. C. P. Harvey in the *Modern Law Review*, Vol. VI (Dec. 1942), p. 41, and in *The Times*, Sept. 15, 1944.

VI. MORE INTERNATIONAL CO-OPERATION AND COMPARATIVE STUDY IN THE FIELD OF CRIMINAL JUSTICE

This is needed in the interest of a more scientific and efficient as well as in that of a more democratic administration of criminal justice. The former argument will hardly be disputed. If it is true that scientific methods of dealing with crime are superior to a purely empirical and amateurish approach, it is equally true that a system of international co-operation and comparative studies is greatly superior to a narrowly nationalistic system. While the former broadens the basis of our scientific knowledge, the latter leads to parochialism and complacency. An international outlook is equally indispensable, however, in the interests of democracy, which means, perhaps more than anything else, an atmosphere of openmindedness and willingness to learn from others. " 'Democracy and internationalism go together,' Hitler often said in his speeches; and he was clearly right. . . . For a democratic community, at least in the sense inspired by the Christian doctrine of equality, always points beyond itself to man as such ".[1] Aloofness and an all too ready belief in the superiority of the particular legal system to which we have grown accustomed, untested by any knowledge of foreign laws and methods, are not only bad politics but also undemocratic. International aspects, thus, are bound to become an integral part of social reconstruction. All this does not imply blind imitation of other laws. As the author has pointed out elsewhere, " there are obvious limits to what nations can learn from one another in this field ". The decision should be based, however, not on ignorance but on the most complete knowledge obtainable.

The purpose of comparative study of criminal law and criminology may simply be to improve our own national laws and penal methods. For the training of the lawyer it is certainly indispensable.[2] It may also be our aim, however, to bring

[1] A. D. Lindsay, *The Modern Democratic State*, Vol. I, p. 251.

[2] " An adequate foundation for legal reasoning is not laid when only the principles of one system of law are taught. The student does not have sufficient relative criteria from which to reason and exercise his imagination " (H. C. Gutteridge, *Journal of Comparative Legislation and International Law*, 3rd series, Vol. 23 (1941), p. 64).

about an assimilation and greater uniformity of the criminal law and penal methods throughout the world.

The amount of labour devoted to these objects by lawyers and criminologists of many countries during the past three-quarters of a century has been immense. A mere enumeration of scientific organizations which have been working in this field, and of international Congresses devoted to better international understanding would fill several pages.[1] In spite of two disastrous breakdowns caused by two world wars, great masses of material have been collected. However, the work has often been of a haphazard character, and its results have but rarely attracted the attention of national legislators and administrators. It was largely due to the untiring labour of the semi-official International Penal and Penitentiary Commission and of the Howard League for Penal Reform that the Fifth Committee of the League of Nations began to take an active interest in matters of penal reform. " Standard Minimum Rules for the Treatment of Prisoners " were drawn up which found at least the theoretical approval of most Governments. The Howard League's International Survey " The Accused ", dealing with the position of untried prisoners, received an equally sympathetic reception. Nevertheless, the tangible results of these efforts have so far been almost nil.

In their practical work, Governments have tended to ignore the unanimous recommendations of international bodies and shown a conspicuous lack of interest in conditions outside their own frontiers. Even Committees set up by Governments to study specific questions of social or penal reform have, more often than not, been satisfied with the scantiest information of a comparative character, or none at all. The absence of adequate library facilities for comparative studies has further contributed to the preservation of the existing ignorance. Private organizations and individual scholars have, from time to time, courageously attempted to brighten the darkness ; [2] but the difficulties are too great to be overcome without State or international assistance. Will the coming World Organization succeed where its predeces-

[1] See for example, W. A. Bonger, *Introduction to Criminology* (1936), Appendix I ; art. " *Kriminalistische Organisationen* ", *Handwörterbuch der Kriminologie*, Vol. II, pp. 237 et seq. ; Léon Radzinowicz, " International Collaboration in Criminal Science ", *Law Quarterly Review*, Vol. 58 (1942).

[2] One recent example of this kind : Prof. Negley K. Teeters, *World Penal Systems* (sponsored and distributed by the Pennsylvania Prison Society, Philadelphia, 1944). Miss Margery Fry's appeal for a new international charter for prisoners (*The Times*, July 12, 1945) was also well timed.

sor has failed? It should be realized that the holding of periodical international Congresses, valuable as it may be as a stimulus, is not enough. As agencies for the promotion of research and the exchange of experiences and ideas such Congresses are of too casual a character. A permanent international Institute for research and teaching in Criminal Law, Criminology, and Penology is required, whose work would have to be supplemented by the provision of corresponding facilities at a number of national Universities, at least at one University in every country. It is only through an organization of this kind that individual Governments would be able to obtain, at any time, all the information required for their legislative work and for a constant overhauling of their administrative machinery of criminal justice.

VII. AND MORE PLANNING

It is perhaps not altogether unnecessary to consider, before anything else, what can be planned in this field: Is it crime itself? Is it the criminal law? Is it the penal system?

(1) *Can crime itself be "planned"?*, i.e., can the likely volume and the types of crime we shall have to deal with be calculated in advance and deliberately regulated by preventive measures? Is it possible to "plan" in a field where everything, and especially the very extent of the evil which has to be mastered, seems to be incalculable? We do not believe any more in Quetelet's static theory of crime as a phenomenon recurring every year in equal numbers and types. Nevertheless, even taking fully into account the many "imponderable" factors which make for crime, the amount of statistical material at our disposal, combined with our growing knowledge of the causative forces at work, enables us to make certain forecasts for the post-war period. In the nature of things, such forecasts cannot be of an absolute character but have largely to depend on such factors as the future conditions of the labour market and the way in which a number of similar social problems will be tackled. No doubt, after a war of unparalleled dimensions and savagery, with its wholesale breaking up of family life and its undermining of social control, allowance will also have to be made for an increase in crimes of violence as the natural result of prolonged mental strain. Even in countries where this did not happen after the 1914 war,[1] it will be wise this time to be prepared for a more difficult situation. Economic crime, however, will again constitute the major mass problem. In both fields, careful preventive work can do much to keep the increase which has to be expected at least within narrow limits. To the student of the period after 1918, it is clear that there are a number of social evils that will have to be avoided at almost any cost: especially prolonged and widespread unemployment, and sudden steep drops in real wages. In spite of the many difficulties confronting the scientific study of the matter, it is fairly safe to say that these two factors were largely responsible for the steady deterioration

[1] See the author's, *Social Aspects of Crime*, pp. 105 and 122; and, for the war years 1914–18, *War and Crime* (1941), pp. 91 and 126.

of the criminological position between the Wars.[1] And, as experience has shown, once a high-water mark of crime has been reached, a reduction can often be achieved only many years after the economic depression has been overcome.[2]

Closely connected with these negative requirements—avoidance of prolonged unemployment, of sudden drops in real wages, etc.—are certain positive changes in the economic and social structure which are likely to reduce economic offences. Criminologists have repeatedly attempted to draw up complete programmes of crime-preventing social and economic reforms.[3] This is not the place to add another comprehensive blue-print of this kind to those already in existence; in Part I of this book several points of outstanding importance have been fully discussed, however. Of a more specific character are the interesting schemes described in recent American publications such as "Preventing Crime".[4] Perhaps the most original and promising among the many experiments in crime preventive planning described in that Symposium are the "Co-ordinated Community Programmes". Whereas the other schemes are largely identified with one or the other social agency of a limited range of activities, such as the School, the Police, Clubs, Child Guidance Clinics, or reformative Institutions of various kinds, these "Co-ordinated Community Programmes" provide for the establishment, in suitable districts, of local agencies which can be placed in charge of the whole preventive work of the community. A more detailed description of these Co-ordinating Councils, of whom there are now more than 700 in the United States, has recently been given by Professor Lowell Juillard Carr of the University of Michigan.[5] It seems to be their chief merit that they bring together representatives of all local organizations, public and private, consisting of both experts and amateurs, who take an active interest in the prevention of crime, and especially of juvenile delinquency. Real planning in this field is hardly possible without the existence of such focal points in each locality which shows the characteristics of an actual or a potential "Delinquency Area". With regard to juvenile

[1] For the details, see *Social Aspects of Crime*, Chapter 5.

[2] *Social Aspects of Crime*, p. 125.

[3] See the excellent critical "Review of Crime-Prevention Programs" in Walter Reckless, *Criminal Behavior* (1940), Chapter XXI.

[4] A Symposium, edited by Sheldon and Eleanor Glueck (1936). This work has now been brought up to date in the brief but informative "Report of the Committee on Crime Prevention" of the American Prison Association (Oct. 1942).

[5] *Delinquency Control* (1941), Parts IV and V.

delinquency, Child Welfare Councils on the Scandinavian model may also form suitable nuclei for organized preventive work.[1] To co-ordinate and to guide the activities of these local Councils, a national Bureau of Crime Prevention would be required.[2]

It is sometimes believed that in a fully planned society a wholesale rise in crime is bound to occur because planning involves more regulations and prohibitions, all of them backed by penalties. True as this argument may be in one way, it overlooks that planning of the kind as here envisaged would, on the other hand, in many fields of human activities replace penal by administrative methods. By enabling the citizen to find out in advance whether his intended action would violate the law ; by erecting administrative barriers ; and, lastly, by removing some of the strongest economic and psychological factors making for crime the actual amount of law-breaking might even be greatly reduced. In theory, the final stage would be reached when this planning would become so perfect as to produce only that minimum volume of crime required to satisfy man's need for a scapegoat. In view of the strongly individualistic human factors involved, this will, however, remain a utopian aim probably for ever. In the first instance, there is a great deal of truth in Durkheim's contention that crime constitutes an essential element of community life which can never be entirely eliminated. Improvements in social behaviour will, therefore, soon result in a raising of the required standards.[3] Secondly, it should be borne in mind that no amount of planning in the economic sphere alone will be enough without corresponding changes in human habits and ways of thinking. The following illustration, perhaps somewhat trivial in itself, shows what might be repeated on a larger scale if such psychological factors are neglected : the introduction of clothes rationing has been held responsible for a considerable increase in female delinquency during the war. As the number of clothing coupons

[1] See above p. 197, and the description of the Swedish Child Welfare Councils in the League of Nations Report on Child Welfare Councils, pp. 53 et seq. It is gratifying to note the recent recommendation made at Norwich by a Conference on juvenile delinquency that a Social Service Department should be formed by the City Council " to co-ordinate the activities of all the Authorities and Committees responsible for social welfare, whether concerned with education, health, or housing, with Juvenile Courts or with Probation " (*Mental Health*, Vol. V, No. 2 (1944), p. 37).

[2] The establishment of such a Bureau for the U.S.A. is recommended in the Report of the Committee on Crime Prevention, p. 24.

[3] Emile Durkheim, *The Rules of Sociological Method* (8th ed., translated by Sarah A. Solovay and John H. Mueller, edited by G. E. G. Catlin), pp. 66 et seq., and Preface to 1st ed., p. xxxviii. Similarly E. Ferri, *Criminal Sociology* (1895), pp. 112, 136 ; Lewis Mumford, *Faith for Living*, p. 169.

provided is the same regardless of the price of the goods bought with them, the system works to the disadvantage of the poorer classes of the community. Working-class girls, even when they earn more than in pre-war years, do not easily acquire the habit of buying more solid and expensive clothes which last longer; therefore, they may need more coupons than well-to-do and better-educated women. A long-range rationing scheme of this kind can be completely successful only with people who are used and able to plan their own affairs far ahead. Unless it is carefully adapted to the individual needs and habits of the different strata of the population, or unless these habits can be adjusted to the economic requirements and the legal system of the community, planning will not substantially reduce the volume of crime. Nationalization of industries, anti-trust legislation, and some measure of rationing are, surely, matters of the very greatest moment in themselves, but if they remain isolated enclaves in an otherwise unplanned society, they may fail not only in their immediate objectives but also as instruments of crime prevention.[1]

(2) What part can the *criminal law* play in the process of planning? The conception of planning is inherent in the very idea of the criminal law. To regulate human behaviour is of its essence. As we have attempted to show in the course of this book, the criminal law has so far, in many respects, inadequately discharged this regulative function: the ideal of "certainty and predictability" has all too often remained a mere phantom, and the ordinary citizen has consequently been unable to find out in advance how this or that form of behaviour would be treated by the courts. Moreover, the line of demarcation between the sphere of penal legislation and that of other methods has sometimes been drawn in the wrong way. Human behaviour should, wherever possible, be regulated by non-punitive techniques of social control. In an unplanned, or a badly planned, society, the criminal law is saddled with a number of problems which should be solved by much more refined techniques. This point, one of the cardinal issues of the present book, is by no means new. The limited practical value of penal legislation was recognized already sixty years ago by Enrico Ferri, to mention only one of the most illustrious names in the history of our science. It was one of the basic contentions of that great Italian criminologist that "penal substitutes" (a misleading term), i.e., suitable measures of economic, social, educational, or legal

[1] See already above, pp. 114–5.

reform, of which he gave many examples, should to a considerable extent replace the Penal Code.[1] It is hardly true to say [2] that Ferri, in his scepticism of penal methods, was inclined to place too much reliance on the preventive value of non-penal legislation. On the contrary, he repeatedly stressed the significance of a great many measures of social reform which could be put into operation without the aid of the legislator. No less was he aware of the dangers inherent in " the immense force of inertia in the habits, traditions, and interests which have to be overcome ". If his ideas on the subject of crime prevention lacked the necessary comprehensiveness and coherence, this is not surprising in the case of an author who wrote so many years before the approach of an age of scientific planning. We do not claim to have given, in the present book, anything like a complete and coherent programme of how the functions of the criminal law should be re-shaped in a post-war world. All we may have been able to do is to show, by means of numerous illustrations, the direction in which this process of re-shaping should be carried out.[3]

In the field of criminal procedure, the question of a Treatment Tribunal will clearly be the central issue of any planning programme.

(3) It is with regard to the *penal system* proper that the need for better planning is perhaps more clearly and widely recognized than anywhere else. One might even be tempted to use the historical development of the penal system as a special example of the general evolution leading from the stage of " discovery " through that of " invention " to that of " planning ".[4] At the earliest stages of penal history, man does not deliberately " punish " ; he " discovers " that evildoers are automatically punished by a superior power. In the second period, disappointed in his belief in divine justice, he proceeds to " invent " and to apply penalties of his own making. It is only at the final stage, however, that of " planning ", that man advances " from the deliberate invention of single objects or institutions to the deliberate regulation and intelligent mastery of the relationships between these objects ",[5] which means prevention of crime

[1] Enrico Ferri, *La sociologia criminale* (1884), here quoted from the English edition *Criminal Sociology* (1895), esp. Chapter II.

[2] Reckless, op. cit., p. 403.

[3] See, in particular, the Summary of Recommendations made in Part I, above, pp. 191–3.

[4] Karl Mannheim, *Man and Society*, pp. 147 et seq.

[5] Karl Mannheim, p. 152.

through effective use and co-ordination of all available resources within the community.

Although this book is not concerned with penal reform as such, it may be briefly indicated that three major problems will have to be satisfactorily solved by those responsible for the planning of the future penal system : the relationship between public and private enterprise ; that between central and local agencies ; and the general co-ordination between the various parts of the machinery.

(*a*) Where should the line of demarcation be drawn between *public and private enterprise* in this field ? [1] English methods of dealing with the lawbreaker offer a particularly interesting example of struggle and compromise between the ideas of public ownership, control and management, and private enterprise. There is an extraordinary wealth of different types, ranging from the one extreme of State owned and managed prisons and Borstal institutions to the other extreme, represented by Q Camps and similar bodies, of an entirely private organization without official sanction or control. Somewhere between stand the Remand Homes, provided by local authorities, with State grants of at present one-half of the expenses and subject to Home Office inspection and rules ; the Approved Schools, owned and managed by either local authorities or private committees, with up to 100 per cent. State and local authority grant and fairly rigid State control ; and the privately owned and managed Probation Homes and Hostels, receiving smaller State grants or no grants at all, with correspondingly less strict State supervision. The Probation Service, after a long period of entirely unofficial activities, has in the end been taken over by the courts (in London by the Home Office), and its complete nationalization is under discussion. Lastly, the systems of After-Care at present employed show hardly less variety of types than the institutions to which they are attached, extending from the semi-public type used for Borstal institutions and convict prisons to the semi-private societies caring for discharged local prisoners. With certain exceptions, it seems to have been the policy so far to strengthen the public character of each individual method of dealing with law-breakers in proportion to its severity. This is

[1] Some of the following sentences are taken from the author's contribution to "*Q Camp. An Epitome of Experiences at Hawkspur Camp*, compiled by members of the Committee and edited by Dr. Marjorie E. Franklin" (no date, 1943), pp. 54 et seq. The author is indebted to the Q Camps Committee for permission to reproduce this material with slight modifications.

reasonable as long as the present combination of public and private elements lasts. In future, however, the part played by public authorities in the administration of the penal system, may it take the form of public ownership or merely of public management, will probably have to be further extended at the expense of the private element. Only by doing so can a uniformly high standard of performance and effective control on the part of the community at large, essential in a democracy, be safeguarded and the casual character inherent in uncoordinated private effort be avoided. Facilities offered by voluntary agencies may have been adequate in former times. Conditions have fundamentally changed, however, as a result of the growing complexity of the problems which have to be faced in the modern treatment of crime and delinquency. For the penal system, too, the principle of the Beveridge Report, that the continuance of private enterprise is justifiable only where it has to contribute something unique which cannot be provided by public authorities, should become the crucial test. In another connection, reference has already been made to the advantages which the institution of a public defender may have over private organization of legal aid.[1] There are certain symptoms that the need for much more public initiative and public effort in penal administration is being recognized. To give but a few illustrations : It is beyond dispute now that the shortage of Approved School accommodation at the outbreak of the 1939–45 war was mainly due to the fact that the Government has no legal power directly to establish institutions of this kind when required. Under the system employed by the Children and Young Persons Act, 1933, the Home Secretary depends in this respect on the good will of local authorities and private management committees.[2] It is common knowledge that the Home Office, to save the situation, has been forced, in the course of the war, to take the initiative : it has formed private management committees and supplied them with the funds needed to establish new Schools. It would be far simpler if the law would provide the responsible Government department with adequate powers, especially as the capital required has anyhow to come from the State. The position is even more difficult in the case of Probation Homes and Hostels, as for them no capital grants

[1] Above, pp. 253–4.

[2] In 1944, of the existing 140 Approved Schools 32 were owned and run by local authorities, and 108 by private committees of management.

can be made by the Government to private bodies willing to establish much-needed institutions of this kind. As a consequence, the shortage is here still more serious, and, as far as staffs are concerned, the conditions of employment contrast very unfavourably with those in Approved Schools.[1]

After a long and chequered history, the treatment of crime and delinquency has now come to be regarded as the duty and prerogative of the State, and, as a rule, there is no reason why the State should be incapable of performing, even more efficiently, the work of private agencies. The Borstal system, the New Hall Camp Prison at Wakefield, and now the Classifying Centres for Approved Schools established by the Home Office, in this country; the Norfolk Community Prison, the Federal Reformatory for Women at Alderson, the Californian Forestry Camps, and many other modern institutions in the United States; Bolshevo and the Gorki Colony in Soviet Russia—to give only a few recent examples—they all demonstrate that State departments can work out new methods and that they are able successfully to experiment, sometimes far in advance of public opinion. Nevertheless, State departments may occasionally be hampered by red tape and treasury control; their tempo may be slow, their schemes too rigid and uniform, and they may have to avoid taking big risks. New and unorthodox ideas, for instance in the field of psychological treatment or of "self-government", may need a place where their value can be tried out on a small scale without committing the State penal system as a whole. Moreover, psychological methods of treating the law-breaker, who is, more often than not, an "unwilling patient"—to refer once more to the masterly analysis of this type made by Dr. Denis Carroll and other medico-psychologists[2]—may easily fail unless the element of coercion is made invisible. Its absence, among other factors, has probably been an important cause of success in the work of the Institute for the Scientific Treatment of Delinquency in London. In State institutions, it is generally more difficult than elsewhere to keep up the appearance of voluntariness. Reflections of this kind may be put forward to justify the continuance of small and carefully selected private institutions as component parts of the penal system, provided they are kept not as relics of the past but as truly experimental units and

[1] Some details are given in Lady Allen of Hurtwood's pamphlet, "Whose Children?" (no date, 1945), pp. 15–18.

[2] *British Journal of Medical Psychology*, Vol. XVII (1938).

pioneers of the future. Only to the extent that they live up to such expectations will they be able to vindicate Cyril Burt's dictum that " nothing can take the place of these voluntary ventures ".[1]

After the War of 1914 to 1918, the task of reforming the English prison system is said to have been greatly aided by the work of a private committee which published its findings and recommendations in 1922.[2] After the second world war, it may well be for an official body, the Advisory Council recently set up by the Home Secretary, to perform a similar function. Nevertheless, for many years to come there will be ample room for the efforts of such private organizations as the Howard League for Penal Reform. To illustrate this point: when the League, with the consent of the Prison Commissioners, recently installed some wireless sets in a few English prisons and arranged correspondence courses for prisoners, this was valuable not because it could not have been done equally well by the responsible authorities, but because such private pioneering may make it easier for State officials to follow suit on a much bigger scale.[3]

Finally, it remains to stress the considerable effect which the taking over of a number of industries would have on the planning of the penal system. With the disappearance of competition in these industries, one of the principal obstacles to a productive employment of prison labour would disappear; and, with a number of factories in the hands of public authorities, it would become easier for After-Care organizations to find suitable work for ex-prisoners. All this, of course, only on the assumption that the attitude of mind of the ordinary man in the street could be accordingly re-shaped so that he would raise no objections to working side by side with ex-prisoners in Government factories.[4]

(*b*) Only second in importance to the question of public or private enterprise is that of how to draw the best line of demarcation between the activities of the State and those of local authorities within the framework of the penal system. The

[1] See also A. D. Lindsay, *The Modern Democratic State*, Vol. I, p. 265; " experiments and pioneer work are much more likely to come from voluntary associations and from individuals ".

[2] *English Prisons To-day*, edited by Stephen Hobhouse and A. Fenner Brockway (1922).

[3] See *Howard Journal*, Vol. VI, No. 4 (1944–5), p. 185.

[4] Similar ideas are expressed in *The Alternatives to Capital Punishment*, The Fifth Roy Calvert Memorial Lecture, by Col. G. D. Turner, formerly Asst. Commissioner of Prisons (1938), p. 10.

guiding principle might well be to leave to local authorities everything that can be dealt with by them equally well or even better than by the Central Government. As proved by recent experiences, however, English law has in some respects tended to impose on local authorities tasks for which they are ill suited. The extent to which crime, its prevention and treatment are national rather than local problems has not always been fully realized. The Children and Young Persons Act of 1933, for instance, by requiring local authorities to provide adequate Approved School and Remand Home accommodation, has undeniably brought about the risk that this duty may be neglected, not only because of occasional incompetence but also wherever local authorities fear that the facilities provided by them at the expense of their taxpayers may be used more in the interest of their neighbours than in their own.[1] Another, even more striking, illustration is provided by the present system of making the cost of maintaining courts of summary jurisdiction a local responsibility falling upon county and borough funds which, on the other hand, receive all court fees and some of the fines imposed by their courts. This system " plays its part in the discredit into which these Courts have fallen ".[2] The Report on Justices' Clerks rightly states that " whatever may have been the theory in times past we do not think it can be longer maintained that the administration of justice in courts of summary jurisdiction is entirely a local concern ", and " When fines are allocated to the authority that maintains the court it may involve the risk or give rise to the suspicion that the justices in fixing the fines might be influenced by the desire to relieve the rates of the area concerned ".[3] It is therefore proposed in the Report that all fees and fines should in future be paid to the Exchequer and different arrangements be made to meet the expenditure of the courts. To the disadvantages of financing legal aid out of local funds attention has already been drawn in another connection.[4]

(*c*) A few observations may be made on the need for better co-ordination as one of the supreme tests of an efficient penal system. Planning in this sphere, as in the field of crime preven-

[1] See for example, Clarke Hall and Morrison's, *Law Relating to Children and Young Persons* (2nd ed., 1941), p. 80 ad. sect. 80 : " It is not clear who are the local authorities ' concerned '. At present, courts often send children to schools outside their own areas, and a shortage of schools does not appear to concern one authority more than another."

[2] R. S. T. Chorley, *The Modern Law Review*, March 1945, p. 16.

[3] Paras. 145 et seq.

[4] See above, p. 251.

tion, implies the existence of some adequate machinery to adjust the work of each individual particle of the system to that of the others. One of the main objects of such machinery is to make sure not only that each of the various functions is entrusted to that particular agency which is best equipped for it, but also that each task is performed at the most suitable stage of the punitive or reformative process. In England, most of the co-ordinating machinery is in the hands of the Home Office which is, altogether or at least to some extent, responsible for the administration of prisons, Borstals, Approved Schools, Remand Homes, and Probation. As already mentioned, its task is sometimes made unnecessarily difficult by the inadequacy of its powers. This weakness may become particularly striking where the need for teamwork with powerful local authorities arises. In the recent Report on London County Council Remand Homes,[1] special attention is drawn to the lack of the necessary means of "easy communication and discussion" between the parties concerned, i.e., the Home Office, the London County Council, juvenile court magistrates, probation officers, and superintendents of Remand Homes. One of the principal recommendations in the Report was, therefore, concerned with the setting up of such machinery. Similar gaps can be encountered in other sections of the system, especially where the authorities primarily responsible for its working are to some extent dependent on the co-operation of others whose responsibility is of a more general and indirect character. Perhaps the most conspicuous case of this kind is that of juvenile courts and probation officers, on the one hand, and education authorities and schools, on the other. In most of the local Reports on juvenile delinquency published during the 1939–45 war, the need for better co-operation between courts, probation officers and schools has been stressed.[2]

Another example may illustrate the significance of the second function of planning, i.e., that of allocating to each stage of the punitive or reformative process the tasks for which it is best suited : the need has long been recognized for the establishment of Observation Centres [3] where accused persons, especially juveniles, can undergo a thorough physical and psychological examination and where their social case histories can be collected.

[1] Report of Committee of Inquiry (1945, Cmd. 6594), paras. 49 et seq.
[2] See, for example, the Reports from Middlesex, Ayrshire, and Bradford.
[3] Criminal Justice Bill, 1938–9, sects. 10 and 11.

Obviously, this is a task to be performed to the best advantage between the finding of guilt and the choice of the most suitable method of treatment. If left to the post-sentencing stage, the information gathered at the centre cannot be available to those who have to decide the question of treatment. Classifying Schools have recently been established by the Home Office, in connection with ordinary Approved Schools, to perform the functions of an Observation Centre for young people already committed to an Approved School by a juvenile court. Welcome and valuable as this new experiment no doubt is, these Classifying Schools could probably be used to even greater advantage if, instead of being confined to the human material sent to Approved Schools, they could begin their work at an earlier stage of the whole process, before the court has decided what to do with the juvenile, i.e., at the Remand Home stage. In this individual case, the overlapping and mixing of different stages and functions may have been inevitable as a consequence of special wartime difficulties. Even in normal times, however, it may recur unless there is thorough re-thinking and timely planning of the whole field.

The immediate post-war period with its expected general overhaul of the network of social and educational services in many lands will be the given moment for such re-planning. Marshal Foch is said to have once exclaimed that what he wanted was a plan—good or bad—but a plan.[1] We do not insist on planning for its own sake ; what we desire is a *good plan* for the administration of criminal justice in a post-war world.

Summary of Recommendations made in Part II

1. The technique of legal draftsmanship should be better adapted to the requirements of modern life and, especially, to the rapid changes in the character of the economic and social problems to be mastered by the criminal law. The use of general formulæ cannot be entirely dispensed with in the framing of criminal statutes. The resulting loss in " certainty and predictability " can, to some extent, be compensated for by creating an administrative machinery to decide certain questions before action is taken by the individual, instead of punishing him after the event (Chapter 10, III, 1).

2. Where narrow terms have to be used in criminal statutes, suitable facilities (delegated legislation, etc.) should exist for permanent observation of the working of the law and for frequent improvements in the wording of the law (Chapter 10, III, 2).

[1] Humbert Wolfe, *Labour Supply and Regulation*, p. 114.

3. Where certain functions which would otherwise devolve upon criminal courts are handed over to administrative agencies, the latter should be of an appropriate composition and standing ; they should use rules of procedure suitable for their task and in accordance with the ideas of natural justice ; and should be subject to a reasonable minimum of court control (Chapter 10, III, 3).

4. The work of the expert in criminal cases should be better integrated. To avoid the suspicion of partisanship and class distinction, the selection of experts should be exclusively a matter for the court, not for the parties (Chapter 11, IV, 1).

5. A central board ("Treatment Tribunal") should be established to advise the courts before a prison sentence is passed. The scope of the indeterminate sentence should be extended ; short prison sentences should be prohibited (Chapter 11, IV, 2).

6. Criminal justice should be administered by magistrates' courts, constituted of highly trained lawyers as chairmen, with well-selected lay assessors, as courts of first instance. Trial by jury should be abolished, except for political cases (Chapter 12, V, 1).

7. The system of legal aid for the defendant should be modernized and extended. If private organizations should fail in this respect, public defenders might be appointed (Chapter 12, V, 2).

8. There should be some permanent organization to ensure international co-operation and comparative research in the field of criminal justice (Chapter 12, VI).

9. A comprehensive planning programme for the reform of criminal justice should be worked out to secure better co-ordination between the various agencies, public and private, which are interested in the subject. The line of demarcation between public and private enterprise in this field, and the distribution of powers and responsibilities among central and local authorities should be re-considered in the light of recent developments and experiences (Chapter 12, VII).

SELECTED READING LISTS

PART ONE,

SECTION ONE

The Protection of Human Life

CHAPTER 1. THE INDIVIDUALISTIC ASPECT

A. Homicide.
C. S. Kenny, *Outlines of Criminal Law* (15th ed., 1936).

B. Suicide.
Emile Durkheim, *Le suicide* (1897).
W. Norwood East, *Medical Aspects of Crime* (1936).
Karl A. Menninger, *Man against Himself* (1938).
art. "Suicide" in the *Encyclopedia of Religion and Ethics*, ed. by James Hastings.

C. Euthanasia.
W. G. Earengay on "Voluntary Euthanasia" in *Medico-legal Review*, April 1940.
Robert Harding, "The Legalization of Voluntary Euthanasia," *Nineteenth Century*, Vol. 124 (1938).
C. Killick Millard, *The Movement in Favour of Voluntary Euthanasia* (Leicester Literary and Philosophic Society, 1936).
Harry Roberts, *Euthanasia and other Aspects of Life and Death* (1936).
Franz Walter, *Die Euthanasie und die Heiligkeit des Lebens* (1935).

CHAPTER 2. THE COLLECTIVISTIC ASPECT : THE POPULATION PROBLEM AND THE CRIMINAL LAW

A. The Extermination of Socially Useless Lives.
Edward Westermarck, *The Origin and Development of Moral Ideas*, Vol. I (1906), Chapter XVII.
art. "Abandonment and Exposure" in *Encycl. of Religion and* Ethics.

B. Sterilization and Castration.
Report of the Departmental Committee on Sterilization, 1934, Cmd. 4485.
Havelock Ellis, *Sex in Relation to Society* (1937).
Arthur E. Fink, *Causes of Crime* (1938), Chapter IX.
J. B. S. Haldane, *Heredity and Politics* (1938).
J. H. Landman, *Human Sterilization* (1932).
Alva Myrdal, *Nation and Family. The Swedish Experiment in democratic Family and Population Policy* (1941).
Walter Reckless, *Criminal Behavior* (1940).
Lord Riddell, *Medico-legal Problems* (1929).

CHAPTER 3. THE COLLECTIVISTIC ASPECT (*continued*)

C. Birth Control.
R. L. Dickinson, *Control of Conception* (2nd ed., 1938).
D. V. Glass, *Population Policies and Movements in Europe* (1940).
Max Hodann, *History of Modern Morals* (1937 ed.).
Claud Mullins, *Marriage, Children, and God* (1933).
Alva Myrdal (see under Chapter 2B).
Frederick Osborn, Preface to Eugenics (1940).

D. ABORTION.
Report of the Inter-Departmental Committee on Abortion (1939).
D. SEABORNE DAVIES, *The Modern Law Review*, Vol. II (1938).
D. V. GLASS (see under C).
MAURICE HINDUS, *Mother Russia* (1943).
MAX HODANN (see under C).
F. J. TAUSSIG, *Abortion, spontaneous and induced* (1936).
DOROTHY THURTLE, *Abortion, right or wrong?* (1940).
SIDNEY and BEATRICE WEBB, *Soviet Communism*, Vol. II.
EDWARD WESTERMARCK (See under Chapter 2 A), Vol. I.

APPENDIX TO SECTION ONE: CRIMINAL NEGLIGENCE

C. S. KENNY (see under Chapter 1 A).
C. H. WADDINGTON, *The Scientific Attitude* (Pelican Books, 1941).

SECTION TWO

THE PROTECTION OF SEXUAL AND FAMILY LIFE

CHAPTER 4. SEXUAL OFFENCES, ESPECIALLY HOMOSEXUALITY.

CLIFFORD ALLEN, *The Sexual Perversions and Abnormalities* (1940).
H. E. BARNES and NEGLEY K. TEETERS, *New Horizons in Criminology*, Chapter XXVI (1943).
RUTH BENEDICT, *Patterns of Culture* (1935).
W. NORWOOD EAST, *Medical Aspects of Crime* (1936).
W. NORWOOD EAST in *Mental Abnormality and Crime*, ed. by L. RADZINOWICZ and J. W. C. TURNER (1944).
W. NORWOOD EAST and W. H. DE B. HUBERT, *The Psychological Treatment of Crime* (1939).
JOSEPH F. FISHMAN, *Sex in Prison* (1934).
MAURICE HINDUS, *Mother Russia* (1943).
KENNETH INGRAM, *Sex Morality To-morrow* (1940).
R. v. KRAFFT-EBING, *Psychopathia sexualis* (English transl. 1939).
PETER NATHAN, *The Psychology of Fascism* (1943).

CHAPTER 5. OFFENCES AGAINST THE FAMILY

LEONARD DARWIN, *The Need for Eugenic Reform* (1926).
C. S. KENNY, *Outlines of Criminal Law* (15th ed., 1936).
CLAUD MULLINS, *Wife* v. *Husband in the Courts* (1935).
ALVA MYRDAL, *Family and Nation* (1941).

Especially on *Incest*:
SIR JAMES FRAZER, *Totemism and Exogamy*, 4 volumes (1910).
SIGMUND FREUD, *Totem and Taboo* (Pelican edition).
LORD RAGLAN, *Jocaste's Crime* (Thinker's Library).
EDWARD WESTERMARCK, *The History of Human Marriage* (5th ed., 1921).
——, *Three Essays on Sex and Marriage* (1934).

SECTION THREE

Economic Crime I

CHAPTER 6. THE PROTECTION OF PROPERTY I: CRITICISM OF THE TRADITIONAL APPROACH

A. Changes in the Economic and Social Structure of Property.

Thurman W. Arnold, *The Folklore of Capitalism* (1937).
A. A. Berle and Gardiner C. Means, *The Modern Corporation and Private Property* (1935).
Franz Neumann, *Behemoth* (1943).
Karl Renner, *Die Rechtsinstitute des Privatrechts und ihre soziale Funktion* (1929).
Thorstein Veblen, *Absentee Ownership and Business Enterprise* (1924).

B. The Law of Theft.

W. W. Buckland and Arnold D. McNair, *Roman Law and Common Law* (1936).
A. S. Diamond, *Primitive Law* (1935).
Jerome Hall, *Theft, Law, and Society* (1935).
H. F. Jolowicz, *Historical Introduction to the Study of Roman Law* (1932).
C. S. Kenny, *Outlines of Criminal Law* (15th ed., 1936).
Plato, *Laws* (transl. by E. B. England).
Pollock and Maitland, *History of English Law* (1895).
R. S. Rattray, *Ashanti Law and Constitution* (1929).
Sir James Fitzjames Stephen, *A History of the Criminal Law of England*, Vol. III (1883).

C. In Particular: the Neglect of Functional Aspects in the Law of Theft.

Ernest Beaglehole, *Property* (1931).
Cyril Burt, *The Young Delinquent* (4th ed., 1944).
Huntington Cairns, *Law and the Social Sciences* (1935).
——, *Theory of Legal Science* (1941).
G. W. Daniels and H. Campion, *The Distribution of National Capital* (1936).
R. T. Ely, *Property and Contract* (1914).
Friedrich Engels, *The Condition of the Working Class in England* (1844, English transl. 1892).
E. C. Gates and T. H. Pear, "An Inquiry into Juvenile Delinquency", in *Social Welfare* (published by the Manchester and Salford Council of Social Service), July 1941.
T. H. Green, *Principles of Political Obligation* (*Works*, Vol. II, (1885–8).
J. A. Hobson, *Property and Improperty* (1937).
Thomas Hodgskin, *The Natural and Artificial Right of Property contrasted* (1832).
Harold J. Laski, *Grammar of Politics* (4th ed., 1938).
Léon Litwinski, "Is there an Instinct of Possession?" in *British Journal of Psychology*, Gen. Sect., Vol. XXXIII (1942).
Anton Makarenko, *The Road to Life* (1936 ed.).
Hermann Mannheim, *Social Aspects of Crime in England between the Wars* (1940).
Karl Mannheim, *Man and Society* (1940).
——, *Diagnosis of our Time* (1943).
Roscoe Pound, *Introduction to the Philosophy of Law* (1921).
Property: its Rights and Duties (ed. by Charles Gore, 2nd ed., 1922).

" Property and Possession ", a Symposium by IAN SUTTIE, M. GINSBERG, S. ISAACS, and T. H. MARSHALL, *British Journal of Medical Psychology*, Vol. XV (1935–6).
WILLIAM SEAGLE, *The Quest for Law* (1941).
W. STARK, *The Ideal Foundations of Economic Thought* (1943).
R. H. TAWNEY, *The Acquisitive Society* (1921).
——, *Religion and the Rise of Capitalism* (Pelican ed.).
JOSIAH WEDGWOOD, *The Economics of Inheritance* (Pelican ed., 1939).

CHAPTER 7. THE PROTECTION OF PROPERTY II: THE NEW APPROACH

A. PUBLIC AND PRIVATE PROPERTY.
MARY STEVENSON CALLCOTT, *Russian Justice* (1935).
NICHOLAS DAVENPORT, *Vested Interests or Common Pool?* (1942).
ELLIOTT DODDS, *Let's try Liberalism* (1944).
ARTHUR FEILER, *The Experiment of Bolshevism* (1930).
MARGERY FRY, *The Ancestral Child* (The fifth Clarke Hall Lecture, 1940).
SAMUEL N. HARPER, *Civic Training in Soviet Russia* (1929).
LEONARD E. HUBBARD, *Soviet Trade and Distribution* (1938).
——, *Soviet Labour and Industry* (1942).
JOHN D. LITTLEPAGE and DEMARÉE BESS, *In Search of Soviet Gold* (1939).
SIR RICHARD LIVINGSTONE, *Education for a World Adrift* (1943).
SIR JOHN MAYNARD, *The Russian Peasant and other Studies* (1942).
R. SCHLESINGER, *Soviet Legal Theory* (1945).
S. and B. WEBB, *Soviet Communism* (2nd ed., 1937).
BARBARA WOOTTON, *Plan or no Plan* (1934).
A. YUGOFF, *Economic Trends in Soviet Russia* (1930).

B. PROTECTION AGAINST DESTRUCTION OF PROPERTY.
SIR WILLIAM BEVERIDGE, *British Food Control* (1928).
R. T. ELY, *Property and Contract* (1914).
W. H. HUTT, *Plan for Reconstruction* (1943).
HERMANN LEVY, *Retail Trade Associations* (1943).
Regulation of Economic Activities in Foreign Countries (Monograph No. 40 published by the American Temporary National Economic Committee, 1941).

C. PROTECTION AGAINST FRAUD.
Report of the Departmental Committee on Share-pushing (1937, Cmd. 5539).
H. E. BARNES and NEGLEY K. TEETERS, *New Horizons in Criminology* (1943).
" Crime in the United States " (*Annals of the American Academy of Political and Social Science*, Vol. 217, 1941, ed. by J. P. SHALLOO).
SIR WILLIAM HOLDSWORTH, *History of English Law*, Vol. VIII.
C. S. KENNY, *Outlines of Criminal Law* (15th ed., 1936).
HERMANN MANNHEIM, *Social Aspects of Crime in England between the Wars* (1940).
FRANK TANNENBAUM, *Crime and the Community* (1938).

SECTION FOUR

ECONOMIC CRIME II

CHAPTER 8. THE PROTECTION AGAINST PROPERTY

A. USURY.

Proceedings of the Joint Select Committee of the House of Lords and House of Commons on the Moneylenders Bill, 1925.
Annals of the American Academy of Political and Social Science, Vol. 196 (March 1938).
JEREMY BENTHAM, *Letters in Defence of Usury* (*Works*, Vol. III).
Encyclopedia of the Social Sciences, art. "Usury".
SIR WILLIAM HOLDSWORTH, *History of English Law*, Vol. VIII.
THEODOR MOMMSEN, *Römisches Strafrecht* (1899).
Our Towns, A Close-up (1943).
F. W. RYAN, *Usury and Usury Laws* (1924).
R. H. TAWNEY, *Religion and the Rise of Capitalism.*
WILLIAM TEMPLE, *Christianity and Social Order* (Penguin Special, 1942).
THOMAS WILSON, *A Discourse upon Usury*, 1572, with an Historical Introduction by R. H. TAWNEY (1925).

B. ECONOMIC CRIME AGAINST THE STATE.

(*a*) PROFITEERING.
SIR WILLIAM BEVERIDGE, *British Food Control* (1928).
LEONARD E. HUBBARD, *Soviet Labour and Industry* (1942).
SIR JOHN MAYNARD, *The Russian Peasant and Other Studies* (1942).
S. and B. WEBB, *Soviet Communism.*
ELLA WINTER, *Red Virtue* (1933).
A. YUGOFF, Economic Trends in Soviet Russia (1930).

(*b*) TAXATION FRAUD.
Debates in the House of Commons (see footnotes).
Encyclopedia of the Social Sciences, art. "Taxation".
A. FARNSWORTH in *The Modern Law Review*, 1942, 1943, 1944.
FERDINAND PECORA, *Wall-Street under Oath* (1939).
JOSIAH WEDGWOOD, *The Economics of Inheritance.*

(*c*) MONOPOLY.
Report of the Departmental Committee on Trusts (1919, Cmd. 9236).
Final Report of the Committee on Industry and Trade (1929, Cmd. 3782).
Report on Anti-Trust Legislation in the British Self-Governing Dominions (1912–13, Cmd. 6439).
THURMAN W. ARNOLD, *The Folklore of Capitalism* (1937).
——, *Bottlenecks of Business* (1940).
A. A. BERLE and GARDINER C. MEANS, *The Modern Corporation and Private Property.*
ELLIOTT DODDS, *Let's try Liberalism* (1944).
GERALD C. HENDERSON, *The Federal Trade Commission* (1924).
W. H. HUTT, *Plan for Reconstruction* (1943).
ROBERT H. JACKSON, *The Struggle for Judicial Supremacy* (1941).
HAROLD J. LASKI, *Reflections on the Revolution of our Time* (1943).
HERMANN LEVY, *The New Industrial System* (1936).
HERBERT MORRISON, "The State and Industry", in *Can Planning be Democratic?* (1944).
E. A. G. ROBINSON, *Monopoly* (1941).

E. F. Schumacher, " An Essay on State Control of Business ", in *Agenda*, Vol. III, 1944.
Carl F. Taeusch, *Policy and Ethics in Business* (1931).
Donald H. Taft, *Criminology* (1942).
William H. Taft, *The Anti-Trust Act and the Supreme Court* (1914).
Ferdynand Zweig, *The Planning of Free Societies* (1942).
American Temporary National Economic Committee: Monograph No. 16: Walton Hamilton and Irene Till, *Anti-Trust in Action* (1940).
——, Monograph No. 38: Milton Handler, *A Study of the Construction and Enforcement of the Federal Anti-Trust Laws* (1941).
——, Monograph No. 40: *Regulation of Economic Activities in Foreign Countries* (1941).

CHAPTER 9. THE PROTECTION OF LABOUR AND THE PROTECTION AGAINST LABOUR

G. D. H. Cole and others, *British Trade Unionism To-day* (1939).
Sir William Holdsworth, *History of English Law*, Vol. VIII.
C. S. Kenny, *Outlines of Criminal Law.*
C. M. Lloyd, *Trade Unionism* (3rd ed., 1928).
Hermann Mannheim, *Social Aspects of Crime in England between the Wars* (1940).
Mass-Observation, People in Production (Penguin Special, 1942).
W. Milne-Bailey, *Trade Unions and the State* (1934).
D. N. Pritt, *Defence Regulation 1AA* (1944).
Sir Henry Slesser and Charles Baker, *Trade Union Law* (3rd ed., 1928).
Sir James Fitzjames Stephen, *A History of the Criminal Law of England*, Vol. III (1883).
Gertrude Williams, *The Price of Social Security* (1944).
Edwin E. Witte, *The Government in Labor Disputes* (1932).
Humbert Wolfe, *Labour Supply and Regulation* (1923).

EPILOGUE TO PART ONE

C. K. Allen, *Democracy and the Individual* (1943).
Leonard Barnes, *Soviet Light on the Colonies* (Penguin Special, 1944).
H. Bradlaugh Bonner, *Penalties upon Opinion* (Thinker's Library, No. 39).
George Ives, *The Continued Extension of the Criminal Law* (privately printed, no date, 1922 ?).
John D. Littlepage and Demarée Bess, *In Search of Soviet Gold* (1939).
K. L. Little, " The Psychological Background of White-Coloured Contacts in Britain ", *The Sociological Review*, 1943.

PART TWO

Re-planning Criminal Justice

CHAPTER 10

ad II. POSSIBLE OBJECTIONS: SEPARATION OF POWERS " ADMINISTRATIVE LAW "—THE RULE OF LAW

Report of the Committee on Ministers' Powers (1932, Cmd. 4060).
Sir Cecil Thomas Carr, *Concerning English Administrative Law* (1941).
——, *Law Quarterly Review*, Vols. 51 and 58.
Joseph P. Chamberlain, Noel T. Dowling, Paul R. Hays, *The Judicial Function of Federal Administrative Agencies* (1942).

ERNST FREUND, *Administrative Powers over Persons and Property* (1928).
F. A. HAYEK, *The Road to Serfdom* (1943).
LORD HEWART OF BURY, *The New Despotism* (1929).
JAMES M. LANDIS, *The Administrative Process* (1938).
IVOR JENNINGS, *The Law and the Constitution* (2nd ed., 1938).
FRANZ NEUMANN, *Behemoth* (1942).
JAMES ROLAND PENNOCK, *Administration and the Rule of Law* (1941).
WILLIAM A. ROBSON, *Justice and Administrative Law* (1928).
——, (ed.), *Public Enterprise* (1937).
E. C. S. WADE, Introduction and Appendix to A. V. DICEY, *Law of the Constitution* (9th ed., 1939).

ad III. IN PARTICULAR: CERTAINTY AND PREDICTABILITY

SIR CECIL T. CARR, Concerning English Administrative Law (1941).
G. D. H. COLE, *British Trade Unionism To-day* (1939).
H. DONNEDIEU DE VABRES, *La Politique criminelle des États autoritaires* (1938).
E. FRAENKEL, *The Dual State* (1941).
STEFAN GLASER in *Journal of Comparative Legislation and International Law*, Third Series, Vol. XXIV, Feb. 1942.
JEROME HALL, *Theft, Law, and Society* (1935).
——, *Readings in Jurisprudence* (1938).
EDWARD JENKS, *The New Jurisprudence* (1933).
C. S. KENNY, *Outlines of Criminal Law* (15th ed., 1936).
HAROLD J. LASKI, *Grammar of Politics* (4th ed., 1938).
——, *Parliamentary Government in England* (1938).
——, *The Socialist Tradition in the French Revolution* (1930).
SIR PETER BENSON MAXWELL, *On the Interpretation of Statutes* (7th ed., 1929).
R. SCHLESINGER, *Soviet Legal Theory* (1945).
F. SCHULZ, *Principles of Roman Law* (1936).
J. SCHUMPETER, *Capitalism, Socialism, Democracy* (1942).
W. T. S. STALLYBRASS in *Law Quarterly Review*, Vol. 49.
R. H. TAWNEY, *Equality* (1931).

CHAPTER 11

ad IV. MAKING THE ADMINISTRATION OF CRIMINAL JUSTICE MORE SCIENTIFIC

(1) THE PLACE OF THE EXPERT.

H. BARNES, "A Century of the McNaghten Rules", in *Cambridge Law Journal*, 1944.
H. E. BARNES and NEGLEY K. TEETERS, *New Horizons in Criminology* (1943).
W. NORWOOD EAST, *Medical Aspects of Crime* (1936).
HAROLD J. LASKI, "Choosing the Planners", in *Plan for Britain* (1943).
——, *Democracy in Crisis* (1933).
A. D. LINDSAY, *The Modern Democratic State*, Vol. I (1943).
A. LAWRENCE LOWELL, *Public Opinion and Popular Government* (1913).
KARL MANNHEIM, *Man and Society* (1940).

(2) THE TREATMENT TRIBUNAL.

American:

Addresses concerning American Law Institute Proposals on Criminal Justice—Youth (no date).
BENEDICT S. ALPER, *Young People in the Courts of New York State*. Legislative Document (1942) No. 55 (April 1942).
H. E. BARNES and NEGLEY K. TEETERS, *New Horizons in Criminology* (1943).

Federal Corrections Act and Improvement in Parole. Hearings before Sub-committee No. 3 of the Committee on the Judiciary; House of Representatives, 78th Congress, First Session, H.R.2139 and 2140 (May 18 and 19; June 10, 1943).
PAUL J. McCORMICK, "A Judge discusses the proposed Federal Corrections Act", in *Federal Probation*, Jan. March, 1944.
Preventing Criminal Careers. A Proposal for a Youth Correction Authority for the State of New York. By Leonard V. Harrison (1941).
Report to the Judicial Conference of the Committee on Punishment for Crime, Washington, D.C. (June 1942).
State Action on the Model Youth Correction Authority Act (The American Law Institute, November, 1941).
Symposium on "The Correction of Youthful Offenders", in *Law and Contemporary Problems*, Vol. IX, No. 4 (Autumn 1942), published by the School of Law, Duke University, Durham, North Carolina.
JOSEPH N. ULMAN, "Dead-End Justice", in *Journal of Criminal Law and Criminology*, Vol. XXXIII (1942).
Youth Correction Authority Act. Official Draft prepared by The American Law Institute (1940).

English:

MARGERY FRY, *The future Treatment of the Adult Offender* (1944).
D. K. HENDERSON, *Psychopathic States* (1939).
HERMANN MANNHEIM, *The Dilemma of Penal Reform* (1939).
——, "New Trends in the Treatment of adolescent Offenders in the U.S.A.", in *Howard Journal*, Vol. VI, No. 1 (1941).
CLAUD MULLINS, *Crime and Psychology* (1943).

CHAPTER 12

ad V. MAKING THE ADMINISTRATION OF CRIMINAL JUSTICE MORE DEMOCRATIC

(1) LAY MAGISTRATES AND JURORS.

Report of the Departmental Committee on Sexual Offences against Young Persons (1926, Cmd. 2561).
Report of the Departmental Committee on Justices' Clerks (1944, Cmd. 6507).
Administration of Justice. A Report of a Sub-Committee set up by the Conservative and Unionist Party Organization (1945).
League of Nations: Child Welfare Councils (1937).
R. S. T. CHORLEY, *Modern Law Review*, Vol. VIII, March 1945.
RAGNA HAGEN, "Norway and the Treatment of Neglected and Problem Children", *Howard Journal*, Vol. VI, No. 4 (1944–5).
HEBER HART, *The Way to Justice* (1941).
SIR WILLIAM HOLDSWORTH, *History of English Law*, Vol. VIII.
HAROLD J. LASKI, *Law and Justice in Soviet Russia* (1935).
HERMANN MANNHEIM, "Trial by Jury in Continental Law", in *Law Quarterly Review*, Vol. 53 (1937).
RALPH MILLNER, *Soviet Justice* (1943).
CLAUD MULLINS, *Crime and Psychology* (1943).
LEO PAGE, *Justice of the Peace* (1936).
GEORGE BERNARD SHAW, *Everybody's Political What's What* (1944).
PAT SLOAN, *Soviet Democracy* (1937).
"Solicitor", *English Justice* (Pelican ed., 1941).
W. J. H. SPROTT, "Plea for trained Magistrates in the Juvenile Court", in *Howard Journal*, Vol. VI, No. 2 (1942).

John A. F. Watson, *The Child and the Magistrate* (1942).
S. and B. Webb, *Soviet Communism* (2nd ed., 1937).

(2) Legal Aid for the Defendant.

Report of the Committee on Legal Aid and Legal Advice in England and Wales (1945, Cmd. 6641).
H. E. Barnes and Negley K. Teeters, *New Horizons in Criminology* (1943).
E. J. Cohn, " Legal Aid for the Poor ", *Law Quarterly Review*, Vol. 59 (1943).
——, The Rushcliffe Report on Legal Aid to the Poor, *The Fortnightly Review*, August 1945.
R. Egerton, *Legal Aid* (1945)
" Frontiers of Legal Aid Work ", *Annals of the American Academy of Political and Social Science*, Vol. 205 (September 1939).
Ralph Millner, *Soviet Justice* (1943).
Charles T. Mishkin, *Journal of Criminal Law and Criminology*, Vol. 22 (1931).
Reginald Heber Smith and John S. Bradway, *Growth of Legal Aid Work in the U.S.A.* (U.S.A. Department of Labor, Bulletin 607, rev. ed., 1936).
" Solicitor ", *English Justice* (Pelican ed., 1941).
J. Zelitch, *Soviet Administration of Criminal Law* (1931).

ad VI. MORE INTERNATIONAL CO-OPERATION AND COMPARATIVE STUDY IN THE FIELD OF CRIMINAL JUSTICE

W. A. Bonger, *Introduction to Criminology* (1936).
Handwörterbuch der Kriminologie, art. " Kriminalistische Organisationen ", Vol. II (1934).
Howard League, International Survey " The Accused " (1937).
Léon Radzinowicz, " International Collaboration in Criminal Science ", *Law Quarterly Review*, Vol. 58 (1942).
Negley K. Teeters, *World Penal Systems* (sponsored and distributed by The Pennsylvania Prison Society, Philadelphia, 1944).

ad VII. AND MORE PLANNING

Lady Allen of Hurtwood, *Whose Children?* (1945).
Lowell Juillard Carr, *Delinquency Control* (1941).
Denis Carroll and others, *British Journal of Medical Psychology*, Vol. XVII (1938).
Emile Durkheim, *The Rules of Sociological Method* (8th ed., translated by Sarah A. Solovay and John H. Mueller, edited by G. E. G. Catlin).
Enrico Ferri, *Criminal Sociology* (1895).
Sheldon and Eleanor Glueck (ed.), *Preventing Crime* (1936).
League of Nations, Report on Child Welfare Councils.
Hermann Mannheim, *Social Aspects of Crime in England* (1940).
——, *War and Crime* (1941).
Karl Mannheim, *Man and Society* (1940).
——, *Diagnosis of our Time* (1943).
Q Camp. An Epitome of Experiences at Hawkspur Camp. Edited by Marjorie E. Franklin (no date, 1943).
Report of the Committee on Crime Prevention of the American Prison Association (1942).
Report on London County Council Remand Homes (1945, Cmd. 6594).

INDEX OF AUTHORS

INDEX OF SUBJECTS

For Product Safety Concerns and Information please contact our EU
representative GPSR@taylorandfrancis.com
Taylor & Francis Verlag GmbH, Kaufingerstraße 24, 80331 München, Germany

www.ingramcontent.com/pod-product-compliance
Ingram Content Group UK Ltd
Pitfield, Milton Keynes, MK11 3LW, UK
UKHW021501240926
475702UK00035B/38

* 9 7 8 0 4 1 5 1 7 7 3 6 8 *